Colonial Families
of the
Eastern Shore of Virginia

Volume 1

Mary Frances Carey
Barry W. Miles
Moody K. Miles

HERITAGE BOOKS
2019

HERITAGE BOOKS
AN IMPRINT OF HERITAGE BOOKS, INC.

Books, CDs, and more—Worldwide

For our listing of thousands of titles see our website
at
www.HeritageBooks.com

Published 2019 by
HERITAGE BOOKS, INC.
Publishing Division
5810 Ruatan Street
Berwyn Heights, Md. 20740

Heritage Books by Mary Frances Carey, Barry W. Miles, and Moody K. Miles, III:

Colonial Families of the Eastern Shore of Virginia: Volumes 1–4

Tombstone Inscriptions of Upper Accomack County, Virginia

Heritage Books by Barry W. Miles and Moody K. Miles, III:

Abstracts of the Wills and Administrations of Accomack County, Virginia, 1800–1860

Marriage Records of Accomack County, Virginia, 1854–1895
(Recorded in Licenses & Ministers' Returns)

Heritage Books by Barry W. Miles:

Cemeteries of the City of Hampton, Virginia, Formerly Elizabeth City County

Cemeteries of the City of Newport News, Formerly Warwick County, Virginia
Barry W. Miles and Gertrude Stead

International Standard Book Number
Paperbound: 978-1-68034-733-3

CONTENTS

PREFACE

This is the first volume of a planned series of Colonial Families of the Eastern Shore of Virginia. The first volume will be devoted to the works of Mary Frances Carey whereas subsequent volumes will also include the works of Barry Miles and M.K. Miles. Mary Frances has devoted many years to research of early Accomack County families and is in the process of turning over her research to Barry and M.K. whose collaboration has generated a database of Accomack County families, initially focusing on the area of upper portion of Accomack County, but which is expanding into the rest of Accomack and Northampton Counties.

In the interest of economy this series does not carry the families much beyond the early 1800s. Nor do we include the verbatim version of wills or other documents. If you would like more detail taking the families into the 1900s. contact either:

Barry W. Miles		M.K. Miles
6641 Whitesburg Rd.	or	13568 Adrian Ct.
Snow Hill, MD 21863		Woodbridge, VA 22191
410-651-4158		703-491-7516
barry@tassnet.net		mkmiles3@comcast.net

Thanks to Mrs. Carey and the Miles cousins (third cousins, by the way) for the enormous progress which is being made. These three individuals have over 25 years of experience each with Accomack County families and the various local records, cemeteries and people still living in Accomack County. Mary Frances has researched and locally printed over 40 family booklets and with Barry and M.K., published the *Tombstone Inscriptions of Upper Accomack County, Virginia* by Heritage Books, Inc. The Miles cousins published the *Marriage Records of Accomack County, VA 1854-1896* in 1997 and the *Abstracts of the Wills and Administrations of Acomack County, Virginia 1800-1860* in 2000, both published by Heritage Books. They have also assembled over 40,000 names in a genealogy database, representing hundreds of Accomack County families. They have 25,000 of these individuals on the Eastern Shore Public Library web page at http://www.espl.org/MilesFiles2/miles.htm which is called the "Miles Files 2.0." They also have a CD based "Miles Files 3.0," which contains over 35,000 individuals.

INTRODUCTION

The Eastern Shore of Virginia, distinct from the Eastern Shore of Maryland, consists of two counties, Northampton and Accomack. The region originally consisted of a single shire or county established in 1634 as Accomack. The population in 1635 was 396.[i] In 1642 the name was changed to Northampton although many persons continued to call the region Accomack. Prior to 23 March 1662/3[ii] the county was divided into two counties, Accomack to the north and Northampton to the south.

Beginning in 1619 patents for land were granted on the basis of 50 acres for each person transported to the colony at the expense of the patentee. Such head rights might include the patentee himself, his wife and children, indentured servants, slaves, and others. A patentee was required to plant or seat his land within three years, or lose it. Ralph Whitelaw, in his *Virginia's Eastern Shore*, discusses the ownership of land tracts which evolved from the early land patents. He has assigned a sequence of numbers to the tracts (consisting of one or more patents) with A or N as a prefix signifying Accomack County or Northampton County. He arrived at 422 tracts for the two counties and created a map showing the relative position of the tracts. The authors of this series sometimes refer to these as the "Whitelaw tracts."

A number of obstacles stand in the way of accurate genealogies of the Shore. Whitelaw cites the lack of early marriage records; frequent intermarriages (sometimes of double first cousins); remarriage of the survivor of a union; and duplication of the same given name among contemporaries.

Familial terms such as cousin, son in law, etc. had meanings oft times different in the colonial period than in today's usage. Cousin was used to indicate a niece, nephew or cousin as defined today. Son in law or daughter in law usually meant a step-child but not always. Sr. and Jr., indicated the respective ages of contemporaries and not necessarily father and son. Sometimes two siblings would have the same given name, even when both survived into adulthood.

Those who have researched a number of families of the Lower Delmarva will find a surprising number of children who are given their mother's maiden name as their first name. This can be especially helpful when the mother's maiden name is otherwise unknown.

For the most part the founders and early settlers of Old Somerset County in Maryland were people from the Eastern Shore of Virginia. They were encouraged to move north by Lord Baltimore who desired to settle these lands, in hopes of legitimizing the land as a part of the Maryland charter. Many of the immigrants from Virginia were Quakers, desiring to get away from the ill treatment by the Virginia government. Many other Virginians came north to obtain available land at reasonable quit rents. By May 1662, the settlements at Manokin and Annemessex numbered fifty tithable persons. In August 1662 the county of Somerset was founded.[iii]

---

[i] Whitelaw:27, citing Colonial Records of Virginia (Extra Virginia Senate Document, 1874).

[ii] It was on this date that the Commissioners for Accomack County took the Oath of Allegiance and supremacy.

[iii] For a thorough treatment of the history of Old Somerset County, the parent of Somerset, Worcester and Wicomico counties, see Clayton Torrence, *Old Somerset on the Eastern Shore of Maryland.*

SOURCES, TERMS AND ABBREVIATIONS

AC – Accomack County, Virginia

AC Surveyors Record No. 3:31. There is a series of books of survey plats (maps) in the Accomack County Clerk's office. These are different than the deeds. Sometimes the plat map was drawn into the deed book, but in most cases they were recorded in a separate set of ledger books, called the Surveyors Record. They are often referred to as plat books.

Acc Parish – Accomac Parish, Accomack County, Virginia

Acc Dist. Ct W&D - Accomack District Court Wills and Deeds

ACD – Accomack County Deeds

Accomack Land Causes - Many of the land causes mentioned can be found in Stratton Nottingham, *Land Causes, Accomack County, Virginia 1727-1826*.

admr. - administrator

admx. - administratrix

b. - born

Bio. Dict. Biographical Dictionary

bur. – buried or burial

c preceding a number – circa, about

Carey - refers to booklets compiled and printed by the author, Mary Frances Carey, 1980-2003. They can now be purchased from M. K. Miles. They include the following:

> *Bonwell to Bonneville, 1998*
> *Bundicks of Metompkin* 1993, *Parksley* 1994, *Bradford Neck* 1995 & *Gargatha* 1996
> *Mason Family of Kegotank, 1990*
> *Messongo Traders, 1998*
> *Thornton Family*, 2004 (printed by M.K. Miles).
> *Wright Family*, 1994

cem – cemetery

Cert. and Rights - *Certificates And Rights, Accomack County, Virginia, 1663-1709*, compiled by Stratton Nottingham, Reprinted by Genealogy Publishing Co., Inc, Baltimore, 1977. (Originally Published in Onancock, Virginia 1929)

Ch - Church

Crowson & Hite, AC 1860 Census - *Accomack County, Virginia 1860 Census*, compiled by E. Thomas Crowson & Susan Crowson Hite, Heritage Books, Inc., Bowie, MD, 1987

d. - died

DAR Library, 1776 D Street, Washington, D.C

dist. – district

Dean Hickman research. Dick Hickman is an associate of the authors from Melfa, Virginia. He possesses 156 three-ring notebooks estimated to contain about 75,000 pages of genealogy notes and charts on Eastern Shore genealogy!

DW – Deeds and wills

DWO – Deeds, Wills and Orders

Edwards, Ames, Mears & Allied Lines - *Ames, Mears and Allied Lines (The American Ancestors of Samuel William Ames and Sarah Anne Edmunds Mears) of Accomack County, Virginia,* compiled by their daughter Lucy Ames Edwards, in collaboration with her sister Nannie Ames Mears, sponsored by The Eastern Shore of Virginia Historical Society, 1967, copyright 1967 by Lucy Ames Edwards. This is a wonderful 393 page-hardbound book that she self printed and sold locally. It has been out of print for many years.

Ep – Episcopal

extr(s). - executor(s)

extx. - executrix

f/o - father of

FA CD309 - Family Archive CD309, 1850 Virginia Census

Family History Resource File, 1880 US Census. Published by The Church of Jesus Christ of Latter Day Saints, Salt Lake City, Utah, copyright 2001 (55 CD set of the entire US 1880 census, keyed and indexed by the LDS Church).

Heir at law - A term carried over from English heraldry wherein the oldest son was entitled to inherit the estate. The rules were applied in England to determine the successor to the throne when a King died. In general it was the oldest son and if he had died it would be his oldest son, not his next oldest brother. This could be key in determining genealogy relationships.

HH# - Household number (as appearing in the federal census)

Hickman, Bonniwell Family. See Dean Hickman [above].

Houston & Mihalyka, *Colonial Residents of Virginia's Eastern Shore*

lic. – marriage license, a written authorization granted by a qualified governmental official to a named man and woman to marry.

m. - married

M.L.B. - marriage license bond

MACM – Barry W. Miles & Moody K. Miles III, *Accomack County Marriages, 1854-1895*

Mark C. Lewis files. Now deceased, Mark C. Lewis was a well know Accomack County genealogist from Parksley, VA whose hand written files are in at the Eastern Shore Public Library (boxes of them).

marriage bond - a financial guarantee that no impediment to the marriage existed, furnished by the intended bridegroom or his friends.

marriage license: a written authorization granted by a qualified governmental official to a named man and woman to marry.

Marshall – James Handley Marshall, *Abstracts of Wills & Administrations*

Northampton County Virginia 1632-1802
Mary Frances Carey – Taken from the research files of Mary Frances Carey.
McKey – JoAnn Riley McKey, *Accomack County, Virginia Court Order Abstracts.*
MD Rev War Mil Lists, MF185:259. See *The Maryland Militia in the Revolutionary War*, by S. Eugene Clements and F. Edward Wright
Mihalyka, NC[Northampton] *Gravestone Inscriptions in Northampton County, Virginia*, compiled by Jean Merritt Mihalyka, edited by Alice B. Deal, Virginia State Library, Richmond, VA 1984
Mihalyka, *NC [Northampton County] Marriages 1660-1854*
MilesW&A – Barry W. Miles and Moody K. Miles, III, Abstracts of the Wills and Administrations of Accomack County, Virginia 1800-1860
MLAC- Jean Merritt Mihalyka & Faye Downing Wilson, *Graven Stones: Inscriptions from Lower Accomack County, Virginia, including Liberty and Parksley Cemeteries*
mos. - months
(N) – Name unknown
NC – Northampton County, Virginia
NC DW&c. - Northampton County Deeds, Wills, & etc.
Nottingham, Accomack Tithables, Tax Lists, 1663-1695. *Accomack Tithables (Tax Lists) 1663-1695*, compiled by Stratton Nottingham, Onancock, Virginia, 1931. Reprinted by Family Line Publications, 1987.
Nottingham Wills –Stratton Nottingham, Wills and Administrations Accomack County, Virginia 1663-1800. The original 1931 version. Pagination will differ with the re-keyed version by Heritage Books and the re-keyed version by Genealogical Publishing Company..
Nugent – Nell Marion Nugent, *Cavaliers and Pioneers*. Abstracts of Virginia Land Patents and Grants (3 vols.)
OB – Order book. There are a series of ledger books, called Order Books, but often called "Orders."
Old Somerset on the Eastern Shore - Clayton Torrence, *Old Somerset on the Eastern Shore of Maryland*
OW – Orders and wills
Pell, Boniwell Family. Rosemarie Bonwell Pell, Loose papers on the Boniwell Family, Oveido, FL, 1992
Pen. Ent. – *The Peninsula Enterprise* (newspaper)
Pollitt, SO Co Marriages 1796-1871 – Roy C. Pollitt, *Somerset County Maryland Marriage Records* 1796-1871
Powell, WO Co Marriages 1795-1865 - *Worcester County, Maryland, Marriage Records, 1795-1865*, compiled by Jody Powell, Roanoke, TX 1990 (privately printed).
Purse and Person –Virginia M. Meyer & John Frederick Dorman, *Adventurers of Purse & Person*

Qualified: A term used to describe that either 1) the person named in a will as the executor was willing and capable of performing the duties of the executor in settling the estate, or 2) someone named at probate to be the executor when the executor named in the will had died or refused to settle the estate. Qualifying to be the executor usually meant they would have to be over age 21 and post a bond or have others post a bond (thus being their security) equal to the value of the estate. This is why some wills stated that the executor should be allowed to qualify without posting a bond. Having someone other then the named executor become the executor at probate most often happened when an under age son was named executor, but did not reach the age of 21 by the time the will was proved, or when a widow refused to "qualify" as the executrix and some more capable friend or family member took her place.

Rev – Revolutionary (War)

Rev Soldiers & Sailors – Stratton Nottingham, Soldiers and Sailors of the Eastern Shore of Virginia in the Revolutionary War

SO Co. – Somerset County Maryland

SOD – Somerset County, Maryland deed books

SORR – Somerset County, Maryland Rent Rolls

SOW – Somerset County, Maryland, Wills

TACM – Nora Miller Turman, *Marriage Records of Accomack County, Virginia, 1776-1854, Recorded in Bonds, Licenses and Ministers' Returns*

Taylor Family, 1663-1974 - Mary Margaret Taylor, *Taylor Family, 1663-1974, James Taylor Branch, Accomack County, Virginia. Photocopied,* Withams, VA, 1973

TUAC – Mary Frances Carey, – Barry W. Miles and Moody K. Miles, III, *Tombstones of Upper Accomack County, Virginia*

W&c. – Wills, etc.

WADR - Walczyk, *Accomack County Death Register, 1853-1896*

Walczyk, 1870 Accomack County, Accomack Parish, Census

Walczyk, Accomack County Indentures, 1798-1835

Walker & Turman, *Accomack Soldiers & Sailors in Revolutionary War*

Whitelaw – Ralph T. Whitelaw, *Virginia's Eastern Shore: A History of Northampton and Accomack Counties*

Whitelaw's tract – In Whitelaw's *Virginia's Eastern Shore*, he established a system of naming tracts by letters and numbers (A for Accomack County and N for Northampton County). Included in this 2 volume set are two maps, one for Accomack and one for Northampton, showing the tracts.

wid. - widow

Wise, Col. John Wise Ancestors & Descendants Jennings Cropper Wise, Col. John Wise of England & Virginia (1617-1695), Virginia Historical Society, printed by the Bell Book and Stationary Co, Richmond, VA 1918

Wise, The Boston Family – Matthew M. Wise, *The Boston Family*

WO Co. – Worcester County, Maryland

WOD – Worcester County, Maryland, deed books

WOW – Worcester County, Maryland, will books

Descendants of James Bonnewell
(Limited to the Bonnewell surname)

Introduction
From the mid 1600s until today, the spelling of this family name has varied greatly. Variations include: Bonnawell, Bonniwell, Bonawell, Bonaville, Boneville, Bonnaville, Bonneville, Bonnivil, Bonnewell, Bonniwell, Bonewell and Bonwell. For the purpose of this work, the Bonnewell was chosen, but the spelling found in the various records sited will also be shown. This work is based primarily on the research of Mary Frances Carey. The branches of the family that she did not trace completely were taken from the research of Dean Hickman of Melfa, VA, with additional research by M.K. & Barry Miles.

First Generation
1. **James[1] Bonnewell I**, b. in England c1620, d. Jul 1667. (Nottingham Wills:2 ((will of James Bonwell))
 He m. 1st c1657, **Sarah (N)** (b. c1620, d. Oct 1659. (Marshall:59 (will of Sarah Bonwell)) She m. c1640, **John Dorman**. (Marshall:44 (adm. of John Derman; Marshall:59 (will of Sarah Bonwell)) He m. 2nd c1660, **Mary (N)** (b. c1630). (Nottingham Wills:2 (adm. of James Bonwell))
 James was named as a headright 13 Dec 1653 in NC. James Bonwell was first named in NC, records on 13 Dec 1653, when he and Neale Mackwellion were headrights for Mr. William Johnson. (NC Orders, Wills & C, 1651-1654:210) Johnson was eligible for a patent of 100 acres of land for paying the passage costs of these two men from England to the Virginia Colony.
 Northampton County records also show that James Bonwell leased 50 acres of "the Secretary Land" from Col. William Claiborne, Secretary of State, on 8 Sep 1658. The lease was to run for 21years, beginning from "the next Feast of St. Thomas the Apostle," and payment was to be one barrel of Indian corn each Christmas. (NC. DW.&c, 1655-1657:19) The Secretary's land consisted of 500 acres, set aside in 1620 by the Virginia Company in London, to support the office of the Secretary at Jamestown. Twenty persons were to be seated on the land, plant it, and pay rent. When a problem developed in keeping tenants on the land, the twenty-one-year lease system was substituted. The land was located north of Cape Charles, on the bay side of Virginia's Eastern Shore, between King's Creek and Cherrystone Creek. The area later became known as Town fields. The following is quoted from the lease: To All to whom these presence shall come, I Coll. William Claiborne Secretary of State for the Collony of Virginia ---greetings: Whereas by Act of Court bearing date the 9th of Ober 1658 It was ordered that the Secretary should lease the Land belonging to his place as by the sd order more att large appeareth. Now know ye that I the sd Coll. Will. Claiborne established in the office and place of the Sec. of State and for all the rights and priviledges thereunto belonging doe by these presence grant, devise and to farme lett unto James Bonwell a piece of Land containing

by survey fifty Acres Bounded from the head of the Little Creek that divideth Wm. Mountneys Land and his owns and bounds upon the Land of John Wilkins to have and to hold the sd fifty ackers of Land unto the sd. James Bonwell his heires Exec: Administr Assigns from the Feast of St. Thomas the Apostle next for and during the tearme of one and twenty years thence to be compleate and ended: Yeilding and payinge unto me the sd Co. Will. Claiborne or my Assigns att the Feast of St. Thomas the Apostle yearely during the sd tearme of twenty one years the fee rent of one Barrel of good Merchantable Indian Corn provided always that if the sd Rent be not yearly payd and satisfied unto the sd Coll. Will. Claiborne his, successors being lawfully demanded by Christmas yearly that then itt shall and may bee Lawfull for the sd Col. Will. Claiborne either to disteame or reorder. In Witnesse whereof I have hereunto sett my hand and seale this 8th of Ober 1658.

In 1660, James Bonwell appeared in court to answer charges of misusing the land belonging to "'ye heir of John Dorman," land that was adjoining the 50 acres leased "from ye Secretary unto James Bonwell." (NC Wills & Deeds, 1657-1666:72) It appears that the 50 acres of leased land was land that Dorman had some interest in and it joined his lands. James Bonwell satisfied the court that when Dorman came of age the 50 acres would be turned over to him. On 13 Dec of the same year, James Bonwell was appointed surveyor of the highway, "from Otterdam Branch to Coaghes (?), including ye marks from Bay Side to Sea Side." (NC OB, 1657-1664:85) The following is a quote from that document: Whereas it appeared In Court a Lease of fifty Acres of Land leased from ye Secretary unto James Bonwell which is adjoyning unto ye Land belonging unto ye heir of John Dorman ye Sd Bonwell being Charged with circumventing ye Heir of ye Sd Dorman who was most Interested In it undoubtedly In answer to which and for full Satisfaction to ye Court ye Sd Bonwell doth here in open Court Declare yt notwithstanding ye Sd Lease be made in ye Sd Bonwells name yet his Sd Intent if & to ye end doth declare & Acknowledge ye Same yt ye Heir of ye ad Dorman Stall enjoy ye Sd fifty acres of Land according to ye Sd Lease when he Shall Come to Age as his own inheritance to him and his Heirs for Ever During Sd Lease & paying ye Rent of ye Sd Land & this Shall be his Sufficent plea for ye Same & a Bars to ye Plea of ye Sd Bonwell any Law notwithstanding to ye Contrary and Manifestation of ye Same ye Sd Bonwell hath herein to Set his hand this 30th of July 1660. Acknowledged in open Court Jno Stringer Wm. Waters.

James bought land 18 Sep 1663 in Onancock, AC. On 18 Sep 1663, James Bonwell bought, from John Nicholls of Pungoteague Creek, 400 acres of land on the north side of Onancock Creek in AC. (AC DW, 1663-1666:21) He paid 4000 pounds of tobacco and casks for this land.

James appears on the list of tithables in AC for 1664. James Bonwell is listed in the AC tax list of 1664 with four tithes, males over 16 years of age. (Nottingham, Accomack Tithables. 1663-1695:2) His name appears in the tithables again in 1666, while in 1667 the "Widdow Bonwell" is shown with two tithes. His land on Onancock Creek stayed in the Bonwell family for many years.

On 16 Jul 1667 Mary Bonwell, widow of James, was appointed to settle his estate. (Nottingham Wills:2 (adm. of James Bonwell))

James Bonnewell I and Sarah (N) had the following child:

+ 2 i. James^2 Bonnewell, b. c1658, d. c1699.

James Bonnewell I and Mary (N) had the following child:

+ 3 ii.Thomas Bonnewell, b. c1663, d. Mar 1718.

Second Generation

2. **James^2 Bonnewell II** (James^1), b. in AC c1658, d. c1699. The other children of the second James Bonwell have been determined from the will of his son James Bonwell, the third, who died unmarried in 1721, leaving an only brother John Bonwell to inherit the land and carry on the line. (AC DW&c 1715-1729:320) This James left 100 acres to his mother, Mary Huebank. He named sisters as Elisabeth Bonwell, Mary Wise, Sarah Wise and Susanna Mychell and his brother John Bonwell.

He m. c1680, **Mary Watson** (b. c1665 in AC, d. 1732), dau. of Robert Watson Sr. and Susan (N). (Nottingham Wills:33 (will of Robert Watson Sr.) She m. c1703, **Henry Hughbank**. (Nottingham Wills:109 (adm. of Mary Hughbank))

James Bonwell petitioned the AC Court on 5 Sep 1675 to change his guardian from Roger Mikeal to Thomas Fowks. The court agreed and ordered Mikeal to deliver up all the estate of the said Bonwell into the hands of Thomas B. Fowkes by the middle of Oct. (AC Wills 1673-1676:313) He would have been at least 14 years of age to choose his own guardian.

On 28 May 1679, James Bonwell, "aged 20 years or thereabout," made a deposition concerning a horse Thomas Williams had borrowed from Robert Dunbar at Thomas "ffokes" home. (AC DWO 1678-1682:82) These two documents indicate this James Bonwell, b. between 1659 and 1661, for he would have been at least 14 years of age to choose his own guardian. He would, then, have been 6 to 8 years of age when his father died.

James' estate was settled 2 Feb 1702 in AC. The inventory and appraisement of his personal property was recorded on 2 Feb 1702. (ACW&c, Part II, 1692-1715:11) This included a long list of household furnishings, tools, a pair of pistols, "cutlass" and a gun, two large Bibles and a small one, sheep, cows, and horses. The inventory was made by John Wise, Senr, John Wise, Junr, John Stanton, and Gervis Baggale. The estate was administered to James Bonwell's widow Mary, who had m. Henry Hewbank by the time the inventory was recorded. Nothing is shown of the children or heirs of this James Bonwell. The inventory and appraisement of James Bonewell's estate was filed 2 Feb 1702 by Mary, relict & admx. together with her now Husband Henry Hewbanck.

James Bonnewell II and Mary Watson had the following children:

+ 4 i. John^3 Bonnewell, b. c1680, d. Mar 1729. (Nottingham Wills:65 (will of James Bonewell))

+ 5 ii. James Bonnewell, b. in AC c1681, d. Mar 1721 leaving a will dated 14 Jan 1721, probated in AC 4 Apr 1721. To mother Mary Huebank land at Ekekses Creek containing 100 acres. To cousins Mary Silverthorne & Susan Wise. Sister Elizabeth Bonewell. Brother John Bonewell. Sister Mary Wise. Sister Susana Mychell. Sister Sarah Wise. Mother extr. Witnessed by William Wise, John Wise Sr., and John Wise Jr. (Nottingham Wills:65 (will of James Bonewell))

+ 6 iii. Elizabeth Bonnewell, b. in AC c1684. Elizabeth was named in her brother's will 14 Jan 1720/1 in AC. (Nottingham Wills:65 (will of James Bonewell))

+ 7 iv. Susana Bonnewell, b. in AC c1688, m. c1706, Simon Michael (b. c1674, d. May 1728), son of John Michael and Anne Tilney. (Nottingham Wills:65 (will of James Bonewell); Nottingham Wills:13 (will of John Michael & 84 (will of Simon Michaell))

Susana was named in her brother's will 14 Jan 1720/1 in AC. (Nottingham Wills:65 (will of James Bonewell))

Susana was named in her husband's will 12 Jan 1727/8 in AC. (Nottingham Wills:84 (will of Simon Michaell))

+ 8 v. Tabitha Bonnewell, b. in AC c1690, m. c1710, Sebastian Silverthorn I (b. c1670). (Mark C. Lewis Files) He m. Susanna Evans c1700.

+ 9 vi. Mary Bonnewell, b. in AC c1690, m. c1715, John Wise (b. c1690, d. Jan 1782), son of William Wise. He m. c1770, Margaret (N). (Nottingham Wills:65 (will of James Bonewell; Nottingham Wills:332 (will of John Wise Sr.); Purse&Person: 553; Wise, *Col. John Wise Ancestors & Descendants*:57)

Mary Wise was named in her brother's will 14 Jan 1720/1 in AC. (Nottingham Wills:65 (will of James Bonewell))

10 vii. Sarah Bonnewell, b. in AC c1695, m. c1720, William Wise (b, c1690, d. Apr 1769), son of William Wise. (Nottingham Wills: (will of James Bonewell); Wise, *Col. John Wise Ancestors & Descendants*:60; Purse&Person: 57, 553; Nottingham Wills:245 (will of William Wise Sr.)) According to Jennings Cropper Wise, he m. Sarah Bonnewell, dau. of James Bonnewell and Mary Watson, and settled in Onancock after disposing of the lands he obtained with his brother from their father. His son was William E. Wise, who married Sarah Evans, dau. of Isaiah Evans; and their son was Isaiah Evans Wise, who m. Ann Abbott; and their son was John Evans Wise, b. at Metompkin, June 5, 1816, d. Jan 17, 1911, who m. Elizabeth Poulson, of Metompkin, b. July 14, 1820, d. Nov 16, 1887, dau. of

5

Erastus Poulson and Katie Bagwell. John Evans Wise and Elizabeth Poulson had John Hastings Wise, late Clerk of the Accomack Court; George Douglas Wise; and William Thomas Wise, b. at Metompkin, Jan 19, 1853, and now resident in Onancock. William Thomas Wise m. Nov 28, 1878, Sadie Parker Bagwell, dau. of Healey Parker Bagwell and Sarah Edmunds, and they had: 1. Elizabeth Bagwell Wise, b. Jan 13, 1881. 2. Henrietta Sarah Wise, b. Feb 12, 1882. 3. Lucy Parker Wise, b. June 9, 1887. 4. Dorothy Edmunds Wise, b. Oct 31, 1892. 5. John Evans Wise, b. Feb 16, 1896.

3. **Thomas**[2] **Bonnewell** (James[1]), b. in AC c1663, d. Mar 1718 (Nottingham Wills:87 (adm. of Thomas Boniwell))

He m. c1685, **Annabella Chambers** (b. c1666), dau. of (N) Chambers and Frances (N). (Whitelaw:956 (Col. John West's 99 year lease Mrs. Frances Chambers; Whitelaw: 956 (Col. John West's 99 year lease Mrs. Frances Chambers))

Thomas bought land 1695 in Kegotank Creek, AC. (Whitelaw:163 (part of tract A121)) Whitelaw states that in 1695 Daniel of St. Thomas and Elizabeth Jenifer sold 300 acres to Thomas Bonwell; it was north of the above and extended westward from Kegotank Creek. In 1758 Thomas Bonnewell left everything to his wife Ann. No clue was found to give the name of Ann's second husband, but in 1771 Ann Stockley, widow, left her plantation to Robert James; there was no explanation of the relationship, if any, and in the probate it was stated that William Bradford was her heir-at-law. In 1787 Robert James (wife Mary) left the north 200 acres to his son William and the balance to his son David. [NOTE: Whitelaw assumed that it was the same Thomas Bonnewell who purchased the land in 1695 that left it to his wife Ann in 1758. However, it is more likely that the Thomas who d. 1758 was the son of the Thomas who bought the land in 1695.]

On 2 Apr 1718 in AC, George Boniwell was appointed to administer the estate of Thomas Boniwell. William Taylor & Sebastian Cropper were the securities. (Nottingham Wills:87 (adm. of Thomas Boniwell)) This Thomas would have been too old to have been a son of the second James Bonnewell (1660-1702), as he purchased 300 acres of land from Daniel Jenifer in 1695 and he would have to have been over age 21 at that time. This would imply he, b. no later than 1674, when the second James Bonnewell would have been only 14 years old. It is therefore assumed that he is a son of the first James Bonnewell.

Thomas Bonnewell and Annabella Chambers had the following children:

+ 11 i. Thomas[3] Bonnewell, b. in AC c1686, d. Jul 1758. (Nottingham Wills:192 (will of Thomas Bonnewell)) He m. Ann Bradford before 1735. (Nottingham Wills:105 (will of William Bradford)) Ann was b. c1714 in AC, d. Mar 1771, dau. of

William Bradford I and Bridget Fisher. (Father's Will; Nottingham Wills:255 (will of Anne Stockley)).

Thomas was named in his brother's will 12 Feb 1720 in AC. (Nottingham Wills:68 (will of George Bonwell)) He was shown as a brother Thomas Bonwell in the will of George Bonwell. He d. leaving a will dated 25 Nov 1753 in AC, probated 25 Jul 1758. To wife Ann Bonnewell whole estate real & personal. Wife extx. Witnessed by David James, Elizabeth James & Thomas Webb. Sheriff's return that George Matthews, one of the heirs at law of Thomas Bonnewell, dec'd, was summoned to appear & that George Stockley, the other heir at law of the said Thomas Bonnewell was not found within his Bailiwick. (Nottingham Wills:192 (will of Thomas Bonnewell))

+ 12 ii. George Bonnewell, b. in AC c1688, d. unm. May 1721. (Nottingham Wills:68 (will of George Bonwell)) George was named as administrator of the estate of his father on 2 Apr 1718 in AC. William Taylor & Sebastian Cropper were the securities. (Nottingham Wills:87 (adm. of Thomas Boniwell))

He left a will dated 12 Feb 1720, probated 6 Jun 1721 in AC. Mentioned: brother Thomas Bonwell, grandmother Mrs. Frances Norton, sister Mary. sister Arabella Bonnewell, friend Solomon Ewell, friend Mason Abbott, John Tankard, Solomon Ewell extr. "I request of the said Solomon his Christian care of my Brethren." Witnessed by Samuel Turner and John Wilkins. (Nottingham Wills:68 (will of George Bonwell))

13 iii. Mary Bonnewell, b. in AC c1693. (Nottingham Wills:68 (will of George Bonwell))

14 iv. Arabella Bonnewell, b. in AC c1696. (Nottingham Wills:68 (will of George Bonwell))

Third Generation

4. **John**[3] **Bonnewell** (James[2], James[1]), b. in AC c1680, d. Mar 1729. (Nottingham Wills:87 (will of John Bonwell))

He m. c1700, **Gratiana Michael** (b. c1682), dau. of John Michael and Anne Tilney. (Whitelaw:894 (the Gratiana Michael part of tract A70; Nottingham Wills:13 (will of John Michael))

John was named in his grandfather's will 24 Jul 1702 in AC. (Nottingham Wills:33 (will of Robert Watson Sr.))

John patented land 16 Dec 1714 in Onancock, AC. On 16 Dec 1714, John Bonwell patented 400 acres of land. (Nugent III:163) This land was located "on Eastern Shore of this Colony on north side of Anancock (Onancock) Creek;

adjacent to Col. Tully Robinson; & Major John Custis: by William Wise's house; & over Round House Gutn." The record says the land had been escheated from John Nicholls, deceased, and John Bonwell was charged two pounds of tobacco for it. It is obvious this land was the same land that John Bonwell's grandfather bought of John Nicholls in 1663. The title to the land must have been in question and a new patent was issued to clear it. Even in those times, 400 acres of land could not have been bought for two pounds of tobacco. John Bonwell sold 100 acres to brother James Bonwell in 1716, and this was the land James left their mother when he died in 1721. (AC DW&c., 1715-1729:38)

He d. leaving a will dated 19 Jan 1728/9, probated 1 Apr 1729, in AC. To sons John & James Bonwell plantation where I now live containing 400 acres, beginning at the head of a gut called Stevens gut. To son Joachim Mikeall Bonewell 200 acres at the sideside which I had by my wife, it being the land formerly of John Mekeall. Sons Thomas & Richard Bonewell. Personal estate to wife for life and then to my 4 children Thomas, Richard, Ann & Sarah. Wife (unnamed) & son James extrs. Witnessed by John Smith, Daniel Fookes and William Wise Jr. (Nottingham Wills:87 (will of John Bonwell))

John Bonnewell and Gratiana Michael had the following children:

15	i.	James[4] Bonnewell, b. c1700, d. May 1767.
16	ii.	John Bonnewell, b. c1702, d. c1790.
17	iii.	Ann Bonnewell, b. in AC c1704, m. c1735, (N) Lee. She was shown as sister Anne Lee in the will of Richard Bonnewell. (Nottingham Wills:148 (will of Richard Bonnewell))

18 iv. Sarah Bonnewell, b. in AC c1706, m. 1st c1729, Nathaniel Brittingham (b. 1692 in AC, d. May 1741), son of William Brittingham and Elizabeth Williams. (Carey, *Bonwell to Bonneville*; and Hickman, *Bonniwell Family*; Nottingham Wills:124 (will of Nathaniel Brittingham. See also The Brittingham Family, vol. 20 of *Colonial Families of the Eastern Shore of Maryland*.)) She m. 2nd c1742, William Wise c1742 (b. c1705, d. Jan 1748/9). (Nottingham Wills:124 (will of Nathaniel Brittingham; MilesW&A:152 (will of William Wise))

Sarah was named in the wills of both husbands. (Nottingham Wills: 124 (will of Nathaniel Brittingham; Nottingham Wills:152 (will of William Wise)) She was given land called *Wises Addition* during her natural life and 1/3 of the shallop called *Sally & Polly* in the will of William Wise.

+	19	v.	Joachim Mikeal Bonnewell, b. c1710, d. May 1783.
+	20	vi.	Thomas Bonnewell, b. c1712, d. Dec 1743.
	21	vii.	Richard Bonnewell, b. in AC c1714, d. Jan 1746/47. He left a will dated 5 Jan 1746/47, probated 27 Jan 1746/7 in AC. Mentioned cousin John Bonnewell; sister Anne Lee; brother Joachim Michael Bonnewell;

8

brother John Bonnewell; brother James Bonnewell; cousin Rachel Bonnewell; brother Joachim Michael Bonnewell extr. Witnessed by Philip Parker, Susanna Wise and Mary Wise. (Nottingham Wills:148 (will of Richard Bonnewell))

Fourth Generation

15. **James⁴ Bonnewell** (John³, James², James¹), b. AC c1700, d. May 1767. (Nottingham Wills:236 (will of James Bonnewell))

He m. c1730, **Hannah Lurton** (b. c1715). Apparently John Bonwell, Senr and his brother James m. sisters, Mary Lurton and Hannah Lurton. The will of John Lurton in 1749 gave his daughters as Hannah, Rachel, Elizabeth, Susanna, and Mary and a son Jacob Lurton. Jacob Lurton, who d. testate in 1770, left property to two of John Bonwell, Senr's children, Mary Bonwell and Stephen Bonwell and also named one child of James Bonwell. (Nottingham Wills:250 (will of Jacob Lurton Sr.); AC Wills 1767-1772:399; ACW&c., 1745-1749:489)

Hannah, b. c1715 in AC, was a dau. of John Lurton and Rachel (N). (Nottingham Wills:152 (will of John Lurton))

He made a will 1765, probated 26 May 1767 in AC. To son John Bonnewell plantation where I now live. To son Michael 200 acres which was my mother's maiden land lying on the seaboard side. To 3 sons John, Michael & James Bonnewell all my right & title of & in an Island called *Tobacco Island* which I purchased of Denwood Turpin, John Wharton & Thomas Upshur. To daughter Hannah. To daughter Leah. To daughter Rachel. Granddaugthers Peggy & Nanny Budd. 3 daughters residuary legatees. Wife (unnamed) & sons John & Michael extrs. Witnessed by Mickeel Bonnewell, Richard Bonnewell, Peter Fitzgerald, Betty Bonnewell & Sarah Bonnewell. (Nottingham Wills:236 (will of James Bonnewell))

On 8 Dec 1769 Michael Bonewell, son of James Bonewell, was named in the will of Jacob Lurton Sr. (Nottingham Wills:250 (will of Jacob Lurton Sr.))

James Bonnewell and Hannah Lurton had the following children:

+ 22   i.   John⁵ Bonnewell Junior, b. c1730, d. Aug 1775.
23   ii.   (d|o James & Hannah) Bonnewell, b. AC c1736, d. before 1765. (Nottingham Wills:236 (will of James Bonnewell)) She was evidently dec'd. when her father James Bonnewell wrote his will in 1765, as he named two granddaus., Peggy and Nanny Budd to share with his other daus. She m. c1755, Zorobabel Budd (b. c1730 in AC).

(d|o James&Hannah) was mentioned (unnamed) in her husband's will 7 Sep 1762 in AC. His wife and James & Michael Bonnewell were the extrs. (Nottingham Wills:238 (will of Zorobabel Budd))
24   iii.   Rachel Bonnewell, b. in AC c1744, d. Dec 1795. She m. 1ˢᵗ c1765, (N) Mears (b. c1740) and m. 2ⁿᵈ c1775,

8

William Martial Richardson (b. c1730 in AC, d. Mar 1781). She was shown as a cousin Rachel Bonnewell in the will of Richard Bonnewell, who was her father's brother. Cousin often mean niece and nephew. (Nottingham Wills:431 (will of Rachel Richardson)) (Nottingham Wills:148 (will of Richard Bonnewell); Nottingham Wills:328 (will of William Martial Richardson) Rachel was named in her husband's will 29 Jun 1780 in AC. (Nottingham Wills:328 (will of William Martial Richardson)) She was given all my lands & 2 plantations & 1/3 of personal estate during her widowhood, she to bring up my son Jacob Richardson & my 3 youngest children. After other bequests the balance was to be divided between my last wife's children.

Rachel left a will 23 Mar 1795, probated in 29 Dec 1795 in AC. (Nottingham Wills:431 (will of Rachel Richardson)) To dau. Peggy Mears Richardson whole estate & should she die without issue to my goddau. Rachel Edwards. McKeel Bonwell Sr. extr. Witnessed by William Bell Sr., William Bell Jr., Mary Budd & Mc. Bonwell. Rachel's estate was settled 26 Jan 1802 in AC. (MilesW&A:444 (settlement of Rachel Richardson)) 26 Apr 1795 (Audit), 26 Jan 1802 (Rec'd) - M. Bonewell admr. Auditors: Robert Snead & Caleb Mears.

+ 25 iv. Michael 'Mikeel' Bonnewell, b. c1746, d. c1805.
26 v. Hannah Bonnewell, b. in AC c1746
27 vi. Leah Bonnewell, b. in AC c1748.
+ 28 vii. James Bonnewell, b. c1750, d. Jan 1799.

16. John[4] Bonnewell Senior (John[3], James[2], James[1]), b. in AC c1702, d. c1790. No will or administration has been found for John Bonwell, Senr. He gave his property away before he died. He gave an estimated 150 acres of land to his son, Jacob Lurton Bonwell, on 3 Sep 1784, "for natural love and affection I bear him." (AC Deeds 1783-1788:162) Son Jacob agreed to furnish his father with "necessary board, washing and lodging during his natural life," Son James, "heir-at-law of John Bonewell, Senr" carne into court "to Contest the probate of said deed Alledging that said John was Insane and Incompetent to the Conveying of his property." (p. 163) The deed was recorded, not withstanding. John Bonwell, Senr gave slaves and a still with worm to his son Stephen Bonewell on 2 Feb 1785. (p. 281) He gave his son James Bonewell slaves, livestock, household furniture and tools on 23 Sep 1785. (p. 281) The above transactions show that John Bonwell, Senr had a dau. Mary and sons James Bonwell, Stephen Bonwell and Jacob Lurton Bonwell.

He married three times. He m. 1st c1745, Mary Lurton. (Nottingham Wills: 250 (will of Jacob Lurton Sr.)) Apparently John Bonwell, Senr and his brother James married sisters, Mary Lurton and Hannah Lurton. The will of John Lurton in 1749 gave his as Hannah, Rachel, Elizabeth, Susanna, and Mary and a son Jacob Lurton. (ACW&c., 1745-1749:489) Jacob Lurton, who d. testate in 1770, left property to two of John Bonwell, Senr's children, Mary Bonwell and Stephen Bonwell and also named one child of James Bonwell. (AC Wills 1767-1772:399) The marriage of John Bonwell, Senr to Mary Lurton could have been a second marriage, as a John and Jane Bonwell witnessed the will of Elizabeth Smith in 1760. (ACW&c., 1757-1761:177) His wife's name could also have been Mary Jane. Mary, b. c1723 in AC, was a dau. of John Lurton and Rachel (N). (Nottingham Wills:152 (will of John Lurton))

He m. 2nd **Jane (N)** before 6 Jan 1755. (Nottingham Wills:197 (will of Elizabeth Smith)) It was on this date that Jane Bonnewell and John Bonnewell witnessed the will of Elizabeth Smith. Jane was either his second wife or his first wife could have been named Mary Jane Lurton. Jane was b. c1730.

He m. 3rd c1785, **Dorothy (N)** (b. c1750). (ACD 1793-1797:420) Only one other reference bearing the name of John Bonwell, Senr has been found. On 20 April 1796, Dorothy Bonwell sold 45 acres to John Wise "that she holds in dower of her late husband, John Bonwell, Senior, deceased, land lying on one of the branches of Onancock Creek. (AC Deeds 1793-1797:420) It is apparent from this deed that John Bonwell, Senr had d. between 1785 and 1796, leaving a widow Dorothy.

On 31 Aug 1768, John Bonwell, Senr entered a petition in AC Court to have a road turned. (AC OB 1768-1769:154) He stated that a road running through his land "down to William Wise's Does Great Damage to him & Praying Leave to Turn the said Road to go along the line between him & John Bonewell, Junr."

On 8 dec 1769 John Bonewell and his dau. Mary Bonewell and son Stephen Bonewell were named in the will of Jacob Lurton Sr. (Nottingham Wills:250 (will of Jacob Lurton Sr.))

On 1 Feb 1770, John Bonwell, Senr and Stephen Bonwell were "each allowed on oath nine days attendance as witnesses for Jacob Bonwell at the Suit of George Hope." (AC OB 1769-1770:347). This John Bonwell was shown in the records as John Senr. to distinguish between him and a nephew of the same name, who was referred to as John Junr.

John Bonnewell Senior had the following children:

+   29   i. Benjamin^5 Bonnewell, b. c1735, d. Feb 1815.
        30   ii. Reuben Bonnewell, b. in AC c1742. (Carey, *Bonwell to Bonneville*)

John Bonnewell Senior and Mary Lurton had the following children:

+   31   iii. James Bonnewell, b. c1746, d. Dec 1802.
        32   iv. Mary Bonnewell, b. in AC c1748. She was named in her uncle's will dated 8 Dec 1769 in AC. (Nottingham Wills:250 (will of Jacob Lurton Sr))
+   33   v. Stephen Bonnewell, b. c1750, d. Feb 1805.
+   34   vi. Jacob Lurton Bonnewell, b. c1752, d. Jun 1791.

19. Joachim Mikeal⁴ Bonnewell (John³, James², James¹), b. in AC c1710, d. May 1783. (Nottingham Wills: 87 (will of John Bonwell; Nottingham Wills:338 (will of Joakim Michael Bonewell))

He m. c1735, **Peggy Bull** (b. c1710 in AC). (Carey, *Bonwell to Bonneville*) dau. of Tobias Bull II and Frances (N).

Joachim left a will dated 18 Jan 1783, probated 27 May 1783 in AC. (Nottingham Wills:338) To son Michael Bonewell land where I live & all my marsh on Gilford. Mentioned dau. Sarah Russell, dau. Betty Bonewell, dau. Peggy, son Thomas - "but should my said son never return from sea I give my said negroes to be equally divided between my Scarburgh Bonewell & my two sons Elijah & Southy Bonewell." Children Sarah, Betty, Peggy, Scarburgh, Thomas, Elijah & Southy residuary legatees. Friends Mr. Thomas Bailey, George Parker Sr. & George Parker Jr. to divide estate. Son Michael Bonewell extr. Witnessed by George Parker Sr., Sarah Parker & Elizabeth Poulson.

Joachim Mikeal Bonnewell and Peggy Bull had the following children:

35   i. Peggy⁵ Bonnewell, b. in AC c1745, m. c1760, James Lewis (b. c1722 in AC, d. Apr 1784). (Nottingham, *Soldiers of the Eastern Shore*:29 (descendants of Thomas Bonwell, an officer in the Virginia Navy) James was the son of John Lewis and Johanna Taylor. (Mark C. Lewis files; Nottingham Wills:343 (will of James Lewis))

Peggy was named as an heir of Rev War Veteran Thomas Bonwell or Bonnewell, formerly an officer in the Virginia Navy. (See below.) Peggy Bonwell, sister of Thomas, married James Lewis, d. leaving three children: Peggy, Sally and William; Peggy Lewis married Robert Russell, d. leaving children unknown; Sally married Laban Gunter and was now his widow; William Lewis died some years since leaving two children: William and John, both of who are dead leaving Sophia Garner, wife of William, their only heir at law. (Nottingham, *Soldiers of the Eastern Shore*:29 (descendants of Thomas Bonwell, an officer in the Virginia Navy))

+ 36   ii. Micheal 'McKeel' Bonnewell (I), b. c1753, d. before 27 Sep 1831).

+ 37   iii. Betsey 'Betty' Bonnewell, b. c1755

38   iv. Thomas Bonnewell, b. in AC c1757. Thomas Bonnewell served in the Rev War c1776 in AC. Based on information in Sally Gunter Sr.'s will of 1832, her uncle Thomas Bonewell served on board the *Galley* in the Rev War. Thomas Bonwell or Bonnewell, formerly an officer in the Virginia Navy went to sea about 40 years ago and has not been heard from since that time, and is supposed to have been drowned. He left no

children or descendants; he left six brothers and sisters of the whole blood: Richard, Southey, Betsey, McKeel, Sarah and Peggy. 1) Richard Bonnewell, brother of Thomas, died some years ago leaving one child his only heir. Rosa who married Savage Crippen, both of whom died leaving John Crippen and Narcissa Crippen, the only heirs at law of the said Rosa Crippen and of said Richard Bonnewell. 2) Southy Bonnewell, brother of Thomas, is dead leaving Levin Bonnewell and Anna Snead, wife of Isaac Snead his only children and heirs at law. 3) Betsey Bonnewell, sister of Thomas, married James Bonnewell, both of whom died some years since leaving Robert, Sally, Betsey, Elijah and Clement Bonnewell their only children and heirs. Robert son of Betsey is dead leaving Betsey Bull, wife of John Bull Jr. his only daughter and heir at law. Sally Bonwell, daughter of Betsey is living. Betsey Bonwell, daughter of Betsey, married McKeel Wise and is now his widow. Elijah Bonwell, son of Betsey is dead leaving Cleme, Harriett, Tabitha, Sally and Leah Bonwell his only children and heirs at law. Clement Bonwell, son of James and Betsey, is dead, leaving Betsey East, widow of Richard, James Bonwell, Robert Bonwell and Elijah Bonwell his only children and heirs at law. 4) McKeel Bonwell, brother of Thomas, died leaving the children: McKeel, Peggy and Elizabeth; McKeel, son of McKeel, is living; Peggy married William West, d. leaving Polly West her only heir at law; Elizabeth is living. 5) Peggy Bonwell, sister of Thomas, married James Lewis, d. leaving three children: Peggy, Sally and William; Peggy Lewis married Robert Russell, d. leaving children unknown; Sally married Laban Gunter and is now his widow; William Lewis died some years since leaving two children: William and John, both of whom are dead leaving Sophia Garner, wife of William, their only heir at law. 6) Sarah Bonwell, sister of Thomas, married first George Russell and last Smith Melson, all of whom are dead; Sarah left by George Russell two children: Robert and Peggy; Robert is living and Peggy married Benjamin West, d. leaving children unknown; said Sarah left by Smith Melson one dau., Scarborough Turnall, widow of Thomas Turnall. Recorded 27 Sep 1831. (Nottingham, *Soldiers of the Eastern Shore*:29 (descendants of Thomas Bonwell, an officer in the Virginia Navy); and MilesW&A:238 (will of Sally Gunter Sr.))

39 v. Scarburgh Bonnewell, b. c1758 in AC.

+ 40 vi. Elijah Richard Bonnewell, b. c1760, d. Dec 1785.

41 vii. Sarah Bonnewell, b. in AC c1762, m. 1st c1780, George Russell (b. c1740 in AC). She m. 2nd c1790, Smith Melson (b. c1765 in AC, d. Mar 1815). (Nottingham, *Soldiers of the Eastern Shore*:29 (Thomas Bonwell descendants; MilesW&A:376 (will of Smith Melson)) Sarah was named as an heir of Rev War Veteran Thomas Bonwell on 27 Sep 1831 in AC. (Nottingham, *Soldiers of the Eastern Shore*:9 (descendants of Thomas Bonwell, an officer in the Virginia Navy)) Sarah left by George Russell two children: Robert and Peggy; Robert was living and Peggy m. Benjamin West, d. leaving children unknown; said Sarah left by Smith Melson one daughter: Scarborough Turnall, widow of Thomas Turnall.

+ 42 viii. Southy Bonnewell, b. c1765

20. Thomas⁴ Bonnewell (John³, James², James¹), b. in AC c1712, d. Dec 1743. (Nottingham Wills: 87 (will of John Bonwell)); 131 (will of Thomas Bonnywell))

He left a will 1 Dec 1743, probated 27 Dec 1743 in AC. To two sons Geroge & Thomas land I bought of Anthony Hudson lying on the head of Mosongo on the north side of Guilford Road containing 100 acres. Mentioned Hannah Bonnywell, wife of James Bonnywell; Sarah Savage; Elizabeth Ewell; brother James Bonnywell. Balance of estate to be reserved for my two son George & Thomas. Brothers James & Joachim Bonnwell extrs. Witnessed by Griffith Savage, Elizabeth Ewell and John Bonnywell. (Nottingham Wills:131 (will of Thomas Bonnywell))

Thomas Bonnewell had the following children:

+ 43 i. George⁵ Bonnewell, b. c1735.

44 ii. Thomas Bonnewell, b. in AC c1737.

Fifth Generation

22. John⁵ Bonnewell Junior (James⁴, John³, James², James¹), b. in AC c1730, d. Aug 1775. (Nottingham w*lls:* 148 (will of Richard Bonnewell); 286 (will of John Bonwell))

He m. c1765, **Mary Wise** (b. c1740 in AC, d. Aug 1810), dau. of William Wise and Sarah Bonnewell. (Carey, *Bonwell to Bonneville;* Nottingham Wills:245 (will of William Wise Sr.; MilesW&A:80 (will of Mary Bonewell))

He was shown as a cousin John Bonnewell in the will of Richard Bonnewell, who was his father's brother. Cousin often mean niece and nephew. (Nottingham Wills:148 (will of Richard Bonnewell))

John left a will dated 22 Sep 1774, probated 29 Aug 1775 in AC. To wife Mary whole estate during her widhood for the maintenance & education of my 5 children, to-wit: Charles, Hannah, Arthur & Smith Bonwell & unborn child, &

14

for the boarding of all my other children. Should my wife marry or die before my 5 children be educated equal to my elder children, then my son James Bonwell to take my estate into his possession & fulfil this my will. Sister Leah Bonwell. Balance of estate to be divided between my wife & children except James when my youngest child arrives to the age of 12 years. To son James Bonwell my plantation where I now live, also my land & marsh on or near Guilford Creek, also the moiety of a water grist mill I now hold in part with Major Ironmonger, lying on the South branch of Onancock. Son Thomas Bonwell. Wife Mary, James Bonwell & Thomas Bonwell extrs. Witnessed by John Smith, Mikeel Bonwell, James Bonwell & William Kennahorn. (Nottingham Wills:286 (will of John Bonwell))

John Bonnewell Junior had the following children:

+   45   i. James[6] Bonnewell, b. 12 Jan 1750, d. 3 Oct 1819.
+   46   ii. Thomas Bonnewell, b. c1762
      47   iii. John Bonnewell, b. in AC c1764, d. Mar 1818.

(MilesW&A:80 (will of Mary Bonewell; 80 (adm. of John Bonewell))

John was named in his mother's will 25 Sep 1807 in AC. (MilesW&A:80 (will of Mary Bonewell))

On 30 Mar 1818 in AC Charles Bonewell was named to settle the estate of John Bonewell. James Poulson, John Bayly, Thomas Snead, John G. Joynes & William Seymour were the securities. (MilesW&A:80 (adm. & settlements of John Bonewell))

John estate was settled 27 Nov 1820 in AC. (MilesW&A:80 (settlements of John Bonewell)) Settlements: 23 & 29 Oct 1821 (Audit & Rec'd) - Charles Bonewell, admr. On 9 Mar 1820 cash was retained in the hands of the admr. on 2 estates until the final statement of the dec'd estate in Kentucky & Ohio. Auditors: Levin L. Joynes & Edward S. Snead. 9 May 1818 (Inventory & Sale), 28 Jan 1819 (1st Audit), 9 Mar 1820 (2nd Audit), 27 Nov 1820 (Rec'd) - Charles Bonewell admr. Buyers: Charles Bonewell, Betty Bull (Negro), McKeel Bonewell Sr., McKeel Bonewell Jr. & John Bonewell of James to Mary Bonewell. Appraisers: McKeel Bonewell, William Lee & Edward S. Snead. Auditors: Thomas R. Joynes & Levin S. Joynes. In 2nd settlement: Cash paid McKeel & Arthur Bonewell for balance of account. On 9 Mar 1820 cash retained in the hands of the administrator until the final settlement of the business of the dec'd in Kentucky & Ohio. The following received $23.79 from the estate of John

Bonewell: William Budd for his wife Betsey's part, Esther Bell for her part, Charles Bonewell for his part, Henry S. Copes for Jacob Bell's part & by the time the receipt was recorded on 27 Nov 1820, Henry S. Copes was dead & his signature was proved by Levin S. Joynes & Thomas R. Joynes & Levin S. Joynes became the guardian of John Bell, orphan of Edward, & Samuel Lumber for his wife Nancy's part of John Bonewell's estate.

John Bonnewell Junior and Mary Wise had the following children:

+	48	iv.	Rev. Charles Bonnewell, b. c1766, d. 1825.
	49	v.	Hannah Bonnewell, b. in AC c1768
+	50	vi.	Arthur Bonnewell, b. c1770, d. Aug 1825.
+	51	vii.	Smith Bonnewell, b. c1772, d. Oct 1801.
	52	viii.	Nancy Bonnewell, b. in AC c1774, m. c1800, (N) Darby. (Dean Hickman research)
	53	ix.	Molly Bonnewell, b. in AC c1775, m. c1795, Major Bell (b. c1770). (MilesW&A: 80 (will of Mary Bonewell))

Molly was named in her father's will 22 Sep 1774 in AC as an unborn child. (Nottingham Wills:286 (will of John Bonwell))

Molly was named in her mother's will 25 Sep 1807 in AC. (MilesW&A:80 (will of Mary Bonewell)) She was shown as dau, Molly, with her 3 children, Esther Bell, Elizabeth Budd & Nancy Bell.

25. **Michael 'Mikeel'^{5} Bonnewell** (James^4, John^3, James^2, James^1), b. in AC c1746, d. c1805 in Elizabeth City Co. (Dean Hickman research)

He m. c1765, **Elizabeth 'Betty' (N)** (b. c1745. (Whitelaw:797 (tract A51); Nottingham Wills:309 (will of Keziah Flud)) In describing the ownership of tract A51, the William Lurton 60-acres part, Whitelaw states that in 1774 Robert Parker left land to his son John, and seven years later (which would have been 1781) John sold it to Mikeel, Thomas & James Bonewell. The next year they, with Betty and Nancy, the wives of the first two, resold to Zorobabel Rodgers. Also, in 1778 Keziah Flud (Floyd) left items to Bettey Bonewell and Cate Bonewell, dau. of Mikeel Bonwell.

Michael was named in his uncle's will 8 Dec 1769 in AC. (Nottingham Wills:250 (will of Jacob Lurton Sr.))

Michael 'Mikeel' Bonnewell and Elizabeth 'Betty' (N) had the following child:

54	i.	Cate^6 Bonnewell, b. in AC c1767. Cate was named as an heir of Rev War Veteran 24 Feb 1778 in AC. It was on this date that Cate Bonwell, daughter of Mikeel Bonwell was named in the will of Keziah Flud. Bettey

Bonwell, evidently her mother, was also named. (Nottingham:309 (will of Keziah Flud))

28. James[5] Bonnewell (James[4], John[3], James[2], James[1]), b. in AC c1750, d. Jan 1799. (Nottingham Wills:458 (will of James Bonwell) ; 236 (will of James Bonnewell))

He m. c1775, **Betsey 'Betty' Bonnewell** (b. c1755 in AC), dau. of Joachim Mikeal Bonnewell and Peggy Bull. (Nottingham Wills:338 (will of Joakim Michael Bonewell))

James left a will dated 11 Dec 1798, probated 28 Jan 1799 in AC. He was shown as James Bonwell, son of James. To wife Betty whole estate during her widowhood. To son Robert all my lands & marsh. Balance of estate to be divided between all my children except Robert. Wife & son Robert extrs. Witnessed by William Gibb, Sarah Rodgers and M. Bonawell. (Nottingham Wills:458 (will of James Bonwell))

James estate was settled 26 Oct 1802 in AC. (MilesW&A:79 (settlement of James Bonewell)) 10 Apr 1799 (Inventory), 29 Jan 1801 (Sale), 24 Oct 1802 (Audit), 26 Oct 1802 (Rec'd) - Robert Bonewell extr. Auditors: William Seymour & George Scarburgh.

James Bonnewell and Betsey 'Betty' Bonnewell had the following children:

- \+   55   i.   Clement[6] Bonnewell, b. c1775, d. Nov 1815.
- \+   56   ii.   Robert Bonnewell, b. c1775.
-        57   iii.   Sally Bonnewell, b. in AC c1778. On 27 Sep 1831 she was named as an heir of Rev War Veteran Thomas Bonwell, she being a dau. of Betsey Bonnewell, sister of Thomas Bonwell. (Nottingham, *Soldiers of the Eastern Shore*:29 (descendants of Thomas Bonwell, an officer in the Virginia Navy))
-        58   iv.   Elizabeth 'Betsey' Bonnewell, b. in AC c1780, m. c1800, McKeely Wise (b. c1780 in AC, d. Jun 1809 at age 28). (Nottingham, *Soldiers of the Eastern Shore*:29 (descendants of Thomas Bonwell, an officer in the Virginia Navy)) (MilesW&A, p.620 (adm. of McKeely Wise))

    On 26 Jun 1809 Elizabeth was named as administrator of the estate of McKeely Wise, AC. John Joynes, Clement Bonewell & William S. Watson were the securities. (MilesW&A, p.620 (adm. of McKeely Wise))

    On 27 Sep 1831 Elizabeth (Betsey) was named as an heir of Rev. War Veteran Thomas Bonnewell (being a dau. of Betsey Bonnewell, sister of Thomas Bonnewell). (Nottingham, *Soldiers of the Eastern Shore*:29 (descendants of Thomas Bonwell, an officer in the Virginia Navy))

- \+   59   v.   Elijah R. Bonnewell, b. c1788, d. Jan 1823.

29. Benjamin[5] Bonnewell (John[4], John[3], James[2], James[1]), b. in AC c1735, d. Feb 1815.

He m. c1756-63, **Mary Parker** (b. c1730), widow of Sacker Parker. (ACD *1757-1770*:182a; Nottingham Wills:186 (will of Sacker Parker))

The only member of the fourth generation, who died without a will naming sons, was John Bonwell, Senr. Since he was married and had three known sons, it is only logical to suppose he had others, one of whom was Benjamin Bonwell.

The name of Benjamin Bonwell first appears in AC records in 1764, when he and his wife Mary sold her one-third dower right in her former husband Sacker Parker's land. (ACD 1757-1770:182a) It can be assumed that Benjamin was at least 20 years of age at this time, placing his birth date not later than 1744. Indeed, he could have been slightly older, for Sacker Parker died testate in 1756, naming wife Mary, his father, brother John, a sister, and an unborn child. (Wills 1752-1757:352) While there is no proof in the records, several other factors point to Benjamin being the son of John Bonwell, Senr. Since this John Bonwell inherited land from his father on the north side of Onancock Creek, and lived there with Fooks, Michells, Parkers, and Wises as neighbors. The land owned by Sacker Parker, called *Ohio*, was located on the south side of Deep Creek, and only slightly north of the Bonwell land. (Whitelaw:967) This shows that Benjamin Bonwell and the widow, Mary Parker, were neighbors. Also supporting this possibility is the fact that Benjamin Bonwell named a son John.

On 28 Dec 1769 Benjamin Bonwell petitioned the court to see that the estate of Sacker Parker deceased be settled according to said Parker's will. (ACO 1769-70:310)

The action upon the Case brought by Benjamin Bonwell plaintiff against Robinson Savage Defendant being at Issue is Continued for tryal till next Court; p. 1.47 - case extended till next Court; p. 189, 7 June 1774 - Came the Parties by their Attorneys and thereupon Came also a Jury - defendant awarded one pound, thirteen shillings and eight pence and to go hence without Day (delay?) and recover against said plaintiff his costs by him about his Defence in his behalf ... (p. 233), 30 Sep 1774 - Ordered that Robinson Savage pay to Thomas Bayly 75 pounds of Tobacco for three days attending this court as a Witness for him at the Suit of Benjamin Bonwell.(ACO 1774-77:82)

Benjamin was living c1775 in WO Co. The records indicate that Benjamin Bonwell moved from AC, after 7 June 1774 when he last appeared in court there, into WO Co., by 1 March 1778, when his name was included on the return of William Hopewell, listing those who had taken Oaths of Fidelity in WO Co. (DAR Library, Wash. D.C.) His name again appeared on a roster of WO Co. militia in 1780, among those of Capt. Walton's Company, Snow Hill Battalion. (DAR Library) Later records show that other members of the 8th Class were neighbors: Joshua Driden (Dryden), Jacob Merrill, Smith Carey, Joshua Riggen, John Redden, Zadok Ardis, Staten Trader and John Allen.

30 Jan 1783 - Thomas Wise, plaintiff against Benjamin Bonwell, defendant - covenant broken. The details of the case are not given, but directly below appear these words - "John Riley of this county came into court and undertakes for the defendant that in case he shall be cast (?) in this suit he shall satisfy and pay the condemnation of the court or render his body to prison in execution for

18

the same or that he the said John Riley will do it for him and therefore the defendant preys and has leave to import till the next court and then to plead." The problem must have been resolved by the time of the next court, for nothing more is found of this case. (AC OB1780-83:429)

The Maryland tax list of 1783 shows that Benjamin Bonwell was raising his family in lower WO Co. The return for Mattapany Hundred, lists Bonwell being taxed for 200 acres called *Wakefield* and 200 acres *Wakefield Discovery*, valued at £305 (Box 6) He owned three horses and ten black cattle, valued at £41.10. Other personal property was valued at £30.10 for a total assessment of £377. He paid £4.14.3 tax and had six males and three females in his household. Mattapony Hundred was the southeastern part of WO Co., adjacent to the AC/MD state line. The 300 acres called *Wakefield* had been patented on 26 March 1687 by William Stevens and assigned to Francis Jenkins "near the Divisional Line on the West side Swanefsett branch." (Md. Land Office. Rent Rolls 9:107) Frances Jenkins had left the land to James Smith of Virginia (Dryden, Land Records of WO Co., p.658) The land had remained in the Smith family until a later James Smith sold part to Thomas Davis on 4 June 1789. (WOD M:546) and the balance to Benjamin Aydellotte on 4 Feb 1791. (WOD N:415) An item of interest is that the 1783 tax assessment for Mattapony Hundred, showing Benjamin Bonwell paying taxes on 200 acres *Wakefield*, also shows a Sacker Parker of Virginia being taxed for the other 100 acres. It is obvious that both men were leasing the land and this Sacker Parker was likely a son of Mary Bonwell by her first husband, the unborn child mentioned in Sacker Parker's will. William Parker, son of John Parker II and wife Bridget Sacker, died testate in AC in 1758, naming a grandson Sacker Parker. (AC Wills 1757-1761. p. 33) This would have been William Parker, father of the first Sacker who died in 1756, and who joined the widow Mary as an extr. of his son's will. (AC Wills 1752-1757:352) Benjamin Bonewell's name first appeared in WO Co. deeds on 13 Nov 1783, when he was named on a bond by Nehemiah Holland. (WOD M:307) He bought his first land in WO Co. on 16 Aug 1790, from John Holland, son and heir of Nehemiah. (WOD N:343) He paid £200 for parts of two adjoining tracts called *Fox Harbour* and *Allens Industry*, totaling 89¾ acres. He bought an additional 10 acres of *Allens Industry* from John Allen, Junr on 31 March 1791 for £22.10. (WOD 0:106) On 11 Feb 1793, Benjamin Bonewell bought 3 acres of *Rotten Quarter* from Ezekiel Brumley (WOD P:55), and on 8 Feb 1800, he purchased a final 7 acres of *Rotten Quarter* from Jebez Brumbly. (WOD T:485). In all, Benjamin Bonewell bought 109 acres of WO Co. land, all of which he owned at the time of his death. The land was located northwest of *Wakefield*, the land he had leased on a head branch of Swansgut Creek. Present-day maps show Holly Swamp Road extending southeast from Goodwill toward Welbourne, through this area.

He left a will dated 4 Apr 1807, probated 10 Mar 1815 in WO Co. To dau. Mary Bonnewell a bed and furniture. He gave son George Bonnwell a hand mill. He directed that the remainder of his estate be equally divided between his five children; Severn Bonnewell, John Bonnewell, George Bonnewell, Edward Hearn Bonnewell, and daughter Mary. He named no extr. (WOW MH#10:86) The will was presented by son Severn Bonnewell on the day it was recorded and John Allen, Senr and Levin Tull, two of the witnesses, gave oaths on the same day that they had seen Benjamin Bonewell sign the will. (WOW MH#10:86) On 22 March 1815, Benjamin Gunby and Nehemiah Holland, arbitrators, signed a statement that they had been appointed by Benjamin Bonnewell's sons to put a valuation on the lands of their father and to award said lands to son George Bonnewell, "he paying unto said Severn Bonnewell, John Bonnewell and Edward Bonnewell the several sums of money." (WOD AL:232) Severn Bonnewell and wife Ann, of Sussex Co., DE, gave a deed to George Bonnwell of WO Co., on 5 Sep 1820, for all his right and title to the 109 acres "that fell to him by his father," including three tracts, *Fox Harbor*, *Allens Industry*, and *Rotten Quarter*. (WOD AL:230) George paid Severn $163 for his share and it can be assumed he paid his other two brothers or their heirs a like amount.

Benjamin Bonnewell and Mary (N) had the following children:

	60	i.	Mary[6] Bonnewell, b. in AC c1765, probably d. before 1815 (as she did not share in the sale of her father's lands as his will directed). (WOW MH-10:86) Mary d. before 1815.
+	61	ii.	Severn Bonnewell, b. c1766, d. 1821.
+	62	iii.	John Bonnewell, b. c1768, d. by 29 Sep 1815.
+	63	iv.	George Bonnewell b. c1770, d. Sep 1837.
+	64	v.	Edward Hearn Bonnewell, b. c1773, d. Aug 1819.

31. **James**[5] **Bonnewell** (John[4], John[3], James[2], James[1]), b. in AC c1746, d. Dec 1802. (ACD *1783-1788*:163) MilesW&A:79 (will of James Bonwell))

On 3 Sep 1784 son James Bonewell, heir-at-law of John Bonewell Senr., came into court "to Contest the probate of said deed Alledging that said John was Insane and Incompetent to the Conveying of his property." (p. 163) The deed was recorded, not withstanding. John Bonwell, Senr gave slaves and a still with worm to his son Stephen Bonewell on 2 Feb 1785 (p. 281) He gave his son James Bonewell slaves, livestock, household furniture and tools on 23 Sep 1785 (p. 281)(ACD *1783-1788*: 163)

He left a will dated 19 Nov 1802, probated 27 Dec 1802 in AC To son John Bonewell my plantation where I live, my yoke of steers, a mare I purchased of John Bonewell, my still &,... To son George Bonewell £100,.. & he to pay son John Bonewell in 5 equal annual payments. To dau, Rachel Bonewell one spinning wheel. Remainder to my dau, Susanna Wise, dau, Rachel, my son George, dau. Mary, dau, Ann Bonewell & dau. Sarah Bonewell. If son John Bonewell dies without heirs, my plantation should go to my son George Bonewell. Son John Bonewell extr. Witnessed by Sarah Rodgers, John Smith & William Guy. Southey Satchell & John Smith securities. (MilesW&A:79 (will of James Bonwell))

James Bonnewell had the following children:

+   65   i.   John^6 Bonnewell, b. c1773
+   66   ii.   George Bonnewell, b. c1775
       67   iii.   Rachel Bonnewell, b. in AC c1777. (MilesW&A:79 (will of James Bonwell))
       68   iv.   Susanna Bonnewell, b. in AC c1779, d. Mar 1850, m. c1800, (N) Wise. (MilesW&A:79 (will of James Bonwell)) She left a will dated 11 Aug 1841, probated 25 Mar 1850 in AC. (MilesW&A:622 (will of Susannah Wise))
       69   v.   Mary Bonnewel, b. in AC c1781. (MilesW&A:79 (will of James Bonwell)
       70   vi.   Ann Bonnewell, b. in AC c1783. (MilesW&A:79 (will of James Bonwell))
       71   vii.   Sarah Bonnewell, b. in AC c1785. (MilesW&A:79 (will of James Bonwell))

33. **Stephen**^{5} **Bonnewell** (John^4, John^3, James^2, James^1),b. in AC c1750, d. Feb 1805. (Nottingham Wills:250 (will of Jacob Lurton Sr.; MilesW&A:82 (will of Stephen Bonewell))

He m. 1st 21 May 1796 (bond), **Peggy Topping** (b. c1775 in AC). (ACM) George Topping was the security on the M.L.B. of Stephen Bonwell and Peggy Topping. He m. 2nd c1800, **Ann 'Nancy' (N)**. (ACM:44 (marriage of George Bull and Ann Bonwell showed her as the widow of Stephen); FA CD309) She m. **George B. Bull Sr.** 6 Jun 1810 (bond) in AC. (ACM) George T. Gibb was the security on the M.L.B. of George Bull of Benjamin and Ann Bonwell, widow of Stephen.

Stephen Bonewell, son of John Bonewell was named in his uncle's will 8 Dec 1769 in AC. (Nottingham Wills:250 (will of Jacob Lurton Sr.))

He left a will dated 15 Feb 1805, probated in AC. To son Jesse Bonewell the land whereon I now live. To dau. Nancy Wise $1. To dau. Rosey Topping $1. Remainder to my son William & dau. Elizabeth, except what shall be given to my wife Nancy. The monies from the sale of my estate to my son William [underage] & he to be bound to some trade or extr. to keep him himself. Friend William Seymour extr. Witnessed by John Bonewell, Susey Wise & Elizabeth Bonewell. John S. Ker & John K. Revell securities. (MilesW&A:82 (will of Stephen Bonewell)) Estate settlement: 26 Feb 1805 (Inventory), 28 Feb 1805 (Sale), 13 Apr 1808 (Order to Audit), 26 Apr 1808 (Rec'd) - Appraisers: Samuel Waples, James Poulson & Charles Snead. Buyers: Nancy Bonewell, Jesse Bonewell, Negro Peter (Wests). Legacy left son Jesse. Cash paid James Wise for legacy left to his wife. Cash received of Negro Peter West. Cash received of Negro Bill (Guys) Cash received of Isaiah Bagwell for Stephen Bonewell.

Stephen Bonnewell had the following children:
       72   i.   Nancy^6 Bonnewell, b. in AC c1770, m. c1795, James Wise (b. c1770). (MilesW&A82 (will of Stephen Bonewell))
       73   ii.   Rosey Bonnewell, b. in AC c1775, m. 24 Dec 1795 in AC, George Topping (b. c1770 in AC). (MilesW&A:82 (will of Stephen Bonewell; ACM)
       74   iii.   Jesse B. Bonnewell, b. in AC c1779, d. Feb 1857. (MilesW&A:82 (will of Stephen Bonewell; FA CD309;

MilesW&A:80 (adm. of Jesse Bonnawell)) He m. 1st 4 Dec 1806 (bond), AC, Peggy Dix (b. c1780 in AC). Reuben Rogers was the security on the M.L.B. of Jesse Bonwell and Peggy Dix. (ACM)

He m. 2nd 6 Oct 1835 (bond) in AC, Nancy Fox (b. c1804 in AC). Thomas R. Joynes was the security on the M.L.B. of Jesse Bonwell and Nancy Fox. (ACM; FA CD309)

Jesse was listed as a head of household in the census of 1850 in St. George Parish, AC. (FA CD309) He was shown as Jessee Bonwell the head of HH#183, a 71 year old farmer with real estate valued at $500. Listed with him were Nancy Bonwell, age 46 and Henry Major, age 12 and black.

Nancy Bonnawell was named to settle Jesse's estate on 23 Feb 1857 in AC. (MilesW&A:80 (adm. of Jesse Bonnawell)) John Fox, James Fox and George W. Custis were the securities.

Stephen Bonnewell and Peggy Topping had the following children:

75   iv.   William Bonnewell, b. in AC c1796. (MilesW&A:82 (will of Stephen Bonewell)) He was shown as an underage son William Bonewell in the will of Stephen Bonewell.

76   v.   Elizabeth Bonnewell, b. in AC c1798, m. 18 Feb 1815 (bond) in AC Thomas Sharrod (b. c1795). (MilesW&A:82 (will of Stephen Bonewell; ACM) John Hogshear & Henry S. Copes were the securities on the M.L.B. of Thomas Sharrod and Betsey Boniwell.

34. **Jacob Lurton[5] Bonnewell** (John[4], John[3], James[2], James[1]), b. c1752 in AC, d. Jun 1791. (ACD *1783-1788:*162; Nottingham Wills:389 (will of Jacob Bonewell))

He m. c1790, **(N) Bishop** (b. c1770 in AC), dau. of Muns Bishop. (MilesW&A:336 (will of Easter Ling))

Jacob received 150 acres as a gift from his father on 3 Sep 1784 in AC. (ACD *1783-1788:* 162) Jacob agreed to furnish his father with necessary board, washing and lodging during his natural life.

He left a will dated 23 Apr 1791 in AC, probated 28 Jun 1791. (Nottingham Wills:389 (will of Jacob Bonewell)) After payment of debts estate to be divided between my 4 children, subject to the provision which the law makes for my wife. Friend Levin Bloxom extr. Witnessed by John Teackle Sr., Southy Bishop and Esther Bishop.

Jacob Lurton Bonnewell and (N) Bishop had the following children:

77   i.   Mary 'Molly'[6] Bonnewell, b. in AC c1790, m. 5 Feb 1825 (bond), Thomas West (b. c1790 in AC). (ACM) Alexander Lang Jr. and Littleton Bloxom were the

securities on the M.L.B. of Thomas West, widower, and Mary Boniwell of Jacob.

Mary was named as an heir of Rev War Veteran 6 Jan 1814 in AC. (MilesW&A:336 (will of Easter Ling)) She was shown as Molly Bonewell (no relationship) in the will of Easter Ling. She was to receive all houses & orchards &,.. after my husband dies. Since Jacob Bonewell had a known dau. Mary who m.Thomas West in 1825 and since a Southy Bishop and an Esther Bishop both wittnessed his will in 1791, this Molly Bonewell is assumed to be a dau. of Jacob Bonewell and it is also assumed that Jacob had married a sister of Esther Ling, thus making Molly Bonewell her niece.

78 ii. Hetty Bonnewell (unproven, but Jacob Bonnewell did have 4 children living when he died in 1791), b. in AC c1790, m. 26 Dec 1809 (bond), Edmund Melson (b. c1785 in AC). (ACM) Robert Melson was the security on the M.L.B. of Edmund Melson and Hetty Bonwell.

36. Micheal 'McKeel'[5] Bonnewell (I) (Joachim Mikeal[4], John[3], James[2], James[1]), b. in AC c1753, d. before 27 Sep 1831. (Nottingham Wills:338 (will of Joakim Michael Bonewell); and Nottingham, *Soldiers of the Eastern Shore*:29 (descendants of Thomas Bonwell, an officer in the Virginia Navy))

He m. 1st c1775, **Molly (N)** (b. c1755) and m. 2nd 16 Feb 1820 (bond) **Margaret Russell** (b. c1786 in AC, d. 26 Oct 1867), dau. of Abel Russell and Leah Chambers. John Watson of John was the security on the M.L.B. of McKeel Bonewell Sr., widower, and Margaret Russell of Abel. The 1850 census puts her birth at 1780 and her tombstone puts it at 1782, but since her parents were married in 1785, she may have been born a little later. Or perhaps her mother was not Leah Chambers, who m. her father Abel Russell in 1785. (ACM; FA CD309; MLAC) Her body was interred in Cokesbury Meth Ch Cem, Onancock, E AC. Her tombstone shows her as Margaret Bonniwell, who d, 26 Oct 1867 at the age of 85 years, 0 months and 0 days.

Micheal was named as administrator of an estate 27 Dec 1785 in AC to settle the estate of Elijah Bonewell. John Bull was security. (Nottingham Wills:345 (adm. of Elijah Bonewell))

Micheal was named as an heir of Rev War Veteran Thomas Bonwell on 27 Sep 1831 in AC. (Nottingham, *Soldiers of the Eastern ShoreL* (descendants of Thomas Bonwell, an officer in the Virginia Navy). McKeel Bonwell, brother of Thomas, d. leaving the children: McKeel, Peggy and Elizabeth; McKeel, son of McKeel, was living; Peggy m, William West and d, leaving Polly West her only heir at law.

Micheal 'McKeel' Bonnewell (I) and Molly (N) had the following children:

+ 79 i. McKeel[6] Bonnewell (II), b. c1779, d. 22 Apr 1856.

80 ii. Peggy Bonnewell, b. in AC c1810, m. c1830, William West (b. c1810 in AC). (Nottingham, *Soldiers of the Eastern*

Shore:29 (descendants of Thomas Bonwell, an officer in the Virginia Navy))

Peggy was named as an heir of Rev War Veteran 27 Sep 1831 in AC. (Nottingham, *Soldiers of the Eastern Shore*:29 (descendants of Thomas Bonwell, an officer in the Virginia Navy)) McKeel Bonwell, brother of Thomas, died leaving the children: McKeel, Peggy and Elizabeth; McKeel, son of McKeel, is living; Peggy married William West, d. leaving Polly West her only heir at law; Elizabeth is living.

Micheal 'McKeel' Bonnewell (I) and Margaret Russell had the following child:

81   iii.   Elizabeth 'Betsey' Bonnewell. b. in AC c1827 (FA CD309; and Nottingham, *Soldiers of the Eastern Shore*:29 (descendants of Thomas Bonwell, an officer in the Virginia Navy; FA CD309) Elizabeth was named as an heir of Rev War Veteran Thomas Bonwell, 27 Sep 1831 in AC. (Nottingham, *Soldiers of the Eastern Shore*:29 (descendants of Thomas Bonwell, an officer in the Virginia Navy)) According to the records McKeel Bonwell, brother of Thomas, d. leaving the children: McKeel, Peggy and Elizabeth; McKeel, son of McKeel, was living; Peggy m. William West and d. leaving Polly West her only heir at law; Elizabeth was living.

On 24 Apr 1837, Elizabeth Boniwell, orphan of McKeel Boniwell, one of the heirs of Thomas Boniwell, officer in the Virginia Navy in the Rev. War, chose Samuel C. White to be her guardian.(Nottingham, *Soldiers of the Eastern Shore*:62 (Eizabeth Boniwell, orphan, chose guardian))

Elizabeth was listed with her mother in the census of 1850 in St. George Parish, AC. (FA CD309) She was shown as Betsey Bonewell, age 23 in HH#1260 headed by Marg't Bonewell, age 70.

37. **Betsey 'Betty'[5] Bonnewell** (Joachim Mikeal[4], John[3], James[2], James[1]), b. in AC c1755. (Nottingham Wills:338 (will of Joakim Michael Bonewell))

She m. c1775, **James Bonnewell** (b. c1750), d. 1799), son of James Bonnewell and Hannah Lurton. Betsey was named in her husband's will dated 11 Dec 1798 in AC. (Nottingham: AC Wills*1663-1800*,:458 (will of James Bonwell) & 236 (will of James Bonnewell))

Betsey was named as an heir of Rev War Veteran Thomas Bonwell on 27 Sep 1831 in AC. Thomas Bonwell or Bonnewell, formerly an officer in the Virginia Navy went to sea about 40 years ago and has not been heard from since that time, and is supposed to have been drowned. He left six brothers and sisters of the whole blood: Richard, Southey, Betsey, McKeel, Sarah and Peggy. Betsey

Bonnewell, sister of Thomas, m. James Bonnewell, both of whom d. some years since leaving Robert, Sally, Betsey, Elijah and Clement Bonnewell their only children and heirs. Robert son of Betsey is dead leaving Betsey Bull, wife of John Bull Jr. his only daughter and heir at law. Sally Bonwell, dau. of Betsey was living. Betsey Bonwell, dau. of Betsey, m. McKeel Wise and was now his widow. Elijah Bonwell, son of Betsey was dead leaving Cleme, Harriett, Tabitha, Sally and Leah Bonwell his only children and heirs at law. Clement Bonwell, son of James and Betsey, was dead, leaving Betsey East, widow of Richard, James Bonwell, Robert Bonwell and Elijah Bonwell his only children and heirs at law. (Nottingham, *Soldiers of the Eastern Shore*:29 (descendants of Thomas Bonwell, an officer in the Virginia Navy))

James Bonnewell and Betsey 'Betty' Bonnewell had the following children:

+ 55 i. Clement[6] Bonnewell, b. c1775, d. Nov 1815.
+ 56 ii. Robert Bonnewell, b. c1775
  57 iii. Sally Bonnewell, b. in AC c1778. Sally was named as an heir of Rev War Veteran 27 Sep 1831 in AC. Betsey Bonnewell, sister of Thomas, m. James Bonnewell, both of whom d. some years since leaving Robert, Sally, Betsey, Elijah and Clement Bonnewell their only children and heirs. Sally Bonwell, daughter of Betsey is living. Nottingham, *Soldiers of the Eastern Shore*:29 (descendants of Thomas Bonwell, an officer in the Virginia Navy))
  58 iv. Elizabeth 'Betsey' Bonnewell, b. in AC c1780, m. McKeely Wise c1800 (b. c1780 in AC, d. Jun 1809. (Nottingham, *Soldiers of the Eastern Shore*:29 (descendants of Thomas Bonwell, an officer in the Virginia Navy)) (MilesW&A, p.620 (adm. of McKeely Wise))

On 26 Jun 1809 Elizabeth Wise was named to settle the estate of McKeely Wise. John Joynes, Clement Bonewell & William S. Watson were the securities. (MilesW&A, p.620 (adm. of McKeely Wise))

Elizabeth was named as an heir of Rev War Veteran Thomas Bonwell on 27 Sep 1831 in AC. Betsey Bonnewell, sister of Thomas, m. James Bonnewell, both of whom died some years since leaving Robert, Sally, Betsey, Elijah and Clement Bonnewell their only children and heirs. Betsey Bonwell, dau. of Betsey, m. McKeel Wise and is now his widow. (Nottingham, *Soldiers of the Eastern Shore*:29 (descendants of Thomas Bonwell, an officer in the Virginia Navy))

+ 59 v. Elijah R. Bonnewell, b. c1788, d. Jan 1823.

40. **Elijah Richard[5] Bonnewell** (Joachim Mikeal[4], John[3], James[2], James[1]), b. in AC c1760, d. Dec 1785 at 25 years of age. (Nottingham, *Soldiers of the Eastern Shore*:29 descendants of Thomas Bonwell, an officer in the Virginia Navy); Nottingham Wills:345 (adm. of Elijah Bonewell))

On 27 Dec 1785 in AC Mickeel Bonewell was named to settle the estate of Elijah Bonewell. John Bull was the security. (Nottingham Wills:345 (adm. of Elijah Bonewell))

Elijah was named as an heir of Rev War Veteran Thomas Bonwell on 27 Sep 1831 in AC. Thomas Bonwell or Bonnewell, formerly an officer in the Virginia Navy went to sea about 40 years ago and has not been heard from since that time, and is supposed to have been drowned. He left six brothers and sisters of the whole blood: Richard, Southey, Betsey, McKeel, Sarah and Peggy. Richard Bonnewell, brother of Thomas, died some years ago leaving one child his only heir. Rosa who married Savage Crippen, both of whom died leaving John Crippen and Narcissa Crippen, the only heirs at law of the said Rosa Crippen and of said Richard Bonnewell. (Nottingham, *Soldiers of the Eastern Shore*:29 (descendants of Thomas Bonwell, an officer in the Virginia Navy))

Elijah Richard Bonnewell had the following child:

> 82   i.   Rosa[6] Bonnewell b. in AC c1785, m. c1805, Savage Crippen (b. c1780 in AC). (Nottingham, *Soldiers of the Eastern Shore*:29 (descendants of Thomas Bonwell, an officer in the Virginia Navy))

42. **Southy[5] Bonnewell** (Joachim Mikeal[4], John[3], James[2], James[1]), b. in AC c1765. (Nottingham Wills:338 (will of Joakim Michael Bonewell))

He m. 27 Mar 1787 (bond) in AC, **Mary Snead** (b. c1765). (ACM) Skinner Wallop was the security on the M.L.B. of Southy Bonewell and Mary Snead.

Southy was named as an heir of Rev War Veteran Thomas Bonwell on 27 Sep 1831 in AC Thomas Bonwell or Bonnewell, formerly an officer in the Virginia Navy went to sea about 40 years ago and has not been heard from since that time, and is supposed to have been drowned. He left no children or descendants; he left six brothers and sisters of the whole blood: Richard, Southey, Betsey, McKeel, Sarah and Peggy. Southy Bonnewell, brother of Thomas, is dead leaving Levin Bonnewell and Anna Snead, wife of Isaac Snead his only children and heirs at law. (Nottingham, *Soldiers of the Eastern Shore*:29 (descendants of Thomas Bonwell, an officer in the Virginia Navy))

Southy Bonnewell and Mary Snead had the following children:

> 83   i.   Levin[6] Bonnewell, b. in AC c1800. In 1831 Levin was living in Mason Co, KY. Levin was named as an heir of Rev War Veteran 27 Sep 1831 in AC. Southy Bonnewell, brother of Thomas, is dead leaving Levin Bonnewell and Anna Snead, wife of Isaac Snead his only children and heirs at law. (Nottingham, *Soldiers of the Eastern Shore*:29 (descendants of Thomas Bonwell, an officer in the Virginia Navy); Dean Hickman research)
>
> Levin was named in his sister's will dated 15 Mar 1849 in AC. (MilesW&A:496 (will of Anna Snead))
>
> 84   ii.   Anna Bonnewell, b. in AC c1802, d. Jul 1849. She m. 25 Jun 1831 (bond) in AC, Isaac Snead. Borden Snead

and James W. Twiford were the securities on the
M.L.B. of Isaac Snead, widower, and Ann Boniwell.
(Nottingham, *Soldiers of the Eastern Shore*:29 (descendants of
Thomas Bonwell, an officer in the Virginia Navy); MilesW&A;
ACM)

Isaac, b. c1780 in AC, m. 1st 3 Dec 1801 (bond),
Nancy Sharwood. John Hogshire was the security on
the M.L.B. (ACM)

Anna was named as an heir of Rev War Veteran
Thomas Bonwell on 27 Sep 1831 in AC. Southy
Bonnewell, brother of Thomas, is dead leaving Levin
Bonnewell and Anna Snead, wife of Isaac Snead his
only children and heirs at law. (Nottingham, *Soldiers of the
Eastern Shore*:29 (descendants of Thomas Bonwell, an officer in the
Virginia Navy))

She left a will dated 15 Mar 1849, probated 30 Jul
1849 in AC. (MilesW&A:496 (will of Anna Snead))

43. **George^5 Bonnewell** (Thomas^4, John^3, James^2, James^1), b. in AC c1735.

He m. c1762, **Elizabeth 'Betty' Hall** (b. c1745 in AC), dau. of Michael
Hall and Betty Cutler. (Dean Hickman research; Edwards, *Ames, Mears & Allied Lines*)

George was named as the extr. of a will 29 Jun 1777 in AC. (Nottingham
Wills:338 (will of William Cullar))

George witnessed a will 2 Mar 1799 in AC. (Nottingham Wills:459 (will of John
Morrison))

George Bonnewell and Elizabeth 'Betty' Hall had the following children:

+ 85   i. Michael Hall^6 Bonnewell, b. 27 Feb 1763, d. Jan 1832.
86   ii. Edward Bonnewell, b. in AC c1766. (Hickman, *Bonniwell
Family*)

Sixth Generation

45. **James^6 Bonnewell** (John^5, James^4, John^3, James^2, James^1), b. in AC 12 Jan
1750, d. 3 Oct 1819 in Brown Co, OH. (Pell, *Boniwell Family*)

He m. 21 May 1783 (bond) in NC, **Mary Robins** (b. c1766 in AC), dau. of
Arthur Robins Jr. and Tillar (N). Arthur Robins Jr. was the security on the
M.L.B. (Mihalyka, *NC Marriages 1660-1854*)

James served in the Rev War in 10 Feb 1776. James served in the VA
militia as a private. He was discharged Feb 1778 at Valley Forge, PA. He was in
the 9th Regiment of the VA Militia commanded by Capt. Levin Joynes. He
fought in the Battle of Brandywine. When he applied for his Rev War pension
on 12 Sep 1818 he gave his age as 68 years, 8 mos. His final payment voucher
for Rev War service was made on 4 Mar 1820. (Pell, *Boniwell Family*)

James Bonnewell and Mary Robins had the following children:

87   i. Bordwin R.^{7} Bonnewell, b. in AC c1789, d. Aug 1853
in Sidney, Fremont Co, IA. (Hickman, *Bonniwell Family*)

88   ii. Arthur R. Bonnewell, b. in AC c1790, d. 25 Sep 1855 in Edgar Co, IL. (Pell, *Boniwell Family*)

89   iii. Margaret Bonnewell, b. c1793. (Pell, *Boniwell Family*)

90   iv. Thomas Bonnewell, b. c1796. (Pell, *Boniwell Family*)

91   v. James Bonnewell, b. 6 Oct 1798, d. 2 Jan 1875 in Edgar Co., IL. (Pell, *Boniwell Family*)

92   vi. Bridget Bonnewell, b. 19 Sep 1802, d. 10 Jan 1866 in OH. (Pell, *Boniwell Family*)

93   vii. John Bonnewell, b. c1805, m. c1830 Alice Robins (b. c1809). (Pell, *Boniwell Family*)

94   viii. Mary Bonnewell, b. c1808. (Pell, *Boniwell Family*)

46. Thomas^6 **Bonnewell** (John^5, James^4, John^3, James^2, James^1), b. in AC c1762.

He m. c1785, **Nancy (N)** (b. c1765). (Pell, *Boniwell Family*)

Thomas was named in his brother's will 26 Sep 1801 in AC. (MilesW&A:81 (will of Smith Bonewell))

Thomas Bonnewell and Nancy (N) had the following children:

95   i. Nancy^7 Bonnewell, b. c1785. (Pell, *Boniwell Family*)

96   ii. Peggy Bonnewell, b. c1788. (Pell, *Boniwell Family*)

97   iii. Amelia Bonnewell, b. c1791. (Pell, *Boniwell Family*)

98   iv. (N) Bonnewell, b. c1800. (Pell, *Boniwell Family*)

48. Rev. Charles^6 **Bonnewell** (John^5, James^4, John^3, James^2, James^1), b. in AC c1766, d. 1825. (Nottingham Wills:286 (will of John Bonwell))

He m. 6 Jan 1816 (bond), **Nancy Scott** (b. c1790). (Mihalyka, *NC Marriages 1660-1854*) They were married by J. Burton.

Charles was named in his brother's will 26 Sep 1801 in AC. (MilesW&A:81 (will of Smith Bonewell)) He was shown as a brother Charles Bonewell and one of the extrs. in the will of Smith Bonewell.

Charles was named as administrator of the estate of John Bonewell on 30 Mar 1818 in AC. (MilesW&A:80 (adm. of John Bonwell)) James Poulson, John Bayly, Thomas Snead, John G. Joynes & William Seymour were the securities.

Rev. Charles Bonnewell had the following child:

99   i. Susan^7 Bonnewell, b. in AC 15 Mar 1792, d. 5 Nov 1848. Her body was interred in Waterford Farm, NC. Her tombstone shows her as Susan Hanby, mother of John T. Scott. (Mihalyka, *NC Gravestones*) (Dean Hickman research)

50. Arthur^6 **Bonnewell** (John^5, James^4, John^3, James^2, James^1), b. in AC c1770, d. Aug 1825 in Brown Co, OH. (Pell, *Boniwell Family*)

He m. 16 Jan 1794 (bond) in NC, **Susanna Toleman** (b. c1770). Wm. Toleman was the security on the M.L.B. They were married by C. Simpkins. (Mihalyka, *NC Marriages 1660-1854*)

Arthur was named in his brother's will 26 Sep 1801 in AC. (MilesW&A:81 (will of Smith Bonewell))

Arthur Bonnewell and Susanna Toleman had the following children:

    100   i.   Nathaniel[7] Bonnewell, b. in AC c1796. (Pell, *Boniwell Family*)

    101   ii.   John Bonnewell, b. in AC c1799. (Pell, *Boniwell Family*)

    102   iii. Mary Ann Bonnewell, b. c1803. (Pell, *Boniwell Family*)

    103   iv. Susan Bonnewell, b. c1805. (Pell, *Boniwell Family*)

    104   v.   Patsey Bonnewell, b. c1808. (Pell, *Boniwell Family*)

    105   vi. Sally Bonnewell, b. c1811. (Pell, *Boniwell Family*)

    106   vii. Eliza Bonnewell, b. c1814. (Pell, *Boniwell Family*)

    107   viii. Harriet Bonnewell, b. c1817. (Pell, *Boniwell Family*)

    108   ix. Margaret Bonnewell, b. c1820. (Pell, *Boniwell Family*)

51. Smith[6] Bonnewell (John[5], James[4], John[3], James[2], James[1]), b. in AC c1772, d. Oct 1801 in Bracken Co, KY. (MilesW&A:81 (will of Smith Bonnewell)) The location of his death was from Dean Hickman's research.

He left a will 26 Sep 1801, probated 26 Oct 1801 in AC. Brothers John Bonewell & Charles Bonewell, extrs. The following except my land in the Kentucky to which I have already willed to my brother Thomas Bonewell & his children. To my brother Arthur Bonewell all the money that he is owing me & also,.. To brothers John Bonewell & Charles Bonewell all the cash. To brother John,.. To brother John & brother Arthur Bonewell,.. To brothers John, Charles & Arthur,.. To brother John Bonewell,.. My Negro man Levi be forever a free man & all the money he has earned, due me in hands of Zorobabel Joynes. Witnessed by Thomas S. Bayly, John O. Twiford & Molly Wise. William Seymour became the admr. with John S. Ker & William Gibb as securities. (MilesW&A:81 (will of Smith Bonnewell))

Smith's estate was settled 28 Jun 1802 in AC. Legacies to Arthur Bonewell, John Bonewell, Charles Bonewell. Auditors: Samuel Waples, John Bayly & Thomas S. Bayly. (MilesW&A:81 (settlement of Smith Bonnewell))

Smith was named in his mother's will 25 Sep 1807 in AC. Mary Ann Bonewell was named as a supposed dau. of Smith Bonewell in the will of Mary Bonewell. (MilesW&A:80 (will of Mary Bonwell))

Smith Bonnewell had the following child:

    109   i.   Mary Ann[7] Bonnewell, b. in AC c1795, m. 13 Jul 1824 in NC, Peter Moore (b. c1795). Charles Bonwell, guardian of Mary Ann was the security on the M.L.B. of Peter Moore, son of Mathey Moore and Mary Ann Bonwell. Thomas Evans & Benja. Kellum were witnesses. They were married by L. Dix. (MilesW&A:80 (will of Mary Bonwell); Mihalyka, *NC Marriages 1660-1854*)

                Mary Ann Bonewell, dau. of Smith Bonewell, was named in her grandmother's will 25 Sep 1807 in AC. (MilesW&A:80 (will of Mary Bonwell))

55. Clement⁶ Bonnewell (James⁵, James⁴, John³, James², James¹, b. in AC c1775, d. Nov 1815. (MilesW&A:79 (adm. of Clement Bonewell); Nottingham, *Soldiers of the Eastern Shore*:29 (descendants of Thomas Bonwell, an officer in the Virginia Navy); Powell, *AC 1800, 1810, 1820 Census*)
He m. 18 Feb 1804 (bond) in AC, **Rachel Russell** (b. c1785 in AC, d. Dec 1817. William White was the security on the M.L.B..(MilesW&A:81 (adm. & settlement of Rachel Bonewell); ACM)
Clement Bonwell, age 26-45, was listed as a head of household in the census of 1810 in St. George Parish, AC Listed with him were 1 male age 0-10; 1 male age 10-16; 1 female age 0-10; 2 females age 26-45; and 1 slave. (Powell, *AC 1800, 1810, 1820 Census*)
On 28 Nov 1815 Levin S. Joynes was named to settle the estate of Clement Bonewell. Edward Snead & Thomas R. Joynes were the securities. Settlement: 12 Dec 1815 (Inventory & Sale), 29 Jan 1820 (Audit), 31 Jan 1820 (Rec'd) - Levin L. Joynes admr. Buyers: Elijah Bonewell, widow & Rachel Bonewell. Appraisers: William Lee, Elijah Bonewell & Purnell O. Twiford. Named in settlement: McKeel Bonewell Jr., Negro Abram, Jesse Bonewell, Negro Comfort. Cash paid Rachel Bonewell's estate for 2 year's board of Elizabeth, MK Bonewell one of the heirs. Same to James Bonewell, Robert Bonewell & Elijah R. Bonewell. John Bonewell. Auditors: William Lee, Jesse Bonewell & George K. Bowman. AC. (MilesW&A:79 (adm. of Clement Bonewell))
Clement was named as an heir of Rev War Veteran 27 Sep 1831 in AC. Betsey Bonnewell, sister of Thomas, married James Bonnewell, both of whom died some years since leaving Robert, Sally, Betsey, Elijah and Clement Bonnewell their only children and heirs. Clement Bonwell, son of James and Betsey, is dead, leaving Betsey East, widow of Richard, James Bonwell, Robert Bonwell and Elijah Bonwell his only children and heirs at law. (Nottingham, *Soldiers of the Eastern Shore*:29 (descendants of Thomas Bonwell, an officer in the Virginia Navy))
Clement Bonnewell and Rachel Russell had the following children:

110   i.   Elizabeth M.C.⁷ Bonnewell, b. in AC 8 Jan 1805, d. 1 Jan 1872. She was shown as Eliz. M.C. Phillips, who d. of cancer. She was the dau. of Clem. & Rachel Boniwell, b. in AC and a widow. Her son-in-law John F. Bull gave the information. Her body was interred in Bull Bur Ground, Melfa, AC. Her tombstone shows her as Elizabeth M.C. Phillips, wife of Smith Phillips, who d. on 1 Jan 1872. (ACM; WADR; Nottingham, *Soldiers of the Eastern Shore*:29 (descendants of Thomas Bonwell, an officer in the Virginia Navy); MLAC)
She m. 1ˢᵗ 5 Jun 1821 (bond) in AC, Richard East (b. c1800 in AC), son of Severn East and Leannah Badger. Carmine Smith was the security on the M.L.B. of Richard East of Severn and Elizabeth M. Bonwell of Clement. Francis Boggs was guardian. (ACM; MilesW&A:182 (will of Severn East (St. George Parish))

She m. 2nd 10 Dec 1834 (bond) in AC, Smith
Phillips (b. 13 Mar 1790, d. 31 Aug 1868), son of
William Phillips and Rachel (N). Laben Phillips was
the security on the M.L.B. of Smith Phillips and
Elizabeth East, widow of Richard. Smith Phillips was
bur. in Bull Bur Gr, Melfa, AC. (ACM; MLAC)
Elizabeth was named as an heir of a Rev War
Veteran 27 Sep 1831 in AC. Thomas Bonwell or
Bonnewell, formerly an officer in the Virginia Navy
went to sea about 40 years ago and has not been heard
from since that time, and is supposed to have been
drowned. He left no children or descendants; he left six
brothers and sisters of the whole blood: Richard,
Southey, Betsey, McKeel, Sarah and Peggy. Betsey
Bonnewell, sister of Thomas, married James
Bonnewell, both of whom died some years since
leaving Robert, Sally, Betsey, Elijah and Clement
Bonnewell their only children and heirs. Clement
Bonwell, son of James and Betsey, is dead, leaving
Betsey East, widow of Richard, James Bonwell, Robert
Bonwell and Elijah Bonwell his only children and heirs
at law., (Nottingham, *Soldiers of the Eastern Shore*:29 (descendants
of Thomas Bonwell, an officer in the Virginia Navy))
Elizabeth Phillips, age 45, was listed with her
husband in the census of 1850 in St. George Parish, AC
(HH#979) headed by Smith Phillips, a 60 year old
farmer with real estate valued at $2,500. (FA CD309)

111   ii. James Bonnewell, b. in AC c1807. James was named as
an heir of Rev War Veteran 27 Sep 1831 in AC.
(MilesW&A:79 (adm. & settlement of Clement Bonewell); and
Nottingham, *Soldiers of the Eastern Shore*:29 (descendants of
Thomas Bonwell, an officer in the Virginia Navy.) See entry for his
sister Elizabeth, above.)

112   iii. Robert Bonnewell, b. in AC c1809. Robert was named
as an heir of Rev War Veteran 27 Sep 1831 in AC.
(MilesW&A:79 (adm. & settlement of Clement Bonewell); and
Nottingham, *Soldiers of the Eastern Shore*:29 (descendants of
Thomas Bonwell, an officer in the Virginia Navy). See entry for his
sister Elizbeth, above.)

113   iv. Elijah Bonnewell b. in AC c1811. Elijah was named as
an heir of Rev War Veteran 27 Sep 1831 in AC.
(Nottingham, *Soldiers of the Eastern Shore*:29 (descendants of
Thomas Bonwell, an officer in the Virginia Navy). See entry for his
sister Elizabeth, above.),

56. Robert[6] **Bonnewell** (James[5], James[4], John[3], James[2], James[1]), b. in AC
c1775. (Nottingham, *Soldiers of the Eastern Shore*:29 (descendants of Thomas Bonwell, an officer
in the Virginia Navy); and Nottingham Wills:458 (will of James Bonwell))
He m. c1800, **Elizabeth Bull** (b. c1780 in AC, dau. of John Bull Sr.
(MilesW&A:99 (will of John Bull Sr.))
Robert was named as an heir of Rev War Veteran 27 Sep 1831 in AC.
Betsey Bonnewell, sister of the veteranThomas Bonwell, m. James Bonnewell,
both of whom d. some years since leaving Robert, Sally, Betsey, Elijah and
Clement Bonnewell their only children and heirs. Robert son of Betsey is dead
leaving Betsey Bull, wife of John Bull Jr. his only daughter and heir at law.
(Nottingham, *Soldiers of the Eastern Shore*:29 (descendants of Thomas Bonwell, an officer in the
Virginia Navy))
Robert Bonnewell and Elizabeth Bull had the following child:

    114   i.   Elizabeth R. 'Betsy'[7] Bonnewell, b. in AC c1805, m. 9
    Feb 1818 (lic.) in WO Co., John Carter Bull (b. c1795
    in AC). (Nottingham, *Soldiers of the Eastern Shore*:29
    (descendants of Thomas Bonwell, an officer in the Virginia Navy);
    FA CD309; MilesW&A:99 (will of John Bull Sr.))
    Elizabeth was named in her grandfather's will dated
    1 Apr 1813 in AC. He left daughter Sally Chandler the
    balance of the land containing 133 acres, but if she has
    no other issue beside her daughter Betsy, then I give
    the land to granddaughter Betsey Bonewell after the
    death of her mother. (MilesW&A:99 (will of John Bull Sr.))
    Eliza R. Bull, age 45, was listed with her son in the
    census of 1850 in St. George Parish, AC (HH#527),
    headed by Francis A. Bull, a 24 year old farmer with
    real estate valued at $10,000. (FA CD309)

59. Elijah R.[6] **Bonnewell** (James[5], James[4], John[3], James[2], James[1], in AC c1788,
d. Jan 1823. (Nottingham, *Soldiers of the Eastern Shore*:29 (descendants of Thomas Bonwell, an
officer in the Virginia Navy); MilesW&A:79 (will of Elijah Bonwell))
He m. 3 Jan 1809 (bond) in AC, **Leah Wise** (b. c1790 in AC, d. Nov
1823). McKeel Bonwell was the security on the M.L.B. of Elijah Bonwell and
Leah Wise. (ACM; MilesW&A:80 (will of Leah Bonwell))
He left a will dated 16 Jan 1823 in AC, probated 27 Jan 1823 in AC. Elijah
was named as an heir of a Rev War Veteran 27 Sep 1831 in AC. Betsey
Bonnewell, sister of Thomas, married James Bonnewell, both of whom died
some years since leaving Robert, Sally, Betsey, Elijah and Clement Bonnewell
their only children and heirs. Elijah Bonwell, son of Betsey is dead leaving
Clement, Harriett, Tabitha, Sally and Leah Bonwell his only children and heirs
at law. (MilesW&A:79 (will of Elijah Bonwell); Nottingham, *Soldiers of the Eastern Shore*:29
(descendants of Thomas Bonwell, an officer in the Virginia Navy))
Elijah R. Bonnewell and Leah Wise had the following children:

    115   i.   Tabitha[7] Bonnewell, b. in AC c1809. Tabitha was
    named in settm't of father's estate 31 Mar 1826 in AC,

receiving 1/5 of the balance of the estate. (MilesW&A:79 (settlement of Elijah Bonwell); and Nottingham, *Soldiers of the Eastern Shore*:29 (descendants of Thomas Bonwell, an officer in the Virginia Navy))

Tabitha was named as an heir of Rev War Veteran 27 Sep 1831 in AC. Elijah Bonwell, son of Betsey is dead leaving Clement, Harriett, Tabitha, Sally and Leah Bonwell his only children and heirs at law. (Nottingham, *Soldiers of the Eastern Shore*:29 (descendants of Thomas Bonwell, an officer in the Virginia Navy))

116   ii. Harriet Bonnewell, b. in AC c1811. She was named in settm't of father's estate 31 Mar 1826 in AC. She received 1/5 of the balance of the estate. (MilesW&A:79 (settlement of Elijah Bonwell); and Nottingham, *Soldiers of the Eastern Shore*:29 (descendants of Thomas Bonwell, an officer in the Virginia Navy))

Harriet was named as an heir of a Rev War Veteran 27 Sep 1831 in AC Elijah Bonwell, son of Betsey is dead leaving Clement, Harriett, Tabitha, Sally and Leah Bonwell his only children and heirs at law. (Nottingham, *Soldiers of the Eastern Shore*:29 (descendants of Thomas Bonwell, an officer in the Virginia Navy))

117   iii. Sally R. Bonnewell b. in AC c1813. She was named in settm't of father's estate 31 Mar 1826 in AC. (MilesW&A:79 (settlement of Elijah Bonwell)) She received 1/5 of the balance of the estate. (MilesW&A:79 (settlement of Elijah Bonwell); and Nottingham, *Soldiers of the Eastern Shore*:29 (descendants of Thomas Bonwell, an officer in the Virginia Navy))

Sally was named as an heir of Rev War Veteran 27 Sep 1831 in AC. Elijah Bonwell, son of Betsey is dead leaving Clement, Harriett, Tabitha, Sally and Leah Bonwell his only children and heirs at law., (Nottingham, *Soldiers of the Eastern Shore*:29 (descendants of Thomas Bonwell, an officer in the Virginia Navy))

118   iv. Leah Scarburgh Bonnewell, b. in AC c1815. She was named in settm't of father's estate 31 Mar 1826 in AC. She was shown as Leah Bonewell and received 1/5 of the balance of the estate. (MilesW&A:79 (settlement of Elijah Bonwell); and Nottingham, *Soldiers of the Eastern Shore*:29 (descendants of Thomas Bonwell, an officer in the Virginia Navy)),

Leah was named as an heir of Rev War Veteran 27 Sep 1831 in AC. (Nottingham, *Soldiers of the Eastern Shore*:29 (descendants of Thomas Bonwell, an officer in the Virginia Navy)) Elijah Bonwell, son of Betsey is dead leaving Clement, Harriett, Tabitha, Sally and Leah Bonwell his only children and heirs at law.

119   v. Elijah Clement Bonnewell, b. in AC c1817, d. 1 Dec
1872 in Lee District, AC of typhoid fever. He was a
widower. Someone named Bridget (no surname) gave
the information. He m. 18 Jul 1840 (bond) in AC,
Sarah 'Sally' Metcalf (b. c1822), dau. of Jesse Metcalf
and Patty (N). Jesse Metcalf was the security on the
M.L.B. of Elijah Bonnewell and Sally Metcalf of Jesse.
(MilesW&A:79 (settlement of Elijah Bonwell); and Nottingham,
Soldiers of the Eastern Shore:29 (descendants of Thomas Bonwell,
an officer in the Virginia Navy); FA CD309; WADR; ACM)
[Elijah] Clement Bonewell was named in the
settm't of father's estate 31 Mar 1826 in AC. He
received 1/5 of the balance of the estate. (MilesW&A:79
(settlement of Elijah Bonwell))
[Elijah] Clement Bonwell, age 33, farmer, was
listed as a head of household in the census of 1850 in
St. George Parish, AC (HH#47). Listed with him were
the following Bonwells: Sally, age 28; Elizabeth, age 8;
Harriette, age 3; and George, age 4/12. Also listed was
Patty Midcass, age 50. (FA CD309)
[Elijah] Clem., age 39, farmer, was head of
household in the census of 1860 in St. George Parish,
AC (HH#193). He possessed personal property valued
at $50. Listed with him were the following Boniwells:
Sarah, age 39; Harriet, age 14; Geo., age 11; John, age
5; and Elijah, age 2. (1860 AC Census)
In 1870 Killmon [probably Clement]Bonewell, age
53, oysterman, was listed as a head of household in the
census of 1870 in Locust Mount PO, St. George Parish,
He possessed person property valued at $250. Listed
with him were Sarah Bonewell, age 49 and keeping
house. Also listed were the following Richardsons:
Harriet, age 25 and at home; John W., a 16 year old
farm laborer; and Ezekiel, a 13 year old farm laborer.
Harriet was evidently his daughter, who had married
Isaiah Richardson. (Walczyk, *1870 Acc Co, St. George Parish,
Census*)

61. **Severn**[6] **Bonnewell** (Benjamin[5], John[4], John[3], James[2], James[1], b. in AC
c1766, d. 1821 in Sussex Co, DE. (WOW MH-10:86; Delaware Probate Vol. A.:16)
He m. c1790, (b. c1770), **Ann 'Nancy'** (N). (Delaware Probate Vol. A)
On 5 Oct 1787 Severn Bonnewell bought 32 acres of land in WO Co. from
Ann Jones for £15. The land was part of *Allens Industry* and began at an oak
standing on a ridge called *Holly Ridge*. (WOD M:243) On 14 Feb 1795 he sold this
land to his brother John Bonnewell for £46.15, indicating he had built a home on
the land. Severn's wife Nancy cosigned the deed. (WOD Q:100)

34

In 1806 Severn Bonnewell, of Broad Creek Hundred, bought 125 acres of land in Sussex Co. for "one Thousand Bushels of Good Merchantable Indian Corn." (SUDELR deeds AB-25:)

He left a will dated 20 Jan 1816 in Sussex Co, DE. He named his wife Ann as extx and daus. Mary, Ann, Lettice, Jane Lecat, and Susan Elliot. Dau. Letty Bonnawell d, testate in Sussex Co. in 1834. Other Delaware records show that dau. Jane had married Levin Lecat; she d. c1833. (Delaware Probate Vol. A.:16; Probate Vol. A#60:14)

Severn Bonnewell and Ann 'Nancy' (N) had the following children:

120   i.   Jane[7] Bonnewell, b. c1790, d. c1833, m. c1810, Levin Lecat (b. c1790). (Delaware Probate Vol. A"16)

121   ii.   Mary Bonnewell, b. c1791. Mary was named in her father's will 20 Jan 1816 in Sussex Co, DE (Delaware Probate Vol. A:16).

122   iii.   Susan Bonnewel, b. c1793, m. c1814 (N), Elliott (b. c1790). (Delaware Probate Vol. A:6, 16)

123   iv.   Ann Bonnewell, b. c1794. (Delaware Probate Vol. A.:16)

124   v.   Lettice 'Letty' Bonnewell, b. c1796, d. 1834 in Sussex Co., DE, leaving a will. (Delaware Probate A:16; A-60:14)

62. **John[6] Bonnewell** (Benjamin[5], John[4], John[3], James[2], James[1]), b. in AC c1768, d. by 29 Sep 1815. (WOW MH-10:86) While there is no one record that gives his approximate age, it appears he was the second oldest son. His name has not been found on a census record. John Bonnawell died just several months after his father, when Daniel Hancock posted bond as his administrator. (General Index to Estates, 1742-1908:17)

He m. 21 Feb 1807 (lic.), **Nancy Hancock** in WO Co. (Powell, *WO Co. Marriages 1795-1865*) He would have been around 35 years of age; later census records indicate his bride was 26 years old.

Nancy, b. 9 Mar 1781 in WO Co. (Dryden, *WO Co. 1850 Census*) The 1850 census puts her birth at 1790. She m. 16 Apr 1816 (lic.), **William Paradise** in WO Co. (Powell, *WO Co Marriages 1795-1865*) He would have been c23 years of age in 1816, when he m. John Bonnawell's widow, and she c35. Nancy and William Paradise had five children, for, when their son Parker Paradise died unm. in 1854, his heirs were given as: Nancy Paradise, his mother; John Paradise, a brother; Nancy Claywell, a sister; Milby Paradise, a deceased brother; Elizabeth Redden" a deceased sister; James Bonnawell, a half-brother; Benjamin Bonnawell, a half-brother; and Eliza Jones, wife of Isaac Jones, a half-sister. (WO Co. Accounts 1853-1857:422)

Nancy d. 9 Jan 1870 at 88 years of age. Her body was interred in Isaac Jones Family Cem, Stockton, WO Co. Robert F. Jones reported some years ago that her tombstone showed her as Nancy Paredis, wife of William, b. 9 Mar 1781, d. 9 Jan 1870. This stone is no longer standing.

On 14 Feb 1795 John Bonnewell of WO Co. bought 32 acres of land from his brother Severn for £46.15. The deed states the boundary of the land began at a white oak on a ridge called *Holly Ridge*. (WOD Q:100)

On 29 Jul 1797 John Bonewell bought an additional, adjoining 9 acres from Giles Jones for £15.15, part of *Allens Industry* and *Peppers Vexation.*,(WOD S:117)

John Bonnewell and Nancy Hancock had the following children:

125   i. James Wise[7] Bonnewell, b. in WO Co. c1810, d. Mar 1882, m. 1st. 11 Apr 1833 (lic.), Sally Banks (b. c1810) in WO Co. (Powell, *WO Co. Marriages 1795-1865;* WO Co. Orphans Court Proceedings 1816-1820:282; Dryden, *WO Co. 1850 Census;* WOW GTB-3:158 (will of James W. Bonnewill))

He m. 2nd 16 Apr 1839 (lic.) in WO Co., Harriet Webb (b. c1816 in WO Co.), dau. of John F. Webb and Henrietta Hudson. (Carey, Bonw*ell to Bonneville;* Powell, *WO Co. Marriages 1795-1865;* Dryden, *WO Co. 1850 Census*)

On 9 Feb 1819, William Paradise, with Daniel Mason and Stephen Redden his securities, posted bond as guardian of James Wise Bonnawell, Benjamin Purnell Bonnawell and Eliza Bonnawell, orphans of John Bonnawell, deceased. (WO Co. Orphans Court Proceedings 1816-1820:282)

James bought 24 ½ acres on 20 Mar 1830 in WO Co., from Daniel Mason for $49. The deed states the land was called *Holly Swamp* and one of the boundaries was "said Bonniwell's land formerly property of John Bonniwell." In 1832 and 1835, he bought the other two portions of his father's land from his brother and sister and then owned c70 acres in the *Holly Swamp* area. He became a large land owner. Some of the WO Co. tracts he purchased were resold, at least two to family members. The balance he left to his children and grandchildren. (WOD AW"84)

James bought 30 acres on 16 Oct 1840 in WO Co., part ot two tracts called *Bacon Quarter* and *Willits Discovery* from Isaac S. Johnson and wife Sarah of Baltimore City for $700. The land was located on the county road from Cottingham's Ferry to Davis Cross Roads, on the east side of Pocomoke River and 1 ½ miles from said river. One of the boundaries was land of William Paradise. (WOD GMH-3:525)

James Boniwell, age 40, farmer, was listed as a head of household in the census of 1850 in First District, WO Co. (HH#1492). Listed with him were the following Boniwells: Harriett, age 34; Sally, age 11; William, age 8; Isaac G., age 6; James, age 4; Martha, age 3; and Benjamin, age 1. (Dryden, *WO Co 1850 Census*) On 6 Aug 1853 James W. Bonnewill and his wife Harriett sold to Ann E. Hancock, 25 acres called *Peters Folly* and 100 acres called *Pilchards Neglect*, both tracts in WO Co. (WOD EMD-5:428) James Bonnewill had bought this land on 6 Nov 1845 from John and Nathaniel Redden and their wives. (WOD EDM-1:212) It was land that had belonged to Capt. Robert Hancock and was located across Lamberson Road from other James W. Bonnewill land.

In 1854 James Bonnawell was named as an heir to Rev War Veteran, Parkier Paradise, his half-brother in WO Co. (WO Co. Acounts, 1853-1857:422 (heirs of Parker Paradise))

James bought 12 ½ acres on 28 Dec 1859 in WO Co. from Levin Horsey and wife Polly, for $100. (WOD WET-2:1) On 24 Oct 1856, he bought 146 acres for $1200 from Peter C. Corbin and wife Rosey. (WOD JAP#11:96) This land was on the northeast side of the road from Cross Roads to Cottinghams Ferry. It appears he moved on this land and called it "my old home farm" in his will. On 3 June 1854, James W. Bonnewill bought 27½ acres, part of *Bridgewater Supply*, from Jacob Riley and wife Charlotte, for $75. (WO Co. EDM#6:43) On 21 Dec 1857, he bought 240 acres from Major T. Hall and wife Julia, for $300. (WOD WET#1:93) The deed places this land on Pocomoke River at Bears Landing, up Carey Creek to Charley Tarr's line, thence to the county road and with the county road to Major W. Jones' land.

James was listed as a head of household in the census of 1860 in Colbourns Dist., WO Co. (Barnes, *WO Co. 1860 Census*) He was shown as James W. Bromwell, head of HH#2998, a 51 year old farmer with real estate valued at $4,000 and personal property valued at $1,000. Listed with him were the following Bromwells: Harriet, age 45; Isaac, age 15; Martha, age 13; George, age 7; and Harriet, age 5.

James Bonnawell, age 61, farmer, was listed as a head of household in the census of 1870 in Snow Hill P.O., WO Co. (HH#252) He possessed real estate valued at $3,800 and personal property valued at $500.

Listed with him were the following Bonnawells:
Harriett, age 50 and keeping house; Jerome, age 26 and
working on farm; Washington, age 18; and Harriett,
age 16. Also listed was Harriett Landing, age 6. (Barnes,
WO Co 1870 Census)

He left a will dated 18 Feb 1882, probated 4 Apr
1882 in WO Co. He left the farm "whereon I now
reside, being on the northwest side of the county road
leading from Pocomoke City to Snow Hill," to his wife
Harriet Bonnewell for her lifetime and then it was to go
to his grandchildren, James E. Bonnewell and Harriet
F. Landing "now the wife of Edward Ardis." He also
left personal property to his wife. James W. Bonnewill
left dau. Ann Elba, the wife of George Hancock, $1.00
and $250 to her children. He gave son Isaac Jerome
Bonnewill $500, to be held for him by son William C.
Bonnewell until "said Isaac Jerome returns home from
his present confinement restored to his right mind." He
left $1.00 to son William C. Bonnewill. He gave dau.
Martha A. Hancock $1.00 and her children $1,000. He
left sons Benjamin E. Bonnewill and George Bonnewill
"lands known as my old home farm lying on the
southeast side of the county road leading from
Pocomoke City to Snow Hill." He gave daus. Harriet
W. Ardis and Sally Landing the farm known as the
Corbin farm, reserving an outlet for both down the lane
near George Hancock's residence. He left Ulysses
Goswelling $50 and appointed son William C.
Bonnewill his guardian. He named friend Benjamin J.
Aydelotte and son Benjamin E. Bonnewill his extrs. It
is evident from his will and from an old map of 1877,
that the land James W. Bonnewill owned was located
on both sides of the road from Pocomoke City to Snow
Hill, at the point this road intersects with present
Lamberson Road, as it extends southeast to Davis
Cross Roads (present Goodwill). (WOW GTB-3:158 (will of
James W. Bonnewill))

126   ii. Benjamin Purnell Bonnewell, b. in WO Co. 1812. (WO
Co. Orphans Court Proceedings 1816-1820:282) He m. (WO Co.
lic. dated 25 Dec 1833), Mary Hall (b. c1812). (Powell,
WO Co Marriages 1795-1865) After his marriage, he
disappeared from WO Co. records, other than being
named as a half-brother when Parker Paradise died in
1854.

38

On 9 Feb 1819, William Paradise, with Daniel Mason and Stephen Redden his securities, posted bond as guardian of James Wise Bonnawell, Benjamin Purnell Bonnawell and Eliza Bonnawell, orphans of John Bonnawell, deceased. (WO Co. Orphans Court Proceedings 1816-1820:282).

In June Court, 1829, Nancy Paradise indentured her son, Benjamin Bonnawell, who was 17 years old, in Nov 1828, to John T. Taylor, shoe and boot maker. (Orphans Court Proc. 1829-1832:25).

Benjamin sold land 21 Jul 1832 in WO Co. (WOD AY:251) He was shown as Benjamin P. Bonnawell when he sold his part of his father's land to his brother, James W. Bonnawell, for $34, when he became of age. This land adjoined George Bonnawell's land.

Benjamin was named as an heir of Rev War Veteran Parker Paradise, his half-brother, in 1854. (WO Co. Acounts, 1853-1857:422 (heirs of Parker Paradise))

127   iii. Eliza Bonnewell, b. c1814 in WO Co. (WO Co. Orphans Court Proceedings 1816-1820:282' Dryden, *WO Co 1850 Census*) Her body was interred in Isaac Jones Family Cem, Stockton, Wor Co, MD. She m. Isaac Jones (b. 1807) (WO Co. lic. dated 22 Dec 1830). (Powell, *WO Co Marriages 1795-1865*)

Isaac, b. 1807 in WO Co., d. 1862. His body was interred in Isaac Jones Family Cem, Stockton, WO Co. (Tombstone readings by Judy T. Howard and Donna S. Clarke)

On 9 Feb 1819, William Paradise, with Daniel Mason and Stephen Redden his securities, posted bond as guardian of James Wise Bonnawell, Benjamin Purnell Bonnawell and Eliza Bonnawell, orphans of John Bonnawell, deceased. (WO Co. Orphans Court Proceedings 1816-1820:282)

Eliza Jones, age 36, was listed with her husband in the census of 1850 in First Dist., WO Co. (HH#1241) with her husband Isaac Jones, a 42 year old farmer. (Dryden, *WO Co 1850 Census*)

Eliza was named as an heir of Rev War Veteran Parker Paradise, her half-brother in 1854. (WO Co. Acounts, 1853-1857:422 (heirs of Parker Paradise))

63. **George**[6] **Bonnewell** (Benjamin[5], John[4], John[3], James[2], James[1]), b. in AC c1770, d. Sep 1837. It was apparently George Bonnewell, aged over 16 years, shown in his father's household by the 1790 census. (WOW MH-10:86; WOW LPS:102)

He m. **Elizabeth 'Betsy' Payne** (b. c1780 in WO Co., d. 1839. (WO Co. lic. dated 16 Dec 1807). (Powell, *WO Co Marriages 1795-1865*; WOW LPS:141)

George Bonnewell, age over 45, was listed as a head of household in the census of 1820 in WO Co.

In 1820 George bought the 109 acres the his father had owned from his brothers, and likely lived there all his life.

He left a will dated 14 Jan 1833, probated 10 Oct 1837 in WO Co. He named his wife Elizabeth and two daus; Hester Ann Bonnewell and Polly S. Payne. He had no sons. (WOW LPS:102)

George Bonnewell and Elizabeth 'Betsy' Payne had the following children:

128   i. Polly S.[7] Bonnewell, b. in WO Co. 1812, d. 1863. (WOW LPS:102; Tombstone records) She m. Samuel A. Payne (WO Co. lic. dated 7 Dec 1830). (Powell, *WO Co Marriages 1795-1865*) Samuel, b. 1808 in WO Co., d. 1873. (Tombstone records)

129   ii. Hester Ann Bonnewell, b. in WO Co. c1818, m. John H. Allen (WO Co. lic. dated 1 Mar 1839). (WOW LPS:102; FA CD309; Powell, *WO Co Marriages 1795-1865*) Hester A. Allen, age 22 (probably 32), b. inVA,was listed with her husband in the census of 1850 in Acc Parish, AC (HH#404) with her husband John H. Allen, a 34 year old farmer born in MD. (FA CD309)

64. Edward Hearn[6] Bonnewell (Benjamin[5], John[4], John[3], James[2], James[1]), b. in AC c1773, d. Aug 1819. (WOW MH-10:86; WOW 1813-1833:289)

He m. **Patsy Barnes** (b. c1780) (WO Co. lic. dated 10 Jan 1799). (Powell, *WO Co Marriages 1795-1865*)

Edward was listed as a head of household in the census of 1810 in WO Co. His age was given as 26 to 45 years, when he had two sons under 10 years in his household and four daus, three of whom were under 10 years and one 10 to 16.

He left a will dated 23 Jun 1818, probated 21 Aug 1819 in WO Co. (WOW 1813-1833:289) He named his wife Patsey, dau. Jane Brittingham, and "four youngest children" as Andrew, Molly, James, and Pattey.

Edward Hearn Bonnewell and Patsy Barnes had the following children:

130   i. Jane[7] Bonnewell, b. in WO Co. c1802, m. Josiah Brittingham (b. c1795). (WO Co. lic. dated Jan 1816). (WOW 1813-1833:289; Powell, *WO Co Marriages 1795-1865*)

131   ii. Andrew N. Bonnewell, b. in WO Co. c1803. (WOW 1813-1833:289) His body was interred in Mt. Moriah Cem, Vandalia, Owen Co, IN. (Hickman, *Bonniwell Family*) He m. Harriett Maddox (SO Co. lic. dated 31 Dec 1827). (Pollitt, *SO Co. Marriages 1796-1871*) Harriett, b. c1799, d. in Mt. Moriah Cem, Vandalia, Owen Co, IN. (Hickman, *Bonniwell Family*)

Andrew Bonewell, age 47, farmer, was listed as a head of household in the census of 1850 in Dublin

Dist., SO Co. (HH#1008). Listed with him were the following Bonewells: Harriett, age 51; Edward, age 21; John, age 18; William, age 16; Sarah, age 14; Littleton, age 10; and George, age 9. (Dryden, *SO Co 1850 Census*)

132   iii. Molly Bonnewell, b. in WO Co. c1806. (WOW 1813-1833:289)

133   iv. James Bonnewell, b. in WO Co. c1808. (WOW 1813-1833:289)

134   v. Pattey Bonnewell, b. in WO Co. c1810. (WOW 1813-1833:289)

65. **John**[6] **Bonnewell** (James[5], John[4], John[3], James[2], James[1]), b. in AC c1773. (MilesW&A:79 (will of James Bonwell))

He m. **Catherine Kellam** (26 Apr 1806 (bond)) in AC. Thomas Snead was the security on the M.L.B. of John Bonwell and Catherine Kellam of Dolly. (ACM)

Catherine, b. c1788 in AC, d. before 21 Feb 1837, dau. of Howson Kellam and Elizabeth 'Betty' Turlington. (MilesW&A:303 (will of Howson Kellam)) She must have died before this date as it was on this date that Howson Kellam named three grandchildren: Betsy, William & George Bonewell, and gave them $1 each.

John Bonnewell and Catherine Kellam had the following children:

135   i. Betsy[7] Bonnewell, b. in AC c1808, named in her grandfather's will 21 Feb 1837 in AC. (MilesW&A:303 (will of Howson Kellam))

136   ii. William Bonnewell, b. in AC c1810. (MilesW&A:303 (will of his grandfather, Howson Kellam))

137   iii. George Bonnewell, b. in AC c1812. (MilesW&A:303 (will of his grandfather, Howson Kellam)

66. **George**[6] **Bonnewell** (James[5], John[4], John[3], James[2], James[1]), b. in AC c1775. (MilesW&A:79 (will of James Bonwell))

George Bonwell was listed as a head of household in the census of 1800 in Acc Parish, AC. He was shown as George Bonwell, age 16-26 with 1 male age 10-16, 1 male age 0-10, 1 female age 16-26, 1 female age 10-16 and 2 slaves. He and Thomas Bonwell were the only 2 Bonwell heads of household in Acc Parish. All the other Bonwell families were in St. George Parish., (Powell, *AC 1800, 1810, 1820 Census:* 6)

George was listed as a head of household in the census of 1810 in Acc Parish, AC. He was shown as George Bonwell, age 26-45 with 1 male age 16-26, 1 male age 10-16, 2 males age 0-10, 1 female age 16-45, 1 female age 10-16, 1 female age 0-10 and 1 slave. He and Rachel Bonwell were the only 2 heads of households in Acc Parish. All the other Bonwell families were in St. George Parish. (Powell, *AC Co 1800, 1810, 1820 Census,*:58)

George Bonnewell had the following child:

138   i. Peter[7] Bonnewell, b. in AC c1795, d. Oct 1824 in AC. (MilesW&A:81) He m. 11 Dec 1817, Elizabeth S. 'Betsy'

Hall (bond dated 5 Dec 1817) in AC. William Holland and John Custis were securities on the M.L.B. of Peter Bonwell of George and Eliza Hall of Henry. (AC Co Marriage Register 1, *1805-1850*; ACM)

Betsy, b. c1785 in AC. (Powell, *AC 1830 Census*:12; and Powell, *AC 1840 Census:*14) Both the 1830 and 1840 censuses place her birth between 1780-1790. Betsy was the dau. of Henry Hall Sr. and Mary 'Molly' Shay. (MilesW&A:247 (will of Mary Hall); ACM)

Peter Bonwell, was listed as a head of household in the census of 1820 in Acc Parish, AC. He was age 16-26 with one female age 26-45 and 5 slaves. He was the only Bonwell in Acc Parish. All the other Bonwell families were living in St. George Parish. (Powell, *AC Co. 1800, 1810, 1820 Census:* 116)

On 25 Oct 1824 Thomas Fletcher was appointed to settle Peter 's estate in AC. Spencer D. Fletcher and William H. Drummond were the securities. Peter's estate was settled 26 Feb 1827 in AC. The order to inventory was dated 29 Nov 1824; the inventory and sale were on 8 Dec 1824. There was a second sale on 7 Apr 1825. The audit was returned on 23 Feb 1827 and recorded on 26 Feb 1827. One of the buyers was Elizabeth Bonewell. One Negro child Charlotte, $50. Appraisers: Thomas Matthews, Spencer Drummond & Michael Robins. Thomas Fletcher admr. Auditors: Spencer Drummond & Michael Robins. (MilesW&A:81)

79. **McKeel**[6] **Bonnewell (II)** (Micheal 'McKeel'[5], Joachim Mikeal[4], John[3], James[2], James[1]), b. in AC c1779, d. 22 Apr 1856. (MilesW&A:79 (settlement of Clement Bonewell); Nottingham, *Soldiers of the Eastern Shore*:29 (descendants of Thomas Bonwell, an officer in the Virginia Navy; FA CD309); MilesW&A:81 (will of McKeal Bonewell)) In the death register he was shown as McKeel Boniwell, who died of cancer at the age of 74 years. He was b. in AC and a farmer, the husband of Susan. His parents were not shown. (Walczyk, *AC Death Register, 1853-1896*)

He married three times. He m. 1st 5 Jan 1803 (bond) in AC, **Sarah Bull** (b. c1780 in AC), dau. of Richard Bull. McKeel Budd was the security on the M.L.B. of McKeel Bonwell Jr. and Sarah Bull of Richard. (ACM)

He m. 2nd 30 Jul 1808 (bond) in AC, **Margaret Salisbury** (b. c1782 in AC). John Bonewell was the security on the M.L.B. (ACM; Hickman to Miles, *Emails, 09/26/2003*)

He m. 3rd 20 Apr 1835 (bond) in AC, **Susan Edwards** (b. c1810 in AC). William Finney was the security on the M.L.B. of McKeel Bonnewell, widower, and Susan Jester, widow of Joseph. She was the dau. of Laban Edwards and Susannah Phillips. She m. **Joseph Jester** 10 Jan 1824 (bond) in AC. John Jester was the security on the M.L.B. of Joseph Jester and Susan Edwards of Laban. (ACM; FA CD309)

McKeel was named as an heir (nephew) of Rev War Veteran Thomas Bonwell on 27 Sep 1831 in AC. (Nottingham, *Soldiers of the Eastern Shore:*29 (descendants of Thomas Bonwell, an officer in the Virginia Navy))

McKeel Bonnawell, age 71, farmer, was head of household (HH#96) in the census of 1850 in St. George Parish, AC. He possessed real estate valued at $800. Listed with him were Susan Bonnawell, age 40 and Margaret Jester, age 24. (FA CD309)

He left a will dated 5 Jan 1856 in AC, probated 28 Apr 1856. He directed that his house & lot be sold if necessary to pay his debts. To my wife Susan Bonewell the whole of my estate during her life & at her death to be disposed of as she may think proper. Wife extx. Witnessed by William Moore, James C. Drummond & John W. Smith. (MilesW&A:81 (will of McKeal Bonwil))

McKeel Bonnewell (II) and Margaret Salisbury had the following child:

139   i.   McKeel 'Heely'[7] Bonnewell (III), b. in AC c1810, d. Jul 1838. (Dean Hickman research; MilesW&A:80 (adm. of Keeley Bonewell)) His body was interred in Onley, AC. (Mears, *Hacks Neck & Its People*) He is buried in a graveyard between Onley and Accomac, about where the 'old road' is intersected by the road to the 'seaside' near the 'new church.' He m. Elizabeth Warrington 28 Nov 1831 (bond) in AC. Robert J. Poulson was the security on the M.L.B. of Heely Boniwell and Elizabeth Warington, ward of Heely Boniwell. (ACM)

       Elizabeth, b. 18 Feb 1810 in AC, d. 18 Jul 1885, m. George W. Scott 21 Feb 1844 in AC. They were shown as George W. Scott and Elizabeth Bonnawell, widow. Her body was interred in St. George Ep Ch Cem, Pungoteague, AC. Her tombstone shows her as Elizabeth Scott, wife of George W. Scott, 18 Feb 1810 - 18 Jul 1885, age 75 years, 5 mos. and 0 days. (ACM; MLAC)

       On 30 Jul 1838 Albert R. Heath was appointed to administer McKeel's estate in AC. John Arlington & Richard P. Rew were securities. (MilesW&A:80 (adm. of Keeley Bonewell))

85. **Michael Hall**[6] **Bonnewell** (George[5], Thomas[4], John[3], James[2], James[1]), b. in AC 27 Feb 1763, d. Jan 1832. (Hickman, *Bonniwell Family*)

He m. 1st c1785, **Mary Moore** (b. c1765). (Dean Hickman research) He m. 2nd 7 Apr 1800, **Elizabeth Lowbar** (b. c1780). (Hickman, *Bonniwell Family*)

Michael Hall Bonnewell and Mary Moore had the following children:

140   i.   George[7] Bonnewell, b. 1786, d. 1855. (Hickman, *Bonniwell Family*)

141   ii.   Samuel Bonnewell, b. c1789. (Hickman, *Bonniwell Family*)

142   iii. William Moore Bonnewell, b. 1796, d. 1864. (Hickman, *Bonniwell Family*)

143   iv. Henry Bonnewell, b. 1798, d. 1865. (Hickman, *Bonniwell Family*)

Michael Hall Bonnewell and Elizabeth Lowbar had the following children:

144   v. Jonathan Bonnewell, b. 1801.(Hickman, *Bonniwell Family*)

145   vi. Maria Bonnewell, b. 19 Mar 1803, d. 25 Feb 1877. (Hickman, *Bonniwell Family*)

146   vii. Margaret Bonnewell, b. c1806. (Hickman, *Bonniwell Family*)

147   viii. Hall Bonnewell, b. 12 Mar 1809, d. 28 Feb 1855. (Hickman, *Bonniwell Family*), b. 12 Mar 1809.

148   ix. James Bonnewell, b. c1812. (Hickman, *Bonniwell Family*)

149   x. Elizabeth Bonnewell, b. 3 Nov 1814, d. 27 Dec 1859. (Hickman, *Bonniwell Family*)

150   xi. Ann Bonnewell, b. c1816. (Hickman, *Bonniwell Family*)

151   xii. Peter Lowber Bonnewell, b. 24 Dec 1824. (Hickman, *Bonniwell Family*)

Descendants of Richard Bundick
(Limited to the Bundick surname)

First Generation

1. **Richard**[I] **Bundick (I), b.** c1620, d. 1693 in NC. (NC OW *1689-98:*224)
He married three times. He m. 1st c1648 in NC, **Dorothy (N)** (b. c1620).
(NC D*W, 1645-51:*163) On 28 Oct 1648, Richard Bundick and Dorothy Bundick, his
wife, signed a bond with their marks agreeing to pay John Foster for the use of a
servant. (NC DW 1645-1651:163) It appears likely that Dorothy was a widow and
owned property when she m. Richard Bundick. Dorothy Bundick d. between 23
May 1663, when she cosigned a deed with her husband, (AC DW, 1663-1666:10),
and 16 Nov 1665, when Ruth was "ye wife of Richard Bundick." (AC DW, 1663-
1666:103)

He m. 2nd c1664, **Ruth (N)** (b. c1630, d. c1680). She previously m. c1650,
(N) Jones. (Mary Frances Carey) Ruth had two children before she m. Richard
Bundick (I), John Jones and Thomas Jones. AC records refer to them at times as
Bundicks. (AC W&c., 1673-1676:242) They apparently left no local heirs, as they
were living in Sussex Co, PA (now Delaware) in 1685, when they sold land in
AC. (AC Deeds, 1676-1690:408) Ruth Bundick was still living in 1680, when she
cosigned a deed with her husband. (AC Deeds, 1676-1690:236). She apparently died
soon thereafter. (NC DW, 1663-66:103)

He m. 3rd c1685, **Elizabeth (N)** (b. c1640). Richard Bundick (I)'s widow
was living on 28 Oct 1698, when she made a gift of her entire estate to Mary
Nottingham. (NC DW, 1692-1707:215) Mary Nottingham, wife of Richard
Nottingham Jr., "is said to have been born a Bundick." (Whitelaw:329) Since she
was not named by Richard Bundick in his will, it appears more likely that Mary
was a dau. of Elizabeth Bundick by a former marriage.

The name of Richard Bundick first appears in Eastern Shore of Virginia
records on 30 Aug 1647, as his name was given with eight other headrights
when John Foster patented 450 acres of land in NC. (NC DW, 1645-1651:110) The
land was located on the sea side, between Nassawadox and
Machipongo,(Whitelaw:365 and map) A colonist was eligible for 50 acres of land for
each person for whom he had paid transportation costs from England. These
persons were called headrights, and agreed to work for their sponsor for several
years, as indentured servants, to repay their cost of transportation. However,
Richard Bundick likely paid for his own passage and assigned his right to 50
acres to John Foster. Richard Bundick made a deposition in NC Court on 21 Jun
1662, giving his age as 41 years or thereabout. (NC OB, 1657-1664:97) This
indicates he was 27 years of age when he came to the Colony of Virginia.
Richard Bundick was granted a patent to 650 acres of land on the south side of
Pungoteague Creek on 21 Nov 1654, a patent that was renewed on 20 Oct 1661.
(Nugent I:296, 412) He sold his 650 acres on Pungoteague Creek to Francis
Moryson on 6 Sep 1672. (NC Deeds, 1668-1680:36) On 23 May 1663, Richard
Bundick, planter, and wife Dorothy deeded 500 acres on the south side of

Pungoteague Creek to Richard Jacob, deceased, saying this land had been purchased from Nicholas Waddelaw (Wallop) and that they had "received full and valuable satisfaction for ye afsd 500 acres" before Jacob died. (AC DW, 1663-1666:9/10) Witnesses to the deed were Evitt Jones and Thomas Fawkes. Richard Jacob's will, written 13 Jan 1663, recorded 2 Mar 1663, apparently left this land to a son Issac and spoke, in his will, of 350 acres he was leaving son Thomas "at Pungoteague on the western part of a main branch of said Creek whereon Richard Bundick presently lives." (NC DW, 1657-1666:140) On 12 Jul 1664, Richard Bundick was granted a patent for 1,400 acres in AC, "at seaboard side beginning at land of Col Edmund Scarburgh, bounded south by Long tone (Long Love) Branch." (Nugent I:524) One of his headrights was a William Wright. On 9 Oct 1672, Richard Bundick patented 600 additional acres, "Being the surplus within bounds of his 1,400 acres at Arcadia." (Nugent II:119) This block of about 2,000 acres is presently called *Parkers Neck*. It is bound south and west by Parkers Creek, the northern branch of which, called Long Love Branch or Poorhouse Branch, crosses U.S. 13 just south of Zion Church. The creek to the north was originally Arcadia Creek and on present-day maps is labeled Bundicks Creek. On 18 Dec 1666, Richard Bundick and Ruth, his wife, sold to Thomas Fowkes 700 acres "being the one half of a patent of fourteen hundred acres granted to me at James City under the hand of ye Honble William Berkeley and sealed wth ye seale of ye Colony the 12 July 1664." (AC DW, 1663-1666:39/40) The consideration was "8,000 pounds of tobacco & Cast, the value thereof in hand." On 14 Feb 1667, Richard Bundick and wife Ruth gave his dau, Elizabeth Sturgis, 200 acres "next unto ye lands sold to Mr. Thomas ffowkes." (AC DW, 1663-1666:63) On 16 Dec 1673, Richard Bundick and Ruth sold 550 acres to John Drummond, stating this was all that could be found of his 9 Oct 1672 patent. (AC W&c, 1673-1676:104) On 16 Nov 1677 Richard Bundick and wife Ruth gave his son Richard 200 acres "next to my son in Law John Sturgis - part of a 1,400 acre Patent." (AC DW, 1676-1690:69) On 18 Nov 1680, Richard Bundick and wife Ruth sold to John Barns 300 acres for 10,400 pounds of tobacco, near Creek called by the name of Arcadia. (AC DW, 1663-1666:236)

Richard Bundick lived to be an old man for the times. He would have been about 72 when he wrote his will on 9 Dec 1692, probated 28 Feb 1692/3 in NC. He owned no land at this tine and was apparently living in NC. He named five children (Richard, Elizabeth, Ann, Dorothy and Grace), each of whom was to receive 100 pounds of tobacco. His remaining estate, after debts were paid, was left to his wife Elizabeth and she was made extx.Witnessed by Mich: Underhill, Edwd: Gunter, and George Green. (NC OW, 1689-1698:224)

Richard Bundick (I) and Dorothy (N) had the following children:

> 2   i.   Elizabeth[2] Bundick, b. in NC c1640. She m. 1st c1660 in NC, John Sturgis (I) (b. c1640, d. 1684). (Mary Frances Carey; AC Co WD 1676-90(vi):383) In his will, dated 6 Mar 1683, John Sturgis named a wife Elizabeth; sons John, Richard (under 21), Jonathan (under 20) and Daniel

(under 16); and daus. Dorothy Nevill and Ann Sturgis. Witnesses were Richard Bundick and David Jones. (AC WD, 1676-90 (vi):383)

> She m. Thomas Jones (b. c1640) after 1683/4. (Mary Frances Carey)

> Elizabeth was living 29 Dec 1692 in NC. (Father's Will)

+   3   ii.   Richard Bundick (II), b. c1656, d. 1731.

     4   iii.   Ann Bundick, b. in NC c1660, m. c1680, Thomas Nixson (b. c1640, d. 1696). (Mary Frances Carey) Thomas Nixson's made a verbal will on 12 Feb 1695, proved 11 Jun 1696 and recorded 16 Jun 1696. He named a mother Ann Nixson and brothers Edward and Richard Nixson. It was proved by Richard Bundick and Jonathan Sturgis. (ACW&c., 1692-1715 (xi):116) Ann was living 29 Dec 1692 in NC.

     5   iv.   Dorothy Bundick, b. in NC c1662, living 29 Dec 1692 in NC.

     6   v.   Grace Bundick, b. in NC c1664. she was living 29 Dec 1692 in NC.

Second Generation

3. Richard[2] Bundick (II) (Richard[1]), b. in NC c1656, d. 1731. (Mary Frances Carey; AC DW, 1729-1737(i):153)

He m. c1700, **Susanna Justice** (b. c1678, d. before 1729), dau. of Ralph Justice and Mary Abbott. (Wife's and Father's Will) Susanna Justice's father, Ralph Justice had m. c1675, so his dau. Susanna was nearly the same age as Richard Bundick (II)'s oldest son George. Ralph Justice d. testate in 1729, leaving property to Susanna Bundick's children when they "come to age or marry." He also named Abbott Bundick and Richard Bundick as grandsons and left them slaves. (AC Wills, 1729-1737:47) It appears that Susanna Justice Bundick d. before her father wrote his will in 1729.

Richard 's will was probated 6 Jul 1731 in AC. (AC DW 1729-1737(i):153) His birth year is based on his being 21 years old when his father deeded him land in Parkers Neck in 1677. On 15 Oct 1691, Richard Bundick deeded John Barns the 300 acres his father had sold Barns in 1680, relinquishing any title he might have in the land. (AC Wills & C Orders, 1682-1697:212) On 23 Jan 1689, Richard Bundick bought 200 acres "near the Seaboard" from Daniel Jenifer for 5600 pounds of good tobacco and cask, land to the north of "the Tann house branch." (AC DW, 1676-1690:491) On 10 Dec 1693, Richard Bundick bought another 74 acres from Daniel Jenifer, called *Gargapha Savannah*, for 2400 pounds of tobacco. (AC W&c, 1692-1715, part 1:69) This land was near the previous purchase. Richard Bundick purchased 299 acres near "Gilford Creek" for 5000 pounds of Tobacco and Casqe" from Edward Nixson, tanner, on 18 Jan 1701. (AC W&c,

1692-1715, part 1:394) The Quit Rents of Virginia in 1704 show Richard Bundick of
AC, the only Bundick listed, as being taxed for 773 acres in that year. (p. 14)
Richard Bundick (II) sold no land. He did give away two 100-acre tracts in May
of 1728, one "near Guilford Branch," to dau. Susanna Onions and her husband
John Onions (AC DW&c., 1715-1729, part 2:206) and 100 acres near Gargatha to son
Richard Bundick Junr (same page).
   Richard Bundick (II) d. leaving a will dated 23 May 1731, recorded on 6
July of the same year. He left son George Bundick his home plantation of 200
acres and made him his extr. He gave son Abbott (under 21) 100 acres in the
woods near Gargathy. He left 73 acres on Gargathy Branch to grandson,
William Bundick Pearson. Son Justis Bundick (under 21) was to inherit 100
acres near Guilford. Son George was left the remainder of Richard's land "at the
head of Guilford. Also mentioned dau. Keziah Bundock (under 21). Pewter to be
divided between daus. Mary Evans, Tabitha Bundock and Keziah Bundock. (AC
DW, 1729-1739, part 1:153) Remainder of my pewter to be equally divided between
my three daus. Mary Evans, Tabitha Bundock and Keziah Bundock. I give to my
three daus. Ann Abbott, Susanna Onions and Mary Evans twelve pence apiece
and to my son Richard Bundock I also give twenty pence. To son George
Bundock, extr., remainder estate after legal and just debts are paid by him.
Witnesses present: Thos. Evans, William Wilson and Willm Hastins. (AC DW,
1729-1739, part 1:153. See the will for more details.)
   Richard Bundick (II) had the following children:
+   7   i. George[3] Bundick, b. c1680, d. 1764.
    8   ii. (d|o Rich II) Bundick, b. in AC c1682, d. before 1731.
            She m. (N) Pearson (b. c1680) before 1731. (Wife's and
            Father's Will)
    9   iii. Ann Bundick, b. in AC c1684, living 23 May 1731, m.
            c1710, (N) Abbott (b. c1680). (Wife's; and Father's Will)
   Richard Bundick (II) and Susanna Justice had the following children:
   10   iv. Susannah Bundick, b. in AC c1700, m. before
            1731, John Onions (b. c1700, d. 1751). (wife's; and
            Father's Will; Whitelaw)
+ 11 v. Richard Bundick (III), b. c1705, d. 1766.
   12   vi. Mary Bundick. b. in AC c1707, m. c1730, Thomas
            Evans (b. c1700). (Wife's and Father's Will) Mary was living
            23 May 1731 in AC. (Father's Will)
+ 13   vii. Abbott Bundick, b. c1712, d. 1784.
   14   viii. Tabitha Bundick. b. in AC c1713, living 23 May 1731
            in AC. (Father's Will)
   15   ix. Keziah Bundick, b. in AC c1714, living 23 May 1731.
            (Father's Will) She m. c1735, John Young (b. c1710).
            (Mary Frances Carey)
+ 16   x. Justice Bundick, b. c1715, d. 1769.

48

Third Generation
7. George³ Bundick (Richard², Richard¹), b. in AC c1680, d. 1764. (Father's Will; AC Wills 1761-67:244)
He m. c1705 in AC, **Elizabeth Abbott** (b. c1685) in AC. (Mary Frances Carey) Elizabeth was the dau. of John Abbott Jr. and Amy Mason. (Nottingham Wills:24 (father's will))
George 's will was probated 23 Feb 1764 in AC. (AC Wills 1761-67:244) George Bundick's birth year is estimated from the fact he had m. by 2 April 1706. On that date, John Abbott Senr, of AC, planter, gave to his dau, Elizabeth Bundick, "now wife of George Bundick" 100 acres "on ye south side of Back Creek Branch wch was given to me by my father John Abbott in 1688." (AC W&c., 1692-1715, part 2:188) On 4 Feb 1718, George Bundick bought 100 adjoining acres from John Abbott of SO Co., son of Robert Abbott, deceased. (AC DW&c., 1715-1729, part 1:99) George Bundick then owned 200 acres of land in the area of present-day Parksley, before his father died in 1731, leaving him 200 acres in Parkers Neck and about 100 acres near Guilford Creek. (Whitelaw:1120) On 28 Jan 1755, George Bundick and wife Elizabeth deeded the latter, as 100 acres, here called *Robins Hole Swamp*, for £20, to John Abbott Bundick (their son) and to Richard Bundick (their grandson). (AC Deeds, 1746- 1757:543)
George Bundick, like his father and grandfather, lived to be an old man. His son and namesake had died 13 years before he made his will on 28 Jun 1763. It was recorded on 23 Feb 1764. He left son John Abbott Bundick the 200 acres "on the seaside where I now live" and made him extr. He gave grandson Richard Bundick, son of his deceased son, George Bundick Junr, 200 acres "where he now lives provided he let his mother, Tabitha Bundick, have a quiet & peaceable living during her widowhood." George Bundick's wife had apparently predeceased him, as she was not named in his will. Two daus. were also deceased. He divided personal property between his son, his grandson, Leah Townsend, dau. of Henry Townsend, daus. Susanna Sturgis and Rachel Satchell, and granddaus Elizabeth Stephens and Betty Turnell. Witnessed by William East, Archibald Barns, Charles Gill. John Walker & Isaac Melson(?) were his securities who entered into and acknowledged a bond for that purpose. (AC Wills, 1761-1767:244)
George Bundick and Elizabeth Abbott had the following children:
+   17   i. George⁴ Bundick Jr., b. c1710, d. 1751.
+   18   ii. John Abbott Bundick Sr., b. c1720, d. 1784.
      19   iii. Susanna Bundick, b. in AC c1722, living 28 Jun 1763 in AC, m. c1750, (N) Sturgis (b. c1730). (Wife's; and Father's Will)
      20   iv. Rachel Bundick, b. in AC c1724, living 28 Jun 1763 in AC, m. c1745, Henry Satchell, son of Henry Satchell and Elizabeth Ansil (b. c1722 in AC, d. 1779). (Father's Will; Husband's Will) In his will, written 13 Nov 1778, Henry Satchell named a son Southy Satchell; daus.

Anne Satchell, Susannah Rodgers, Molly Satchell, Elizabeth Bonnewell and Esther Satchell. A wife was mentioned, but not by name. To wife whole estate during her widowhood. To son Southy plantation where I live, he to pay his sister Anne ½ of the value of the negro Philip. To dau. Elizabeth Bonnewell, she to pay ½ of the value of the negro Sybal to my dau. Esther. Children were residuary legatees. Wife and son Southy to be extrs. Witnesses were David Bowman, William Steavens, Phillip Parker West. In order of probate Rachel Satchell & Southy Satchell qualified. (AC W&c., 1777-80:239)

21   v. Elizabeth Bundick, b. in AC c1726, d. before 1763. She m. c1750, Christopher Stevens (b. c1730, d. 1751). In his will, written 24 Apr 1751, Christopher Stephens, named sons John Stephens (under 21), George and William Stephens and a dau. Elizabeth Stephens. At probate, the wife was named as Elizabeth Stephens. Wife to have the use of my plantation during her widowhood and then all my lands and plantation to descend to my son John Stephens. Balance of estate to wife during her life or widowhood then to be divided between my 3 children George, William and Elizabeth Stevens. Wife to be extx. Witnesses were Thomas Ryley, Richard Grinalds, Martha Sturgis, John Abbott Bundick. In order of probate, John Abbott Bundick was appointed guardian to John Stephens, heir at law to the testator. Elizabeth Stevens, widow of the testator qualifed. (AC Wills, 1749-52:327); Mary Frances Carey)

22   vi. (1d|o Geo.) Bundick, b. in AC c1728, d. before 1763. (Father's Will) She m. c1745, Robert Tunnell (b. c1720 in AC, d. 1763). In his will, written 13 Apr 1762, Robert Turnall named sons George, William, Robert and John "Turnal;" a dau. Betty Turnal, and a grandau. Amy Turnal. Cattle and sheep to be divided between my wife and all my daus. and my granddau Amy Turnal. Balance of estate to wife and all my children execpt son Robert. To sons Robert and John. Son Robert and Thomas Riley to be extrs. Witness were William Young and Richard Bundick. (Mary Frances Carey; AC Wills 1761-67:196)

23   vii. (2d|o Geo.) Bundick, b. in AC c1730, d. before 1763. (Father's Will) She m. c1750, Henry Townsend (b. c1730). (Wife's; and Father's Will)

11. **Richard³ Bundick (III)** (Richard², Richard¹), b. in Parkers Neck, AC c1705, d. 1766 in AC. (Grandfather's Will; Mary Frances Carey; AC Orders 1765-67:33)

He m. c1728, **Ann Nock** (b. c1710 in AC), dau. of John Nock and Rose (N). Ann Nock's father named her as Ann Bundick in his will dated 24 Dec 1739 and named her husband, Richard Bundick (III) as an extr. along with his son, George Nock. (AC Wills, 1737-43:222); Mary Frances Carey;)

Richard Bundick (III), b. in Parker's Neck, on land his father had been given in 1677 by Richard Bundick (I). On 7 May 1728, his father gave Richard Bundick (III), 100 acres near Gargatha, "part of land I bought of Colonel Jenefer." (AC DW&c., 1715-1729, part 2:206) When Richard Bundick (III), d. testate in 1731, he left son Richard 12 pence in his will; he mentioned that land he was leaving son Abbott Bundick adjoined son Richard's land. This Richard Bundick was also named in the 1728 will of his grandfather, Ralph Justis, who left him a slave (AC WD, 1729-1737, part 1:47) Richard Bundick (III), lived his entire adult life on the 100 acres of land east of Gargatha that his father gave him in 1728. He d. intestate in 1766, his land descending to his oldest son, Richard Bundick (IV), called "Piper" in local records. Note that Whitelaw:1160, has this 100 acres confused with the 72/74 acres Richard Bundick II, left grandson William Bundick Pearson in 1731, apparently being unaware he had deeded this 100 acres to son Richard before he died. Whitelaw locates the land behind the present Arcadia Nursing Home, to the east of U.S. 13, and on both sides of Gargatha Landing Road.

On 27 May 1766, John Bundick was named to administer the estate of Richard Bundick. John would have been Richard's younger son and he gave his brother, Richard Bundick (Richard (IV) or "Piper"), as his security. The inventory of Richard Bundick's personal estate, valued at £18.19.1, was returned on 26 Nov 1766. It was signed by the appraisers John Kittson, Charles Bagwell and William Nock. It was divided into five lots, one for each of his children. (AC Wills, 1761-1767:2/3)

Richard Bundick (III) and Ann Nock had the following children:

+ 24 i. Richard 'Piper'⁴ Bundick (IV), b. c1730, d. 1790.

    25 ii. (d|o Rich III) Bundick, b. in Gartahta, AC c1730 (AC Wills 1761-67:673) She m. c1750, Edmund Mason (d. Apr 1768), son of Bennett Mason and Bridget Bagwell. She was living 26 Nov 1766 in AC. (Distribution of Wife's Father's Estate; Nottingham w*lls:*229 (will of Bennet Mason)); Nottingham Wills:231 (adm. of Edmund Mason))

+ 26 iii. John 'Long' Bundick, b. c1732, d. 1800.

    27 iv. Susanna Bundick, b. in Gargahta, AC, c1734, living 26 Nov 1766 in AC. (AC Wills 1761-67:673) She m. c1760, John Wimbrough (b. c1730). (Distribution of Wife's Father's Estate)

28   v. Ann Bundick, b. in Gargatha, AC, c1736, living 26
           Nov 1766 in AC. (AC Wills 1761-67:673) She m. c1760,
           (N) Holt (b. c1730). (Distribution of Wife's Father's Estate)
13. **Abbott**[3] **Bundick** (Richard[2], Richard[1]), b. c1712, d. 1784. (Father's Will; AC
W&c 1784-87:48)
    He married three times. He m. 1st c1735, **Sophia Bagwell** (b. c1715). (Mary
Frances Carey) He m. 2nd c1760, **Mary Sanders** (b. c1720), dau. of Richard
Sanders and Rachel (N). (Mary Frances Carey) He m. 2nd c1770, **Keziah Bell** (b.
c1740 in AC). (Husband's Will) Keziah was the dau. of (N) Bell and Rachel (N).
(Mother's Will)
    Abbott left a will dated 7 Mar 1784, probated 1 Sep 1784 in AC. He named
a son Elias; and 5 daus: Rachel, Leah, Tabitha, Patience and Keziah Bundick.
To wife Kesiah Bundick my plantation during her widowhood, with reversion to
son Elias Bundick and for want of heirs to 5 daus. Personal estate to wife for life
and then to 5 daus. Wife and Stephen Bell extrs. Witnesses were Robert James,
Thomas Taylor and William Taylor. (AC W&c 1784-87:48)
    Abbott Bundick and Sophia Bagwell had the following children:
    +   29   i.   Levin[4] Bundick, b. c1750, d. before 1784.
          30   ii. Peggy Bagwell Bundick, b. in AC c1755. (Mary Frances
                     Carey)
    Abbott Bundick and Keziah Bell had the following children:
          31   iii. Patience Bundick, b. in AC c1770, m. c1790, William
                 .   Baker (b. c1760, d. Sep 1846. (Wife's; and Brother's Land
                     Cause; MilesW&A:26 (will of William Baker Sr.))
          32   iv. Rachel Bundick, b. in AC c1772, m. c1790, Richard
                     Baker (b. c1760). (Wife's; and Brother's Land Cause)
          33   v.   Leah Bundick, b. in AC c1774, m. c1795,Thomas West
                     (b. c1760). (Wife's; and Brother's Land Cause)
          34   vi. Tabitha Bundick, b. in AC c1776, m. 3 Nov 1796 in
                     AC, William Hinman (b. c1760 in AC), son of Moses
                     Hinman and Scarburgh (N). (ACM; AC Wills 1788-94:306).
          35   vii. Keziah Bundick, b. in AC c1780, d. 1816. (Mary Frances
                     Carey)
          36   viii. Elias Bundick, b. in AC before 1784, d. before 28 Oct
                     1805 in AC. On 28 Oct 1805, in a partition suit it was
                     stated that Elias Bundick was lately seized of 100 acres
                     in the Parish of Accomack, and on the _ day of _ 1805
                     departed this life intestate, leaving Leah wife of
                     Thomas West, Tabitha wife of William Hinman,
                     Patience wife of William Baker, and Keziah his sisters,
                     and also Preeson Baker, Tabitha Baker, Richard Baker
                     and Rachel Baker, infants, his nephews and nieces,
                     being the children of Rachel Baker, another sister of
                     Elias Bundick, and Sally Bundick his niece, being the
                     dau. of Levin Bundick brother of the half blood of Elias

Bundick - John Nock appointed guardian to the infant
defendants to defend this suit. (AC Land Causes 1773-
1805:313)

16. **Justice³ Bundick** (Richard², Richard¹), b. in AC c1715, d. 1769. (AC W&c
1767-72:252)

He m. c1740, **Sarah (N)** (b. c1720). In describing the ownership of
Whitelaw's tract A112, it is noted that in 1769 the extr. of Justice Bundick was
joined by the widow Sarah in a sale of the 100 acres to Jacob Mason.
(Whitelaw:1116)

Justice d. leaving a will dated 15 Dec 1768, probated 1 Feb 1769 in AC.
(AC W&c 1767-72:252) He named 2 daus. Susannah and Beersheba Bundick as
residuary legatees. He mentioned Robert Jones, Thomas Bloxom, Richard
Bundick, and Rachel "Sandrews." Thomas Crippen and Charles Bagwell to be
extrs. Witnesses were Richard Onions and John Riggs. In order of probate
Richard Onions was appointed guardian to Tabitha Bundick, one of the co-heirs
of the testator. (AC W&c., 1767-72:252)

Justice Bundick and Sarah (N) had the following children:

    37   i. Susannah⁴ Bundick, b. in AC c1750. She was living 15
             Dec 1768. (Father's Will)

    38   ii. Beersheba Bundick, b. in AC c1752, m. c1780, John
             Taylor (b. c1750). (Mary Frances Carey)

    39   iii. Tabitha Bundick, b. in AC c1754, m. 31 Oct 1775 in
             AC, Robert Rogers (b. c1750 in AC). (ACM)

Fourth Generation

17. **George⁴ Bundick Jr.** (George³, Richard², Richard¹), b. in AC c1710, d.
1751. (Mary Frances Carey; AC Wills 1749-52:259)

He m. c1732, **Tabitha (N)** (b. c1710). George Bundick Jr. wife's given
name, Tabitha, is first found on 21 Aug 1751, when George's inventory was
returned by extrs., Tabitha Bundick and Richard Bundick, and again when his
father's will was recorded in 1764, at which time she had not remarried. (Mary
Frances Carey; AC Wills, 1749-52:290)

George d. leaving a will dated 14 Apr 1751, probated 30 Jul 1751 in AC.
(AC Wills 1749-52:259) George Bundick Jr. inherited no land, for he died before his
father. He apparently lived on his father's land, in an area that became the
present-day Parksley, for this was where his widow and son were living when
his father died in 1764. In his will George Bundick Jr. named a son Richard and
daus. Ann and Elizabeth Bundick. He left personal property to son Richard
Bundick and to daus. Ann Bundick and Elizabeth Bundick. Wife (unnamed) to
have use of personal estate during her widowhood, then to be divided between
children. Wife and son Richard to be extrs. Witnesses were Henry Satchell,
Richard Onions, and John Abbott Bundick. (AC Wills, 1749-52:259) An inventory of
the estate of George Bundick Junr was filed in Aug 1751 (2 full pages of items).
(AC Wills, 1749-52:290)

George Bundick Jr. and Tabitha (N) had the following children:
+   40   i. Richard⁵ Bundick Sr., b. c1732, d. 13 Mar 1805.
      41   ii. Ann Bundick, b. in AC c1736, living 14 Apr 1751 in
            AC. (Father's Will)
      42   iii. Elizabeth Bundick, b. in AC c1740, living 14 Apr
            1751. (Father's Will)
18. **John Abbott⁴ Bundick Sr.** (George³, Richard², Richard¹), b. in AC c1720,
d. 1784. (AC Wills 1780-84:480)
      He m. c1745, **Elizabeth Satchell** (b. c1726 in AC), dau. of Henry Satchell
and Elizabeth Ansil. (Wife's; and Father's Will)
      He m. c1760, **Bridget (N)** (b. c1740). (Husband's Will) She m. 30 Nov 1784 in
AC, **William Nock.** (ACM) Bridget, the wife named in John Abbott Bundick's
will, dated 13 Jul 1780, was his 2nd wife as shown by a deed of 3 Mar 1791,
when Bridget and her next husband, William Nock, released her dower interest
in land John Abbott Bundick's son George sold, saying she had m. "aforesaid
George's father." (AC Deeds, 1788-1793:469a) Had she been George's mother, this
deed would have been worded differently. William Gibb was the security on the
1784 AC M.L.B. of William Nock and Bridget Bundick. On 27 Apr 1791,
William Nock and wife Bridget joined William Bundick and wife Agnes in
selling their 54 acres, *Robins Hold* to Crippen Taylor. (AC Deeds, 1788-1793:470)
John Abbott Bundick, Junr sold his interest in the same land on the same day.
(AC Deeds, 1788-1793:471)
      John was paid for public service during Rev War. 1781-1783 in AC. (Walker
& Turman, *Acc Soldiers & Sailors in Rev*)
      John Abbott Bundick Sr, who was named for his maternal grandfather,
inherited 200 acres from his father George in 1764, "on the seaside where I now
live." This tract was in the northern part of Parkers Neck, part of the first
Richard Bundick patent of 1664, the 200 acres he gave his son Richard in 1677
and that Richard (II) left son George in 1731. John Abbott Bundick and his
nephew, Richard Bundick, had been given the 100 acres called *Robins Hole
Swamp* by his parents in 1755. John Abbott Bundick sold no land in his lifetime,
except for 200 acres his son, John Abbott Bundick Junr. (with wife Nancy and
mother-in-law Mary Dix), deeded him on 22 Feb 1779. (AC Deeds, 1777-1783:113),
land that he deeded back to his son the next day. (AC Deeds, 1777- 1783:127) This
was evidently a transaction to clear the title to the land.
      John Abbott Bundick d. leaving a will dated 13 Jul 1780, probated 30 Mar
1784 in AC. His will was a long one. He left his home plantation of 200 acres to
his son George Bundick. He left his swamp land and marsh to sons John Abbott
Bundick and William Bundick (unmarried). He left his wife Bridget household
furniture, "200 weight of meat" and livestock. He left furniture to other of his
children, but son George seems to have inherited most of his personal property
including livestock, a still and "1/3 my fishing boat." Negroes were to be divided
"equally amongst all my children." He also named a grandson as John Bundick,
son of George. John Abbott Bundick's residuary estate was divided among his

heirs on 25 Nov 1785. As his widow, Bridget received 1/3, amounting to £104.14.1 1/4 pence. Sons John Bundick and William Bundick received a like amount, as did Thomas Lillaston, Parker Barnes, Archibald Barnes, and Richard Hickman. These four men had m. John Abbott Bundick's four daus. Son George Bundick was not named in this division. (AC Wills, 1784-1787:269) An item of interest is that on 1 May 1783, the AC Court made a list of persons who had supplied Revolutionary War forces or persons "Impressed for Continental Purposes." Among those listed are John A. Bundick Senr "for carting 25 bushels oats 17 miles" at a cost of 7 shillings, 1 pence and John A. Bundick Junr for 150 bushels fodder at 4 shillings, 4 pence. (AC Orders, 1780-1783:529 & 531) Witnesses: Spencer Barnes, Jacob Sturgis, John Barnes. William Parramore and John Custis, securities. (AC Wills, 1780-1784:480)

John Abbott Bundick Sr. and Elizabeth Satchell had the following children:

+   43   i.   George 'of Metompkin'[5] Bundick, b. c1745, d. 1819.

        44   ii.   Anne Bundick. b. in AC c1747, d. 1796. (Father's Will; AC W&c 1794-96:404) She m. c1765, Richard Hickman (b. c1750in AC, d. 1787). (Wife's Will; AC W&c 1784-87:375) In his will, written 21 Nov 1786, Richard Hickman named a son Hampton Hickman and a dau. Elizabeth, the wife of Isaiah Hickman. To wife all the remainder of my estate, real and personal, during her widowhood, and then to my son Hampton Hickman all my lands and the remainder of my personal estate to my dau. Elizabeth. Wife (unnamed) and son Hampton Hickman and Isaiah Hickman extrs. Witnesses were Geroge Bundick, Tabitha Bundick, and Thomas Hickman. In order of probate Anne Hickman, Isaiah Hickman and Hampton Hickman qualifed. (AC W&c., 1784-87:375) It is assumed that the Anne Hickman that qualified was his wife, since his wife was named as an executrix.

                 Anne 's will was probated 25 Jul 1796 in AC. In her will, written 10 Sep 1793, prorbated 25 Jul 1796, Anne Hickman named a son Hampton Hickman and granddaus Rebeckah & Peggy Hickman, daus. of Isaiah Hickman. To my said granddaus all the estate devised to their mother by the last will of my husband, which estate was left in my care during my natural life. John A. Bundick and Parker Barnes to be extrs. Witnesses were Leah Barnes and Susanna Barnes. (AC W&c., 1794-96:404)

+   45   iii.   John Abbott Bundick Jr.. b. c1752, d. 1805.

+   46   iv.   William Bundick, b. c1755, d. 1795.

John Abbott Bundick Sr. and Bridget (N) had the following children:

47   v. Leah Bundick, b. in AC c1760, living 13 July 1780.
          (Father's Will) She m. c1775, Parker Barnes (b. c1742 in
          AC), son of William Barnes and Susannah Parker. (Mary
          Frances Carey; Nottingham Wills:271 (father's will))
48   vi. Shady Bundick, b. inAC c1764, m. c1790, Thomas
          Lilliston (b. c1760). (Mary Frances Carey)
49   vii. Attalanta 'Lanter' Bundick, b. in AC c1766, m. c1790,
          Archibald Barnes (b. c1760). (Mary Frances Carey)
24. **Richard 'Piper'**[4] **Bundick (V)** (Richard[3], Richard[2], Richard[1]), b. c1730 in
Gargatha, AC, d. 1790. (AC Wills 1761-67:673; AC Wills 1788-94:306)
    He m. c1755, **Lucretia 'Lukey|Suke' (N)** (b. c1730 in AC). (Husband's Will)
    On 27 May 1766 Piper Bundick was named by his younger brother John to
be his security on the administration of their father's estate. (AC Orders 1765-67:33)
    On 26 Nov 1766, Piper, as the elder son of Richard Bundick III, inherited
the 100 acres of land at Gargatha his father had been deeded in 1728 by Richard
Bundick II, land Richard II bought in 1689. He was called 'Piper' in many local
records to distinguish him from other Richard Bundicks in Acc Parish. (AC Wills
1761-67:672/3)
    No record has been found indicating he played a musical instrument,
smoked a pipe, or built four-barrel casks, which were known as pipes. However,
his inventory did include 7 casks, 5 tubs, 2 open barrels and 1 keg. (AC Wills 1788-
94:306)
    On 23 Aug 1788 Richard Bundick and Luky his wife sold 8 acres, 3 roods
and 11 perches to Meshack Mears for £22. (AC Deeds, 1788-1793)
    He d. leaving a will dated 19 Feb 1789 in AC, probated 29 Apr 1790. In it
he named a wife Suke; sons George, Richard, John, William, Abbott, and
Justice; daus. Susanna Bundick and Sally Bundick; grandchildren: Richard
Bundick, son of his son George, Nancy Garrett, dau. of John Garrett, and Tabby
Garrett, Betsy Garrett and Thomas Garrett, the children of Richard Garrett;
brother John Bundick and his wife Sarah, who was the widow of James Foster.
He left his entire estate to his wife Luke during her widowhood and the "use of
the plantation where I live" was to go to son George Bundick for his lifetime. At
George's death it was to be sold and the money to be divided between "such of
my children and grandchildren as shall be alive, viz: son Richard, John, William,
Abbott, Justice, Susanna Bundick, Sally Bundick and my grandchild Richard
Bundick, son of my son George." He left his brother John Bundick the
plantation where he now lives, "which was conveyed to me by his wife Sarah."
He named his wife and son William as extrs. Friend Charles West was to be the
overseer. Witnesses were Moses Hinman, and William Hinman, son of Moses,
and John Riggs. When 'Luke' Bundick and William Bundick qualified as extrs.,
George Bundick was named as heir-at-law of the testator, implyng that he was
the oldest son.
    On 25 May 1793, George Bundick was joined by Richard Bundick, Abbott
Bundick, Hezekiah Baker Junr and wife Susanna, and William Onions Junr and

wife Sally, in selling their father's land at Gargatha to their brothers William and Justice Bundick. George Bundick received £50 and each of the other children £6. This deed does not mention their mother's dower interest in the land, but does say that brother John "died during the lifetime of his father," and that George was the eldest son. (AC Deeds 1793-1797)

On 1 Dec 1795, a survey was made of the land, which then contained 91 acres. William Bundick received 50.5 acres and Justice Bundick received 40.5 acres. The survey shows the land north of present-day Gargatha Landing Road, with a small frontage on Wallops Road, present-day U.S. 13.(AC Surveyor's Rec 2, 1794-1799)

Richard 'Piper' Bundick (IV) and Lucretia 'Lukey|Suke' (N) had the following children:

	50	i.	(1d	o Rich)^5 Bundick, b. in AC c1756, d. before 1789. (Father's Will) She m. c1777, John Garrett (b. c1755). (Wife's; and Father's Will) He m. 28 Mar 1787 (bond) in AC, Sarah 'Sally' Taylor. George Trewet Taylor was the security on the M.L.B. of John Garrett and Salley Taylor. (ACM)
	51	ii.	(2d	o Rich) Bundick, b. in AC c1758, d. before 1789. (Father's Will) She m. c1779, Richard Garrett (b. c1750). (Wife's; and Father's Will)
+	52	iii.	George Bundick, b. c1760, d. before 1817.
	53	iv.	Richard Bundick, b. in AC c1763. (Father's Will) Richard was listed as a head of household in the census of 1800 in Acc Parish, AC. He was shown as age 26 to 45. He had two males in his household age 16 to 26 and another male under age 10. Three females were age 16 to 26, age 10 to 16 and under age 10. He had apparently m. c1785, but no record of his marriage has been found. His name has not been found in AC records after 1800. It is not known when he died or the names of his children, if they survived.
	54	v.	John Bundick, b. in AC c1765, d. before 29 Apr 1790. (Father's Will)
+	55	vi.	William Bundick, b. 28 Nov 1768, d. 1 Feb 1845.
+	56	vii.	Abbott Bundick, b. c1770, d. 1833-1840.
	57	viii.	Susanna Bundick, b. in AC c1771, d. before 1817. (Father's Will) She m. c1791, Hezekiah Baker Jr. (b. c1770 in AC). (Mary Frances Carey) He m. Tabitha Baker 7 Jun 1816 (bond) in AC. (ACM) Ezekiel Baker was the security on the M.L.B. of Hezekiah Baker and Tabitha Baker of Rich.
+	58	ix.	Justice Bundick, b. c1772, d. 1818.

59   x. Sally Bundick, b. in AC c1774. (Father's Will) She m. 6
Dec 1792, Rev. William Selby Onions (b. c1760 in AC,
d. Aug 1818). (ACM; MilesW&A:403 (will of William Onions
Sr.))
26. John 'Long'⁴ Bundick (Richard³, Richard², Richard¹), b. in Gargatha, AC,
d. 1800. (AC Wills 1761-67:673; AC W&c 1800-04:342)
He m. 1ˢᵗ c1755, Beersheba Wimbrough (b. c1740), dau. of Joseph
Wimbrough. (Wife's; and Father's Will) On 26 Feb 1763, John and Beershiba
Bundick witnessed the will of Jonathan Bunting. (AC Wills, 1761-1767:251) Jonathan
Bunting owned land southwest of Accomac. (Whitelaw:899) Joseph Wimbrough
wrote his will on 9 Sep 1767, recorded on 29 Jan 1771. (AC Wills, 1767-1772:494)
He named a dau. as Beersheba Bundick. Before the will was recorded, John
Bundick, who m. one of the heirs of the decedent, was called into court "&
having nothing to object the said will was admitted to probate," clearly
indicating that John Bundick m. Beersheba Wimbrough, whose father Joseph
owned land near Jonathan Bunting. (Whitelaw:900/1)
He m. 2ⁿᵈ 1774, Sarah Whaley (b. c1735, d. before 1800), dau. of Thomas
Whaley and Barbara (N). (Mary Frances Carey; AC Deeds (General Reference), 1770-77:287)
She m. c1770, James Foster. (Will of Wife's 2nd Husband's Brother; AC Census of 1800)
On 29 March 1774, John Bundick Junior, and Sarah his wife, dau. and heir of
Thomas Whaley, gave a deed of trust to Richard Bundick, Junior (his brother
Richard (IV) or "Piper"), for five shillings for 100 acres of land on Burton's
Branch in the Parish of St. George. The said John and Sarah were to keep
possession of the land during their lives. (AC Deeds, 1770-1777:287) When Richard
Bundick (IV) died in 1790, his will directed that his brother John Bundick have
"the plantation where he now lives, which was conveyed to me by his wife
Sarah, which was the widow of James Foster." (AC Wills, 1788-1794:306)
John d. leaving a will dated 4 Oct 1796, probated 27 Oct 1800 in AC. John
"Long" Bundick was most likely named for his maternal grandfather, John
Nock. He, b. near Gargatha and raised on the land his father had been deeded in
1728 by Richard Bundick (II). As a younger son, John Bundick inherited no
land from his father. John Bundick would have been of age to have m. by 1755.
John Bundick was the first Bundick to live in St. George Parish, the southern
parish of Accomack County. Apparently he lived southeast of Accomac on his
father-in-law's land during his first marriage and moved to the land his second
wife owned c1774. This land on Burton's Branch would have been between
Melfa and Onley and east of U.S. 13. John Bundick is shown in St. George
Parish by the 1787 personal property tax lists when he was called "Long John."
He was also on the 1788 tax list as "Long Jno." The 1800 Federal Census lists
"John Bundick, Long" as over 45 years, still the only Bundick in St. George
Parish. His household included two other males, one 10 to 16 years and the other
16 to 26 years old. Two females were both 16 to 26 years old. Apparently he had
lost his second wife by 1800. John Bundick wrote his will on 4 Oct 1796. He
gave "unto my two sons George Bundick and John Bundick all my lands and for

58

it to be equally divided between them." If either should die without an heir then the other should have his half. If both George and John should die without heirs, the land was to go "unto my Grandson William Bundick Reed," then to grandson Laben Phillips. He devised to his wife Sarah his "Riding Chear" and after her death or marriage it was to go to his two sons. Dau. Nancy Phillips inherited "one beehive." Dau. Susanna Outten was devised "all the articles that she carried away which is one bed and furniture one linen wheel one iron pot" and these were to go to her son William Outten after her death. He gave son George "my shooting Gun" and son John "ten dollars cash to buy him a Gun." Grandson William Outten was to have five pounds for schooling.The remainder of his estate was to be divided between his wife & Sarah and sons George and John. Wife & Sarah and son George were to be extrs. Witnessed by William James and Abel Badger. Teackle Elliott & Charles Elliott were security. (AC Wills, 1800-1804:342)

On 7 Jul 1801, George Bundick and John Bundick deeded to John Shephard Ker and William Seymour, for £81.5, 100 acres land devised by John Bundick, dec'd. father of George and John. The land was bordered by lands of James Kellam, Benjamin Floyd, George Taylor and William Gibb. (AC Deeds, 1800-1804:139) Both George and John were unm. as no wives signed the deed. This was apparently a mortgage, as two other deeds followed. On 31 Aug 1802, George Bundick and wife Rachel sold to Littleton Ward 50 acres in St. George Parish for £100, land bound north by William Gibb Senr, northeast by James Kellam, southeast by Benjamin Floyd, and southwest by Burton's Branch joining land of George Taylor. (AC Deeds: 364) On 27 Jan 1803, John Bundick of John (unm.) deeded to Littleton Ward 50 acres of land with the same boundaries, for £100. (AC Deeds:363)

John 'Long' Bundick and Beersheba Wimbrough had the following children:

    60   i. (d|o John 'Long')[5] Bundick, b. in AC c1765, d. before 1796, m. c1785, (N) Read (b. c1760). (Wife's; and Father's Will)

    61   ii. Nancy Bundick, b. in AC c1767, living 4 Oct 1796, m. c1790, (N) Phillips (b. c1760). (Wife's; and Father's Will)

    62   iii. Susanna Bundick, b. in AC c1769, living 4 Oct 1796, m. c1790, (N) Outten (b. c1770). (Wife's; and Father's Will)

John 'Long' Bundick and Sarah Whaley had the following children:

  + 63 iv. George Bundick, b. c1778

  + 64 v. John S. 'of Long' Bundick, b. 4 May 1781, d. 4 Aug 1861.

29. **Levin[4] Bundick** (Abbott[3], Richard[2], Richard[1]), b. in AC c1750, d. before 1784. (Brother's Land Cause; Father's Will)

Levin served as a seaman during the Rev War, 1775-1783 in AC. (Walker & Turman, *Acc Soldiers & Sailors in Rev*; AC OB 1829-1832:475) An order of 29 May 1832 states that Edmund Bundick was the only heir of Levin Bundick, who served in the State Navy of Virginia during the Rev War.

Levin Bundick had the following child:

+   65   i.   Sarah 'Sally'[5] Bundick, b. c1780.

Fifth Generation

40. **Richard[5] Bundick Sr.** (George[4], George[3], Richard[2], Richard[1]), b. in AC c1732, d. 13 Mar 1805 in AC. (Father's Will; AC Land Cause 1773-1805:317) He m. c1755, **Rachel Andrews?** (b. c1735). (Mary Frances Carey) Richard Bundick Sr. likely m. Rachel Andrews, a granddau. of Richard Andrews, who d. testate in 1759, naming a granddau. as Rachel Bundick. (AC Wills, 1757-1761:126) A Rachel Bundick witnessed his will and that of William Andrews in 1763. (AC Wills, 1761-67:225)

Richard Bundick Sr. would have been about 19 years of age when his father died in 1751 and 23 years old in 1755 when his grandparents, George and Elizabeth Bundick, deeded the 100 acres called *Robins Hole Swamp* to him and his uncle, John Abbott Bundick, for £20. (AC Deeds, 1746-57:543) He would have been about 32 years of age when he inherited the 200 acres from his grandfather George in 1764, land "where he now lives." A survey of this land after his death shows the 200 acres were actually 221 acres. (Acc Survey Rec #3:115) It was later to become the eastern part of the present-day Parksley. (Whitelaw:1120) The same survey shows that Richard's part of *Robins Hole Swamp* contained 84 ½ acres and that it was a separate tract located near Guilford. The name of Richard Bundick, "Clk," appears on the 1784 tax list and on a survey. (AC Survey Rec #1:59) " No explanation for this designation after his name has been found. The records have been searched, looking for his appointment as clerk to some office, to no avail. It seems certain it was used to distinguish him from Richard Bundicks of other Acc Parish areas. In 1784, he owned five slaves, four horses and eleven cattle. He was taxed £3.11.3 on his real estate and £2.10.9 on his personal property. By the time the Federal Census was taken in 1800, Richard Bundick Senr was over 45 years of age (about 68). He then owned six slaves. Another male in his household was 16 to 26 years of age and the only female was 26 to 45. Richard Bundick had died intestate by 27 Feb 1805 when William Grinalds was named to administer his estate. (AC OB, 1804-05:225) William Grinnalds returned an audit of the estate on 28 Jun 1805. (AC Wills, 1804-06:507), and a division of the personal property was made on the same day. (Ibid:508) It is apparent that Richard Bundick's wife was deceased by 1805, for his personal estate was divided between four children, each of whom received £76.9.4. On 7 Aug 1805, in a partition suit it was stated that Richard Bundick Sr. was seized of two tracts of land and marsh containing 300 acres in Acc Parish, and being so seized died intestate on 13 Mar 1805 leaving children, to wit: Nancy Grinnalds, wife of William Grinnalds, Betsy Vessels, wife of Arthur Vessels, and Richard Bundick, and also grandchildren, to wit: Tabitha Taylor, wife of James Taylor, William Bundick, Betsy Bundick, and Sally Bundick, children of one George

Bundick, a deceased son Richard Bundick Sr. Tabitha Bundick (Taylor?) appointed guardian of Betsy and Sally Bundick, two of the infant defendants to this suit. (AC Land Causes, 1773-1805:317) The lands of Richard Bundick were surveyed on 24 Sep 1805, for a division among his heirs. (AC Survey Rec #3:115) The four children of deceased son George Bundick received 20 to 25 acres each, totaling 90 acres. William Grinnalds and wife Nancy received 70 ½ acres, and Arthur Wessells and wife Betsy received 60 ½ acres. 84 ½ additional, separate acres "lying Robins Hole near Guilford," went to Richard Bundick, son of Richard.

Richard Bundick Sr. and Rachel Andrew/Andrews had the following children:

66   i. George[6] Bundick, b. in AC c1758, d. 1804 in AC. (Father's Land Cause; AC OB 1804-05:148) He m. c1779, Tabitha (N) (b. c1760 in AC, d. 1818). (Mary Frances Carey; AC W&c., 1817-18:333) In her will, written 1 Jan 1818, Tabitha Bundick left personal property to 3 of her children and the remainder of her estate, both real and personal, was to be divided between all her children. The 4 surviving children of George and Tabitha inherited a total of 90 acres from his father in 1805. This George Bundick's name appears directly under that of Richard Bundick, Clk, in the 1784 tax list as "George Bundick, his son," indicating he had m. and was head of a houshold by that time. He owned only 2 horses and was taxed 14 shillings. The 1800 Federal Census lists "George Bundick, Rich. Clk" as 26 to 45 years of age (42?). He had one other male in his household, at 16 to 26 years, and 5 females, one being his wife, also 26 to 45 years. 2 females were under 10 years, one was 10 to 16 and another 26 to 45 years. George Bundick d. intestate the year before his father, for on 31 Oct 1804, his widow, Tabitha Bundick, was qualified to administer his estate. (AC OB, 1804-05:148)

67   ii. Nancy Bundick, b. in AC c1765, living 7 Aug 1805 in AC, m. c1785, William Grinnalds Sr. (b. before 1765 in AC, d. Oct 1821 in AC), son of Elijah Grinnalds and Sarah (N). (Wife's; and Father's Land Cause; Powell, *AC 1800, 1810, 1820 Census;* MilesW&A:234 (will of Elijah Grinalds)) He m. 21 Sep 1814 (bond) in AC, Sarah 'Sally' Joynes. (ACM) William White, BS, was the security on the M.L.B. of William Grinnalds Sr. and Sally Joynes of William dec'd.

68   iii. Richard Bundick Jr., b. in AC c1766, d. 1818. (Father's Land Cause; Mary Frances Carey) He m. c1787, Rachel

Fitchett(?) (b. c1765 in AC, d. 1822). (Mary Frances Carey; AC W&c., 1821-23:125) In Rachel Bundick's will of 7 Aug 1820 she named the same three children as were named in her husband, Richard Bundick's will, Richard, John, and Damaris Bundick. Rachel left land to son John F. Bundick, saying he was under 21 years of age, and other land to dau. Daisy Parks, now wife of Benjamin Parks. She also named a granddau, Eunice P. Rogers. Rachel's land was surveyed on 13 Mar 1822 and it contained 41 acres, 4 rods. She had sold 6 acres to Southy Taylor and 8 acres were to go to son John F. Bundick, while the balance was to be sold at public auction. Her land was located 2 ½ miles "in a south direction from Guilford." (AC Survey Rec #5:100)

In his will, Richard Bundick Junr left his plantation called *Robin Hole*, of 84 acres to his son Richard A. Bundick. He named another son John T. (F?) Bundick, his wife Rachel, a dau. Damaris Bundick and granddau. Emma Rodgers. (MilesW&A:105)

69   iv.   Elizabeth 'Betsy' Bundick, b. in AC c1770, d. 1839 in AC. (Father's Land Cause; AC Wills 1828-46:305) She m. 11 Jan 1794 in AC, Arthur Wessells Jr. (b. c1775 in AC, d. 1813 in AC), son of Arthur Wessells Sr. In his will of 20 Aug 1806 Arthur Wessels Jnr. named: a wife Elizabeth; sons Arthur (under 21) and Richard; daus. Nancy, Sally E., Betsey, and Catherine Wessels; and extrs. wife and friend Charles Bagwell. Witnesses were Charles Bagwell, George Bell, and William Young. Securities for probate were Thomas M. and Richard D. Bayly. Evidently Arthur had several other children between the time he wrote his will and his death in 1813 for there are additional children named in his wife's will of 1837. (Nottingham, *AC MLB 1774-1806; P*owell, *AC 1800, 1810, 1820 Census*; Brother Ephriam's Will of 1807; AC W&c., 1812-14:333)

Elizabeth 's will was probated 26 Aug 1839 in AC. Although she died by 26 Aug 1839, she was evidently listed as a head of an 1840 household, age 50-60, with 6 males, 2 other females and 4 slaves in the household. There were 4 males 30-40, one male 20-30 and one male under 5; one female 20-30 and one female under 5. In her will dated 21 Jan 1837 Elizabeth (Bundick) Wessels named sons Arthur <u>W.</u> ("F." in probate), Richard, John, Samuel and Ephraim; daus. Nancy

Wessels (w/o Thomas Wessels), Elizabeth Somers, and
Cally Young; and her father Richard Bundick; and extr.
son Arthur Wessels. Witnesses were George H. Ewell,
Robert S. Taylor and Thorougood Dix. Apprasors were
George H. Ewell, David Mears, L.A. Hinman and John
Parks (of John). Securities for probate were John H.
Wessels, Samuel Wessels and Raymond Riley. (AC Wills
1828-1846:305)

43. **George 'of Metompkin'**[5] **Bundick** (John Abbott[4], George[3], Richard[2],
Richard[1]), b. in AC c1745, d. 1819. (AC W&c., 1819-21:129)

He m. 1st c1775, **Ann 'Nancy|Nanney' Warrington** (b. c1750 in AC), dau.
of Abbott Warrington and Elizabeth Millechoppe. (Mary Frances Carey; Grandmother's
Will) While there is no record of Ann Warrington's marriage to George Bundick,
from later deeds it is clear that she was Ann Warrington, who inherited
Warrington land "on Assawoman." She was called Ann and Nancy in the deeds
and Nanney Warrington by Tabitha Warrington, who named her and Elizabeth
Warrington as grandchildren in her will, written 28 Mar 1768 and recorded on
27 Aug 1771. (AC Wills, 1767-1772:573) While Tabitha Warrington did not mention
land in her will, she did name an only surviving son, George Warrington.
Stephen Warrington d. testate in 1745 naming his wife as Tabitha and five sons,
the youngest of whom was George. (AC Wills, 1743-1749:239) He left 40 acres to his
eldest son, Abbott Warrington. Abbott Warrington left his land to his son
Stephen in 1760. (AC Wills, 1757-1761:282) Abbott Warrington, wife Elizabeth, also
had a son John, a dau. Betty, and an unborn child. The unborn child apparently
was Ann "Nancy/Nanney" Warrington and she and her sister Elizabeth "Betty"
inherited the land at the death of their brothers.

He m. 2nd 15 Dec 1815 in AC, **Milly Hickman** (b. c1770). Stephen
Hickman and Richard D. Bayly were securities on the 1815 AC M.L.B. (ACM)

George 's will was probated 28 Dec 1819 in AC. (AC W&c., 1819-21:129) On
20 Dec 1779, George Bundick of Metompkin bought 75 acres of land from
Elizabeth Warrington, of NC, "one-half that tract of land on the Sea Board in
Parish and County of Accomack formerly the Right of a Certain Stephen
Warrington deceased grandfather of said Elizabeth, 2500 pounds current
money." (AC Deeds, 1777-1783:200) On 3 Mar 1791, George Bundick and wife Ann
sold to Susannah Nock, for £100, 50 acres "on Assawoman," land George and
Ann got from "late Tabitha Warrington where George Warrington deceased
lived." (AC Deeds, 1788-1793:508) On 28 Jul 1806, George and Nancy Bundick "of
Metompkin" deeded to John A. Bunting, "son of George and Nancy (John A.
Bundick of Drummond town)," for 1 shilling, 100 acres of land near
Assawoman. (AC Deeds, 1804-1807:622) According to this deed George and Nancy
owned this land "in the right of Nancy," giving the names of adjacent owners as
Thomas Abbott, John Teackle Senr, Ayres Tatham and John Finney, and stating
that they, George and Ann, were to have the use of the land for their lifetime and
after their death it was for the "benefit of George Warrington Bundick, a

younger son not 21 years as yet," and if he should die, for their younger daus. Tabitha and Nancy. After son John A. Bundick of Drummond Town d.in 1816, apparently this land reverted back to his parents for, on 17 Feb 1817, George Bundick Senr deeded to George Bundick Junr, for 10 shillings, 150 acres, bound by the heirs of John Finney, by Ayres Tatham, by Thomas Abbott, deceased, and by Arthur Watson. (AC Deeds, 1817-1818:18) The extra 50 acres was likely Elizabeth Warrington's part of the George Warrington land. George Bundick's name appears on the 1784 tax list, when he was taxed £7.0.3 for his real property and £2.18.3 for personal property. He owned 4 slaves, 3 of whom were under sixteen years of age, 3 horses, 9 cattle and 2 "wheels." There were two other George Bundicks listed in 1784, one the son of Richard Bundick "Clk." (Richard Bundick of the *Robins Hole* and Parksley area) and George Bundick, son of Richard Bundick (IV) (Piper) of the Gargatha area. The 1800 census lists one George Bundick with "Mkn" after his name. By this time, there were four George Bundicks in Acc Parish. George Bundick of Metompkin, in 1800, was over 45 years of age. He had a son of 16 to 26 and another son under 10 years. His wife was 26 to 45 and there were four other females in his household, one under 10, two 10 to 16 and one 16 to 26. George Bundick of Metompkin owned no slaves in 1800, but there were ten free blacks in his household. In 1810, George Bundick was again over 45, with a son between 10 and 16 and two females aged 16 to 26, plus four free blacks. Apparently wife Nancy Warrington Bundick died between 1806 and 1810 and his younger daus. were keeping house for him and his younger son. On 15 Feb 1817, George Bundick Senr, "sea side" and Milly his wife, sold to Thomas Cropper 200 acres for $4,000, the "tract of land and plantation whereon Daniel Baker now lives." (AC Deeds, 1815-1817:515) This land was bound on the north by "Alicado" Creek and was the 200-acre part of the original Richard Bundick patent of 1664. George Bundick Senr reserved the family graveyard and, in another deed, was to get $200 each year for life and $2,480 at his death "for his children." (AC Deeds, 1815-1817:516/7) This family graveyard is no longer in existence. It is apparent that George Bundick of Metompkin did not live on Assawoman Creek on the Warrington land. It seems equally certain he was not living on his inherited 200 acres in Parkers Neck, at least when he sold it in 1817, or afterwards. No record has been found of him buying land elsewhere.

George Bundick left a will dated 27 Nov 1819, probated 28 Dec 1819. He did not mention his wife or his daus. He lent his real and personal property to his son, George W. Bundick, and at his death "to my grandson, John A. Bundick." Witnessed by Elijah Hickman (?), Stephen Hickman, John F. Only. (AC Wills, 1819-1821:129)

George 'of Metompkin' Bundick and Ann 'Nancy/Nanney' Warrington had the following children:

70   i. John A.[6] Bundick, b. in AC c1778, d. Mar 1816. (Mary Frances Carey; AC W&c., *1814-1816:* 518) He m. 24 May 1806 in AC, Elizabeth 'Betsy' Twiford (b. c1785), dau. of

Robert Twiford. (ACM; MilesW&A:553 (will of Robert Twiford of Drummond Town))

John 's will was probated March 1816 in AC. Robert Twiford was the security on the 1806 AC M.L.B. of John A. Bundick and Elizabeth Twiford. On 7 Jun 1815, John A. Bundick and Betsy his wife sold to Thomas Cropper, for £210, ½ of the store house and tenement in Town of Drummond lately occupied and kept by Cropper & Bundick. (AC Deeds, 1815-17:211) He had no children, for he named only his wife, two sisters and nephews in his will. (AC Wills, 1814-16:518)

71 ii. Betsy Bundick, b. in AC c1780. (Brother's Will) She m. c1800, (N) Bradford (b. c1780. (Wife's; and Brother's Will)

Betsy was living Mar 1816 in AC. (Brother's Will) Betsy Bradford was named as a sister by John A. Bundick of Drummond Town in his will, as were two of her sons, Nathaniel Bradford and George Bundick Bradford. (AC Wills, 1814-16:518)

72 iii. Sarah 'Sally' Bundick, b. in AC c1785. (Brother's Will) She m. 1st 5 Oct 1801 in AC, William Finney (b. c1775 in AC, d. before 1816). (ACM) She m. 2nd 8 Jul 1816 (bond) in AC, Charles Rew Jr. (b. c1795 in AC). George Snead was the security on the M.L.B. of Charles Rew Jr. and Sarah Finney, widow of William. (ACM)

Charles was son of Charles Rew Sr. and Comfort Hickman. (MilesW&A:442 (will of Charles Rew)) He m. Hetty Baker 31 May 1818 (bond) in AC. Charles Rew Sr. was the security on the M.L.B. of Charles Rew Jr. and Hetty Baker of Solomon. (ACM)

Edmund Bayly was the security on the 1801 AC M.L.B. of William Finney and Sally Bundick. She was named as Sally Finney in the will of her brother, John A. Bundick. (AC Wills, 1814-16:518)

73 iv. Tabitha Bundick, b. in AC c1788. (Mary Frances Carey)

74 v. Ann 'Nancy' Bundick, b. in AC c1792. She m. 23 Dec 1816 (bond) in AC, James Wright Sr. (b. c1792 in AC). John H. Bayly was the security on the M.L.B. of James Wright and Ann Bundick of Geo. (ACM)

James Wright, b. c1792 in AC, d. Jun 1831, son of George Wright and Sally Dix. He m. 14 Apr 1827 (bond) in AC, Mary Ann Finney. William W. Dix was the security on the M.L.B. of James Wright and Mary Ann Finney of William, dec'd. ((ACM; Nottingham, *AC Land*

*Causes, 1728-1825:*125 (Partition Suit Wright &c. vs. Wright); MilesW&A:626 (will of James Wright))

75   vi. George Warrington Bundick, b. in AC c1798, d 6 Nov
1854 in AC. The death register shows him as age 54
and dying of old age. His occupation was surveyor.
Edward H. Hickman, a friend gave the information. He
m. 25 Oct 1816 in AC, Elizabeth Hickman (b. c1795, d.
before 1842), dau. of Richard Hickman and Nancy (N).
Levi Dix was the security on the M.L.B. of George W.
Bundick and Elizabeth Hickman. (AC Death Register(s)
1853-1896; FA CD309; ACM; AC Deeds (General Reference),
1842-43:140)
   George was listed with another family in the cenus
of 1850 in St. George Parish, AC. He was shown as
Geo. W. Bundick, age 52 and a tutor, in HH#1046
headed by Jno. Langsdale, age 42, born in MD and a
farmer with real estate valued at $3,000. There were
several young children in the household. On 2 Jan
1819, George W. Bundick and wife Elizabeth sold to
John W. Watson, for $500, 170 acres "in the
neighborhood of Assawoman," land bound by Arthur
Watson, by Thomas Abbott, deceased, and by John
Finney, deceased. (AC Deeds, 1818-1819:241) George W.
Bundick would have been the male in his father's
household in the 1800 census, under 10 years, and in
1810, aged 10 to 16. In 1820, he was listed as head of a
household at 18 to 26 years of age. He then had a wife
of 16 to 26 years and a son under 10 years. By 1830,
his age was given as 30 to 40 years, as was that of his
wife. Their household included a son of 10 to 15 years
and another, aged 5 to 10 years. They also had a dau. of
5 to 10 years. In the 1840 census, George W. Bundick
was 40 to 50 years old. His wife was also 40 to 50 and
one son was 15 to 20, while another was 20 to 30, and a
dau. was 15 to 20. In 1850, George W. Bundick's age
was given as 52 (56?) He was then living in the
household of John Longsdale, as a tutor. His wife was
deceased by 1842. (AC Deeds, 1842-1843:140) George W.
Bundicks "son of George" d. 6 Nov 1854 at 54 (60?), as
reported by a friend, Edward Hickman. (AC Reg. of
Deaths:6) His occupation was given as "Surveyor." John
A. Bundick was named to administer the estate of
George W. Bundick on 26 Feb 1855. (AC OB, 1854-
1857:179) George W. Bundick had been appointed AC

Surveyor and took the oath of office on 31 Mar 1840. (AC OB, 1840-1842:11) On 28 May 1830, Jacob Warner, trustee, transferred to John A. Bundick and William H. Bundick, "the heirs at law of Elizabeth Bundick, wife of George W. Bundick, 20 acres of land near Metompkin. (AC Deeds, 1829-1830:515) This land was bordered northeast by George P. Barnes, west and northwest by the sea side county road, south and southwest by lands of John Snead and east by George P. Barnes. George W. Bundick and wife Elizabeth had sold 52 acres "near Metompkin" to Jacob Warner on 8 Jan 1824, for $450. (AC Deeds, 1822-1824:539) The deed states that this was land that had become Elizabeth's at the death of her father, Richard Hickman, and was bound on the east by Metompkin Bay. George W. Bundick was a colonel in the 99th Regiment of AC Militia by 1830. In Jan 1840, he assumed command of the 99th Regiment in Upper AC. (Acc Parish) He resigned his commission by 1843. (Pungoteague to Petersburg, Vol. I,:118, 119, 138)

45. John Abbott[5] Bundick Jr. (John Abbott[4], George[3], Richard[2], Richard[1]), b. in AC c1752, d. 1805. (Father's Will; AC W&c., 1804-06:328)

He married three times. He m. c1775, **Nancy Dix** (b. c1755 in AC), dau. of Richard Dix and Mary (N). (AC Deeds (General Reference), 1777-83:113; Mary Frances Carey) He m. 2nd c1784, **Elizabeth Savage?** (b. c1760). (Mary Frances Carey) He m. 3rd 13 Sep 1802 in AC, **Elizabeth Hannaford** (b. c1775). (ACM)

John A. Bundick was paid for public service during Rev War. 1781-1783 in AC. (Walker & Turman, *Acc Soldiers & Sailors in Rev*)

John 's will was probated 1805 in AC. (AC W&c., 1804-06:328) Edmund Bayly was the security on the 1803 AC M.L.B. of John A. Bundick and Elizabeth Hannaford. John Abbott Bundick Junr left 200 acres of Dix land "near head of Metompkin on the Branches of Parkers Creek" to his son William, "if he ever returns to the County of Accomack" and if he should not return, to his other son, John S. Bundick. He also named a dau. as Mary Savage Bevans (Barnes?), who was the wife of George P. Barnes by 9 Apr 1806, when the slaves of John Abbott Junr. were divided between his widow and children. Evidently, son William did not return, for John S. Bundick died testate by 2 May 1821. (Accomack District Court Wills, 1807-1830:250) and mentioned "Lands on the Sea Side that fell to me by my Father's will."

John Abbott Bundick Jr. and Nancy Dix had the following child:

      76   i.   William[6] Bundick, b. in AC c1778, living 1805 outside AC. (Father's Will)

John Abbott Bundick Jr. and Elizabeth Savage? had the following children:

77   ii. John S. Bundick, b. in AC 1 Feb 1785, d. 2 May 1821.
His body was interred in Warner/Bundick, Plot,
Pastoria, AC. (MLAC) He m. 19 Nov 1811 in NC, Ann
Custis West (b. 9 Aug 1794, d. 12 Dec 1850) Her body
was interred in Warner/Bundick, Plot, Pastoria, AC.
(MLAC) She m. 28 Sep 1822 (bond) in AC, Samuel M.
Taylor. George W. Bundick was the security on the
1822 AC M.L.B. of Samuel M. Taylor and Ann C.
Bundick, widow of John A. Bundick. (ACM)
John's will was probated 2 May 1821 in AC. (Acc
Dist Ct Wills 1807-30:250) Charles West was the security on
the 1811 NC M.L.B. of John S. Bundick and Ann
Custis West. John was of AC. He named his wife as
Ann Custis Bundick in his will probated in 1821 and
named her as extx. He had two daus, both underage in
1821.

78   iii. Mary Savage Bundick, b. in AC c1787, m. before 1806,
George P. Barnes Sr. (b. c1779 in AC, d. Sep 1850),
son of Parker Barnes and Leah Bundick. (Mary Frances
Carey; FA CD309; MilesW&A:28 (will of George P. Barnes Sr.))
He m. c1815, Eliza Givans. (MACM: 230 (marriage of John
W. Matthews and Mary A.P. Selby show her as the dau. of George
Barnes & Eliza Givins)) (will of George P. Barnes Sr.))

46. William⁵ Bundick (John Abbott⁴, George³, Richard², Richard¹), b. in
AC c1755, d. 1795. (AC W&c., 1794-96:257)

He m. c1783, **Agnes Gilchrist** (b. c1758 in AC, d. 1796 in AC), dau. of
Andrew Gilchrist and Tabitha Bayly. (Wife's; and Brother's Will; AC OB 1796-98:158)
On 26 Dec 1796, administration of Agnes Bundick's estate was granted to
George Bundick, with John A. Bundick and Americus Scarburgh securities. (AC
OB, 1796-98:158)

William d. leaving a will dated 31 Oct 1795, probated 28 Dec 1795 in AC.
To wife Agnes Bundick whole estate during her widowhood to bring up my 3
children Lewis, George and William. Unborn child to be brought up and
educated as my other children. At the death of my wife estate to be equally
divided between my 3 sons above named and unborn child. Wife to be
executrix. Witnesses were George Wright, Major Hinmon and Charles Stockly.
(AC W&c., 1794-96:257) It appears his widow died soon after the birth of her fourth
child, for on 26 Dec 1796, William's brother, George Bundick, was named to
administer the estate of Agnes Bundick. (AC OB, 1796-98:158)

William Bundick and Agnes Gilchrist had the following children:

79   i. Lewis⁶ Bundick, b. in AC c1784. On 30 Sep 1799,
Lewis Bundick was bound to the firm of Dennis &
Teackle of SO Co., "to learn the art and mystery of
merchandize." (AC OB, 1798-1800:198)

80   ii.   George Gilchrist Bundick, b. in AC c1786. On 30 Sep 1799, George Gilchrist Bundick came into Court and made choice of George Bundick for his guardian. (AC OB, 1798-1800:199)

81   iii.   William Bundick, b. in AC c1788. On 29 Oct 1799, John Burton was appointed guardian to William Bundick, "orphan of William." (AC OB, 1798-1800:208)

82   iv.   John Satchell Bundick, b. in AC c1796. John Satchell Bundick, "orphan of William and Agnes Bundick," had his accounts returned by his uncle George through 1807. (AC Orphan's Accounts, 1800-05: 508 and 1805-18:209) At this point in time his entire family disappeared from AC records.

52. **George**[5] **Bundick** (Richard 'Piper'[4], Richard[3], Richard[2], Richard[1]), b. in AC c1760, d. before 1817. His brother Justice Bundick stated in his will, written 23 Jan 1817, that his brother George was deceased by that time. He apparently d. between 1810 and 1817, without a will with an estate too small to warrant an administration. Census records suggest that George Bundick may have had 6 sons and 3 daus. Only 3 sons are named in the records: Richard, Joseph and William.

He m. 25 Aug 1785 (bond) in AC, **Elizabeth 'Betty' Laws** (b. c1765, d. before 1820), dau. of William Laws (I) and Hannah (N). Caleb Broadwater was the security on the M.L.B. (ACM; Mary Frances Carey) This may have been George's 2nd marriage, as he had at least one son born c1778, but the name of the first wife is unknown.

Neither a will nor an administration has been found for Betty Laws Bundick and her name does not appear on the 1820 census. Local records indicate that a branch of the Laws family lived near Assawoman Creek, east of Mappsville. For more on this Laws family, see a booklet by Mary Frances Carey titled, *The Laws Family of Accomack County, Virginia.*

George appears on the list of tithables in Acc Parish, AC, for 1783. He was shown as "Son of Piper Rich," an indication that he was married and head of a household by that year.

George was named in his father's will 19 Feb 1789 in AC. He was about age 29 at the time. His father left him, after his mother's death, what was then 91 acres of land at Gargatha for his lifetime.

George appears on the list of tithables in Acc Parish, AC for 1792. He was again shown as "Geroge Bundick (of Piper)."

On 25 May 1793 in AC George Bundick was joined by Richard Bundick, Abbott Bundick, Hezekiah Baker Junr and wife Susanna, and William Onions Junr and wife Sally, in selling their father's land at Gargatha to their brothers William and Justice Bundick. George Bundick received £50 and each of the other children £6. This deed does not mention their mother's dower interest in the land, but does say that brother John "died during the lifetime of his father," and that George was the eldest son. (AC Deeds 1793-1797)

It appears that he continued living in this area until 1800. Apparently he had moved to the Assawoman area by 1810, where he would have rented land where his wife's family lived. It should be noted that George Bundick's wife did not sign the 1793 deed with him, when he sold his father's land. This does not indicate that she was deceased, but only that she had no interest in the land and no reason to sign, since George would have inherited only a lifetime interest at his mother's death, and his wife could not have claimed a dower right to the land.

George Bundick of Gargatha, was listed as a head of household in the census of 1800 in Acc Parish, AC. He was age 26 to 45 (he would have been 40) and there were four other males in his household, two under age 10 and two between age 16 and 26, another proof of a former marriage. His wife was also age 26 to 45 and there were two daus. under age 10. He owned no slaves at this time.

George was listed as a head of household in the census of 1810 in Acc Parish, AC. He was shown as "George Bundick, Assom" (meaning of Assawoman), over age 45 (he would have 50). He again had two sons under age 10 and one age 26 to 45. His wife was over age 45 and one dau. was under age 10 and another was age 16 to 26. He owned two slaves at this time. This George Bundick's name does not appear on a later census.

George Bundick had the following children:

83   i. George[6] Bundick Jr., b. in AC c1778, d. before 31 May in AC. (Mary Frances Carey; (FA CD309) He m. 28 Jun 1811 (bond) in AC, Nancy Holt (b. c1793 in AC). Tommy Abbott was the security on the M.L.B. of George Bundick Jr. and Nancy Holt. (FA CD309; (ACM)

George was listed as a head of household in the census of 1820 in Acc Parish, AC. He was shown as age 18 to 28 with a wife age 16 to 26 and a son under age 10.

George was listed as a head of household in the census of 1830 in St. George Parish, AC. He was shown as "George Bundick, Senr" age 50 to 60 (actually about 40) with a wife age 30 to 40, two sons under age 15 and three daus. under 20.

George signed a deed of mortgage 26 May 1831 in AC. (AC Deeds, 1830-1832; Whitelaw:1068 and map.) It was on this date that "George Bundick, Senr," became indebted to Southy W. Bull, who was guardian of Charles and Polly Mason, infants of Charles Mason, deceased, "in sum of $221 for rent of lands of said Charles and Polly for 1831." George put up "crops of corn and oats" and other personal property as security. This land of Charles Mason's was near Accomac, in the vicinity of the present day Mary Nottingham Smith Middle School.

George was listed as a head of household in the census of 1840 in St. George Parish, AC. He was shown as "George Bundick, Senr" age 50 to 60 (actually age 50) with 2 sons, one age 10 to 15 and the other age 15 to 20.

George was listed as a head of household in the census of 1850 in St. George Parish, AC. He was shown Geo. Bundick as the head of HH#199, age 72 and a farmer, with a wife Nancy, age 57. Also living with him were Jno Bull, age 16 and a farm hand and Jim Dix, age 9 and black. (FA CD309)

The estate of George Bundick, Senr, was administered 31 May 1852 in AC by George T. Bundick (a son) and Charles H. Mason (a son-in-law). (AC OB 1851-1854:218)

84   ii.   John Bundick, b. in AC c1778, d. 1810. (Mary Frances Carey) He m. 27 Dec 1798 (bond) in AC, Sarah 'Sally' Nock (b. c1780, d. by 26 Jul 1819 in AC. William Baker was the security on the M.L.B. of John Bundick and Sally Nock. (ACM; AC Census of 1800; AC OB 1817-19:410.) On 26 Jul 1819 Noah Bundick, orphan of Sally, was bound out by the overseers of the poor to Elijah Wright to learn farming.

John was listed as a head of household in the census of 1800 in Acc Parish, AC. He was listed as "John Bundick, Garga," age 16 to 26 (he was 22), with a wife of the same age and a dau. under age 10. He apparently d. before 1810, as his name has not been found in the census of that year, but Sarah Bundick, age 26 to 45, was head of a household that included a dau. under age 10 and a son under age 10. This family does not appear at all in 1820.

85   iii.   Richard Bundick, b. in AC c1780, d. after 1860. (Grandfather's Will; Barnes, *SO Co 1860 Census*) He m four times. He m. 1st 4 Dec 1804 (bond) in AC, Lany Nelson (b. c1790). (ACM) He m. 2nd 8 Nov 1825 (bond) in AC, Molly (N) (b. c1790 in AC). Sacker Scott was the security on the M.L.B. of Richard Bundick, widower, and Molly Lewis, widow of William. Molly m. c 1810, William Lewis c1810. (ACM)

He m. 3rd 4 Feb 1829 (bond) in AC, Rachel
Bunting (b. c1800), dau. of Solomon Bunting. (ACM)
Custis Hargis was the security on the M.L.B. of
Richard Bundick, widower, and Rachel Fosque, widow
of John. She m. previously c11 May 1816 (bond) in
AC, John Fosque. John Crowson was the security on
the 1816 AC MLB of John Fosque of George and
Rachel Bunting of Solomon. (ACM)

He m. 4th 5 Oct 1838 (bond) in AC, Nancy (N) (b.
c1800. John L. Snead was the security on the M.L.B. of
Richard Bundick, widower, and Nancy Hickman,
widow of Joseph. Nancy m. Joseph Hickman c1820.
(ACM)

Richard was named in his grandfather's will dated
19 Feb 1789 in AC. (AC Wills 1788-94:306.) Richard was
given an interest in 91 acres of land when his
grandfather Richard 'Piper' Bundick wrote his will, land
that his father George sold to his two brothers in 1793.

On 6 Jan 1801 Richard gave his uncles, Justice and
William Bundick, a deed for his interest in the land his
father sold them in 1793. He had apparently come to
age at this time. His grandmother, Luke Bundick,
signed the deed with her mark as one of the witnesses.
(Acc Dist Ct W&D 1800-06:134.)

Richard was listed as a head of household in the
census of 1810 in Acc Parish, AC. He was shown as
"Richard Bundick of G" age 26 to 45.

Richard was listed as a head of household in the
census of 1820 in Acc Parish, AC. He was shown as
"Richard Bundick of G" age 26 to 45.

Richard was listed as a head of household in the
census of 1830 in St. George Parish, AC. He was
shown as age 50 to 60 with 5 other males in his
household: two age 5 to 10, one age 10 to 15, one age
15 to 20, and one age 20 to 30. He was not listed as a
head of household in the 1840 AC census. He had
likely lost his last wife by that year and was the male,
age 60 to 70 (he would have been 60) in the household
of his oldest son, David Bundick.

Richard was listed with his dau. in the census of
1850 in Acc Parish, AC. He was shown as Richard
Bundick, age 70 in HH# 665, headed by John L. Snead,
age 37 and a farmer, and his wife, Tabitha, age 25, who
was Richard's dau. (FA CD309)

Richard was listed with his son in the census of 1860 in Brinkleys Dist., SO Co. He was shown as age 90 (he was probably age 80), b. in VA and blind in HH# 990, headed by his son David, age 48 and a farmer.

George Bundick and Elizabeth 'Betty' Laws had the following children:

86   iv.   Joseph Bundick, b. in AC c1787, d. c1848. (AC OB, *1812-1814*:106) This date is used since he was listed in the 1840 census and his wife Margaret Bundick, age 40 with 3 children, was listed as a head of household in 1850.

He married three times. He m. 1st 24 Feb 1808 (bond) in AC, Molly Baker (b. c1785 in AC). William Baker was the security on the M.L.B. of Joseph Bundick and Molly Baker. (ACM)

He m. 2nd 26 Aug 1815 (lic.) in WO Co., Rachel Baker (b. c1790). (Powell, *WO Co. Marriages 1795-1865*)

He m. 3rd 7 Feb 1831 (bond) in AC, Margaret 'Peggy' Bloxom (b. c1810 in AC). George Bundick was the security on the M.L.B. of Joseph Bundick and Margaret Bloxom. (Crowson & Hite, *AC 1860 Census*; FA CD309; ACM)

Joseph was listed as a head of household in the census of 1810 in Acc Parish, AC. He was shown as age 16 to 26 (he was 23), with a wife of the same age and a dau. under age 10.

Joseph Bundick, son of George was ordered to be tax free on 29 Jun 1812 in AC, "due to infirmity." His infirmity must have improved by 1818, for he dug his uncle, Justice Bundick's, grave. (AC OB, *1812-1814:*106)

Joseph sold land 2 Apr 1819 in AC. The deed showed that Joseph Bundick and his wife Rachel sold 4 acres to James Gibbons for £17.8. (AC Deeds 1818-1819; AC Surveyor's Rec 3) This land was east of Gargatha, between Woodbury Church and Gargatha Landing Road, and "descended to wife of said Bundick by my (her) uncle Elias Bundick." Joseph's second wife, Rachel, was therefore the dau. of Richard Baker and his wife, Rachel Bundick Baker, and would have been a first cousin of Joseph's father George Bundick.

Joseph, under age of 26 (actually c33), was listed as a head of household in the census of 1820 in Acc Parish, AC; he had a son under age 10 and two daus.

under age 10. He was not listed as a head of household in 1830 in AC.

Joseph was listed as a head of household in the census of 1840 in St. George Parish, AC. He was shown as age 40 to 50 (he would have been 53) with a wife age 30 to 40 and one other male age 5 to 10.

87   v.   Esther Bundick, b. in AC c1790. (Mary Frances Carey) (FA CD309)

She m. 1st 27 Dec 1816 (bond) in AC, James Gillespie (b. c1795 in AC), son of John Gillespie. Edmund Bell and John Bull were the securities on the M.L.B. of James Gillespie and Esther Bundick. (ACM)

She m. 2nd 15 Dec 1828 (bond) in AC, George Bloxom Sr. (b. c1790, d. Nov 1829). Joseph P. Godwin was the security on the M.L.B. of George Bloxom Sr., widower, to Esther Gillispie, widow of James. (ACM; MilesW&A:71 (will of George Bloxom Sr.))

Esther was named in her husband's will dated 28 Oct 1829 in AC, the will of George Bloxom Sr. He left her all personal estate & the tract of land whereon I now live during her life or widowhood & at her death or marriage then the land to go to Ann M. Gillespie, Edward J. Gillespie & Leah Gillespie orphans of James Gillespie dec'd, children of my wife Esther. (MilesW&A:71 (will of George Bloxom Sr.))

Esther Bloxom was listed as a head of household in the census of 1850 in Acc Parish, AC (HH#512), age 60 with real estate valued at $1,000. Listed with her was Leah Bloxom, age 95. She would have been one of George Bundick's daus. under age 10 in 1800 and the dau. in his household in 1810 age 16 to 26. (FA CD309)

88   vi.   Nancy Bundick, b. in AC c1791. (Mary Frances Carey; FA CD309) On 26 Feb 1821 "Nancy Bundick, orphan" was bound out by the Overseers of the Poor to William Beavans, Senr until of lawful age to learn spinning and weaving. The 1850 census puts her birth at 1791; however this would indicate that she was 30 years old in 1821 when she was bound out as an orphan. (AC OB 1819-22::270.)

On 1 May 1822 Nancy Bundick mortgaged personal property to Jaxkson Laws. The list of her property was a short one, consisting of a bed with covers and a spinning wheel. (AC Deeds 1822-1824)

In the 1850 census of Acc Parish, AC Nancy Bundick, age 59, was living in HH# 636, headed by Dainy Copes, age 50 (female). (FA CD309)

89   vii.   William Bundick, b. in AC c1805,d. c1845 in NY. (Uncle Justice Bundick's Will; Mary Frances Carey) He evidently moved his family to New York after 1830, where he worked as a teamster until his death there c1845. Nothing more is known of his widow or surviving daus. He m. 8 May 1827 (bond) in AC, Polly Prescott. George Bundick (his brother) and Richard D. Bayly were securities on the M.L.B. of William Bundick and Polly Prescott, dau. of Thomas. (ACM)

Polly, b. c1791 in AC, d. 1861, dau. of Thomas Prescott. Her body was interred at Bundick Plot, Parksley, AC. (Crowson & Hite, *AC 1860 Census;* ACM; TUAC) Polly's father, Thomas, was a soldier in the Continental Army during the Rev War.

William was listed as a head of household in the census of 1830 in Acc Parish, AC. He was shown as William Bundick Junr, age 20 to 30, with a wife of the same age, a son under age 5, a dau. under age 5 and another female age 5 to 10. There is no other documented evidence of William Bundick of George in AC after this date. The mother of one of the authors, Mary Frances Carey, Lena (Bundick) Trader, wrote on the back of her grandfather Bundick's picture that his father, a teamster in New York, died when he was young and that his mother was a Preston. She also wrote that her grandfather was an only child, likely meaning he was the only son.

William was listed as a head of household in the census of 1840 Schenectady Co, NY, age 30 to 40, with a wife of the same age, a son age 5 to 10 (would have been age 11), and seven other females. There were other Bundicks in New York in 1840, but none in 1830. He would have been one of the two males in George Bundick's Assawoman household in the 1810 AC census under age 10. He was likely named for his grandfather, William Laws, and was only about age 12 in 1817, when his uncle Justice Bundick wrote his will, leaving William Bundick, "son of my deceased brother George," one fourth of his estate should Justice's dau, Elizabeth Blackstone, die without issue.

55. William⁵ Bundick (Richard 'Piper'⁴, Richard³, Richard², Richard¹), b. in AC 28 Nov 1768, d. 1 Feb 1845, bur. Bundick Cem, Gargatha, AC. (TUAC) The family plot is east of Gargatha and north of Gargatha Landing Road. His has daus. and a grandson bur. in this plot. This burial plot stands on land that had been in his family since 1689 and could be the final resting place of a number of his ancestors.

He m. c1790, **Nancy Mears** (b. 1770 in AC, d. 25 May 1832, bur. Bundick Cem, Gargatha, AC), dau. of Meshack Mears and Susannah 'Sukey' Northam. (Wife's and Father's Wills; TUAC) Nancy Bundick was named in the will of her father, dated 3 Feb 1790 and in the will of sister, Caty Hoff dated 2 Jul 1791. (AC W&c., 1794-96:42; AC Wills, 1788-94:559)

William, age 26 to 45, was listed as a head of household in the census of 1800 in Acc Parish, AC, with a wife of the same age, and four daus. under age 10. In the 1810 census the household consists of himself, age 26-45, with three daus, two under age 10 and one age 10 to 16. In 1820 he appears with wife, both over age 45 with two daus., ages 16 to 26. In 1830 he and his wife were both shown as age 50 to 60.

He d. leaving a will dated 6 Oct 1843, probated 24 Feb 1845.in AC. He left land called *Conquest's* and *Taylor lot* to grandchildren, John Hope, William Hope and Elizabeth Hope, after the death of their mother, Molly Pettit. He also left them the tract of land and mill attached called *Hinman's* and "the store houses and lot in Drummond (Town)." He gave to dau. Molly Pettit one half his personal estate and half his slaves. He gave his grandson William B. Jacobs and his mother Nancy Mears, "my dau," the other half of his personal estate and slaves. He left his dau. Nancy Mears "the farm whereon I now live with all the land adjoining the same" and at her death it was to go to her son William B. Jacobs. Grandson William B. Jacobs was also to inherit the farm lying at the head of Gargatha Creek called *Savage's*, the house and lot and store house and lot in Modest Town and other land near Modest Town. He left his silver spectacles to dau. Nancy Mears and his wearing apparel to grandson William Hope. He gave granddau Mary Pettit $200. James W. Custis and grandson William B. Jacobs were named extrs. and William Bundick signed his will with his mark. He added a codicil on 23 Dec 1844. This dealt with requiring grandson William B. Jacobs to repay a loan and stipulated that grandson Gillett Mears was to receive $200. (AC Wills 1828-46:535)

Whitelaw indicates his first home was on the south side of Gargatha Landing Road, behind present-day Arcadia Nursing Home, where the remains of an old house on the property, which once had a brick end, had bricks marked "W N Bundick 1797." It is believed that the initials are for William, son of "Piper" and his wife Nancy Mears. It could have been moved there. Kirk Mariner, in an article in the 9 Feb 1994 issue of *The Eastern Shore News*, shows a picture of William Bundick's later home that was moved to near Huntingtontown, MD, in 1971 and restored. Mariner locates the original site of this house on the east side of U.S. 13, at Littleton Road, south of Nelsonia. This study would place it nearer to Arcadia Nursing Home, and the family burial plot. (Whitelaw:1160)

The inventory of William Bundick's personal estate covers twelve pages. He owned seven slaves, various notes from sixteen local people to whom he had lent money, eight lots of books, numerous livestock and stuffs, farming equipment, and extensive household articles, including silver flatware, two walnut tables, a walnut desk, two mahogany bureaus and a mahogany secretary.(AC Inventories, 1842-46:387)

William Bundick and Nancy Mears had the following children:

90   i.   Elizabeth^6 Bundick, b. in AC 1791, d. 10 May 1816, bur. Bundick Cem, Gargatha, AC. (TUAC)

91   ii.   Mary 'Molly' Bundick, b. in AC 4 Aug 1796, d. 26 Oct 1859, bur. Ebenezer Meth Ch Cem, Modest Town. (ACM; TUAC) She m. 1st 27 Dec 1813 (bond) in AC, Kendall Hope. Kendall Hickman was the security on the M.L.B. of Kendall Hope and Molly Bundick of Wm. (ACM)

Kendall, b. 18 Jun 1791 in AC, d. 11 Apr 1833, bur. Bundick Cem, Gargatha, AC, son of George Hope and Nancy 'Nanny' (N). (TUAC; MilesW&A:273 (will of George Hope)) and 274 (will of Nancy Hope))

She m. 2nd 7 Jan 1836 (bond) in AC, Capt. William M. Pettitt (b. 11 Oct 1806 in AC, d. 20 Feb 1881, bur. Ebenezer Meth Ch Cem), son of Thomas Pettitt and Nancy (N). (ACM; TUAC; MACM) He m. 2nd 1 May 1860 in AC, Elizabeth D. White. (Miles & Miles, *AC Marriages, 1854-1895*) He m. 3rd 27 Nov 1869 in AC, Mary Jane Cook. (MACM)

Mary was named in her husband's will 4 Oct 1830 in AC. (MilesW&A:274) She was named as the extx. in the will of George Hope.

Mary was listed with her husband in the census of 1850 in AC. (FA CD309) She was shown as Mary Pettit, age 53 in HH#661 headed by William Pettit, a 45 year old farmer.

92   iii.   Sally Bundick, b. in AC 1799, d. 20 Oct 1828, bur. Bundick Cem, Gartha. (TUAC; ACM) She m. 30 Dec 1822 (bond) in AC, William C. White, son of Arthur White and Annie (N). Wm. Justice Sr. was the security and Wm. Bundick gave consent on M.L.B. of William C. White and Sally Bundick of Wm. (ACM; FA CD309; TUAC)

William m. 2nd 4 Dec 1829 (bond) in AC, Elizabeth 'Betsy' Bundick Solomon Ewell Sr. & Littleton P.

Henderson were the securities on the M.L.B. of William C. White, widower, and Elizabeth Blackstone, widow of Wm. William m. 3rd 30 Dec 1833 (bond) in AC, Henrietta Wright. George Hickman was the security on the M.L.B. of William C. White, widower, and Henrietta Copes, widow of John. (ACM)

William d. 27 Jul 1871 at 82 years of age at Metompkin, bur. Gibbons Cem, Metompkin. (TUAC; WADR) Jas. S. White gave the information.

93   iv. Nancy Bundick, b. in AC 12 May 1800, bur. Bundick Cem, Gartha. (TUAC) She m. 1st 12 Dec 1821 (bond) in AC, John B. Jacob (b. c1800 in AC). William B. Blackstone was the security and William Bundick gave consent on the M.L.B. of John B. Jacobs and Nancy Bundick of Wm. (ACM)

She m. 2nd c1842 in AC, William W. (of M.) Mears (b. c1816 in AC, d. of dropsy on 25 Jul 1878 in AC), son of Meshack Mears II and Margaret]Peggy' Baker. (Mary Frances Carey; FA CD309; WADR; MilesW&A:371 (will of Meshack Mears)) . He m. c1853, Mary S. (N). (1860 AC Census; WADR)

Nancy, age 49, was listed with her husband in the census of 1850 (HH#218) in Acc Parish, AC. (FA CD309)

56. **Abbott^5 Bundick** (Richard 'Piper'^{4}, Richard^3, Richard^2, Richard^1), b. in AC c1770, d. 1833-40.

He m. 11 Sep 1791 (bond) in AC, **Betsy Taylor** (b. c1770). Isaac Taylor was the security on the M.L.B. of Abbott Bundick and Betsy Taylor. (ACM)

Abbott sold land 25 May 1793 in AC. (AC Deeds 1793-1797) The deed showed that Abbott Bundick was joined by George Bundick, Richard Bundick, Hezekiah Baker, Junr and wife Susanna, and William Onions, Junr and wife Sally, in selling their father's land at Gargatha to their brothers, William Bundick and Justice Bundick. Abbott's share was £6.

Abbott was listed as a head of household in the census of 1800 in Acc Parish, AC. He was shown as 'Abbott Bundick, Ridd, Piper' age 26 to 45 (he would have been 30) with a wife age 16 to 26 and a son and dau, both under age 10.

In the 1810 census in Acc Parish, he was shown as age 26 to 45 with a wife of the same age. They had a son and dau. under age 10 and a son age 10 to 16.

Abbott was listed as a head of household in the census of 1820 in Acc Parish, AC. His age was shown as over 45 with a son age 10 to 16 and two daus, one age 10 to 16 and one under age 10. This census lists the households in the order they were enumerated, rather than in their usual alphabetical order. From the names of his neighbors, it appears that he was living in the Hunting Creek area, possibly a waterman.

Abbott was listed as a head of household in the census of 1830 in Acc Parish, AC. He was shown as age 60 to 70 with a male age 20 to 30, also his wife age 50 to 60 and two females age 15 to 20.

Abbott was order to be tax free on 25 Jul 1831 in AC due to age and infirmity. (AC OB1829-1832:302)

On 20 Jul 1833 Abbott Bundick and his wife Elizabeth joined James Taylor of Isaac and wife Caty in selling Edmund Parks 4 ½ acres for $18, described as "land Edmund Parks purchased of Joseph Melson." (AC Deeds, 1835-1837 (28):94) This is the last record that has been bound of Abbott Bundick. He apparently died without a will or administration between 1833 and 1840, when his name does not appear in the census.

Abbott Bundick and Betsy Taylor had the following children:

94   i.   (d|o Abbott)[6] Bundick, b. in AC c1705. (AC Census of 1800)

95   ii. Jabez Bundick, b. in AC c1798, d. by Sep 1830 when his children were named in AC Orphan's Court. He m. 7 Jan 1819 (bond), Tabitha Taylor (b. c1799 in Guilford, AC), dau. of Charles Taylor Sr. and Tabitha Miles. She later m. 28 Feb 1831, Levi Annis. They were all of the Guilford area and were most likely watermen. Abbott Bundick was the security on the M.L.B. of Jabez Bundick of Abbott and Tabitha Taylor of Charles. William Taylor was the security on the M.L.B. of Levi Annis and Tabitha Bundick. (ACM; AC Orphan's Accts, 1826-1836:276/7; FA CD309; MilesW&A:518 (will of Charles Taylor Sr.)

96   iii. Tullie Bundick, b. in AC c1805, d. before 1850. (1840 AC Census) He m. before 1830, Mary 'Molly' Wright (b. c1810 in AC, d. 10 Dec 1881), dau. of Henry Wright IV and Ann 'Nancy' Savage. (Crowson & Hite, *AC 1860 Census;* WADR) She m. David Sparrow 2 Feb 1857 (lic.) in AC. (MACM) He was shown as David Sparrow, widower, and she as Molly Bundick, widow.

Mary d. 10 Dec 1881 in Acc Parish, AC. She was shown as Mary Sparrow, who died of pneumonia at the age of 70 years. She was a dau. of Henry Wright, born in AC, a housekeeper and the wife of David Sparrow. Her son-in-law, Elijah Colonna gave the information. (WADR)

Tullie was listed as a head of household in the census of 1830 in AC. age 20 to 30, with a wife, but no children. Tullie would have been a son of Abbott Bundick, for the records indicate he lived at Lee Mont.

97   iv. Mahala 'Neary' Bundick, b. in AC c1812. (ACM; FA CD309) She m. 1st 26 Nov 1832 in AC, Henry P. Berry (b. c1810 in AC). David Mears and Nathaniel Bird were securities on the 1832 AC M.L.B. of Henry P. Berry and Mahala Bundick of Abbott. (ACM)

        She m. 2nd 24 Mar 1842, Edward C. Smith (b. c1822 in AC). (ACM; FA CD309)

        Mahala Smith, age 38, was listed with her husband in the census of 1850 in Acc Parish, AC, HH#1043. Edward Smith, was listed as a 28 year old farmer. Also in the household were her 4 children by Henry Berry, Sarah, Harriet, Wm. H., and Nancy, and her 3 children by Edward Smith, Susan, Edward, and Samuel. (FA CD309)

        Mahala as Neary Smith, age 47, appeared with her husband, 39-year old farmer, Edw'd Smith, in the census of 1860 in Acc Parish, AC in HH#1009. (Crowson & Hite, *AC 1860 Census*)

98   v. Catherine 'Caty' Bundick, b. in AC c1814, m. 1st 26 Dec 1831 (bond) in AC, Robert Andrews (b. c1805 in AC. David Mears and Littleton A. Hinman were securities on the 1831 AC M.L.B. of Robert Andrews and Catherine Bundick of Abbot. (ACM; FA CD309)

        She m. 2nd 17 Feb 1841 (bond) in AC, William F. Fisher, a shoemaker (b. c1816 in Acc Parish, d. 13 Feb 1888 of consumption, in Acc Parish) s|o Fairfax? (ACM) James B. Andrews (who had married Nancy Fisher, dau. of Fairfax Fisher, in 1829) and Nathaniel Topping were the securities on the M.L.B. of William F. Fisher and Caty Andrews, widow of Robert. (FA CD309; WADR (information given by friend Archibald Annis))

        Catherine, age 36, was listed with her husband in the census of 1850 in Acc Parish (HH#486). The household was headed by William Fisher, a 34 year old laborer. Also listed was Robert Andrews, age 9, assumed to be her son by her first marriage. (FA CD309)

        Catherine was listed with her husband in the census of 1860 in Acc Parish. (1860 AC Census) Catherine was listed with her husband in the census of 1870 in Metompkin District, AC. She was shown as Catherine Fisher, age 58 in HH#MT517 headed by William Fisher, a 50 year old shoemaker. (Walczyk, *1870 AC, Acc Parish, Census*)

58. Justice^{*5*} **Bundick** (Richard 'Piper'*⁴*, Richard*³*, Richard*²*, Richard*¹*), b. in AC
c1772, d. 1818. (Whitelaw)

He m. c1795, **Leah Laws** (b. c1780 in AC), dau. of William Laws (II).
(Whitelaw; Mary Frances Carey)

On 25 May 1795 Justice Bundick and his brother William bought 40 ½
acres of their father's land from their other brothers and sisters. He and his wife
Leah sold this to his brother William in 1806. (AC Deeds 1793-1797:46)

On 18 May 1800 Justice bought 46 ¼ acres near his father's land in AC for
£3.10 per acre, from William Parramore Junr and wife Margaret. (AC Deeds 1797-
1800:432)

On 30 Jun 1806 Justice bought 60 acres for £700 from Samuel Crippen,
described as "land on the head waters of Gargatha Creek," bound on the east by
the creek and on the west by the main county road. This property contained a
water grist mill on the creek. (AC Deeds, *1804-1807*)

On 30 Jun 1806 Justice sold the land he bought from William Parramore to
Samuel Crippen for £470, described as "where said Justice now resides." (AC
Deeds, *1804-1807*)

On 6 Apr 1815 Justice bought 38 acres, 1 rood, 5 ½ perches by survey,
from John Teackle for $574.26, land that joined his other land on the west. Since
the main county road was then the old stage coach road or what is now known as
the sea side road, it appears Justice Bundick's land was east of Gargatha and
south of present-day Gargatha Landing Road. (AC Deeds, *1815-1817*)

Whitelaw states that Justice Bundick's land was in the vicinity of Mutton
Hunk and that an old story-and-a-half house with two brick ends stood there in
1951, that may have been built by Justice Bundick after his 1815 purchase.
(Whitelaw:1146)

He left a will dated 23 Jan 1817 in AC, probated 26 Oct 1818 in AC.
Justice Bundick owned 98 acres when he wrote his will. He left his entire estate
to his wife Leah for her widowhood. It was then to go to his dau. Betsy
Blackstone, but if she should die without issue, her husband, William
Blackstone, was to have the use of it until he died or remarried. The whole estate
was then to be sold, "my negros excepted," and the proceeds were to be equally
divided between "Harriet White, dau. of my deceased sister-in-law Lacey
White," (Lacy Laws had m. James White in 1801), "Hetty Baker, dau. of my
deceased sister Sufsannah Baker," William Bundick, son of my deceased brother
George Bundick" and "George Onions, son of my sister Sally Onions."

Justice Bundick and Leah Laws had the following child:

       99   i. Elizabeth 'Betsy'*⁶* Bundick. b. in AC c1796, d. before
              24 Nov 1834 inAC. (AC OB1832-1836:378.) She m. 1st 11
              Mar 1816 in AC, William B. Blackstone (b. c1790, d.
              1828 in AC). John Custis and William P. Custis were
              securities on the M.L.B. of William B. Blackstone and
              Elizabeth Bundick of Justice. dau. of Laben. (AC
              OB1827-29:217; ACM)

She m. 2nd 4 Dec 1829 (bond), William C. White.
Solomon Ewell Sr. & Littleton P. Henderson were the
securities on the M.L.B. (ACM)
  Elizabeth 's estate was administered 24 Nov 1834
in AC. (AC OB1832-1836:378.)
  William, b. c1790 in AC, son of Arthur White and
Annie (N). (FA CD309; TUAC) He m. 1st 30 Dec 1822
(bond) in AC, Sally Bundick. Wm. Justice Sr. was the
security and Wm. Bundick gave consent on M.L.B. of
William C. White and Sally Bundick of Wm. (ACM)
  He m. 3rd 30 Dec 1833 (bond) in AC, Henrietta
Wright. George Hickman was the security on the
M.L.B. of William C. White, widower, and Henrietta
Copes, widow of John. (ACM)
  William C. White d. 27 Jul 1871 at Metompkin of
old age (85). (TUAC; WADR (Jas. S. White gave the
information.)) He was bur. Gibbons Cem, Metompkin,
AC. His tombstone shows him as William C. White, the
son of Arthur & Annie White, who d. on 27 Jul 1871 at
the age of 82 years. (TUAC)

63. **George**[5] **Bundick** (John 'Long'[4], Richard[3], Richard[2], Richard[1]), b. in AC
c1778.
  He m. 1st 23 Mar 1802 (bond) in AC, **Rachel Mason** (b. c1780 in AC).
George Taylor was the security on the M.L.B. (ACM)
  He m. 2nd 11 Jun 1811 in AC, **Elizabeth Kellam** (b. c1790). Evande
Cameron was the security on the M.L.B. (ACM)
  George Bundick's name has not been found in the 1810 census or that of
1820. He was apparently deceased by 11 Sep 1822, when Thomas H. Bradford
mortgaged 100 acres to Elizabeth Bundick. (AC Deeds, 1829-1830:27) The children
of George Bundick are unknown, with the possible exception of a Samuel C.
Bundick, who lived in the Locustville Wachapreague area. He was a miller in
1860 and 1870 and had apparently d. by 1880. His widow d. 20 Dec 1892. (AC
Register of Deaths) Samuel and Sally had three children: Elijah Thomas Bundick, b.
c1840; William S. Bundick, b. c1844; and Sarah A. "Sally" Bundick, b. c1847,
m. 1867, Harry Groton. (AC Marr. Reg. #3:19)
  George Bundick and Rachel Mason had the following child:
    100   i. Samuel C.[6] Bundick, b. in AC c1805, d. before 1880.
            (Mary Frances Carey; FA CD309) He m. 14 Dec 1836 in AC,
            Sarah 'Sally' Bunting. Samuel Bundick and Walter
            Lewis were securities on the 1836 AC M.L.B. of
            Samuel C. Bundick and Sally Bunting of Solomon.
            (ACM) Samuel C. Bundick lived in the Locustville-
            Wachapreague area. He was a miller in 1860 and 1870
            and had apparently died by 1880.

Sarah was born c1808 in AC, d. 20 Dec 1892 in AC, dau. of Solomon Bunting. (FA CD309; ACM; AC Death Register(s) 1853-1896) Samuel was listed as a head of household in the census of 1850 in St. George Parish, AC. He was shown as Samuel Bundick the head of HH#631, age 45 and a laborer, with wife Sally, age 42 and children: Elijah, age 10; Wm., age 6; and Sally, age 3. (FA CD309) Samuel was listed as a head of household in the census of 1850 in St. George Parish, AC (HH#1039), age 46, laborer, with wife Sally, age 43 and children: William, age 7 and Sally A., age 4. (FA CD309) Samuel was listed as a head of household in the census of 1860 in St. George Parish, AC (HH#405), age 54 and a miller, with wife Sarah, age 50 and sons Elijah, age 20 and a fisherman and Wm., age 15. (Crowson & Hite, *AC 1860 Census*)

6. **John S. 'of Long'**[5] **Bundick** (John 'Long'[4], Richard[3], Richard[2], Richard[1]), b. in AC 4 May 1781, d. 4 Aug 1861, bur. John S. Bundick Cem, Melfa, AC. (MLAC; Death Register(s) 1853-1896)

He m. 1st 8 Dec 1808 in AC, **Jane 'Jinney' Bradford** (b. 7 Jan 1776 in AC, d. 28 Apr 1855 in 2nd dist., AC). (ACM; AC Death Register(s) 1853-1896) Jane was the dau. of Zephaniah Bradford and Elizabeth (N). (AC Surveyor's Record #1:205) She m. 1st c1800, **George Taylor**. (Husband's Will) The death register shows her dying of palsy at age 79 years, 3 mos., 19 days. Her body was interred in John S. Bundick Cem, Melfa, AC. (MLAC) Jane Bradford's father, Zephaniah, owned 538 acres, land and marshes in the lower end of Bradford Neck, next to Upshur Neck and between Machipongo Creek and Upshur Bay. Jane inherited 92 acres of this land from her father in 1792. (AC Surveyor's Record #1:205) Her first husband was George Taylor of John who d. testate in 1804. (AC Wills, 1804-06:206) He and his wife Jane had three children, including an only son, Charles Taylor, to whom he left his home land. George Taylor also left land to dau. Polly Taylor (1801-1866) who m. John Belote. and to dau. Sally Taylor, who m. John Downing of John and was deceased by 1848. (AC Chancery Orders, 1856-1869:279)

He m. 2nd 22 Mar 1857 in Crossroads, AC, **Mary Gunter** (b. c1793 in AC). They were married by Benjamin T. Ames. She was the widow of John West and dau. of Laben Gunter. She m. c1815, **John West**. (Wife's 2nd Marriage) (AC Marriage Register 3, *1853-1896*)

John was listed as a head of household in the census of 1850 in St. George Parish, AC. He was shown as John (L. or S.) Bundick the head of HH#1203, a 70 year old farmer with real estate valued at $8,000. Listed with him were the following Bundicks: Jane, age 74; Susan, age 28. Also listed was William Mears, age 42 with an occupation shown as "none" and "idiotic." (FA CD309)

John was listed as a head of household in the census of 1860 in St. George Parish, AC. He was shown as the head of HH#547, age 79 and a farmer, living alone. John Bundick of Long or John S. Bundick, unmarried, sold the land he had inherited from his father in Jan 1803, when he would have been 22 years of age. His land joined that of George Taylor an the southwest. John Bundick "long" bought 100 acres from Charles W. Taylor and wife Melinda on 31 Dec 1830 for $225.29, part of George Taylor's land. (AC Deeds, 1830-1832:62) John S. Bundick bought 54 acres, for $530, from James R. Garrison on 7 Dec 1834. (AC Deeds, 1834-1835:312) John S. Bundick bought 50 acres, "part of Taylor land on which John S. Bundick now resides," for $200 on 20 Sep 1848, the Sally Taylor Downing part. (AcC Deeds, 1849-1851:43) He bought 32 acres for $270 from George W. Scott an 16 Oct 1848. (AC Deeds, 1848-1849:308) In Jun 1849, John S. Bundick bought 20 acres for $240 from William B. Finney. (AC Deeds, 1848-1849:602) He bought 20 additional acres from Louis C.H. Finney in Nov 1849. (AC Deeds, 1849-1851:111) On 15 Jul 1857,John S. Bundick deeded 23 acres for $5.00 to his son John B. Bundick, land lying in Bradford Neck. (AC Deeds, 1855-1858:485) His new wife did not cosign the deed. On 17 Nov 1858, John S. Bundick and wife Mary, "who was Mary West, widow of John" signed papers agreeing "to live separate and apart. (AC Deeds, 1858-1860:275) The 1860 census shows John S. Bundick, at 79 years, living alone.

John S. Bundick left a will dated 14 Feb 1861; it was recorded on 26 Aug of the same year. He gave his son John B. Bundick his Garrison land. He left his home farm to daus. Ann Mason and Susan Ward. His Scott and Finney lands were given to dau. Elizabeth "Dunckin." He left a slave named Mary to his son and gave money to his children and grandchildren. purchased of James R. Garrison adjoining the lands of Edwin Roberts and others. At the death of my dau. Ann Mason I give her one half to my grandson George B. Mason, and if my dau. Susan Ward shall have a child or children that shall live to be twenty one years of age then I give her one half of said farm to them and their heirs forever but if my dau. Susan Ward leaves no child or children or if they should not live to the age or twenty one years then I give the said half or said farm to my grandson John P. Bundick to him and his heirs forever. [I leave my farm called *Scot and Finney land* that is to say all the land I purchased of the Finneys and George Scot to my dau. Elizabeth Dunckin. To son John B. Bundick Negro woman Mary. To son John B. Bundick's children $200 each. To the children of dau. Ann Mason $200 each. To daus. Ann Mason, Elizabeth Dunckin and Susan Ward, $100 each. To son John B. Bundick $600, chest, clothes and books. Son John B. Bundick extr. Witnesses were John E. Ames and James P. Haley. (AC Wills, 1846-1882:329) John S. Bundick and his wife Jane were buried on his home farm, the Taylor land. (Whitelaw:848) Their stones stand in a family burial plot between Melfa and Onley, about one mile east of U.S. 13, with those of their daus. and their husbands.

John S. 'of Long' Bundick and Jane 'Jinney' Bradford had the following children:

101   i. John B.^{6} Bundick, b. in AC 19 Jan 1810, d. 28 May 1888. His body was interred in Old Homestead Cem, Quinby, AC. (MLAC) He m. 8 Apr 1846 in AC, Margaret E. Floyd (b. 23 Sep 1827 in AC, d. 1 Jun 1883. (ACM; MLAC) Her body was interred in Old Homestead Cem, Quinby, AC. Margaret Bundick's obituary, under Savageville News, states she was "formerly of this locality but of late a resident of Bradford's Neck." She died of paralysis. (Pen. Ent., 7 Jun 1883) The tombstone at the "Old Homestead" cemetery slighty north of present-day Quinby reads, "Margaret E. Bundick, nee Floyd, died 1 Jun 1883 aged 55 years 8 months 8 days."

John B. Bundick was listed as a head of household (HH#933) in the census of 1850 in St. George Parish, AC, age 40, and a farmer with real estate valued at $1,000. With him were his wife Margaret E., age 23 and children: William, age 3; Mary J., age 1 and Elizabeth S., age 2 mos.. Also living with him was John Bradford, age 16. (FA CD309)

John was listed as a head of household in the census of 1860 in St. George Parish, AC. (HH#944) He was age 50 and a farmer, with a wife Margt. E., age 32 and children: Wm. S., age 13; Mary J., age 11; Elizt., age 10; Susan, age 7; John F., age 5; Charles B., age 4; James E., age 2; and Margt. R., age 7 mos. Also living with him were 3 black farm laborers. (Crowson & Hite, *AC 1860 Census*)

On 27 Jul 1847, John B. Bundick bought, for $825, from Thomas F. Floyd and wife Margaret E., their interest in 67 acres. (AC Deeds 1846-1848:523) This land was bordered west by Matchapungo Creek, east by the Broadwater (present Upshurs Bay), north by Joshua Burton and south by Elizabeth Barnes' land. The deed of 1857, to John B. Bundick from his father, for 23 acres in Bradford Neck, gives the same boundaries on the east and west. On 17 May 1866, John B. Bundick bought at public auction 96 acres for $2,400. (AC Deeds, 1865-1867:474) The land bordered on the west by Matchapungo Creek, east by Broadwater, and south by Nathaniel Lecato. He then owned 186 acres in Bradford Neck, between Wachapreague and Quinby, and his land appears to have been the land his mother Jane inherited from her father, Zephaniah Bradford, in 1790

and that of his uncle Abel Bradford. (Whitelaw:771/2)
John B. Bundick sold 54 acres to Francis S. Smith on
27 Mar 1885, for $1,230. (AC Deeds, 1884-1885:327) This
was apparently the Garrison land he inherited from his
father.
   The 1850 Federal Census shows John B. Bundick
at 40 years, a farmer, in household #933 in St. George
Parish. His wife, Margaret E., was 23. Their household
included three children: William at 3 years, Mary J. a
1-year-old, and Elizabeth S. of 2 mos. By 1860, there
were five other children: Susan at 7 years, John F. at 5
years, Charles B. at 4 years, James E. at 2 years and
Margaret R. at 7 mos. In 1870, John B. Bundick was 60
years of age and still farming. His older son was no
longer in his household, but there were three additional
children: Amanda A. at 9 years, Fluranna J. at 7 years
and George E.L. at 3 years. The 1880 census lists John
B. Bundick, a 70-years old, farmer, in household
#207/237 of Pungoteague District. Wife Margaret E.
Bundick was 52 and eight of their children were living
at home, the youngest being George E. at 13 years.
   George W. LeCato was named to administer the
estate of John B. Bundick on 25 Jun 1888. (AC OB 1886-
1889:552) On 31 Jul 1888, the children of John B.
Bundick "lately deceased," deeded to George W.
LeCato, trustee, the land they inherited from their
father in Bradford's Neck, three tracts bound northwest
by Machipongo Creek, southeast by Upshur's
Broadwater, northeast by George W. James and
southwest by the heirs of William LeCato, deceased.
(AC Deeds 60:31) George W. Lecato, Trustee, sold lot #3
to John T. Powell, on 25 Oct 1888, as 61 acres for
$700. (AC Deeds 60:230) He sold lot #2 to Benjamin T.
Eichelberger on the same date, 67 acres for $1,406. (AC
Deeds 60:234) On 18 Nov 1889, George W. LeCato,
trustee of the estate of John B. Bundick, sold lot #1, 23
acres, to Charles B. Bundick for $655. (AC Deeds 67:503)
Charles B. Bundick and wife Virgie B. sold this 23
acres, "land near Quinby in Bradford's Neck" to James
A. Eichelberger on 17 Jun 1911 for $1,250. (AC Deeds
97:363) The obituary of John B. Bundick appeared in the
2 Jun 1888 issue of The Peninsula Enterprise under
Wachapreague news. It states he was of Bradford's
Neck and left 11 children. John B. Bundick is buried in

86

a family plot called "Old Homestead," slightly north of present-day Quinby.

102   ii. Ann 'Nancy' Bundick, b. in AC 11 Jan 1814, d. 13 Jun 1891 in St. George Parish, AC, bur. John S. Bundick Cem, Melfa. (Father's; MLAC; WADR; MLAC) She m. 9 Sep 1839 (bond) in AC, George W. Mason. John Belote was the security on the M.L.B. (ACM)

George, b. 23 Feb 1818 in AC, d. 8 Jan 1898, farmer, bur. John S. Bundick Cem, Melfa, was son of Edmund C. Mason and Elizabeth 'Betsy' James. (MLAC; MACM; MILESW&A:352 (will of Edmund Mason)) He m. 2nd 27 Oct 1892 in Only, Virginia Susan Mears, dau. of Joseph G. & Virginia Belote.

Ann was listed with her husband in the census of 1850 in St. George Parish, AC, HH#164. (FA CD309)

103   iii. Elizabeth Bundick, b. in AC 2 Feb 1816, d. 7 Aug 1877, bur. John S. Bundick Cem, Melfa. (MLAC) She m. 13 Sep 1843, John H. Duncan (b. c1814, bur. John S. Bundick Cem, Melfa). (AC Marriage Register 1, *1805-1850*; 1860 AC Census; MLAC)

Elizabeth was listed with her husband in the census of 1860 in Pungoteague PO, St.George Parish, AC, HH#1227. (1860 AC Census)

104   iv. Susan J. Bundick, b. in AC 26 Jul 1819, d. 13 Jan 1861, bur. John S. Bundick Cem, Melfa. (MACM; FA CD309; MLAC) She m. 4 Aug 1858 in AC, John L. Ward (b. 25 May 1826, d. 9 Oct 1898), son of Lancelott Ward & Mary A. East. John is also bur. in John S. Bundick Cem. (AC Marriage Register 3, *1853-1896;*.MLAC; FA CD309; MACM)

John m. 1st Melinda Kellam 7 Jun 1848 in AC. (FA CD309) They were shown only as John Ward and Malinda Taylor.

65. Sarah 'Sally'^{5} Bundick (Levin^4, Abbott^3, Richard^2, Richard^1), b. inAC c1780. (Father's; and Brother's Land Cause)

On 16 Jan1807 Sarah sold the 9 acres of land she inherited from Elias Bundick to William Baker of Isaiah. (AC Deeds, *1804-1807*)

Sarah 'Sally' Bundick had the following child:

105   i. Edmund^6 Bundick, b. in AC c1795, d. before 1840. (AC OB1829-1832:475) His apparent wife, Polly, was head of an 1840 household. He m. c1818, Polly Topping(?) (b. c1800).*

*AC records have been throughly searched for direct proof of Polly Bundick's husband. Since direct proof has not been found and since all other Bundicks in Accomack County have been researched and positively placed in the Bundick family, it is concluded that she married Edmund Bundick, the son of Sarah, who was the dau. of Levin Bundick. This conclusion is based on the above and the following series of facts and land ownership.(1) Edmund's widow Polly and their descendents were found living among other Bundicks of the Gargatha line and the use of the given names Edward, Edmund and Elias by their descendants. (2) In 1840, his widow Polly was living near Ezekiel Baker, who inherited land across from Woodbury Church. (3) The 100 acres of land across from Ezekiel Baker's land and north of Woodbury Church, "in the woods near Gargathy," as left to Abbott Bundick by his father, Richard Bundick (II), in 1731. Abbott died testate in 1784, leaving his plantation to wife Keziah for life, then to son Elias Bundick, and if he had no heirs, to five daus. Abbott had an older son Levin Bundick, who was apparently deceased by 1784. Elias Bundick died intestate by 28 Oct 1805, when his land was ordered to be divided. It was subsequently divided between his five sisters and a half-niece, Sarah Bundick, "dau of Levin, deceased." As a half-niece, Sarah got only 9 acres of Elias' land, which she sold on 16 Jan 1807 to William Baker of Isaiah.(4) Nothing more has been found of Sarah, but an order of 29 May 1832 states that Edmund Bundick was the only heir of Levin Bundick, who served in the State Navy of Virginia during the Revolutionary War. This implies that Sarah, dau. of Levin, apparently had a son Edmund Bundick. Based on this information it is concluded that Edmund, who was not listed in any AC census, had lived with other family members on or near his mother's (Sarah) land until his death before the 1840 census, leaving his widow Polly living in this vicinity near Ezekiel Baker in 1840. When his son, John E. Bundick married the second time in 1896, the marriage license gave his parents as Elijah Russell and Polly Bundick. When his other son, Thomas E. Bundick married for the second time in 1899, the license states he was the son of Elijah Bundick and Polly his wife. These records could indicate that their mother Polly was not married at all, or that her husband was Elijah Russell Bundick. No Elijah Bundick of the right age has been found in the records. It seems logical to suppose that both John E. and Thomas E. had forgotten their father's name by this time and/or were saying their father was Elias (Thomas E.'s middle name), having heard that their grandmother Sarah had inherited part of Elias Bundick's land. (Sources for the above facts are noted with those individuals' records.).

Descendants of William Mason
(limited to the Mason Surname)

Introduction

The name Mason has been found spelled several different ways. In early records it appears as Mafon, Mafson and Marfon, where the letter "s" was written as a "f." Later, in addition to Mason, it was spelled as Maison, Mayson or Maysen. This work is based primarily on the research of Mary Frances Cary contained in her *The Mason Family of Kegotank, Accomack County, Virginia,* dated Sep 17, 1990. The branches of the family that she did not trace completely were traced further by M.K. and Barry Miles.

Except for one early Mason in Northampton County, there appears to have been none there until the mid-1800s. SO Co. had two early Mason men, and an Abraham Mason on tax lists of 1723 and 1724, but no Masons are listed there in the 1850 census. WO Co. records show: Edmund Mason selling personal property in 1746; William Mason who died intestate in 1774; a John Mason dying intestate in 1778; and Bennet and Daniel Mason as members of the Snow Hill Battalion of the county militia in 1780. These men appear to be related to or descendants of the first William Mason of Accomack County and evidently moved into Maryland from the Messongo area. The 1850 census shows eleven Mason men and their families in WO Co., concentrated in District #1, that of Newtown (present-day Pocomoke area). Some of their descendants moved south across the Maryland/Virginia line, into the upper Accomack County area of New Church, Horn Town, and Chincoteague Island.

The Masons of Messongo had apparently either died out or moved on by 1820. One of their descendants could have been James Mason, whose dau. Tinny married Bennet Mason, of the Kegotank Masons, in 1814. James Mason, b. c1760. He was listed by the 1800 census, living on Wallops Road (present U.S. 13), aged 26-40 years. He had married Betty Northam in 1789. The Northams lived between Messongo Creek and Wallops Road. James Mason bought land in the Kegotank area after 1800. He died testate in 1823, naming only dau. Tinny Mason and her son James Mason. He had one other dau, Elizabeth Mason, who married William Thornton, Junr in 1814. The parentage of James Mason has not been found. It appears likely he was a son of Middleton Mason, who had land dealings with Southy Northam in 1768 and 1771 and was deceased by 1780.

The Kegotank Masons had sold their entire 100 acres of land there by 1821, land that their great-grandfather, Bennet Mason, bought in 1728, and male descendants were no longer in the area after 1831.

The only Accomack County Mason who served during the Revolutionary War was an Adam Mason, who was a soldier in the county militia. He was a descendant of Thomas Mason, brother to Edmund Mason of Kegotank, and lived in Saint George Parish.

The earliest record of a Mason on the Eastern Shore of Virginia was a Richard Mason, who was a headright for William Cole, when Cole was granted a land patent in NC in 1642. (County Court Records 1640 - 1645:204) True's Biographical Dictionary shows a John Mason receiving a grant for land in Accomack County in 1640, but the original record clearly states the patentee was John Major. (Deeds & Wills 1663 - 1666:74) Richard Mason's name appears in Northampton County records at least twice after 1642; on 23 March 1643, when he was a witness at court, and on 10 April 1644, when he gave a deposition (p. 349 and p. 358). No record of his death in Northampton County or in Accomack County has been found. There is no record of Richard Mason having married. However, a widow or dau, Ann Mason, could have married Captain William Kendall, Junr, who d. testate in NC in 1696, naming one dau. as Mason Kendall. (Whitelaw:659;.NC XVII, AC OB:384) Mason Kendall had married Samuel Welbourne, of Horn Town, by 1724, when she and her husband joined a sister and a father brother in selling AC land they inherited from their father Col. Solomon Ewell. (ACDW&c., 1715 - 1729, part I:540) The land was called *Ewell's Forest* and later became known as *Pocomoke Swamp*. (Whitelaw:1262) It was located near Messongo Creek, which empties into Pocomoke Sound. William Mason, son of William Mason , bought 460 acres of this land in 1734, land he left his son John Mason in 1759. This suggests the possibility of a family connection. (ACDW 1729 - 1737:388),

George Mason and Robert Mason were named as headrights for Ambrose White in 1668 and 1670, as White patented land in Accomack County. (Cert. and Rights:38,42) The former does not appear again, but Robert Mason d. testate in 1678, naming only two daus. (ACDW 1676 - 1690:86) He had married Temperence, the dau. of Nicholas Wadallow/Wallop. (Whitelaw:701)

A William Mason patented 100 acres, called *Mason's Adventure*, in SO Co., in 1687. (SO Co. Land Records:281) There is no record of him selling this land. John Whitty had patented the same land in 1685, as *Whitty's Lot* (p. 420) and later records show it reverted to Whitty's heirs. (SORR 1666 - 1723:281) William Mason m. 18 Aug 1680, Anne Deane. (SO Co. Deeds JKL:167) He registered a cattle mark on 14 June 1680 (p. 13), and then disappeared from SO Co.

Joseph Mason bought 41 acres of SO Co. land from Ambrose London in 1678. (SO Co. Deeds MAO6:21) His name does not appear in the grantor index as selling this land. He did not die testate in SO Co. or WO Co. It is possible that Joseph Mason was the father of William Mason, who m. in SO Co. in 1680, or his brother.

Of these early Mason men on the Eastern Shore of Virginia and Maryland, the records suggest, without proof, that William Mason , subject of this Mason Family Report, could have been the son of Richard Mason of NC. Many early immigrants to NC moved northward into AC and SO Co., as land became available in these areas, some settling in Sussex Co., DE (called Sussex Co., PA, in early records).

First Generation

1. **William**[1] **Mason**, b. c1644, d. 1710. (Nottingham Wills:52 (adm. of William & Sarah Mason)) The administration of the estates of both William and his wife Sarah was granted to their son, William Mason, on 1 Aug 1710. (AC OB 1710 - 1714:7)

He m. c1685, **Sarah Bennett** (b. c1667, d. 1710), dau. of Thomas Bennett. (Nottingham Wills:52 (adm. of William & Sarah Mason))

On 27 Sep 1692, William Mason, age c48, gave a deposition in AC Court. (AC OB 1690 - 1697:42) He would have been 22 years of age when his name was listed as a headright in 1666. It is likely he had married when his name first appeared on the AC list of tithables in 1681. (AC Tithables (Tax List) 1663 - 1695:27) While no record has been found as proof, it appears his wife and the mother of his children was Sarah Bennet. Thomas Crippen, who d. testate in 1735, had a dau. who had m.Thomas Bennet. (AC DW 1729 - 1737:411) The Crippen name appeared many times in the settling of the estates of the Kegotank Masons, suggesting some family relationship. Thomas Bennet was a headright for Edmund Scarburgh in 1664. (Certificates and Rights:15) He could have had a dau, Sarah Bennet, who m. William Mason, in addition to the son who m. Elizabeth Crippen.

In 1695 William, ship carpenter, was living near Pungoteague Creek, AC. This is shown by a document he had recorded on that date, stating he had paid John Revell "a valuable consideration" to move a shallop he had built "on a Plantation in the woods near Pungoteague and having no way whereby to convey and Carry down the Said Shallop from the place where it is built to ye water side to Launch but over the land of Mr. John Revell." The boat was built for Col. Charles Scarburgh. (Wills & C Orders 1682 - 1697:270)

On 6 May 1707, Edmund and wife Elizabeth Scarburgh sold 121 acres to William, Mason for 4000 pounds of tobacco and cask. (ACW&c., 1692 - 1715, part II:235) This land was at "ye head of Little Matompkin alias Burton Branch" and was inland from Pungoteague Creek.

On 1 Aug 1710 William Mason was named to settle the estates of his parents, William & Sarah Mason in AC. On 21 Aug 1710, the inventory and appraisal of the estates was presented by John Warrington and John Wylie, two of the appraisers, and recorded. (ACW&c., 1692-1715, part III:1) Transcript of inventory of William and Sarah Mason: one tabble and bedstead; 3 cowes & one yearling & one five year old; 2 old blankets; one pro of Gloves and two pare of slippers; one peaberat (?) & a hackle made of nailes; 2 earthen potts and sum small Triffles; one small trunk & some small triffles; an apron and a small piece of Rope; one Lining wheal; 2 matts y one of them old; 1 old Wig(?); 1 old Psalm book; 1 spit & 1 flesh pork; a peas of Cane; 2 peases of Leather and a powder home; 2 par of wool cords one old; one par of beads(?); 10 pound of Cole (?); 1 old bed ye wate 31 (?); an old wheale and 2 old Chests; an old Runlet (?) & hackle; an earthen pot &. Gimlet; an old hat It a fire piece(?); one book &. one tub; 2 old wheales; an old stock lock 2 pair of Knitting needles and thimble; one needle Case and thimble both silver; an old petticoat Linen; 7 pd of soape; one par of Cotton Gloves; 1 virginia Cloath percale (?); 2 blue aprons, 1 sifter; 8 yards ½ of bagging; 1 bocat (bonnet?); one yard ½ of Linen; 1 Vial and 5 glafs bottles; 1 pound of Cotton yarne one pound ½ of Cotton; 3 pds of woolen yame; 3 womans Cape and 2 toualls (?); 4 pound ½ of pewter; 2 pocket knives and 2 small iron wedges; 1 Iron pot; an old earthen pot 2; pieces of Rope; an Earthen Stien; 22 pd of old iron; for a mare which I have sold for 6 hundred pds of Toba ffor 3 pd sowshead (?) which I have used and about a pound and halfe of sugar and about a pint of Rum and pint Molasses which I have made use of. (Nottingham Wills:52 (adm. of William & Sarah Mason))

Besides the known son, William Mason, and one dau, other children of William and Sarah Mason can only be deduced. The fact that William Mason could have had brothers nearby complicates this. The name of Richard Mason does not appear after he was named as a headright in 1666. Edmund Mason got in trouble with the law in 1706 for "keeping an unlawfull Tipling house." (AC OB 1703-1709:83a) After this date, his name does not appear in the records. John Mason was listed as a tithable in 1692,1693,1694 and in 1695. (AC Tithables (Tax List) 1663-1695:54, 55, 58, 61) No record of his death has been found. Taking these facts, and the prevalence of similar given names, into consideration, the next generation of Masons in AC are deemed to be the children of William Mason and his wife Sarah.. The names of four men, who could have been brothers or a father with three sons, appear in the list of headrights given by David Williamson, when he was granted a patent for 6000 acres in AC on 16 Feb 1666. (AC DW 1663 - 1666:115) They were William Marfson, Edward (Edmund) Mafson, John Mafon, and Richard Mafsons. Although each of their last names were spelled slightly different, there seems little doubt but that they were all Masons. The land that David Williamson patented in 1666 was bound on the north by Crooked Creek (present-day Bullbegger Creek) and on the south by Messongo Creek. (Nugent I:554) It was near the land William Mason's son bought in 1713.

William Mason and Sarah Bennett had the following children:
+   2   i. William² Mason, b. c1685, d. Nov 1759.
    3   ii. Katherine Mason, b. in AC c1687. (Carey, *Mason Family of Kegotank*) Thomas Webb, planter, made a gift of a cow, "with a calf by her side" and a heifer to his goddau, Katherine Mason, dau. of William Mason, carpenter, on 18 Sep 1688. (AC WD 1678-1690:481)
    4   iii. Abraham Mason, b. c1690. On 6 Oct 1719 in AC, Abraham Mason brought a suit against James Conner's estate. (AC OB 1719-1724:8) Abraham appears on the tax list of SO Co. for 1723 and 1724.
+   5   iv. Bennett Mason, b. c1695, d. Dec 1766.
+   6   v. John Mason, b. c1700, d. before 5 Sep 1738.
    7   vi. Edmund Mason, b. in AC Aug 1710. Edmund Mason, orphan, "who will be 15 years of age next Aug," was bound out to Sabastian Delastatius, Junr on 2 March

1725, "to learn to read and Right and the Art of a wheel Right." This Edmund Mason apparently moved into WO Co. He sold personal property there on 9 Jan 1746. (WOD A, P 469)

Second Generation

2. **William**[2] **Mason** (William[1]), b. in AC c1685, d. Nov 1759. (Nottingham Wills:195 (will of William Mason Sr.))

He m. c1708, **Eleanor (N)**, apparently the widow and second wife of Thomas Middleton, who d. testate in 1708, naming his "now wife Eleanor." William Mason was a witness to the will. (AC Wills 1692-1715:442)

Eleanor, b. c1685 in AC, d. Apr 1760, m. c1705, **Thomas Middleton**. (Nottingham Wills:38 (will of Thomas Middleton; Nottingham Wills:171 (adm. of Eleanor Mason))

William inherited his father's land in AC, in 1710 and exchanged it with John Collins on 4 May 1713 for land elsewhere. (AC W&c., 1692-1715, part III:123) He and wife Eleanor sold the new land to Richard Rodgers on 10 Oct 1713. (p. 153) On the same date, William Mason (carpenter) bought 200 acres on the north side of Messongo Creek from Thomas Preeson for 10,000 pounds tobacco and cash. (p. 166)

On 2 Oct 1716, they reported "ye Rebackah Lister Servt woman by Indenture bound to them Absented herself by runing away." (AC OB 1714-1717:24)

He left a will dated 12 Feb 1758, probated 28 Nov 1759 in AC. He left 200 acres on the south side of Messongo Creek to his oldest son, Middleton Mason, "where he now lives." He left 100 acres, bought of Ann Drummond, to son William Mason "where he now lives." He left 450 acres, purchased of Solomon Ewell, to son John Mason. William Mason left his son, Bennet Mason, 200 acres "where I now live" (north side of Messongo Creek). He named daus. as Ann Pilchor [Pilchard], Hannah Major, Susanna Andrews, and Eleanor Howard. He left his wife, Eleanor Mason, half his home plantation for her lifetime. He left a slave to William Mason, son of son John "if he comes to live in this county." He named another grandson as Daniel Mason and left property to grandson Ismael Mason/Andrews. Wife and son Bennet were the residuary legatees & extrs. William Beavans, Ephraim Waggaman & Henry Fletcher were to appraise the estate. Witnessed by John Milligan, Daniel Howard and Lewis Biswick. Besides those named in his will, William Mason had two other children. Middleton Mason was named the heir at law, implying that he was the oldest son. (Nottingham Wills:195 (will of William Mason Sr.))

Ede Mason wrote her will on 17 May 1748, recorded 29 Nov 1748. (AC Wills 1745-1749:469) Her will was witnessed by brothers Middleton Mason, Bennet Mason, and Zorobable Mason. (AC OB 1744-1753:295)

Of William and Eleanor's four sons, only Bennet Mason appears to have left descendants in the Messongo area.

William Mason and Eleanor (N) had the following children:

+   8   i. Middleton[3] Mason, b. c1710, d. c1780.

9   ii. William Mason, b. in AC c1712, d. 1774 in MD, probably WO Co. (Nottingham Wills:195 (will of William Mason Sr.; Carey, *Mason Family of Kegotank;* Index to Estates 1742-1908) He m. c1740, Comfort (N) (b. c1712). (Carey, *Mason Family of Kegotank*) William and wife Comfort, sold his inherited land in 1761. (AC Deeds 1757-1770:163)

+ 10   iii. John Mason, b. c1714, d. c1778.

+ 11   iv. Bennett Mason, b. c1716, d. Mar 1768.

12   v. Ann Mason, b. in AC c1718, m. Francis Pilchard (b. c1715) before 12 Feb 1758. (Nottingham Wills:195 (will of William Mason Sr.)) Ann was named in her father's will 12 Feb 1758 in AC. She was shown as a dau. Ann Pilchor, wife of Francis Pilchor in the will of William Mason Sr. (Nottingham Wills. Note: Nottingham showed the spelling as Pickeran, not Pilchor.)

13   vi. Zorobable Mason, b. in AC c1720, d. 1748. (Nottingham Wills:151 (will of Ede Mason; Carey, *Mason Family of Kegotank; AC OB* 1774-1753:295) Zorobable witnessed a will 17 May 1748 in AC. (Nottingham Wills:151 (will of Ede Mason

14 vii. Hannah Mason, b. in AC c1722. (Nottingham Wills:195 (will of William Mason Sr.)) She m. before 12 Feb 1758, (N) Major (b. c1720 in AC). (Nottingham Wills:195 (will of William Mason Sr.))

15 viii. Susannah Mason, b. in AC c1724, m. c1742, William Andrews (b. c1720 in AC), son of William and Mary Andrews. (Nottingham Wills:195 (will of William Mason Sr.); 216 (will of William Andrews))

16   ix. Eleanor Mason, b. in AC c1726, m. Daniel? Howard. (Nottingham Wills:195 (will of William Mason Sr.))

17   x. Ede Mason, b. in AC c1728, d. Nov 1748, leaving a will dated 17 May 1748, probated 29 Nov 1748. To Middleton Mason. father & mother residuary legatees. Mother extr. Witnessed by Middleton Mason, Bennet Mason & Zorobable Mason. Middleton Mason relinquished his legacy. (Nottingham Wills:151 (will of Ede Mason)

5. Bennett² Mason (William¹), b. in AC c1695, d. Dec 1766. (Nottingham Wills:229 (will of Bennet Mason))

He m. 1ˢᵗ c1720, **Bridget Bagwell** (c1700 in AC). (Carey, *Mason Family of Kegotank*) Bennet Mason's wife Bridget was likely a Bagwell. She was apparently the mother of his older children and it is likely he married a second time after her death. He named no wife in his will.

He m. c1745, **(2nd w|o Bennet Mason) (N)** (b. c1720).

The name of Bennet Mason first appears in AC records on 7 May 1728, when he bought 100 acres of land from William Huse (Hughes) for 3250 pence. The land was located "in the woods on the Westermost Side of Kecotanke (Kegotank) Branch near the sea Side." (ACDW&c., 1715 - 1729, part II:204) This tract can be located on present-day maps at Nelsonia, extending eastward on both sides of the road to Modest Town. (Whitelaw:1161)

On 30 Nov 1743, Bennet Mason and his wife Bridget brought a suit against Abbot Bundick and wife Sophia "in case for Words." (AC OB 1737 - 1744:526) Sophia Bundick was found guilty of "speaking the words" and fined. (AC OB 1744 - 1753:6)

Bennet Mason bought 150 acres on the south side of Onancock Creek from Littleton Lurton for £65 in 1750. (AC Deeds 1746 - 1757:302) This land was not far from his father's land.

He left a will dated 17 Apr 1762, probated 30 Dec 1766 in AC. He left the plantation where he lived to son Edmund Mason. He left to son Thomas Mason where he now lives adjoining the White Marsh. He called two other sons, Jeremiah Mason and Jacob Mason, "boys" and left them his gold and silver, household furniture and slaves. He named three daus. as Bridget Mason, Susannah Clemmons and Nanny Mason. John Kitson, Thomas Crippen and Richard Justice were named to divide the estate. Sons Thomas & Jeremiah extrs. Witnessed by John Cowley, Solomon Wimbrough & William Goodday. (Nottingham Wills:229 (will of Bennet Mason)) Edmund Mason was named heir at law.

Bennett Mason and Bridget Bagwell had the following children:

+ 18   i. Edmund³ Mason, b. c1720, d. Apr 1768.
+ 19   ii. Thomas Mason, b. c1725, d. before 1810.
  20   iii. Susannah Mason, b. in AC c1725, m. c1745, Stephen Clemmons (b. c1720, d. Jan 1786 in AC). Susannah was named in her husband's will dated 16 Feb 1782. (Nottingham Wills:229 (will of Bennet Mason) & 360 (will of Stephen Clemmons))
  21   iv. Bridget Mason, b. in AC c1740, m. c1765, (N) Bell. (Nottingham Wills:229 (will of Bennet Mason)) Bridget Mason was unm. in 1762, when her father wrote his will, and m. to Bell when his estate was divided in 1768. (AC Wills 1767 - 1772:99)
  22   v. Ann 'Nanny' Mason, b. in AC c1742, m. c1765, (N) Bloxom. (Nottingham Wills:229 (will of Bennet Mason))

Bennett Mason and (2nd w|o Bennet Mason) (N) had the following children:

+ 23   vi. Jacob Mason, b. c1745, d. Mar 1810.
+ 24   vii. Jeremiah Mason, b. c1747, d. c1805.

6. **John² Mason** (William¹), b. in AC c1700, d. before 5 Sep 1738 when his inventory and appraisal was returned by Mary Mason, his administratrix. (AC OB

1737-1744:96) He left five small children, William Mason, Elizabeth Mason, Miles Mason, and Thomas Mason; and an older son, Solomon Mason, who sold his father's land in 1749 and 1750. (AC Deeds 1747-1757:211, 297) He m. c1730, **Mary** (N) (b. c1710 in AC, d. by 5 Sep 1738). She probably m. c1740, **Thomas Lucas** c1740. After 1750, this family disappeared from AC records. (AC Deeds 1747-1757:192) John Mason bought land in the Messongo area in 1726 and 1728. (AC DW&c., 1715-1729, part II:65, 215, 216) He and wife Mary sold the land in 1728. John Mason bought land in the Messongo area in 1726 and 1728. (ACDW&c.., 1715-1729, part II:65, 215, 216) On 5 Sep 1738 his the inventory and appraisal of his estate was returned by Mary Mason, his administratrix. (AC OB 1737-1744:96) He left five small children, William Mason, Elizabeth Mason, Miles Mason, and Thomas Mason; and an older son, Solomon Mason, who sold his father's land in 1749 and 1750. (AC Deeds 1747-1757:211, 297)

John Mason had the following child:

    25   i. Solomon[3] Mason, b. in AC c1725. Solomon sold land 1749 & 1750 in AC. Solomon Mason sold his father's land in 1749 and 1750. (AC Deeds 1747-1757:211, 297)

John Mason and Mary (N) had the following children:

    26   ii. William Mason, b. in AC c1730.
    27   iii. Elizabeth Mason, b. in AC c1732.
    28   iv. Miles Mason, b. in AC c1734.
    29   v. Thomas Mason, b. in AC c1736.

Third Generation

8. **Middleton[3] Mason** (William[2], William[1]), b. in AC c1710, d. c1780. (Orders 1780-1783:72)

He m. c1745 in AC, **Rachel Byrd** (b. c1727 in AC), dau. of Daniel Bird. (Nottingham Wills:191 (will & settlement of Daniel Bird; AC Wills 1752-1757:547)

On 29 Apr 1760 Middleton Mason was named to settle the estate of Eleanor Mason. Littleton Armitrader was the security. (Nottingham Wills:171)

Middleton Mason and wife Rachel sold his inheritance in 1768. (AC Deeds 1757-1770:550, 551)

Middleton Mason and Rachel Byrd had the following children:

    +   30   i. John[4] Mason, b. c1745.
         31   ii. Daniel Mason, b. in AC c1746. (Nottingham Wills:195 (will of William Mason Sr.)), Daniel was named in his grandfather's will 12 Feb 1758 in AC. (Nottingham Wills:195 (will of William Mason Sr.))

              Daniel Mason was a captain in the WO Co. Militia in 1780.

              Daniel appears on the tax list of in WO Co. for 1783. Daniel Mason had two grown sons in 1783. (WO Co. Tax List)

32   iii.   Bennett Mason, b. in AC c1748, d. before 1792. (Carey, *Mason Family of Kegotank*) Bennet Mason also served in the WO Co. Militia in 1780.
Bennett appears on the tax list of WO Co. for 1783. Bennett Mason had three grown sons in 1783. (WO Co. Tax List)

+   33   iv.   James Mason, b. c1750, d. Dec 1823.

10. **John³ Mason** (William², William¹), b. in AC c1714., d. c1778 in MD. (Nottingham Wills:195 (will of William Mason Sr.)) It appears it was he who died intestate in WO Co. in 1778. (Index to Estates, 1742-1908)

In 1760 John was living in Sussex Co, DE when he sold his inherited land. (AC Deeds 1757-1770:133)

John Mason had the following child:

34   i.   William⁴ Mason, b. c1740. (Nottingham Wills:195 (will of William Mason Sr.)) William was named in his grandfather's will 12 Feb 1758 in AC. He was shown as a William Mason, son of John, and given a slave in the will of William Mason Sr., if he comes to live in this county. (Nottingham Wills:195 (will of William Mason Sr.))

11. **Bennett³ Mason** (William², William¹), b. in AC c1716, d. Mar 1768. (Nottingham Wills:151 (will of Ede Mason), 195 (will of William Mason Sr.; Nottingham Wills:209 (adm. of Bennet Mason))

He m. c1755 **Ann** (N) (b. c1735 in AC. (Carey, *Mason Family of Kegotank*)

Bennett witnessed a will 17 May 1748, probably that of his sister, in AC.,(Nottingham Wills:151 (will of Ede Mason))

On 30 Mar 1768 Anne Mason was named to settle the estate of Bennet Mason. Littleton Armitrader, John Bunting & Thomas Bloxom were the securities. (Nottingham Wills:209 (adm. of Bennet Mason)) On 1 Nov 1769 in AC the audit of Bennet Mason's personal estate was recorded by Ann Mason, administrix. (AC Wills 1767-1772:357) After a number of bills were paid, the balance was divided into three parts, for William Mason, Bennet Mason, and Eleanor Mason. On 28 Aug 1771, Jacob Bird was appointed guardian of William Mason, Bennet Mason and Nelly Mason, orphans of Bennet Mason. (AC OB 1770-1773:231) William Mason, as eldest son, inherited his father's land. Of William and Eleanor's four sons, only Bennett Mason appears to have left descendants in the Messongo area. He did not sell his inherited land.

Bennett Mason and Ann (N) had the following children:

+   35   i.   William⁴ Mason, b. c1765, d. Feb 1788.
+   36   ii.   Bennett Mason, b. c1768, d. Mar 1816.
37   iii.   Eleanor 'Nelly' Mason, b. in AC c1770, m. c1790, Benjamin Parks (b. c1770). (Carey, *Mason Family of Kegotank*)
On 28 Aug 1771, Jacob Bird was appointed guardian of William Mason, Bennet Mason and Nelly Mason, orphans of Bennet Mason. (AC OB 1770-1773:231)

18. Edmund³ Mason (Bennett², William¹), b. in AC c1720, d. Apr 1768.
(Nottingham Wills:229 (will of Bennet Mason); 231 (adm. of Edmund Mason))
He m. c1750 **(d|o Rich III) Bundick** (b. c1730 in Gargatha, AC, dau. of
Richard Bundick (III) and Ann Nock. (AC Wills 1761-67:673)
On 26 Nov 1766 when the estate of Richard Bundick III was divided, by
John Kitson, Charles Bagwell, William Nock, and administrator John Bundick,
between his five children, Edmund Mason was allotted Lot #3, valued at
£3.12.10. (AC Wills 1761 - 1767:673) This indicated that Edmund Mason had married
one of the three daus. of Richard Bundick III; her name was not given. Richard
Bundick III had m. Ann Nock, dau. of John Nock. He was the son of Richard
Bundick II and his wife, Susanna Justice, dau. of Ralph Justice. Richard
Bundick II was the only son of Richard Bundick I (died testate in NC in 1692).
Richard Bundick I patented 1400 acres in AC in 1664 and an additional 600
acres in 1672, land that is now called *Parkers Neck*. (Whitelaw:1132).
On 26 Apr 1768 Thomas Mason was named to settle the estate of Edmond
Mason. Stephen Coleman & Stephen Bloxom were the securities. Edmund
Mason died intestate within two years of both his father and father-in-law.
Thomas Mason was evidently his brother. Solomon Bird, Thomas Bloxom,
Arnold Morgon and John Kitson were named to appraise his personal estate.
The inventory, appraisal, and division of the estate were recorded on 27 May
One third went to an unnamed widow and the balance was divided equally
between five children: Susanna, Bennett, Ann, William and Bagwell. (Nottingham
Wills:231 (adm. of Edmund Mason); AC Wills 1767 - 1772: 412, 413, 414, 415)
Edmund Mason and (d|o Rich III) Bundick had the following children:
+   38   i.   Bennett⁴ Mason, b. c1757, d. Jun 1808.
       39   ii.   Susanna Mason, b. in AC c1759.
+   40   iii.   William Mason, b. c1760, d. Feb 1806.
+   41   iv.   Bagwell Mason, b. c1762, d. before 1800.
       42   v.   Ann Mason, b. in AC c1765.
19. Thomas³ Mason (Bennett², William¹), b. in AC c1725, d. before 1810 (not
listed in 1810 census). (Nottingham Wills:229 (will of Bennet Mason)) Besides son Caleb,
it can be assumed he was the progenitor of Masons listed in St. George Parish of
AC (Lower AC) by the 1800 census. These included: Thomas Mason, Senr
(himself, over 45?), Thomas Mason of Thomas (d. testate 1821, naming sons
William Mason and Bagwell Custis Mason); William Mason (died testate 1806,
wife Rachel, son John); Babel Mason (d. testate 1821, sons John and Charles H.
Mason); George Mason (d. testate 1815, wife Suffiah, son Edmund Mason); and
Adam Mason (d. intestate 1833, son William Mason). Thomas Mason's
descendants continued to live in Saint George Parish. Some of them had moved
into NC by 1850.
He m. 1ˢᵗ c1745, **Tabitha (N)**, (b. c1725 in AC, d. before 1780). He m. 2ⁿᵈ
c1780, **Temperance (N)** (b. c1750 in AC).
He was shown as a son Thomas Mason in the will of Bennet Mason. When
his father died in 1766, Thomas Mason inherited the 150 acres of his father's

land near Onancock Greek "adjoining the White Marsh where he now lives." On 1 Jan 1774, Jacob Mason gave Thomas Mason (both mentioned as sons of Bennet Mason) a quitclaim to the White Marsh land. (AC Deeds 1770 - 1777:290)

Thomas sold land before 25 Feb 1778 in AC. Thomas Mason had sold 100 acres of his land to Severn East by 25 Feb 1778. (AC Deeds 1777 - 1783:53)

Thomas and wife Temperance sold 8½ acres to East in 1782. (AC Deeds 1783 - 1788:13) and Thomas Mason, alone, sold other small tracts to East through 1789.

Thomas was listed as a head of household in the census of 1800 in St. George Parish, AC. (Powell, *AC 1800, 1810, 1820 Census*) He was shown as Thomas Mason Senr, over age 45.

Thomas Mason and Tabitha (N) had the following children:

+	43	i. William[4] Mason, b. c1745, d. Sep 1806.
+	44	ii. George Mason, b. c1750, d. Oct 1815.
+	45	iii. Caleb Mason, b. c1750, d. c1805.
+	46	iv. Adam Mason, b. c1752, d. Dec 1833.
+	47	v. Thomas Mason, b. c1760, d. Feb 1822.
+	48	vi. Zorobabel 'Babel' Mason, b. c1765, d. Oct 1825.
+	49	vii. Henry Mason, b. c1765.

Thomas Mason and Temperance (N) had the following child:

+	50	viii. Ezekiel Mason, b. c1785, d. before 25 Dec 1848.

23. **Jacob[3] Mason** (Bennett[2], William[1]), b. in AC c1745, d. Mar 1810. (Nottingham, *Acc Land Causes, 1728-1825*:113 (Mason &c. vs. Suit for dower & division, Sterling & wife.)) He d. leaving a wife Mary and children; Zadock Mason; Sally, wife of Griffin Bishop; Susannah, wife of Elijah Bayly; Lovey, wife of John Sterling; "all of full age, also Nancy Mason, Betsy Mason & Benney Mason, infants. (Land Causes 1812 - 1821:235)

He m. c1765, **Mary 'Molly' Riley** (b. c1745, d. Feb 1836). In his will Mary's father, William Riley, named her children as: Sally Mason, Zadock Mason, William Mason, and Mary Riley Mason, the last two of whom were apparently deceased when their father died in 1810. (Nottingham Wills:392 (will of William Riley; MilesW&A:354 (will of Molly Mason))

On 29 Jun 1769 Jacob Mason bought 100 acres for £18 from Justice Bundick's extrs. (AC Deeds 1757 - 1770:635) The land was located at Guilford. (Whitelaw:1115)

On 12 Sep 1780 Jacob and wife was Mary sold 25 acres of the land he purchased in 1769 to his brother, Jeremiah Mason. (AC Deeds 1777 - 1783:258)

Jacob was named in a land cause 30 Aug 1810 in AC. It was a suit for dower & distribution. That Jacob Mason, father to your complainants except Mary, to whom he was husband, being seized in his demesne as of fee in and to a tract of land situate near Guilford, in the Parish & county of Accomack, containing 73 acres, departed this life intestate on the _ day of March 1810, leaving the complainants Zadock Mason, Sally, who intermarried with Griffin Bishop, Susannah, who m. Elijah Bayly, his children, and of full age, also Nancy Mason, Betsy Mason & Benney Mason infants & his children, and Mary

Mason, his widow, and Lovey Sterling who m. John Sterling also his dau. &c. (Nottingham, *Acc Land Causes, 1728-1825*:113 (Mason &c. vs. Suit for dower & division, Sterling & wife))

Jacob Mason d. intestate. On 28 Apr 1812 Jacob's estate was administered by Charles Bagwell. Thomas M. Bayly was the security. (MilesW&A:353 (adm. of Jacob Mason; AC OB 1812 - 1814:60)

Jacob Mason and Mary 'Molly' Riley had the following children:

51   i. Sally[4] Mason, b. in AC c1776, m. c1795, Griffin Bishop (b. c1775 in AC). (Nottingham Wills:392 (will of her grandfather William Riley); Nottingham, *Acc Land Causes, 1728-1825*:113 (Mason &c. vs. Suit for dower & division, Sterling & wife.))

52   ii. Zadock Mason, b. in AC c1778. (Nottingham Wills:392 (will of his grandfather William Riley dated 18 Sep 1785))

In her will written 9 Feb 1842, Sally Bishop gave her cousin Leah C. Topping all her interest in the Negroes that my uncle Zadock Mason of Norfolk County gave me. (MilesW&A:68 (will of Sally Bishop))

Zadock was named in a land cause 30 Mar 1810 in AC. (Nottingham, *Acc Land Causes, 1728-1825*:113 (Mason &c. vs. Suit for dower & division, Sterling & wife))

53   iii. Susanna Mason, b. in AC c1780, m. 6 Sep 1803 (bond) in AC, Elijah Bayly. Henry Trader was the security on the M.L.B. (Nottingham, *Acc Land Causes, 1728-1825*:113 (Mason &c. vs. Suit for dower & division, Sterling & wife; ACM)

Elijah, b. c1780 in AC, d. May 1815 in AC, son of Robert Bayly and Nancy (N). (MilesW&A:(admin of Elijah Bayly); Nottingham Rev Soldiers & Sailors; and MilesW&A:36 (will of Robert Bayly))

Susanna was named in her grandfather's will 18 Sep 1785 in AC. (Nottingham Wills:392 (will of William Riley))

She was the plaintiff in a law suit against an unknown person 30 Aug 1810 in AC. She was named as Susannah, dau. of Jacob Mason, who had m. Elijah Bayly, in a land cause to divide his land and settle his estate. (Nottingham, *Acc Land Causes, 1728-1825*:113 (Mason &c. vs. Suit for dower & division, Sterling & wife))

54   iv. William Mason, b. in AC c1782, d. before Mar 1810. He was not listed as an heir of Jacob Mason in the land cause showing Jacob's other children. (Nottingham Wills:392 (will of William Riley); Nottingham, *Acc Land Causes, 1728-1825*:113 (Mason &c. vs. Suit for dower & division, Sterling & wife))

William was named in his grandfather's will 18 Sep 1785 in AC. (Nottingham Wills:392 (will of William Riley))

55   v. Lovey Mason, b. in AC c1784, m. 24 Dec 1805 (bond) in AC, John Young Sterling (b. c1780 in AC). Jacob Mason was the security on the M.L.B. of John Sterling and Lovey Mason. They evidently m. 1 Jan 1806, as another record shows a John Starling (sic) and Lovey Mason were m. on that date. (Nottingham, *Acc Land Causes, 1728-1825*:113 (Mason &c. vs. Suit for dower & division, Sterling & wife); FA CD309; ACM)

Lovey Sterling, age 66, was listed as a head of household (HH#1031) in the census of 1850 in Acc Parish, AC. She possessed real estate valued at $300. Listed with her was Mary J.W. Shreaves, age 7. Mary was evidently her granddau. (FA CD309)

56   vi. Mary Riley Mason, b. in AC c1784, d. before Mar 1840 She was not listed as an heir of Jacob Mason in the land cause showing Jacob's other children. (Nottingham Wills:392 (will of William Riley); Nottingham, *Acc Land Causes, 1728-1825*:113 (Mason &c. vs. Suit for dower & division, Sterling & wife))

Mary was named in her grandfather's will 18 Sep 1785 in AC. (Nottingham Wills:392 (will of William Riley))

57   vii. Nancy Mason, b. in AC c1795. Nancy was named in a land cause Mar 1810 in AC. Nancy was named in her mother's will 14 Jan 1836 in AC. (Nottingham, *Acc Land Causes, 1728-1825*:113 (Mason &c. vs. Suit for dower & division, Sterling & wife); MilesW&A:354 (will of Molly Mason))

58   viii. Elizabeth 'Betsy' Mason, b. in AC c1797. Elizabeth was named in a land cause Mar 1810 in AC. (Nottingham, *Acc Land Causes, 1728-1825*:113 (Mason &c. vs. Suit for dower & division, Sterling & wife.))

59   ix. Benny Mason, b. in AC c1799. Benny was named in a land cause Mar 1810 in AC. (Nottingham, *Acc Land Causes, 1728-1825*:113 (Mason &c. vs. Suit for dower & division, Sterling & wife))

24. **Jeremiah[3] Mason** (Bennett[2], William[1]), b. in AC c1747, d. c1805. There is no record of his death - his name appears on the 1800 census and on a deed, with his wife, Ann on 6 Aug 1804. (AC Deeds DC 1804 - 1807:116); However, he was not named in his wife's will of 10 Jan 1805 nor listed in the 1810 census.

He m. c1775, **Ann (N)** (b. c1750 in AC, d. Feb 1805. (MilesW&A:351 (will of Ann Mason))

In 1780 Jeremiah Mason bought 25 acres of land at Guilford, AC, in 1780.

On 3 Jan 1800 Jeremiah and his wife Ann sold 3 acres of the land he bought in 1780 in Guilford, AC, to Major Mason. (AC Deeds 1797 - 1800:449) Major Mason was mentioned as their son in this deed.

Jeremiah Mason and Ann (N) had the following children:

\+   60   i. Major[4] Mason Sr., b. c1778, d. Apr 1854.

61   ii. Sacker Mason, b. in AC c1780, m. 5 Dec 1808 (bond) in AC, Elizabeth 'Betsy' Ironmonger. Major Mason was the security on the M.L.B. of Sacker Mason and Elizabeth Ironmonger, alias Monger (widow of Zadock). (ACM)

Elizabeth , b. 1775 in AC, d. Feb 1823 in AC, dau. of Charles White and Catharine (N), m. c1800 in AC, Zadock Ironmonger. (Nottingham Wills:360 (will of father Charles White); MilesW&A:386 (Husband Zadock Monger's administration and estate settlement.); MilesW&A:352 (will of Elizabeth Mason)) (Assigning him as son of Jeremiah Mason is based soley on his 1808 M.L.B. wherein Major Mason was the security, suggesting that he was probably a brother of Major Mason.)

62   iii. Bridget Mason, b. in AC c1780. (MilesW&A:351 (will of Ann Mason)) She m. 5 Jun 1803 (bond), George Crosley in AC. Clement Bonwell was the security on the M.L.B. of George Crowley and Bridget Mason. (ACM)

George Crosley, farmer, b. c1781 in AC, d. 1 Dec 1859 in AC. He m. c1823, Caroline (N). He died of cancer at the age of 78 years. His son Thos. Crosly gave the information recorded in the Death Register. (FA CD309; WADR:136. (Death of Mary S. Saulsbury shows her as the dau. of Geo. & Caroline Crosley.)

Bridget was named in her mother's will 10 Jan 1805 in AC.(MilesW&A:351 (will of Ann Mason)) (Note: Since this was a verbal will, could the Custis have been Crosley? A Bridget Mason did marry George Crosley in 1803 and no other parents for her have been found and no other record of a Bridget Custis has been found to date.)

+   63   iv. Agnes Mason, b. c1790

Fourth Generation

30. **John**[4] **Mason** (Middleton[3], William[2], William[1]), b. in AC c1745. (Carey, *Mason Family of Kegotank*)

He m. c1765, **Barsheba (N)** (b. c1745 in AC). (Carey, *Mason Family of Kegotank*)

John bought land 1784 in AC. He was apparently the John Mason who bought 475 acres of Great Fox Island in 1784 (AC Deeds 1783-1788:181), and whose children, John Mason, George Mason, and Rachel Mister deeded *Fox Island* to their brother, Middleton Mason in 1810. (AC Deeds 1810-1812:97)

John Mason and Barsheba (N) had the following children:

64   i. John[5] Mason. b. in AC c1773. (Carey, *Mason Family of Kegotank*)

65   ii.   Middleton Mason, b. in AC c1775, d. before 1850.
(Carey, *Mason Family of Kegotank*)
He m. 1st 13 Apr 1802 (lic.) in SO Co., Rosey
Ellender Tyler (b. c1780). (Pollitt, *SO Co. Marriages 1796-1871*)
He m. 2nd 17 Mar 1842 in AC, Margaret R. Custis.
(ACM) He was shown only as Middleton Mason and she
as Margaret R. Ewell. Margaret R. Mason inherited an
interest in land at Chesconessex from her first husband,
Francis Onley, land that she and Middleton Mason sold
to John C. Wise in 1843. John C. Wise sold the same
land to Henry A. Wise, who became Governor of
Virginia in 1855. (Whitelaw:944, 945)
Margaret, b. c1775 in AC, the dau. of (f|o Margt &
Geo) Custis. She m. 1st c1800, Francis Onley. She m.
2nd 8 Jul 1833 (bond) in AC, John Ewell. John
Arlington was the security on the M.L.B. of John Ewell
and Margaret Onley, widow of Francis. (ACM) Another
record from this same source showed they m. 10 Jul
1833. (Powell, *AC 1830 Census*; MilesW&A:403 (will of Francis
Onley named wife's brother George Cusits))
Middleton Mason and wife Rosey sold *Foxes
Island* for $800 on 29 June 1830. (AC Deeds 1829-
1830:498) On the same date, he bought 130 acres "on
head of Chefssonefsex Creek" plus pasturage on
Tobacco Island, from Thomas Snead for $1005. (AC
Deeds:496)
Middleton Mason and son William bought a "Store
House" near Onancock in 1841. (AC Deeds 1842-1843:79)
66   iii.   George Mason, b. in AC c1778. (Carey, *Mason Family of
Kegotank*)
67   iv.   Rachel Mason, b. in AC c1780. (Carey, *Mason Family of
Kegotank*) She m. 21 Oct 1803 (bond) in AC, James F.
Mister (b. c1785). Robert Saulsbury was the security on
the M.L.B. (ACM; FA CD309) He m. 5 Feb 1812 (bond),
Catherine 'Caty' Salisbury. McKell Bonwell was the
security on the M.L.B. (ACM)

33. **James**[4] **Mason** (Middleton[3], William[2], William[1]), b. in AC c1750, d. Dec
1823. (Carey, *Mason Family of Kegotank*; MilesW&A:353 (will of James Mason))
He m. 30 Jun 1789 in AC, **Elizabeth 'Betty' Northam** (b. c1760 in AC).
He left a will dated 21 Oct 1822, probated in AC. To grandson James
Mason all my estate except that which my dau. Tinny Mason is to possess the lot
& houses whereon I now live &... to support herself & family; but if she is
wasteful or diminishes the value of the property, then to be sold for the benefit

of my grandson James Mason. My extr. to provide for my grandson James Mason & give him good schooling until age 21. Everything to grandson James Mason. Witnessed by Isaac Young, John Savage Jr. & William Powell. Codicil: 2 Jan 1823 - If dau. Tinny Mason does not care for lot & house or moves away, then lot & house to grandson mentioned in will. John Cole Jr. & George Warner Jr. extrs. Witnessed by Isaac Young, William Powell & John Savage Jr. Thorowgood Taylor & William Bird securities. (MilesW&A:353 (will of James Mason))

James Mason and Elizabeth 'Betty' Northam had the following children:

68   i. Elizabeth[5] Mason, b. in AC c1790, m. 19 Jan 1814 (bond) in AC, William Thornton (b. c1790 in AC). Jesse Clayton was the security on the M.L.B. (Carey, *Mason Family of Kegotank;* ACM)

69   ii. Matilda 'Tinny' Mason, b. in AC c1792. She m. 1st 17 Dec 1814 (bond) in AC, Bennett Mason. Covington Mason & James Mason were the securities on the M.L.B. of Bennett Mason and Tinney Mason, dau. of Jas. (Lewis, *AC MLB 1806-1835*

Bennett , b. c1792 in AC, son of Bennett Mason and Nanny Rodgers Clemmons. Bennett. (Carey, *Mason Family of Kegotank*) He d. by 15 June 1825, when Matilda Mason, widow of Bennet, was issued a bond to marry John Bayly. (p. 10) Bennet Mason and wife Tinny/ Matilda had at least two sons. Her father, James Mason d. testate in 1823, leaving his property to dau. Tinny Mason and her son, James Mason. (Wills 1823 - 1824:318) This James Mason m. Tinny/Matilda Jester by license of 25 Aug 1835. (WO Co. Mar Rec. 1795 - 1855:125) They sold part of his inherited land in 1836. (AC Deeds 1835 – 1837:462, 268, 583) On 10 Oct 1853, Bennet Mason and wife Sarah Ann, joined by Matilda Mason, "Widow of James, deceased," sold 9 acres of land that had been "devised to James Mason (brother of said Bennet) by James Mason whose will was recorded in 1823."

She m. 2nd 15 Jun 1825 (bond) in AC, John Bowman (b. c1795 in AC). Reuben Rew was the security on the M.L.B. of John Bowman of Levin and Matilda Mason, widow of Bennett. (ACM)

35. **William**[4] **Mason** (Bennett[3], William[2], William[1]), b. in AC c1765, d. Feb 1788, m. c1785, **Margaret 'Peggy'** (N) (b. c1765 in AC). (Nottingham Wills:370 (adm. of William Mason))

In 1787 William and his wife Margaret sold 10 acres of his father's land in AC. (AC Deeds 1788-1793:24)

On 26 Feb 1788 William 's estate was administered by James Benston in AC. Peggy Mason, widow of the deceased, relinquished her right to qualify.

Jabez Pitt & Thomas Sandford were the securities. (Nottingham Wills:370 (adm. of William Mason))

William Mason and Margaret 'Peggy' (N) had the following child:

70   i. Bennett[5] Mason , b. in AC c1786. (Orphan's Accts, 1780-1805:53)

36. **Bennett[4] Mason** (Bennett[3], William[2], William[1]), b. in AC c1768, d. Mar 1816. (Carey, *Mason Family of Kegotank;* W&A:351 (will of Bennett Mason Sr.))

He m. 11 Mar 1799 (bond) in AC, Rachel Duncan (b. c1780 in AC), dau. of James Duncan. Solomon Johnson was security on the M.L.B. (ACM; MilesW&A:179 (will of James Duncan))

Benett Mason Sr. of Acc Parish left a will dated 10 Mar 1816, probated 26 Mar 1816 in AC. To son William Mason all the land where I now live & all other lands & Negro Edmund & woman Lucy. To dau. Harriet Major Mason... & my Negro woman Keziah, girl Bett, girl Charity &... &... that was her mother's. To Pamela Andrews Mason,.. & Negro woman Judah & Leah & girl Love &,.. that was her mother's & also ½ of a note I gave James Duncan Sr. dec'd which he in his will gave to my 2 daus. to be divided, now in the hands of Jesse Duncan his extr. To dau. Harriet M. Mason the other ½ of that note. Jacob Northam to be guardian to son William Mason until he comes of age. Friend Arthur Watson to be guardian to dau. Harriet M. Mason until she comes of age & friend Southey Northam to be guardian to my dau. Pamela A. Mason until lawful age. Friends Southey Northam, Jacob Northam & Arthur Watson extrs. Witnessed by Johannas Bird, Edmund Duncan & Southey Northam. Nicholas P. Godwin & Isaiah Johnson securities. (MilesW&A:351 (will of Bennett Mason Sr.))

Bennett Mason and Rachel Duncan had the following children:

71   i. Pamela Andrews[5] Mason, b. in AC c1800, d. in 1850. (MilesW&A:179 (adm. of Permelia Duncan)) She must have died months before the administration of her estate, as she was not listed in the 1850 census. She m. 26 Nov 1821 (bond) in AC, James K. Duncan. Thorowgood Taylor and Isoial Johnson were the securities on the M.L.B. of James Duncan, orphan of Jesse and Parmelia A. Mason, orphan of Bennet. (ACM)

James, b. c1800 in AC, d. Jan 1846, son of Jesse Duncan and Kesziah Taylor. (ACM; MilesW&A:179 (will of James K. Duncan))

Pamela was named in her grandfather's will 6 Feb 1813 in AC. (MilesW&A:179 (will of James Duncan)) She was named in her husband's will 7 Jul 1840 in AC. (MilesW&A:179 (will of James K. Duncan))

On 30 Dec 1850 Pamela's estate was administered in AC by William S. Horsey. (MilesW&A:179 (adm. of Permelia Duncan)) James H. Fletcher & Thomas W. Twiford were securities.

72   ii. Harriet Major Mason, b. in AC in AC c1805, d. before
          1836. She m. 26 Feb 1827 (bond) in AC, William
          Godwin. Nathaniel Fitchett & Felix Bull were the
          securities on the M.L.B. of William Godwin of
          Edmund and Harriet Mason of Bennett. She was not
          named in the 20 Aug 1836 will of her husband William
          Godwin. (Lewis, *AC MLB 1806-1835*); MilesW&A:231 (will of
          William Godwin); ACM)
          William , b. c1807 in AC, d. Aug 1836, son of
          Edmund Godwin and Anne Gray 'Nancy' Godwin.
          (Chesser, *Godwin Ancestry*; ACM; MilesW&A:231 (will of William
          Godwin))
          Harriet was named in her grandfather's will 6 Feb
          1813 in AC. (MilesW&A:179 (will of James Duncan)
73   iii. William Mason, b. in AC c1810. He m. c1830, Mary J.
          (N). (MACM:230 (marriage of Samuel H. Matthews and Margaret
          Mason))

38. Bennett⁴ Mason (Edmund³, Bennett², William¹), b. in AC c1757, d. Jun 1808.
(Carey, *Mason Family of Kegotank*)
He m. c1780 in AC, his first cousin, **Nanny Rodgers Clemmons** (b. c1760
in AC), dau. of Stephen Clemmons and Susannah Mason. (Nottingham Wills:360
(will of Stephen Clemmons))
His uncle John Bundick was appointed his guardian on 25 Oct 1768. (AC
OB 1768 - 1769:205). Bennet Mason chose Jeremiah Mason (another uncle) for his
guardian on 31 July 1771. (AC OB 1770 - 1773:215).
He left a will dated 9 Feb 1808, probated 27 Jun 1808 in AC. To wife
Nancy,.. To eldest son Ayres part of my plantation whereon I now reside
adjoining the Market Road & Guy's land & also a wood lands adjoining John
Laws & Joseph Brimer's line. To my 3rd son Covington the residue of my
plantation whereon I reside lying between my ditch & Wallops Road. To 2nd
son Teackle all the land called *Clemons' Place* containing 42 ½ acres. To son
Ayres,.. To son Teackle,.. To son Covington $30 for a horse. Sell all the land I
purchased of Caleb Brimer & estate of Kesire Stephens & the Andrews land &
the proceeds to youngest son Bennett. To son Bennett all the residue of my
personal estate. My son Ayres is to board & school my son Bennett for 2 years
at his expense. Friend Samuel Crippen extr. Witnessed by Samuel Crippen,
David James & James Mason. Jonathan Mears & Henry Custis securities. (Note:
It was his his father's land he divided between sons Ayres and Covington.)
(MilesW&A:351 (will of Bennett Mason Sr.))
Bennett Mason and Nanny Rodgers Clemmons had the following children:
74   i. Ayres⁵ Mason, b. in AC c1782, d, before Mar 1823. On
          18 Mar 1823, Polly Mason, widow of Ayres, m.
          William Johnson, widower. He m. 18 Jan 1808 (lic.) in
          WO Co., Mary 'Polly' Aydelotte (b. c1795). (ACM;
          Powell, *WO Co Marriages 1795-1865*)

Mary m. 2nd 18 Mar 1823 (bond) in AC, William Johnson 18 Mar 1823 (bond) in AC. Walter Douglass & Henry Harvey were the securities on the M.L.B. of William Johnson, widower, and Polly Mason, widow of Ayres. (ACM)

On 25 Nov 1816 Ayres Mason and his wife Mary sold the 50 acres he had inherited, to Galen Hinmon for $1,525. (AC Deeds 1815 - 1817:464) There is no evidence that Ayres Mason had children.

75   ii. Teackle Mason, b. in AC c1785, d. Oct 1821. (MilesW&A:354 (will of Teackle Mason)) He m. three times. He m. 1st 27 Jul 1807 (bond) in AC, Sally Savage (b. c1785, d. 1812). Richard R. Savage was the security on the M.L.B. of Teackle Mason and Sally Savage. (ACM)

He m. 2nd 17 Mar 1812 (bond) in AC, Hester 'Hetty' James (b. c1780, d. 1816). Dennis Bloxom & Coventon Mason were the securties on the M.L.B. (ACM) Hester was the dau. of Robert James and Mary (N). ((Brother's Will; Acc Land Caus 1821-1826:289) Dennis Bloxom and Coventon Mason were the securities on the 1812 AC M.L.B. of Teackle Mason and Hetty James. On 27 Nov 1821 it was determined that Hetty Mason, formerly Hetty James, late of this county, d. in 1817 leaving one child named Delight Mason.

Hetty and her husband Teackle Mason owned 35 acres of land on Kegotank Creek, which had been left to her by her brother William James. Delight Mason d. intestate, an infant, and without issue in 1819, and Teackle Mason d. in 1821. Elizabeth Warner, wife of George Warner Jr., was a whole sister. David James, deceased, was a whole brother and left children Elizabeth, Mary and Sarah Ann James. Robert J. Broadwater, who d. in 1820 intestate, was a half brother and left children Rosanna, Sarah and Robert J. Broadwater. Nancy Savage, deceased, was a whole sister, and left children Mary Anne and Sally C. Savage (AC Land Causes, 1821-26:289)

He m. 3rd 21 May 1816 (lic.), in WO Co., Nancy Tunnell (b. c1795 in AC). (Powell, *WO Co Marriages 1795-1865*)

Teackle was listed as a head of household in the census of 1820 in Acc Parish, AC. (Powell, *AC 1800, 1810, 1820 Census*) He was shown as Teackle Mason, head of a household, aged 26 to 45 years. There was a male in the household aged 10 to 16 years. If this male were a son by his first marriage, it appears he would have been mentioned in his father's will.

He left a will dated 1 Oct 1821, probated 29 Oct 1821 in AC. My black girl Esther to be free at age 21 & her increase to serve my wife Nancy Mason until they are age 21. The whole of my estate to wife & my land containing 35 acres to be sold. William Nock of Z. extr. Witnessed by Walter M. Custis & Nancy Mason. (MilesW&A:354 (will of Teackle Mason))

76   iii.   Covington Mason, b. in AC c1787, d. Dec 1831. (MilesW&A:352 (adm. of Covington Mason))

Covington sold land 5 Oct 1821 in AC. No record can be found of Covington Mason having married. His name did not appear as head of a household in census records. No wife signed deeds with him in 1810, 1815, 1816 and 1821. He sold his land on 5 Oct 1821 to Jackson Laws. (AC Deeds 1821 - 1822:381)

On 26 Dec Covington 's estate was administered by Samuel C. Savage. (MilesW&A:352 (adm. of Covington Mason)) James Justice (of R.) & David D. Abbott were securities.

77   iv.   Bennett Mason, b. in AC c1792. (Carey, *Mason Family of Kegotank*) He m. 17 Dec 1814 (bond) in AC, Matilda 'Tinny' Mason. Covington Mason & James Mason were the securities on the M.L.B. of Bennett Mason and Tinney Mason, dau. of Jas. (Lewis, *Acc MLB 1806-1835*)

Matilda, b. c1792 in AC, dau. of James Mason and Elizabeth 'Betty' Northam. (MilesW&A:353 (will of James Mason); Lewis, *AC MLB 1806-1835*) She m. 15 June 1825 (bond) in AC, John Bowman. Reuben Rew was the security on the M.L.B. of John Bowman of Levin and Matilda Mason, widow of Bennett. (ACM)

Bennet Mason, Junr. chose Covington Mason as guardian on 25 June 1810. (AC OB 1808 - 1810:167). He was deceased by 15 June 1825, when Matilda Mason, widow of Bennet, was issued a bond to marry John Bayly. (p. 10) Bennet Mason and wife Tinny/Matilda had at least two sons. Her father, James Mason d. testate in 1823, leaving his property to dau. Tinny Mason and her son, James Mason. (Wills 1823 - 1824:318) This James Mason m. Tinny/Matilda Jester by license of 25 Aug 1835. (WO Co. Mar Rec. 1795 - 1855:125) They sold part of his inherited land in 1836. (AC Deeds 1835 –

108

1837:462, 268, 583) On 10 Oct 1853, Bennet Mason and wife Sarah Ann, joined by Matilda Mason, widow of James, deceased, sold 9 acres of land that had been devised to James Mason (brother of said Bennet) by James Mason whose will was recorded in 1823.

40. **William**[4] **Mason** (Edmund[3], Bennett[2], William[1]), b. in AC c1760, d. Feb 1806. (MilesW&A:355 (will of William Mason)) He m. c1785, **Esther Anderson** (b. c1765 in AC, d. Dec 1808). (MilesW&A:352 (adm. of Esther Mason))

William appears on the list of tithables in AC for 1787. William Mason was listed next to his brother, Bennet Mason, on the 1787 tax list for AC.

William was listed as a head of household in the census of 1800 in Acc Parish, AC. The 1800 census shows him living near brother Bennet Mason at Kegotank, in Acc Parish. His age was here given as 26 to 45. He had two males in his household under 10 years and one male 10 to 16 years of age. The only female in the household, his wife, was over 45 years.

On 30 Apr 1805 William Mason bought 3, acres of land from John Laws and wife Adah for £13.16. (AC Deeds 1804 - 1807:432) The deed shows this tract beginning at Bennet Mason's gate and running east on the Market Road (present road from Nelsonia to Modest Town), to the land of Robert James, deceased.

He left a will dated 13 Nov 1805. probated 24 Feb 1806, in AC. To wife Esther Mason all my lands & property as long as she lives my widow or dies & then the land to son Bagwell Mason & my property to the rest of my children William Mason, Samuel Mason & Sally Mason. Son Bagwell Mason extr. Witnessed by Levin Bloxom, Dennis Bloxom & Bennett Mason. (MilesW&A:355 (will of William Mason)) Bagwell Mason & the widow both relinquished & Levin Bloxom became the admr. with John Cole & Bennett Mason as securities.

William Mason and Esther Anderson had the following children:

78   i.   Bagwell Anderson[5] Mason, b in AC 15 Feb 1788, d. 22 Aug 1855 in Streator, IL. His body was interred in Streator, IL. (Family Records) He m. 1st 14 Mar 1810 (lic.) in WO Co., Elizabeth 'Betsy' Tarr (b. c1790, d. before 9 Dec 1825). (Powell, *WO Co Marriages 1795-1865*) John Tarr, who d. testate in WO Co. by 11 Feb 1826, left property to Gatty and Sally Mayson. (WOW MM, 1822 - 1833:200) They were likely daus. of his dau. Elizabeth Tarr (dau-in-law?), who had m. Bagwell Mason in 1808. It appears their mother was deceased by 9 Dec 1825, when John Tarr wrote his will.

He m. 2nd c1821,Nancy B. Butler (b. 1801 in Baltimore, MD, d. 1863. Her body was interred in Streator, IL. (Family Records)

Bagwell was named as administrator of the estate of Esther Maston on 26 Dec 1808 in AC. (MilesW& A:352

(adm. of Esther Mason)) Samuel Cirppen & John Laws were
securities.

On 26 Jun 1809 an account of the sales, audit and
settlement of the estate of Esther Mason, deceased, was
returned by Bagwell Mason and recorded. (AC OB 1807 -
1809:322) On the same date, a deed of conveyance was
also recorded, from Bagwell Mason of AC to Ayres
Mason, for 3 acres for £51. (AC Deeds 1807 - 1810:292) The
plot was bordered on the southwest by the lands of the
said Ayres Mason, northeast by John Laws, and
southeast by Robert Savage. The deed was witnessed
by Samuel Crippen and George Warner, Junr. Bagwell
Mason signed the deed alone, without a wife's co-
signature.

Bagwell Mason, aged 26 to 45, was listed as a head
of household in the census of 1810 in WO Co.
(Obviously he was only 22 years of age in 1810.) There
were two children in his household, a male under 10
years and a female under 10, suggesting he had married
a widow with two young children.

Bagwell sold land 1 Dec 1812 in AC. It is apparent
that Bagwell Mason was married when his mother's
estate was administered to him on 26 Dec 1808 and
when he sold his father's land to his cousin, Ayres
Mason, on 26 June 1809. Since this deed did not give
therefore a clear title, another deed was recorded on 1
Dec 1812. (AC Deeds 1812 – 1815:32) This deed was from
Bagwell Mason and wife Elizabeth to Ayres Mason, for
3 acres (the same land) for $170. It was signed by both
Bagwell Mason and Betsy Mason.

Bagwell was listed as a head of household in the
census of 1820 in WO Co. He was again listed as 26 to
45 years by the WO Co. census of 1820. He then had a
male under 10 years in his household and two females
under 10 years. His wife was over 45. He was not listed
in either AC or WO Co. in 1830.

WO Co. deeds have been searched from 1800 to
1834 for a Bagwell Mason buying or selling land or
personal property in Maryland. His name does not
appear in these records. Neither does his name appear
in the WO Co. Index to Estates, 1742 - 1908. Family
records give the information that Bagwell A. Mason
left WO Co., soon after the death of his first wife,
apparently in late 1820. He m. 2nd c1821, Nancy B.

Butler (1801 - 1863), b. in Baltimore, MD. He and his family moved first to OH and then to Streator, IL, where he is buried with his second wife..

79   ii.   William Mason, b. in AC c1795, d. before 20 Sep 1806.

80   iii. Samuel Mason, b. in AC c1797.

On 30 Jun 1806 Esther Mason was appointed guardian to William Mason, Sally Mason, and Samuel Mason, orphans of William Mason. (AC OB 1806 - 1807:116) No other record has been found of him in AC or WO Co.

81   iv.   Sally Mason, b. in AC c1802.

On 30 Jun 1806 Esther Mason was appointed guardian to William Mason, Sally Mason, and Samuel Mason, orphans of William Mason. (AC OB 1806 - 1807:116)

41. **Bagwell[4] Mason** (Edmund[3], Bennett[2], William[1]), b. in AC c1762, d. before 1800, m. c1790, **Mary (N)** (b. c1770 in AC).

The name of this Bagwell Mason does not appear again in AC records after his father's settlement. He was not named on the 1787 or the 1792 tax list as were his brothers. The 1800 census gives the names of brothers Bennet Mason, Senr and William Mason at Kegotank. With them is listed a Mary Mason, who was apparently Bagwell Mason's widow. Her household included one male, under 10 years. A reasonable supposition is that this son was named Bagwell Mason for his father and was the Bagwell Mason who m. Ann Townsend by bond of 15 March 1821. (WO Co. Mar. Rec. 1795 - 1865:79)

The inventory, appraisal, and division of the estate of Edmund Mason was recorded on 27 May 1770. (Wills 1767 – 1772:412, 413, 414, 4l5) One third went to an unnamed widow and the balance was divided equally between five children: Susanna, Bennett, Ann, William and Bagwell..

Bagwell Mason and Mary (N) had the following child:

82   i.   Bagwell[5] Mason , b. in AC c1795, m. 13 Mar 1821 (lic.) in WO Co., Ann Townsend (b. c1800), (Powell, *WO Co Marriages 1795-1865)*

43. **William[4] Mason** (Thomas[3], Bennett[2], William[1]), b. in AC c1745, d. Sep 1806.

He m. c1770, **Rachel (N)** (b. c1755 in AC.

He left a will dated 16 Jun 1806, probated 30 Sep 1806 in AC. To dau. Sarah Pitts £5. To dau. Polly Sterling £5. To son John Mason Negro man Moses, woman Letty & her child Candis. To son John,.. To dau. Susanna Mister Negro boy Simon & girl Sarah. To dau. Betsy Rodgers Negro boy Peter & girl Lucy &,.. To dau. Frances Custis Colonna Negro man Isaac & boy Moses. To wife Rachel Negro girl Tamer &,.. Remainder to wife Rachel, son John Mason, daus. Susanna Mister, Betsy Rodgers & Frances Custis Colonna. Friend John Rodgers

Sr. extr. Witnessed by Peter Rodgers, Peter Cutler & Edward Mason.
(MilesW&A:355 (will of William Mason Sr.))

William Mason and Rachel (N) had the following children:

83   i. Sarah[5] Mason, b. in AC c1772, m. before 16 Jun 1806, (N) Pitts (b. c1770 in AC).

84   ii. Polly Mason, b. in AC c1774, m. before 16 Jun 1806, (N) Sterling (b. c1770 in AC).

85   iii. John Mason, b. in AC c1776, d. Oct 1807. (MilesW&A:353 (adm. of John Mason)) He m.11 Nov 1802 (bond) in AC, Margaret 'Peggy' Onley. Major Rodgers was the security on the M.L.B. of John Mason and Margaret Onley. (ACM)

Margaret, b. c1780 in AC, m. 13 Feb 1809 (bond) in AC, William Charnock. Owen Charnock was the security on the M.L.B. of William Charnock and Peggy Mason. (ACM)

On 27 Oct 1807 John Joynes was named to settle the estate of John Mason. John Bull Jr. & Ephraim Outten were securities. (MilesW&A:353 (adm. of John Mason))

John's estate was settled 1 Sep 1812 in AC. (MilesW&A:353 (settlement of John Mason)) 13 Nov 1807 (Invy & Sale), No Date (Audit), 1 Sep 1812 (Rec'd) - John J. Joynes extr. Buyers: widow & Daniel Rone (Negro) Named in settlement: Rachel Mason & Peggy Mason. Cash received by John Rodgers for his part of his father's estate. Auditors: John Leatherbury & George Scarburgh. (Note: Rachel could have been his mother and Peggy could have been his wife.)

86   iv. Susanna Mason, b. in AC c1778, m. before 16 Jun 1806, (N) Mister (b. c1775 in AC).

87   v. Elizabeth 'Betsy' Mason, b. in AC c1780, m. 11 Nov 1802 (bond) in AC, Major Rogers (b. c1780 in AC). John Mason was the security on the M.L.B. (ACM)

88   vi. Frances Custis Mason, b. in AC c1782, m. before 16 Jun 1806 (N) Colonna (b. c1780).

89   vii. Walter? Mason, b. in AC c1785. (Carey, *Mason Family of Kegotank*)

44. **George[4] Mason** (Thomas[3], Bennett[2], William[1]), b. in AC c1750, d. Oct 1815. (Carey, *Mason Family of Kegotank;* MilesW&A:352 (will of George Mason, St. George Parish))

He married **Sophia 'Suffiah' (N)** c1775 (MilesW&A:352 (will of George Mason, St. George Parish)) Sophia, b. c1750 in AC, d. Oct 1837. (MilesW&A:354 (will of Sophiah (Sophine) Mason))

George Mason, St. George Parish, left a will dated 25 May 1812, probated 30 Oct 1815, in AC. To wife Suffiah Mason the whole of my moveable estate during her life time & at her death my moveable estate to my children then living. To son Edmund Mason the whole of my lands & if he dies without heirs, then to dau. Mary Mason. To dau. Peggy Edwards,.. To dau. Mary Mason £20. Wife Suffiah Mason extr. Witnessed by Nathaniel Badger, Mary Badger & Rosey Watkinson. (MilesW&A:352 (will of George Mason, St. George Parish))

George Mason had the following children:

90   i.   George[5] Mason, b. in AC c1768. (Carey, *Mason Family of Kegotank*; FA CD309) He m. 1st 1 Oct 1803 (bond) in AC, Scarburgh Turner (b. c1780). William Mister was the security on the M.L.B. (ACM)

He m. 2nd 17 Aug 1805 (bond) in NC, Susanna 'Sukey' Wilkins (b. c1780 in NC, d. Aug 1810). Johannes Wise was the security on the M.L.B. of George Mason and Susana Wilkins. They were married by J. Elliott. (Mihalyka, *NC Marriages 1660-1854*) Susanna was the dau. of Henry Wilkins and Anne Drummond. (Nottingham, *Acc Land Causes, 1728-1825*:101 (Wilkins vs. Northam &c., partition suit))

He m. 3rd 2 Dec 1848 in AC, Sarah Phillips. (ACM) George Mason Jr. (Sr.?), age 82, was listed with his son in the census of 1850 in St. George Parish, AC in HH#989 headed by Edward Mason, a 33 year old farmer. (FA CD309)

91   ii.   Nancy Mason, b. in AC c1780. (Carey, *Mason Family of Kegotank*)

George Mason and Sophia 'Suffiah' (N) had the following children:

92   iii.   Esther Mason, b. in AC c1776, d. Dec 1815. (MilesW&A:354 (will of Sophiah (Sophine) Mason); MilesW&A:218 (adm. of Esther Fox)) She m. c1795 in AC, Golden Fox (b. c1760 in AC, d. Apr 1807 in AC). (MilesW&A:218 (adm. of Golden Fox))

On 30 Oct 1809 Esther Fox was named as the widow for 1/3 of the estate of Golden Fox. (MilesW&A:218 (esttlement of Golden Fox))

On 25 Dec 1815 Esther 's estate was administered in AC by William Fox. Zorobabel Mason, John Mason & Charles Mason were the securities. (MilesW&A:218 (adm. of Esther Fox)) Esther's estate was settled 30 Aug 1816 in AC. (MilesW&A:218 (settlement of Esther Fox)) 28 Dec 1815 (Inventory & Sale), 25 Dec 1815 (Order to Audit), 30 Aug 1816 (Rec'd) - William Fox admr. Buyers: William Fox, John Fox, Sally Fox, Nancy Fox & Thomas Fox. Auditors: H. G. Copes & John Wise. Since Sophiah Mason named a granddau (probably great-granddau) Mary Fox, and since James Fox had a dau. Mary, who would have be about age 12 at the time, it is assumed that James' mother Esther was a dau. of Sophiah.

93   iv. Margaret 'Peggy' Mason, b. in AC c1785. (MilesW&A: 352 (will of George Mason, St. George Parish); 354 (will of Sophiah (Sophine) Mason)). She m. 29 Feb 1808 (bond) in AC, William Edwards (b. c1780). William Badger was the security on the M.L.B. of William Edwards and Peggy Mason. (ACM)

Margaret was named in her father's will [see above] and her mother's will dated 10 Oct 1835 in AC. (MilesW&A:354 (will of Sophiah (Sophine) Mason))

94   v. Edmund C. Mason, b. in AC 8 Sep 1793, d. 4 May 1849, bur. Mason Cem, Melfa. (MLAC; MilesW&A:352 (will of George Mason, St. George Parish; MLAC) His tombstone shows him as Edmund C. Mason, the son of Geo. & Sophia Mason, who d. 4 May 1849 at the age of 55 years, 7 mos., 26 days. He m. 4 Nov (bond) in AC, Elizabeth 'Betsy' James. (ACM) Zorobabel Chandler was the security on the M.L.B. of Edmund Mason and Betsy James of Patience.

Elizabeth, b. 10 Aug 1789 in AC, d. 16 Nov 1868, dau. of William James and Patience (N). She d. of dropsy at the age of 78 years, 3 mos., 6 days, bur. in Mason Cem, Melfa. Her son Geo. W. Mason gave the information recorded in the death register. (MLAC; MilesW&A:283 (will of Patience James); WADR)

Her tombstone shows her as Elizabeth J. Mason, the wife of Edmond C. Mason & the dau. of Wm. & Patience James. (10 Aug 1789 - 16 Nov 1868)

Edmund was named in his father's will [see above] and extr. in mother's will dated 10 Oct 1835 in AC. (MilesW&A:354 (will of Sophiah (Sophine) Mason))

He d. leaving a will dated 25 Feb 1848, probated 28 May 1849 in AC. To my wife Elizabeth Mason all my estate & at her death or marriage ¼ of my property & land to the hands of my sons George W. & Zorobabel C. Mason to pay over to my dau. Susan J. Parker as she calls for it. ¾ of all my real & personal estate to my 2 sons George W. Mason & Zorobabel C. Mason by their paying my son William J. Mason ¼ of my real & personal estate. My sons George W. Mason & Zorobabel C. Mason, extrs. Witnessed by John S.

Gibb, Edmond Leatherbury & Mary H. Parker. John B. Bundick & John E. Ames, securities. (MilesW&A:352 (will of Edmund Mason))

95   vi. Mary A. 'Molly' Mason, b. in AC 24 Jul 1798, d. 13 Jul 1881. (ACM; MLAC) Her body was interred in James Place, Locustville, AC. (MLAC) She m. 29 Jan 1816, Thomas James (b. c1793 in AC), son of William James and Patience (N). Levin James and Robert Kellam were the securities on the M.L.B. of Thomas James of Wm. and Molly Mason of Geo. (ACM)

Mary was named in her father's will [see above] and in her mother's will dated 10 Oct 1835 in AC. (MilesW&A:354 (will of Sophiah (Sophine) Mason))

Mary was listed as a head of household in the census of 1850 in St. George Parish, AC. (FA CD309) She was shown as Mary James the head of HH#1000, age 50 with real estate valued at $5,000. Listed with her were the following of the James family: Emma, age 17; Margaret, age 15; and Sarah A., age 12.

45. **Caleb[4] Mason** (Thomas[3], Bennett[2], William[1]), b. in AC c1750, d. c1805.

On 30 Oct 1759 Caleb Mason, orphan of Tabitha, aged c9, was bound out to Peter Hack, shoemaker. (AC OB 1753 - 1763:313) There seems little doubt that Caleb was Thomas Mason's son, for the Hacks were of Hacks Neck, near Onancock Creek, and in the early 1800s a Bennet Mason of Caleb and Thomas Mason of Caleb were both issued marriage bonds. (MLB 1806 - 1832:93).

Caleb appears on the list of tithables in AC for 1783 and 1786. Caleb was listed as a head of household in the census of 1800 in AC.

Caleb Mason had the following children:

96   i. Bennett[5] Mason, b. in AC c1775, d. Sep 1810. (MilesW&A:351 (adm. of Bennett Mason)) He m. 28 Nov 1805 in AC, Aroda 'Arody' Heath (b. c1780 in AC). William Doughty was the security on the M.L.B. of Bennet Mason of Caleb and Aroda Heath. (Nottingham, *AC MLB 1774-1806*)

Bennett 's estate was administered 24 Sep 1810 in AC by Arody Mason. George S. Fisher & James Hornsby were securities. (MilesW&A:351 (adm. of Bennett Mason))

97   ii. Thomas Mason, b. in AC c1780. He m. 12 Dec 1816 (bond) in AC, Ann 'Nancy' Snead b. c1790), dau. of Bowdoin Snead and Polly Kellam. Bowdoin Snead was the security on the M.L.B. of Thomas Mason of Caleb and Ann Snead of Bowdoin. (ACM)

Nancy m. 12 Jan 1830 (bond), Major Budd.
Edward Gunter was the security on the M.L.B. of
Major Budd and Nancy Mason, widow of Thomas.
(ACM)

46. **Adam⁴ Mason** (Thomas³, Bennett², William¹), b. in AC c1752, d. Dec 1833.
(Carey, *Mason Family of Kegotank;* MilesW&A:351 (will of Adam Mayson))
He d. leaving a will dated 29 Jul 1833, probated 30 Dec 1833 in AC. To
Nancy Shepherd 1/3 of my estate & the other 2/3 to son William Mason. The
money which will be received for my soldier's pay which is $96 a year to John
G. Joynes. Witnessed by John C. Kellam, John Coleburn & Thomas Coleburn.
(MilesW&A:351 (will of Adam Mayson))
Adam Mason had the following child:
98   i. William⁵ Mason, b. in AC c1776. (FA CD309) He m. 25
1806 (bond) in AC, Esther Howard (b. c1785 in AC).
John Howarth and Edward Mason were the securities
on the M.L.B. of William Mason and Esther Howarth.
(Note: It is assumed that Howarth was Howard.) (ACM)
William was listed with his son in the census of
1850 in St. George Parish, AC. (FA CD309) He was
shown as Wm. Mason, age 74 in HH#486 headed by
Stephen Mason, a 40 year old farmer.

47. **Thomas⁴ Mason** (Thomas³, Bennett², William¹), b. in AC c1760, d. Feb
1822 in AC. (Nottingham Wills:355 (will of Thomas Mason Sr.))
He m. c1790, **Nancy Edwards** (b. c1768 in AC), dau. of David Edwards.
(Nottingham Wills:451 (will of Sacker Edwards); Nottingham Wills:382 (will of David Edwards))
He left a will dated 29 Jan 1822 in AC, probated 25 Feb 1822 in AC. At the
death of my wife Nancy the land whereon I now live (which I heired from my
son William to whom it was devised by Sacker Edwards dec'd) to my sons
Bagwell C. Mason & Thomas Mason,.. To dau. Betsey,.. Remainder to my 2
sons Bagwell Custis Mason & Thomas Mason & dau. Betsey Mason. Friend
Levin S. Joynes & son Bagwell C. Mason extrs. Witnessed by Levin S. Joynes,
Smith R. Carmine & John Edwards. John Hargis & John A. Edwards, securities.
(Nottingham Wills:355 (will of Thomas Mason Sr.))
Thomas Mason and Nancy Edwards had the following children:
99   i. William⁵ Mason, b. in AC c1792, d. before 29 Jan
1822. (Nottingham Wills:451 (will of Sacker Edwards))
William was named in his uncle's will 5 Nov 1797
in AC. (Nottingham Wills:451 (will of Sacker Edwards)) He was
shown as William Mason, son of my sister Nancy
Mason & her husband Thomas Mason.
100   ii. Bagwell Custis Mason, b. in AC c1800. (FA CD309) He
m. 1ˢᵗ 10 Oct 1831 (bond) in AC, Margaret East.
Edmund Mason was the security on the M.L.B. of
Bagwell C. Mason and Margaret East of Severn. (ACM)

Margaret, b. c1810 in AC, was the dau of Severn East and Tabitha 'Tabby' Phillips. (MilesW&A:182 (will of Tabitha East); ACM)

Bagwell m. 2nd 24 Nov 1851 in AC, Anna Simpson Arlington. (ACM) He was shown as Bagwell C. Mason, widower, and she was shown as Ann Rayfield, widow of Levi.

Anna, b. 24 Feb 1812 in AC, was the dau. of Thomas B. Arlington and Elizabeth Simpson. She m. 1st 7 Jan 1829 (bond) ni AC, Levi R. Rayfield. Henry P. Mister was security on the M.L.B. of Levi R. Rayfield and Ann S. Arlington of Tho. Anna d. 21 July 1852, bur. in Arlington Plot, Mt. Nebo, Slutkill Neck, AC. Her tombstone shows her as Ann S. Mason, 24 Feb 1812 - 21 Jul 1852, erected by her grandmother Hannah Topping. (MLAC; ACM)

Bagwell was listed as a head of household in the census of 1850 in St. George Parish, AC. (FA CD309) He was shown as Bagwell C. Mason, the head of HH#520. a 50 year old farmer with real estate valued at $300. Listed with him were the following Masons: Sarah A., age 18; William T., a 16 year old student; Susan J., age 13; Caroline, age 10; John, age 5; and Mary, age 3.

Bagwell was named as administrator of the estate of Ann R. Mason on 26 Jul 1852 in AC. William H. Belote & John E. Ames were securities. (MilesW&A:351 (adm. of Ann R. Mason))

Bagwell C. Mason was listed as a head of household in the census of 1860 in Savageville P.O., St. George Parish, AC (HH#659), a 61 year old farmer with real estate valued at $6,000 and personal property valued at $400. Listed with him were the following Masons: William T., a 26 year old carpenter; Susan J., age 22; Caroline, age 20; John, age 14; and Mary, age 13. Also listed was Geo. Coruthus, age 12; and Peter Bevans, age 14 and black.

101   iii. Thomas Mason, b. in AC c1805. He m. 1 Aug 1838 (bond), in AC, Ann C. 'Nancy' Phillips. Bagwell C. Mason was the security on the M.L.B. of Thomas Mason and Ann Phillips of William. (ACM)

Ann, b. 22 Jan 1809 in AC, d. 6 Feb 1889 in St. George Parish, AC, dau. of William Phillips and Mary 'Molly' Savage. (MLAC; MilesW&A:426 (will of William Phillips Sr.); ACM; WADR) Her AC death record shows her

as Nancy Mason, who d. 5 Feb 1889 (one day before
the date on the tombstone) of pneumonia at the age of
79 years and 10 mos. She was the dau. of Wm. Phillips,
born in AC and a widowed housekeeper. Her son James
H. Mason gave the information for the death register.
Her body was interred in John Phillips Plot, Melfa,
AC. (MLAC) Her tombstone shows her as Nancy G.
Mason, the wife of Thomas Mason.

102   iv. Elizabeth 'Betsey' Mason, b. in AC c1811, m. 9 Dec
1837 (bond) in AC, Samuel S. Tignal. Edward Poulson
was the security on the M.L.B. (ACM)
Samuel, b. 1808 in AC, d. 23 Jul 1895 in AC, was
son of John Tignal and Mary (N). (MLAC; MACM) He m.
4 Feb 1869 in AC, Mary Anne Lewis. (MACM) He was
shown as Samuel Tignal, a 45 year old widowed
farmer, the son of John & Mary Tignal and she was
shown as Mary Johnson, a 28 year old widow of Alfred
F. Johnson & the dau. of Samuel K. & Sallie Thomas
Lewis. They were married by Edward S. Grant. Sam'l
Tignall d. of paralysis at the age of 86 years. He was a
farmer and the husband of Mary Tignall. His son (N)
Tignall gave the information. (WADR) His body was
interred in Onancock Cem, AC. (MLAC) His tombstone
shows him as Samuel Tignal, husband of Mary A.
Tignal.
Elizabeth was listed with her husband in the census
of 1850 in St. George Parish, AC. She was shown as
Betsey Tignal, age 39 in HH#1181 headed by Sam'l
Tignal, a 39 year old carpenter with real estate valued
at $1,000. (FA CD309)

48. **Zorobabel 'Babel'**[4] **Mason** (Thomas[3], Bennett[2], William[1])(Carey, *Mason Family
of Kegotank*), b. in AC c1765, d. Oct 1825. (MilesW&A:355 (will of Zorobabel Mason))
He m. 1st 23 Jan 1790 (bond) in AC, **Ann 'Nancy' Bull** (b. c1770 in AC).
(ACM)
He m. 2nd 5 Feb 1817 (bond) in AC, **Sally Johnson** (b. c1780 in AC).
William Kendall was the security on the M.L.B. of Zorobabel Mason, widower,
and Sally Kelly, widow. (ACM)
Sally m. 4 Mar 1800 in AC, **Richardson(?) Kelly**. (ACM)
On 25 Dec 1815 Zorobabel Mason, John Mason and Charles Mason were
the securities on the administration of Esther Fox. (MilesW&A:218 (adm. of Esther
Fox))
He left a will dated Jun 1821 in AC, probated 31 Oct 1825 in AC.
Everything to 2 sons John Mason & Charles Mason who were extrs. Witnessed
by Thomas Cropper & William Harvey. Proved by Thomas Cropper who made

oath that the will was executed in the month of May or Jun 1821. John Mason relinquished his right as extr. to Charles Mason with William Nock & Sebastian Cropper, securities. (MilesW&A:355 (will of Zorobabel Mason))

Zorobabel 'Babel' Mason and Ann 'Nancy' Bull had the following children:

103   i.   Charles H.⁵ Mason, b. in AC c1791, d. May 1830. He was evidently over age 21 in 1825 when he took over as extr. of his father estate. (MilesW&A:352 (will of Charles Mason)) He m. 21 Apr 1812 (lic.) in WO Co., Polly Warner (b. c1793 in AC), dau. of William Warner and Elizabeth (N). (Powell, *WO Co Marriages 1795-1865;* Nottingham Wills:565 (will of William Warner))

On 25 Dec 1815 Zorobabel Mason, John Mason and Charles Mason were the securities on the administration of Esther Fox. (MilesW&A:218 (adm. of Esther Fox))

Charles left a will dated 6 Apr 1830, probated 31 May 1830, in AC. To son Charles C. Mason that part of my plantation on which I now live which formerly belonged to my father Zorobabel Mason dec'd containing 140 acres. To dau. Polly Mason that part of my plantation which I purchased from James Ironmonger containing 140 acres. To dau. Ann Bull that part of my plantation which formerly belonged to Littleton Parker dec'd containing 60 acres. Slaves Moses, Adah, George & Rachel to be free when I die. Remainder of my slaves to be free as they arrive at age 21: Ansley, Mary, Dick, Raner & Henry. Remainder to my 3 children Charles C. Mason, Polly Mason & Ann Bull. William P. Custis extr. Witnessed by P. P. Mayo, James J. Ailworth & Zorobabel Fox. Southey Bull, who had m. Ann, one of the daus. of Charles Mason, appearing by Vespasian Ellis his attorney, contested the will. The will was proved by the oaths of Peter P. Mayo, James J. Ailworth & Zorobabel Fox. Thomas R. Joynes, Thomas Lewis Sr. & George P. Scarburgh were securities. (MilesW&A:352 (will of Charles Mason))

104   ii.   John Mason, b. in AC c1792. (MilesW&A:355 (will of Zorobabel Mason))

He m. 1ˢᵗ 15 Jul 1813 (bond) in AC, Susan Matthews. Charles H. Mason & Sam'l H. Mathews were securities on the M.L.B. of John Mason and Susan Mathews, dau. of Sally Mathews who gave consent. They were married by I. Bratten. (Mihalyka, *NC Marriages*

1660-1854) Susan , b. c1795 in NC, was the dau. of Sally Matthews, widow? (Mihalyka, *NC Marriages 1660-1854*)
He m. 2nd 27 Nov 1831 (bond) in AC), Charlotte Upshur (b. c1800 in AC). John Bull Sr. & Southy W. Bull were the securities on the M.L.B. of John Mason, widower, and Charlotte Upshur. (ACM)
On 25 Dec 1815 Zorobabel Mason, John Mason and Charles Mason were the securities on the administration of Esther Fox. (MilesW&A:218 (adm. of Esther Fox))

49. **Henry⁴ Mason** (Thomas³, Bennett², William¹), b. in AC c1765. (Carey, *Mason Family of Kegotank*)
He m. c1792, **Sarah Rayfield Rayfield? Sterling?** (b. c1770 in AC, d. Mar 1821). She m. c1790, **(N) Davis.** (MilesW&A:354 (will of Sarah Mason))
Henry appears on the list of tithables in AC for 1787.
Henry Mason had the following child:
105   i.   Rosey⁵ Mason, b. in AC c1785, d. by 4 Mar 1812. She m. 27 Nov 1809 (bond) in AC, Luther Bunting. George Smith was the security on the M.L.B. of Luther Bunting and Rosey Mason of Henry. (ACM)
       Luther, b. c1780 in AC, m. 4 Mar 1812 (bond) in AC, Elizabeth 'Betsy' (N). Andrew Tunnell was the security on the M.L.B. of Elizabeth Lewis and Luther Bunting. (ACM)

Henry Mason and Sarah Rayfield Rayfield? Sterling? had the following children:
106   ii.   Ephraim Mason, b. in AC c1794. (MilesW&A:354 (will of Sarah Mason)) He m. 3 Jun 1834 (lic.) in SO Co., Sarah 'Sirah' Linton (b. c1800). (Pollitt, *SO Co Marriages 1796-1871)*
       Ephraim was named in his mother's will 13 Apr 1819 in AC. (MilesW&A:354 (will of Sarah Mason)) He was shown as son and extr. Ephraim Mason in the will of Sarah Mason.
107   iii.   Henry Mason, b. in AC c1796. (MilesW&A:354 (will of Sarah Mason)) He m. 4 May 1829 (bond) in AC, Elizabeth 'Betsy' Custis (b. c1785), dau. of Revel Custis. James Russell was the security on the M.L.B. of Henry Mason and Betsy Bonwell, widow of John. (ACM)
       Elizabeth m. 10 Sep 1807 (bond) in AC, John Bonnewell. John Joynes was the security on the M.L.B. of John Bonwell and Elizabeth Custis of Revel. (ACM)
       Henry was named as extr. in his mother's will 13 Apr 1819 in AC. (MilesW&A:354 (will of Sarah Mason))

108   iv.   Elizabeth 'Betsey' Mason, b. in AC c1798. (ACM; MilesW&A:354 (will of Sarah Mason; FA CD309) She m. 14 May 1822 (bond) in AC, Andrew B. Wyatt (b. c1800 in AC, d. Dec 1841). Ephraim Mason & Custis Rayfield were the securities on the M.L.B. of Andrew B. Wyatt and Elizabeth Mason of Sarah. (ACM; MilesW&A:627 (adm. of Andrew B. Wyatt))
Elizabeth was named in her mother's will 13 Apr 1819 in AC. (MilesW&A:354 (will of Sarah Mason))
Elizabeth was listed with her son in the census of 1850 in St. George Parish, AC. She was shown as Betsey Wyatt, age 52 in HH#791 headed by Jno. Wyatt, a 25 year old laborer. Also listed were Andrew Wyatt, a 20 year old laborer and Jane Wyatt, age 16, who were evidently her children as well. (FA CD309)

50. **Ezekiel**[4] **Mason** (Thomas[3], Bennett[2], William[1]), b. in AC c1785, d. before 25 Dec 1848. (Carey, *Mason Family of Kegotank;* Powell, *AC 1830 Census;* MilesW&A:352 (adm. of Ezekiel Mason)) He may have died years earlier, since he was not shown in the 1840 AC Census.

He m. 1st 25 Jan 1805 (bond) in AC, **Sally Matthews** (b. c1780 in AC). Charles Smith was the security on the M.L.B. (ACM)

He m. 2nd 3 Aug 1814 (bond) in AC, **Tabitha Watson** (b. c1790 in AC), dau. of William Watson. William Watson was the security on the M.L.B. of Ezekiel Mason and Tabitha Watson of Wm. (ACM)

Ezekiel Mason, age 40-50, was listed as a head of household in the census of 1830 in St. George Parish, AC. Listed with him were the following males: 2 age 0-5; 2 age 5-10; 2 age 10-15; and the following females: 1 age 0-5; 1 age 20-30; 1 age 30-40 and 1 age 50-60. (Powell, *AC 1830 Census*)

On 25 Dec 1848 Samuel W. Mason was named to settle the estate of Ezekiel in AC. Francis Kellam & Edward L. Bayly were securities. (MilesW&A:352 (adm. of Ezekiel Mason))

Ezekiel Mason and Tabitha Watson had the following children:

109   i.   Samuel W.[5] Mason, b. in AC c1817, d. Mar 1852. (FA CD309; MilesW&A:354 (adm. of Samuel W. Mason)) He m. 10 Feb 1842 in AC, Elizabeth J. 'Eliza' Smith. (ACM)
Samuel was named as administrator of the estate of Ezekiel Mason on 25 Dec 1848. Francis Kellam & Edward L. Bayly were securities. MilesW&A:352 (adm. of Ezekiel Mason))
Sam'l W. Mason, a 33 year old farmer, was listed as a head of household in the census of 1850 in St. George Parish, AC (HH#834. Listed with him were the following Masons: Eliza, age 31; Jas. O., age 2; and

Jno. T., age 1. Also listed was Jno. Bivins, an 18 year old black laborer. (FA CD309)

On 29 Mar 1852 George S. West was named as administrator of Samuel 's estate. Mitchell W. West & George S. Rodgers were the securities. (MilesW&A:354 (adm. of Samuel W. Mason))

Elizabeth, widow of Samuel Mason, b. c1819 in AC, dau. of Charles Smith and Sally Mears, m. 2nd 26 May 1858, John W. Lingo, a 31 year old widowed farmer, son of Robt. & Marg't Lingo. They were m. by Montcalm Oldham. (FA CD309; MACM)

110   ii. Edward W. Mason, b. in AC c1825, d. Nov 1853 in First Dist. He died of infection at the age of 30 years. He was the son of E__ & Tabitha Mason, born in AC, a farmer and unmarried. A friend A.J.T. Kellam gave the information. He m. Jane (N) c1848 (b. c1830). (WADR; FA CD309)

Edward W. Mason, a 25 year old farmer, was listed as a head of household in the census of 1850 in St. George Parish, AC (HH#850). Listed with him were Jane Mason, age 20; and Ahah Roberts, age 73. (FA CD309)

He left a will dated 15 Nov 1853, probated 28 Nov 1853 in AC. To my friend George W. Cutler the whole of my estate. Friend George W. Cutler extr. Witnessed by John W. A. Mears, Edward T. Ayres & Custis S. Turner. Richard P. Read & Levi D. Dix securities. (MilesW&A:352 (will of Edward W. Mason))

60. **Major**^{4} **Mason Sr.** (Jeremiah^3, Bennett^2, William^1), b. in AC c1778, d. Apr 1864. (FA CD309; MilesW&A:353 (will of Major Mason Sr.))

He m. c1800, **Rachel Parks** (b. c1782 in AC, d. 8 Aug 1870 in Metompkin Dist., AC. (AC Surveyors Record No. 3:31; FA CD309; WADR) She was shown as Rachel Mason, who d. at the age of 91 years, 6 mos., wife of Major Mason Sr. Her son Rich. Mason gave the information for the death register.

In 1837 Major Mason bought 130 acres (Whitelaw's tract A109) from Mary P. (Polly) Stran. This would have been on the south side of Guilford Creek. (Whitelaw:1102 (tract A109, the Polly Stran part))

In 1842 Major Mason bought 182 acres of land on the north side of Guilford Creek from Robert W. and his wife Mary C. Williams. (Whitelaw:1197) In 1854 he left it to his son Thorowgood Mason and in time it had other owners and in 1937 was purchased by Herbert V. Ewell. The house on this parcel (Whitelaw's A126D) is known as the Mason House. The quaint little house has always been intriguing to visiting architects, as the stairs definitely are very old, seemingly older than the house itself. There seems some reason to believe that originally the house was a frame structure with two brick ends, and that at some later, but still ancient date, a brick veneer was added in front and rear, as well as at the ends below the eaves line. Should this theory be right, the house as originally built could date from before 1700 and be attributed to Richard Hinman. A clue to the period of the change mentioned has not been found, but it would probably be some time before the death of William Andrews Sr. The brickwork in the gable ends is different from that below the eaves line, as well as from the work in the front and rear walls; also the widening of the house necessitated the flare of the roof line at the eaves. The treatment of the later brickwork is most unusual in that around the doors and windows, and at the corners of the house, the bricks are set forward a little to produce a panel effect; there is a one-brick offset at the eaves line, where the new bricks were added to the end walls, and a two-brick offset at the water table. The porch has gone since the picture was taken, but it had a brick floor. The hallway has double doors at the front entrance, but a single one at the rear to give access to a much more modern addition. The stairway, with its simple newel post, heavy rail and turned balusters, and bolection-moulding closed stringer, is most ancient. The doorway to the parlor at the left has eight panels. In that room the windows, with twelve panes in each sash, are deep-set, with the walls and plaster beleved towards them. The mantel has some hand-carving or reeding and fretwork, but it must be a later addition, perhaps shortly before 1800. The mantel in the dining room is plain; to the right of it are two small sections of paneled wainscoting, but elsewhere in the whole first floor there is no other indication of any paneling, nor was there any chair rail or conrnice, as the plaster is unmarked. The inside hall walls have clay nogging. Each of the second-floor bedrooms has a tiny fireplace with mantel, and the ceilings, as well as theat in the upper hall, have exposed beaded beams, this being one of the few such examples on the Shore. (Whitelaw tract A126)

Major Mason Sr. was listed as a head of household in the census of 1850 in Acc Parish, AC (HH#940), a 72 year old farmer with real estate valued at $8,000. Listed with him were the following Masons: Rachel P., age 68; Thorogood, a 24 year old laborer; and Elizabeth, age 23. Also listed was Parker Justice, a 16 year old laborer. (FA CD309)

He left a will dated 8 Sep 1853, probated 24 Apr 1854 in AC. To my son Major Mason the land on which he lived in 1851, a part of which was purchased by me from Richard Bundick & the balance was purchased from Thomas Lewis & is called *The Gray land*. To son Richard Mason the plantation whereon he now lives, being the land I purchased from Arthur Wessells, which is separated from the lands of my son Samuel Mason & my son-in-law Samuel Justice by a line beginning at two gums near the Gladding land & thence,.. near Samuel Wessells' land. To son Zadock Mason the plantation whereon he now lives, which is the land I purchased from Nathaniel Topping. To son William Mason the plantation whereon he now lives, being part of the land I purchased from Mary P. Stran which lies to the northwest & southwest of a line commencing at the Mill branch thence,.. to George White's land. To my dau. Mary A. Justice the plantation whereon she now lives, part of which was purchased by me at a Sheriff's sale & formerly belonging to William Ewell & the balance of which I purchased from Ann Bagwell. The Ewell land given here is separated from a small part of the same land given to my son Samuel Mason, by a line of marked trees running from the land of Samuel Wessells to the land of Jacob Matthews' heirs. To son Samuel Mason the plantation whereon he now lives which includes all the land I purchased from John Lewis & Spencer Lewis, also the Monger land, also a small piece of the Ewell land, separated from the rest of the Ewell land given to my dau. Mary A. Justice. To my son Thorowgood Mason the part of the plantation on which I now reside which lies to the southwest of a line,.. near Dennis Clayton Sr.'s land,.. cornering on Zadock Nock's land & also the land I purchased from Higginbotham, called *Bayly's Ridge* & also the land I purchased of Richard Justice called the *John Russell Ridge* & also a small tract of land called *Robins Hole* adjoining the land of William Mason & others. To my son James Mason the balance of the land on which I reside lying northeast of the line,.. now occupied by my son James, but is part of the same tract on which I reside & which formerly belonged to Thorowgood Taylor. To my son Zorobabel Mason the plantation on which he now resides which includes the land I purchased of Mary P. Stran not given to my son William Mason & also the land purchased by me at public sale formerly belonging to Southey Grinnalds. To my children: Major, Zorobabel, Richard, David, Zadock, William, Samuel & Mary A., marsh land near Back Creek adjoining the land of William Justice with a road leading from the public road to the marsh land. The tract of land I purchased of Crippen Taylor's extr. called *Robins Hole* shall be sold & the money to all my children except my son Thorowgood. To wife Rachel Mason during her life my Negro woman Chloe & her share of my estate as if I had died intestate,.. To son Thorowgood Mason the balance including the increase of slave Chloe during my wife's life & Chloe herself at my wife's death. Son Thorowgood Mason extr. & he not be required to give security. Witnessed by John Parks, Jesse Dickerson Jr., Parker W. Parks & Jesse Dickerson Sr. (MilesW&A:353 (will of Major Mason Sr.))

Jeremiah Mason and his wife Ann sold 3 acres of the land he bought in 1780 to son Major Mason on 3 Jan 1800. (AC Deeds 1797 - 1800:449)

Major Mason Sr. and Rachel Parks had the following children:

111　　i.　Richard[5] Mason, b. in AC c1803. (ACM; WADR:103 (death of Rachel Mason); FA CD309) He m. 26 Nov 1827 (bond) in AC, Elizabeth 'Betsy' Justice. Littleton P. Henderson and Isaiah Justice were the securities on the M.L.B. of Richard Mason of Major and Elizabeth Justice of Isaiah. (ACM)

Elizabeth, b. c1805 in AC, d. before 8 Sep 1849, dau. of Isaiah Justice Jr. and Sarah 'Sally' Lewis. Her children Nancy and Charles Mason were named in the will of Isaiah Justice Sr., 8 Sep 1849, wife Sally. (ACM; MilesW&A:297 (will of Isaiah Justice Sr., 8 Sep 1849, wife Sally))

Richard Mason was listed as a head of household in the census of 1850 in Acc Parish, AC (HH#353), a 47 year old farmer with real estate valued at $1,500. Listed with him were Nancy Annis, age 60 and deaf; Nancy Mason, age 21; and Charles Mason, age 18. (FA CD309)

In the census of 1860 in Acc Parish, AC Richard was shown as the head of HH#449, a 58 year old farmer with real estate valued at $4,900 and personal property valued at $4,500. Listed with him were Nancy Annis, age 70 and Charles Mason, a 28 year old farmer. (1860 AC Census)

On 8 Oct 1870 Richard Mason reported the death of his sister Mary Justice, who d. of dropsy at the age of 50 years. (WADR)

112   ii. Major Mason Jr., b. in AC 11 Oct 1805, d. 11 Mar 1885 in Acc Parish, AC. He d. of cold chills at the age of 79 years, 5 mos. The death register shows him b. in AC, a farmer and the husband of Netty. His son, Henry Mason of M. gave the information. His body was interred in Mason Plot, Bloxom, AC. His tombstone shows him as Major Mason Sr., the son of Major & Rachel Mason. (WADR; MilesW&A:353 (will of Major Mason Sr.); TUAC)

He m. 1st 25 Dec 1826 (bond), Ann 'Nancy' Grinnalds. James Berry and William Taylor were the securities on the M.L.B. of Major Marson Jr. and Nancy Grinnalds orphan of South. (ACM)

Ann, b. c1807 and d. 1 Mar 1854 in Guilford, AC, was the dau. of Southey B. Grinnalds and Ader West. She was shown as Nancy Mason, a slave (which must have been in error) of M. Mason, who d. of consumption at the age of 48 years. She was the dau. of S. Grinalds, born at Guilford, and unm. Her owner gave the information. (Note: She must have erroneously been reported as an unm. slave.) (FA CD309; ACM; WADR)

He m. 3 Jan 1856 (lic.) in AC, Bernette 'Netty' Justice. He was shown as Major Mason, widower, and she was shown as Bernetta Justice of Samuel. Robert Ayres said both were over age 21. (ACM; MACM)

Bernette , b. c1829 in AC, dau. of Samuel R.
Justice and Priscilla Hornsway, m. 2nd 26 Feb 1890 in
Parksley, AC, John (of B.) Parks. (MACM) He was
shown as John Parks, a 64 year old widowed carpenter,
the son of Benjamin Parks and she was shown as
Bernetta Mason, a 60 year old widow, the dau. of
Samuel Justis. They were m. by H.S. Dulany. (FA
CD309; ACM; MACM)

In the 1850 census of Acc Parish, AC, Major
Mason, Jr., was listed as a head of HH#362, a 44 year
old farmer with real estate valued at $1,350. Listed
with him were the following Masons: Nancy, age 43;
Ann E., age 21; Polly, age 18; Margaret, age 16;
Southey, age 14; George, age 12; and Eveline, age 8.
Also listed with him were Elizabeth Parker, age 8; and
Adam Custis, age 6 and black. (FA CD309)

In the 1860 census Major Mason was head of
household (HH#623), a 55 year old farmer with real
estate valued at $8,500 and personal property valued at
$1,500. Listed with him were the following Masons:
Bennette, age 32; Jeremiah, a 24 year old farmer;
Eveline, age 18; Major, age 10; Henry, age 2; and Mary
J., age 7/12. Also listed was Isaac Wessels, a 23 year
old hired hand; Elizabeth P. Grinnalds, age 16; and
John Custis, a 16 year old apprentice farmer. (1860 AC
Census)

In the 1870 census in Metompkin District, AC he
was shown as Major Mason the head of HH#MT62, a
64 year old farmer with real estate valued at $4,000 and
personal property valued at $2,000. Listed with him
were the following Masons: Burnetta, age 40 and
keeping house; Major, a 19 year old farm laborer; and
Henry, a 13 year old farm laborer. Also listed were
George Littleton, a 22 year old farm laborer and Harriet
Justice, a 15 year old mulatto domestic servant.
(Walczyk, *1870 AC, Acc Parish, Census*)

113   iii. Zorobabel 'Babel' Mason, b. in AC 27 Aug 1807, d. 18
Apr 188, bur. Mason Cem, Maswell St., Parksley, AC.
He m. 27 Dec 1830 (bond) in AC, Polly Grinnalds.
Major Mason Jr. was the security on the M.L.B. of
Zorobabel Mason and Polly Grinnalds, orphan of
Southy. (MilesW&A:353 (will of Major Mason Sr.); TUAC; ACM)

Polly, b. 15 May 1810 in AC, dau. of Southey B.
Grinnalds and Ader West, d. 25 Mar 1884. Her body

was interred in Mason Cem, Maswell St., Parksley,
AC. (TUAC; ACM)

In the 1850 census in Acc Parish, AC, Zorobabel
was listed as a head of HH#927, a 40 year old farmer
with real estate valued at $1,500. Listed with him were
the following Masons: Polly, age 32; Rachal, age 15;
Nancy, age 13; Zerobabel W., age 3; Henry P., age 7;
and Margaret, age 1. Also listed were George Dix, a 21
year old laborer and John H. Grinalds, age 9. (FA CD309)

In the 1860 census Zerobabel was listed as a head
of HH#577, Acc Parish, AC, a 53 year old farmer with
real estate valued at $6,000 and personal property
valued at $2,700. Listed with him were the following
Masons: Polly, age 45; Henry, age 16; Zerabbabel, age
14; Margaret, age 11; and Frank, age 6. Also listed was
Nancy Lewis, a 19 year old hired servant. (1860 AC
Census)

In the 1870 census of Metompkin District, AC
Babel Mason was head of HH#MT673, a 62 year old
farmer with real estate valued at $4,000 and personal
property valued at $500. Listed with him were the
following Masons: Polly, a 53 year old house keeper;
William, a 23 year old farm laborer; Margaret, age 18
and at home; and Frank, a 16 year old farm laborer.
Also listed with him were the following Mears: Nancy,
a 30 year old house keeper; Jennie, age 9; John, age 7;
and Mary, age 5. (Note: Nancy was his dau.) Also
listed was Joseph Mason, a 14 year old black farm
laborer. (Walczyk, *1870 AC, Acc Parish, Census*)

114   iv. William Mason, b. in AC 11 Oct 1809, d. Mar 1900.
His body was interred in Mason Fm Plot, west of
Parksley, AC. He m. 24 Jan 1833 (bond) in AC,
Tabitha Justice. Josiah Justice was the security on the
M.L.B. (MilesW&A:353 (will of Major Mason Sr.); TUAC; ACM)

Tabitha, b. 28 Feb 1812 in AC, D. 30 Apr 1897,
was dau. of Isaiah Justice Jr. and Sarah 'Sally' Lewis.
Her body was interred in Mason Fm Plot, west of
Parksley, AC. (TUAC; MilesW&A:297 (will of Isaiah Justice Sr.,
8 Sep 1849, wife Sally))

In the 1860 census William Mason was listed as a
head of household #506 in the census of 1860 in Acc
Parish, AC, age 50. With him were the following
Masons: Tabitha, age 47; Sally, age 16; Caroline, age
16; Vienna, age 12; Thorogood, age 10; and Arinthia,

age 3. Also listed were Betsey Justice, age 28; Noah Justice, age 8; and Samuel Dix, age 22 and farming. (Crowson & Hite, *AC 1860 Census*)

William Mason was listed as a head of household in the census of 1870 in Metompkin Dist., AC, HH#MT676, a 60 year old farmer with real estate valued at $3,000 and personal property valued at $300. Listed with him were the following Masons: Tabitha, age 57 and keeping house, Thorogood, age 19 and a farm laborer; and Arinthia, age 12 and at home. Also listed were Mordicai B---, a 30 year old farm laborer; Laney Lewis, a 55 year old black domestic servant; and Henry Lewis, a 12 year old black farm laborer. (Walczyk, *1870 AC,, Acc Parish, Census*)

115 v. David L. Mason, b. in AC 23 Nov 1811, d. 14 Feb 1894. His body was interred in Mason Plot, Lee Mont, AC. He m. c1838, Catherine C. Scott (b. 28 Jan 1820 in AC, d. 12 Jun 1890), dau. of John Scott and Tabitha Lewis. Her body was interred in Mason Plot, Lee Mont, AC. (MilesW&A:353 (will of Major Mason Sr.); TUAC)

In the 1850 census of Acc Parish, AC, David was listed as a head of household, HH#360, a 38 year old farmer with real estate valued at $1,400. Listed with him were the following Masons: Catharine, age 28; James S., age 7; Mary E., age 5; Virginia, age 3; and Emily S., age 1. (FA CD309)

In the 1860 census of Acc Parish, AC, David Mason was listed as a head of household, HH#1138, a 48 year old farmer with real estate valued at $3,000 and personal property valued at $660. Listed with him were the following Masons: Catharine, age 47; Jas. S., age 17; Mary E., age 14; Virginia, age 12; Emily S., age 11; Edw'd P., age 10; Malinda, age 9; and Richard T., age 3. (1860 AC Census)

116 vi. Zadock Mason, farmer, b. in AC 20 Aug 1813, d. 28 Apr 1866 in AC. He d. of consumption at the age of 52 years. His son (unnamed) gave the information for the death register. His body was interred in Mason Cem, Hopeton, AC. He m. 8 Oct 1835 (bond) in AC, Leah Grinnalds. Major Mason Jr. was the security on the M.L.B. (TUAC; WADR; MilesW&A:353 (will of Major Mason Sr.); ACM)

Leah, b. 1815 in AC, d. 2 Oct 1892. The 1850 census places her birth at 1820, but her tombstone puts it at 1815. Leah was the dau. of Southey B. Grinnalds and Ader West. Her tombstone shows her as Leah Mason, wife of Zadock, who d. 2 Oct 1892 at the age of 77 years. Her body was interred in Mason Cem, Hopeton, AC. (Family Archive CD309, *1850 Census*; TUAC; Carey, *Mason Family of Kegotank*)

In the 1850 census Zadock Mason was listed as a head of household in Acc Parish, AC, HH#348, a 36 year old farmer with real estate valued at $400. Listed with him were the following Masons: Leah, age 30; William T., age 13; Littleton, age 11; James H., age 9; Gilet, age 6; and Amanda, age 1. Also listed with him were Ada Grinalds, age 15 and George Mitchell, a 16 year old laborer. (FA CD309)

In the 1860 census Zadock Mason was listed as a head of household in Acc Parish, AC, HH#450, a 49 year old farmer with real estate valued at $3,000 and personal property valued at $1,000. Listed with him were the following Masons: Leah, age 49; William, age 23; Middleton, age 21; James H., age 19; Gilbert, age 16; Amanda, age 12; and Betty, age 8. Also listed was Nancy Custer, age 22 and black. (1860 AC Census)

117 vii. Samuel Mason, b. in AC c1818, m. 8 Jan 1845 in AC, Adeline W. Wessells. Another record from this same source shows that Samuel Mason m. Adeline Metcalf on this same date. (MilesW&A:353 (will of Major Mason Sr.); FA CD309; ACM)

Adeline, b. c1825 in AC, was the dau. of Ephraim Wessells Sr. and Shady Bell Taylor. (FA CD309; AC Wills 1828-46:458)

In the 1850 census Samuel Mason was listed as a head of household in Acc Parish, AC (HH#632), a 32 year old farmer with real estate valued at $350. Listed with him were the following Masons: Adeline W., age 25; Susan A., age 4; Eveline T., age 2; and Samuel C., age 3 mos. (FA CD309)

In the 1860 census Samuel Mason was listed as a head of household in Acc Parish, AC. (HH#1146), a 42 year old farmer with real estate valued at $7,000 and personal property valued at $5,460. Listed with him were the following Masons: Adeline, age 36; Susan A., age 14; Eveline, age 12; Sam'l C., age 1; Thos., age 2; and unnamed male, age 4/12. Also listed was Jas. Drummond, age 14 and black. (1860 AC Census)

118   viii. Mary Ann Mason, b. in AC 4 Apr 1820, d. 8 Oct 1870
in AC. As Mary Justice, she d. of dropsy at the age of
50 years, 6 mos., 4 days, dau. of Major & Rachel
Mason, unm. housekeeper. Her brother Richard Mason
gave the information for the death register. Her body
was interred in Justice Plot, Parksley, AC. Her
tombstone shows her as Mary A. Justis, wife of
Samuel, son of I., who d. 21 Oct 1870 at the age of 47
years, 3 mos, 23 days. She m. Samuel (of I.)) Justice
c1840. (MilesW&A:353 (will of Major Mason Sr.); WADR;
TUAC)

Samuel, b. 21 Oct 1816 in AC, son of Isaiah Justice
Jr. and Sarah 'Sally' Lewis. His obituary puts his birth
at 1818, but the 1850 census puts it at 1813. (Crowson &
Hite, *AC 1860 Census*; FA CD309; *Peninsula Enterprise*, obituary;
MilesW&A:297 (will of Isaiah Justice Sr., 8 Sep1849, wife Sally)

He m. 28 Feb 1872 in Woodstock (Lee Mont), AC,
Mary A. White. The marriage register shows him as
Samuel Justice, a 45 year old widowed farmer, the son
of Ismaih (probably Isaiah) & Sally Justice and she is
shown as Mary A. White, age 35 and single dau. of
Henry B. & Hetty White. They were m. by Deniy A.
Woodson. (AC Marriage Register 3, *1853-1896*)

Samuel d. 9 Mar 1898 in Parksley, AC, age 81. The
obiturary states that Mr. Samuel Jusice, of I.,
d.Wednesday night at his home near Parksley, in his
80th year. Survivors included 2 daus. and 1 son, all of
whom were listed, and a second wife, who was not
listed. The 1850 & 1860 transcribed censuses show him
as son of J., but the initial I. and J. in the old and
writting are very similiar. (Peninsula Enterprise, 12 Mar 1898)

His body was interred in Justice Plot, Parksley,
AC. (TUAC) His tombstone shows him as Samuel Justis,
son of I. (burried beside Mary A. Justis).

Mary A. Justice, age 26, was listed with her
husband in the census of 1850 in Acc Parish, AC, in
HH#720 headed by Samuel Justice of J., a 37 year old
farmer. Also listed was Elizabeth Taylor, age 11, who
may have been her dau. by a previous marriage or a
younger sister. (FA CD309)

Mary A Justice, age 36, was listed with her
husband in the census of 1860 in Acc Parish, AC, in
HH#504 headed by Samuel Justice of J., a 47 year old
farmer. (Crowson & Hite, *AC 1860 Census*)

119   ix. Henry Mason, b. in AC c1820, d. Jul 1852. Henry was listed as a head of household in the census of 1850 in Acc Parish, AC (HH#719), a 30 year old farmer. Listed with him was Alfred Annis, age 11. ((FA CD309; Carey, *Mason Family of Kegotank*; MilesW&A:353 (adm. of Henry Mason))

      On 26 July 1852 Zadock Nock was named to settle Henry 's estate in AC. Littleton Nock & Samuel T. Taylor were the securities. (MilesW&A:353 (adm. of Henry Mason))

120   x. James Mason, b. in AC 1822, d. 1895, b. in AC 1822. He married three times.

      He m. 1st 16 Feb 1848 (bond) in AC, Sarah Ann Byrd. Henry Mason was the security on the M.L.B. of James Mason of Major and Sarah A. Bird of John A. (ACM; MACM; Carey, *Mason Family of Kegotank*)

      Sarah Mason, b. 14 Nov 1830, d. 25 Feb 1877 in Acc Parish, AC, dau. of John W. Byrd Sr. and Nancy Bloxom. (Father's Will; WADR) She d. of kidney failure. She was a housekeeper and the wife of Jas. Mason of M., who gave the information. AC. (Carey, *John Bird of Muddy Creek*)

      James Mason m. 2nd 23 Jan 1884, Guilbord Ch, AC, Pamelia Mary Barnes. He was shown as James Mason, a 62 year old widowed farmer, the son of Major Sr. & Rachel Mason and she was shown as Pamelia Mary Lewis, age 42 and widowed, the dau. of Sam'l & Lydia Barnes. They m. by John W. Carroll, a Methodist minister. (MACM)

      Pamelia, b. c1843 in AC, was the dau. of Samuel Barnes and Lydia Lewis. She m. 12 Oct 1871 in AC, Richard Lewis. They m. by Drury A. Woodson, a Baptist minister, at the residence of Samuel Barnes. Richard was age 75, a widowed farmer, and Mary was age 28 and single. (MACM)

      James Mason, m. 3rd 17 Apr 1895 in AC, Mary Elizabeth Killmon. He was a 65 year old widowed farmer, the son of Major & Rachel Mason and she was shown as Mary E. Poulson, a 50 year old widow, the dau. of Samuel & Nancy Killman. They were m. by Daniel G.C. Butts, a Methodist minister. (MACM)

      Mary, b. 30 Dec 1841 in AC, was the dau. of Samuel Killmon Jr. and Nancy Riggs. She m. 31 Jan 1859 (lic.) in AC, John Edward Poulson. He was shown as John E. Poulson and she as Mary E. Killman, the

dau. of Erastus, but Samuel Kilman gave consent for
his dau. Mary E. Killman. (Note: John was the son of
Erastus Poulson.) John C. Wessel said the groom was
over the age of 21. (TUAC; MACM; FA CD309)
  Mary d. 9 Apr 1922, bur. in Bethel Bapt Ch Cem,
Mears, AC. (TUAC)
  James was listed with another family in the census
of 1850 in Acc Parish, AC. He was shown as James
Mason, a 25 year old sailor in HH#1241, headed by
Maria Lewis, age 35. Listed below him was Elizabeth
Mason, age 9, who may have been his niece. (FA CD309)
  In the 1860 census in Acc Parish, AC, James
Mason was listed as a head of HH#688, a 39 year old
farmer with real estate valued at $3,000 and personal
property valued at $1,400. Listed with him were the
following Masons: Sarah, age 39; John, age 11;
Virginia, age 9; Henry, age 7; Olivia, age 5; Oswell,
age 3; and Matilda, age 1. (1860 AC Census)
  James Mason was listed as a head of household in
the census of 1870 in Metompkin Dist., AC, head of
HH#MT419, a 48 year old farmer with real estate
valued at $2,000 and personal property valued at $500.
Listed with him were the following Masons: Sarah, age
39 and keeping house; Major, a 20 year old farm
laborer; Virginia, age 18; William, a 17 year old farm
laborer; Olevia, age 15; Oswell, a 13 year old farm
laborer; Matilda, age 11; Franklin, a 9 year old farm
laborer; Richard, age 4; and Sallie, age 2. (Walczyk, *1870
AC, Acc Parish Census*)
  James Mason was listed as a head of household in
the census of 1880 in AC, a 59 year old farmer. Listed
with him were the following Masons: Francis, a 19 year
old son, keeping house; Rich'd, a 13 year old son;
Sallie, an 11 year old dau; Amelia, a 10 year old dau;
and Leonora, a 7 year old dau. (Family History Resouce File,
1880 US Census)

121 xi. Thorogood Mason, b. in AC c1826, d. 1 Jul 1902. His
body was interred in Mason Cem, Guilford, AC. His
tombstone shows him as Thorogood Mason who d. 1
Jul 1902 at the age of 78 years. He is buried next to
Elizabeth Mason.
    He m. c1848 in AC, Elizabeth A. Hickman (b.
1827, d. 9 Feb 1922). Her body was interred in Mason
Cem, Guilford, AC. Her tombstone shows her as

Elizabeth A. Mason, wife of Thorogood Mason, who d. on 9 Feb 1922 at the age of 87 years. (FA CD309; MilesW&A:353 (will of Major Mason Sr.; TUAC)

Thorogood was listed with his parents in the census of 1850 in Acc Parish, AC as a 24 year old laborer in HH#940 headed by Major Mason Sr., a 72 year old farmer with real estate valued at $8,000. (FA CD309)

Thorogood was listed as a head of household (HH#1314) in the census of 1860 in Acc Parish, AC, a 33 year old farmer. Listed with him were the following Masons: Eliz't, age 25; Eugene, age 5; Alice, age 3; Unnamed, age 6 mos.; and Rachael, age 80. Also listed were Wm. Taylor, a 30 year old black hired hand; Jane Wessells, age 18; and Pamelia Pitts, age 26. (Crowson & Hite, *AC 1860 Census*)

63. **Agnes**[4] **Mason** (Jeremiah[3], Bennett[2], William[1]), b. in AC c1790. (MilesW&A:351 (will of Ann Mason)), b. in AC c1790.

She m. 31 Dec 1832 (bond) in AC, **John Parker** (b. c1810 in AC, son of Sacker Parker). Custis Annis was the security on the M.L.B. of John Parker of Sacker and Agnes Mason. (ACM)

Agnes was named in her mother's will 10 Jan 1805 in AC. (MilesW&A:351 (will of Ann Mason)

Agnes Mason had the following child:

122   i. Ann Aydelotte[5] Mason, b. in WO Co. 28 Nov 1808, d. 10 Mar 1885 in Odessa MO. She m. 1st 15 Nov 1832 (bond) in AC, Asa J. Merrill. Peter Hargis was the security on the M.L.B. of Asa J. Merrill and Ann A. Mason of Agnes. Asa , b. c1805 in WO Co., d. 1834 in Lexington, Lafayette Co., MO. (ACM; Byrd, *Hist & Gene Byrd Family*)

She m. 2nd 1837, in MO, Nathaniel J. Byrd (b. 8 Feb 1812 in Muddy Creek, AC, d. Jan 1904 in Springfield, MO). He was the son of Daniel T. Byrd Sr. and Nancy Gillespie. (Byrd, *Hist & Gene Byrd Family*)

Descendants of Edward Thornton
(Limited to the Thornton surname)

First Generation
1. **Edward**[1] **Thornton (I)**, b. c1650, d. Sep 1703. (Nottingham Wills:34 (will of Edward Thornton))
He married c1677, **Patience (N)** (b. c1661). (Nottingham Wills:34 (will of Edward Thornton))
Edward bought land 1677 in AC. It appears that all AC Throntons are descended from an Edward Thornton, who purchased 250 acres of Whitelaws tract A140 in 1678. This was land described by John Stockley in his will of 1673 as one neck of land to the northward of Christopher Stanley's plantation, which I give to my wife Elizabeth to be at her own disposing. In 1674 she sold 100 acres at the south end to Edward Vaughan. She then married John Stratton of NC and the next year (1675) they sold the balance as 250 acres to James Powell, who resold to Edward Thornton three years later (1678). This was located north of the present road from Temperanceville to Atlantic, probably nearer the road from Horsey to Atlantic. (Whitelaw:1234)
Edward Thornton appears on the list of tithables in AC for 1679 with one tithable. Jno. Stratton and Edw'd Vahun were on the list near him. (McKey, *AC Court Orders, 1678-1682,* 6:65)
Edward witnessed a will 1682 in AC. (Nottingham Wills:12 (will of Edward Vahan)) In either late 1682 or early 1683 William Stockley, John Stratton & Edward Thornton witnessed the will of Edward Vahan, who left his dau. Elizabeth the plantation where I now live.
Edward sold land 1685 in AC. In 1683 Edward Vahan (wife Ann) left a 150 acre plantation to his dau. Elizabeth, this being 50 acres more than he had bought, but two years later Edward Thornton sold 50 acres to Elizabeth, so perhaps her father had contracted for it before his death. This was part of Whitelaw's tract A140. (Whitelaw:1234)
Edward appears on the list of tithables in AC for 1690. He was shown on Mr. Tho. Welburne's precincts list as Edw'd Thronton, with 1 tithable. Edward appears on the list of tithables in AC for 1691. Capt. Wallop's precincts for 1691 showed Edw'd Thorneton with 1 tithable. (McKey, *Acc Court Orders, 1682-1690, Vol* 7:321, 36)
Edward appears on the list of tithables in AC for 1692. He was shown as on Capt. Wallop's precincts list as Edw'd Thronton, with 1 tithable. (McKey, *Acc Court Orders, 1682-1690, Vol* 7:352)
He left a will dated 16 May 1703, probated 6 Oct 1703 in AC. To son Edward Thornton 100 acres where I now live. Son Thomas. Son Jonathan. To son William 100 acres being the other 1/2 of my 200 acres. Wife Patience residuary legatee & extx. Sons under 18 - daus. (unnamed) under 16 - Witnessed by Thomas Perry, Nathaniel Rackcliffe, Jr., Joseph Staton, Jr. (Note: Mary Frances Carey's Thorton file shows Edward Thornton's will of 1703 and names a

134

fifth son as James, omitted in Nottingham's will book.) It appears that present
day Thorntons on the mainland of the Eastern Shore can be traced back to either
son Edward or William Thornton. According to Whitelaw, Edward got the
southern part and William got the northern part of the original tract. All the
Thorntons of Chincoteague can be tracted back to their brother James Thornton.
(Nottingham Wills:34 (will of Edward Thornton))
   Edward Thornton (I) and Patience (N) had the following children:
+   2   i.   Edward^2 Thornton, b. c1688, d. Nov 1759.
       3   ii. Thomas Thornton, b. in AC c1690.
+   4   iii. Jonathan Thornton , b. c1692, d. before 29 Apr 1746.
+   5   iv. William Thornton, b. c1694, d. Nov 1758.
+   6   v.   James Thornton, b. c1696, d. Jan 1741/42.
       7   vi. Daus., mentioned (unnamed) in their father's will.

Second Generation
2. **Edward^2 Thornton (II)** (Edward^1), b. in AC c1688, d. Nov 1759. (Nottingham
Wills:34 (will of Edward Thornton; ACWills&c 1757-61:162)
   He m. c1745, **Tabitha (N)** (wid. of Wm. Sharpley). In describing the
ownership of tract A147 (in the Hallwood - Temperanceville area), Whitelaw
states that Edward Thornton married Tabitha by 1750. She was the widow of
William Sharpely who d. by 30 Mar 1742. (Whitelaw::1255 (tract A147))
   Tabitha , b. c1680, m. c1700 **William Sharpley**. (Nottingham Wills:125 (will
of William Sharpley))
   Edward left a will dated 8 Nov 1759 in AC, probated 27 Nov 1759 in AC.
To dau. in law Rachel Thornton the plantation where she lives during her
widow. Mentions dau. Susannah Taylor, son John Thornton, dau. Rhody
Wheelton, dau. Scarburgh Broadwater, dau. Esther Broadwater. Children
Edward Thornton, Rachel Thornton, Comfort Warrington & Ann Mary Taylor
residuary legatees. Son Edward Thornton & dau. in law Rachel Thornton, extrs.
Witnessed by Joshua Beavans, Edmund Warrington, William Dunston.
(Nottingham Wills:195 (will of Edward Thornton Sr.)) William Beavans guardian to
Edward Thornton, infant heir at law to the testator. (ACW&c., 1757-61:162)
   Edward Thornton (II) had the following children:
+   8   i.   John^3 Thornton, b. c1725, d. before 27 Nov 1759.
       9   ii. Esther Thornton, b. in AC c1730, m. c1750, Caleb
                Broadwater (b. c1722 in AC, d. Nov 1784), son of Elias
                Broadwater and Phebe (N). In his will, written 15 Nov
                1784, Caleb Broadwater named a wife Esther; sons
                Joseph, Ezekiel, Elias, Caleb and Edward Broadwater;
                daus. Mary Sterling and Martha Broadwater. To wife
                Esther Broadwater 125 acres purchased of William
                Harris during her widowhood and then to my 2 sons
                Joseph and Ezekiel Broadwater, they paying my
                youngest son Edward Broadwater £7.10. Son Elias,

extr. Witnesses were Jacob Broadwater and William
Burton. Codicil - Children Elias Broadwater, Mary
Sterling, Caleb, Joseph, Martha, Ezekiel and Edward
Broadwater residuary legatees. (ACW&c. 1784-87:80)

10   iii. Susannah Thornton, b. in AC c1732, m. before 1759,
(N) Taylor.

+   11   iv. Edward Thornton (III) , b. c1734, d. Jul 1799.

12   v. Rhody Thornton, b. in AC c1736, m. (N) Whealton
before 1759.

13   vi. Scarburgh Thornton, b. in AC c1738, m. (N)
Broadwater before 1759.

14   vii. Comfort Thornton, b. in AC c1740, m. before 1759,
William Warrington (b. c1730 in AC, d. Jan 1768).
Comfort was named in her husband's will dated 27 Jul
1767 in AC. Comfort and her brother Edward Thornton
were named as extrs. (Nottingham Wills:239 (will of William
Warrington))

15   viii. Mary Ann Thornton, b. in AC c1742, m. (N) Taylor
before 1759.

16   ix. Rachel Thornton, b. in AC c1744.

4. **Jonathan**[2] **Thornton (I)** (Edward[1]), b. in AC c1692, d. before 29 Apr 1746. It
was on this date that Jonathan Thornton, orphan of Jonathan deceased, was
bound to Isaac McHenny until he became 18 years of age. This first Jonathan
Thornton left no will, nor is there an account of the administration of his estate.
He may have been father of William Thornton, whose descendants have been
found in the area of Wallops Neck and would have included a William Thornton
of Charles, who m. Polly Rowley, widow of William Rowley, and who was the
widow of John Young when she married William Rowley. Another son was
evidently James Thornton. In tracing other lines, it has been noted that the name
Jonathan often turned into John, a name that seems to persist in this line. (AC
OB1744-53:127)

He m. before 1725, **Jane (N)**. (Carey, *Thornton Files*)

Jonathan inherited land 13 Mar 1730 in Wattsville, AC. In his will of this
date, Joseph Blake left son Charles Blake 165 acres where I now live & for want
of issue to unborn child & for want of heirs to Rachel Wilson. Jonathan
Thornton to have free possession of a parcel of land on Jengoteague Branch
where he now lives for 14 years, being 150 acres provided he pay the Quit Rents
& plant 150 apple trees, and after the expiration of the said 14 years I give the
said land to my unborn child & for want of heirs to my brother in law John
Morris. To brother Gilbert Morris. Wife Rebecca & brother Dennis Blake extrs.
Witnessed by Uriah Collins, William Watts, John Melten. According to
Whitelaw (tract A174) this could have been the same land that John Blake sold
to John Collins Sr. in 1704 and was located on the water, between Atlantic and
Wattsville. (Nottingham Wills:96 (will of Joseph Blake); Whitelaw:1331 (tract A174))

Jonathan Thornton (I) and Jane (N) had the following child:

17   i.   Jonathan³ Thornton, b. in AC May 1732. On 29 Apr
1746 Jonathan Thornton, age 13 last May, orphan of
Jonathan deceased, was bound to Isaac McHenny until
he became 18 years of age. (Carey, *Thornton Files*; AC
OB1744-53:127)

5. **William² Thornton (I)** (Edward¹), b. in AC c1694, d. Nov 1758. (Nottingham
Wills:193 (will of William Thornton))

He m. c1740, **Sarah (N)** (wid. of Nathaniel Tunnell). (Nottingham Wills:193
(will of William Thornton); Whitelaw:1232 (tract A140)) In describing the ownership of
tract A140, land between Mappsville and Temperanceville, Whitelaw notes that
after Nathaniel Tunnell d. in 1739, his widow Sarah m. William Thornton. In
1754 there was an involved land suit against William and Sarah Thornton, who
were in possession of part of this tract. It resulted in a General Court deed from
Woodman Stockley III to Sarah and William Thronton in trust for her son
William Tunnell. The title was transferred to William Thornton Jr. (Whitelaw
indicates that he was a son of Sarah and William Thornton, but he was probably
older than Sarah's son William Tunnell, as so was William Thornton Sr.'s son
before he married Sarah) during the life of Sarah and then it was to go to his
step-brother, William Tunnell, who finally in 1778 (wife Mary) left to his son
Nathaniel.

Sarah , b. c1710 in AC, m. c1725, **Nathaniel Tunnell**. (Nottingham Wills:120
(will of Nathaniel Tunnell))

He left a will dated 14 Nov 1758 in AC, probated 28 Nov 1758. Mentioned
wife Sarah, son William, son David Thornton, son Thomas Thornton, grandau.
Jacaman Thornton, dau. Mary Thorp. Two elder sons extrs. Witnessed by
Bartholomew Taylor, Mary Broadwater, Mary Tunnel, Thomas Matthews. His
will did not mention land. He was succeeded by a son William who d. intestate
the next year, his estate being administered by his wife Anne. Both before and
after the turn of the century, a Joshua Thornton was shown by surveys and
bounds of adjacent lands to have been the owner - he may have been the son of
the last William. (Nottingham Wills:193 (will of William Thornton); Whitelaw:1235)

William Thornton (I) had the following children:

+   18   i.   (son of Wm.)³ Thornton , b. c1718
+   19   ii.   William Thornton (Assawoman), b. c1720, d. 1759.
     20   iii.   David Thornton, b. in AC c1722. David witnessed a
will 23 Mar 1753 in AC. (Nottingham Wills:178 (will of
Nicholas Milman))

David Thornton was granted a license to keep an
ondinary in 1761. (Carey, *Thornton Files*)
+   21   iv.   Thomas Thornton , b. c1724, d. Jan 1767.
     22   v.   Mary Thornton, b. in AC c1726.

6. **James² Thornton** (Edward¹⁾, b. in AC c1696, d. Jan 1741/42. (Carey, *Thornton
Files*), Nottingham Wills:125 (will of James Thornton))

He m. c1720, **Bridget Collins** (b. c1695 in AC), dau. of John Collins.
(Nottingham Wills:130 (will of John Collins))
    James was named as administrator of an estate 4 Oct 1732 in AC.
(Nottingham Wills:109 (adm. of John Collins))
    On 13 Jul 1736 James Thornton bought 600 acres for 1500 lbs. of tobacco
from Samuel Taylor and wife Jeminia. The land began at the mouth of
Gingoteague Inlet, which marsh and hammocks are commonly called *Samuel
Taylor's Island,* alias *William's Island.* The deed states that the sale included
houses, buildings, orchards, fences, woods, etc. It was probably near the land of
Jonathan Thornton in 1732. The purchase of island land near Wallops Neck
suggests that the Thorntons of Chincoteague Island were of this line. (ACDW
1729-1737(ii):27)
    On 25 Jan 1740 in AC James Thornton, planter, sold to Thomas Townsend,
son of Henry, for £5, 300 acres of marshy lands near Jingoteague Inlet
commonly called *Samuel Taylor's Marsh.* This sale left James Thornton still
owning 300 acres at the time of his death. (Carey, *Thornton Files*; AC Deeds 1737-
45:205)
    He left a will dated 20 Nov 1741 in AC, probated 26 Jan 1741/2.
Mentioned sons John Thornton, James Thornton, Southy Thornton, William
Thornton and Thomas Thornton; dau. Sarah Thornton; 3 youngest children:
Southy, William & Thomas. Wife Bridget. Wife & 6 children residuary legatees
Wife extx. Witnessed by John Wallop, Thomas Townsend, Henry Townsend.
(Nottingham Wills:125 (will of James Thornton))
    James Thornton and Bridget Collins had the following children:

+	23	i.	John[3] Thornton , b. c1722, d. c1805.
+	24	ii.	James Thornton Sr. , b. c1725, d. after 1813, prob. settled on Chincoteague Island.
	25	iii.	Sarah Thornton, b. in AC c1728
	26	iv.	Southy Thornton, b. in AC c1730.
	27	v.	William Thornton, b. in AC c1732
+	28	vi.	Charles (William?) Thornton , b. c1732, d. after 1775.
	29	vii.	Thomas Thornton, b. in AC c1734.

Third Generation
8. **John[3] Thornton** (Edward[2], Edward[1]), b. in AC c1725, d. before 27 Nov
1759. (Nottingham Wills:195 (will of Edward Thornton Sr.))
    He m. c1745, **Rachel Warrington** (b. c1727), dau. of Walter Warrington.
John Thornton and Rachel Warrington had the following children:

	30	i.	Polly[4] Thornton, b. in AC c1748. (Carey, *Thornton Files*)
	31	ii.	Leah Thornton, b. in AC c1750. (Carey, *Thornton Files*)
	32	iii.	Rachel Thornton, b. in AC c1752. (Carey, *Thornton Files*)
+	33	iv.	Edward Thornton, b. c1755, d. Jan 1795. (Carey, *Thornton Files*)

11. **Edward[3] Thornton (III)** (Edward[2], Edward[1]), b. in AC c1734, d. Jul 1799.

In Nov 1759 William Beavans was named guardian to Edward Thornton, infant heir at law to his father. This indicates he was under age 21 in Nov 1759 when the will of his father was probated and that he was the oldest living son.

Edward was named as the extr. of the will of William Warrington dated 27 Jul 1767. (Nottingham Wills:239) Wife Comfort Warrington and her brother Edward Thornton were named as sxtrs. in the will of William Warrington.

Edward was paid for public service during Rev War, 1781-83. (Walker & Turman, *Acc Soldiers & Sailors in Rev*)

He d. leaving a will dated 22 Apr 1799, probated 29 Jul 1799. To dau. Sally Thornton for life, but if she marries with Matthew Taylor, son of Parker, I give the above named property to my grandson John Thornton, son of John. To son Southy Thornton. 4 sons John, William, Southy & George residuary legatees. Son John Exr. Witnessed by David Watts, Simson Bloxom. (Nottingham Wills:467)

Edward Thornton had the following children:

+   34   i.   John[4] Thornton , b. c1765
+   35   ii.   William Thornton , b. c1767, d. Feb 1805.
      36   iii.   Southy Thornton, b. in AC c1769, m. 8 Dec 1802 (bond), Polly Vernelson. Zadock McMath was the security on the M.L.B. of Southy Thornton and Polly Vinnalson. (ACM)

            Polly, b. c1784 in AC, was the dau. of Elisha 'Lisha' Vernelson. (MilesW&A:555 (will of Elisha Vernelson))

      37   iv.   George Thornton, b. in AC c1771.

            George was listed as a head of household in the census of 1800 in Acc Parish, AC. (Powell, *AC 1800, 1810, 1820 Census*) He was shown as George Thornton, of Edw'd, age 26-45. Listed with him were 1 male, age 0-10; 1 female, age 10-16; and 1 female, over age 45.

      38   v.   Sally Thornton b. in AC c1772, m. 12 Aug 1799 (bond), John Collins (b. c1775). John Watson was the security on the M.L.B. (ACM)

18. (son of Wm.)[3] Thornton (William[2], Edward[1]), b. in AC c1718. He had the following child:

      39   i.   Jacaman[4] Thornton, named in her grandfather's will dated 14 Nov 1758. (Nottingham Wills:193 (will of William Thornton))

19. William[3] Thornton (II) (Assawoman) (William[2], Edward[1]), b. in AC c1720, d. 1759. He m. c1755, **Anne (N)** (b. c1735). (Nottingham Wills:170 (adm. of William Thornton))

Sometime between Dec 1758 and May 1759 Anne Thornton was named to settle the estate of William Thornton. Joseph Feddiman & Warrington Staton were securities. (Nottingham Wills:170)

William Thornton (II) (Assawoman) and Anne (N) had the following children:

+   40   i. Joshua[4] Thornton, b. c1755, d. Apr 1806.

       41   ii. William Thornton, b. in AC c1757. William Thornton was under age 14 in 1761 when a guardian was appointed. (Carey, *Thornton Files*)

       42   iii. Elizabeth Thornton, b. in AC c1759 (under age 14 in 1763 when a guardian was appointed. (Carey, *Thornton Files*)

21. **Thomas[3] Thornton** (William[2], Edward[1]), b. in AC c1724, d. Jan 1767. He m. c1750, **Martha (N)** (b. c1725).

    Thomas 's estate was administered 27 Jan 1767 in AC.by Martha Thornton. Samuel Bevans & William Patterson were the securities. (Nottingham Wills:208 (adm. of Thomas Thornton))

Thomas Thornton and Martha (N) had the following child:

+   43   i. William[4] Thornton Sr. (Guilford) , b. c1760.

23. **John[3] Thornton** (James[2], Edward[1]), b. in AC c1722., d. c1805. Evidently, he had a son James Thornton who inherited the 100 acres of Charles Taylor Island or Willises Island and who applied for a military pension in 1829.

    John m. c1750, **Mary (N)** (b. c1725). (Carey, *Thornton Files*)

    On 24 May 1744 John Thornton, eldest son of James Thornton, deceased, sold 150 acres of the same land and marsh to William Marshall for £3, "near the mouth of Jengoteague Narrows, which said Island late belonged to Samuel Taylor." (AC Deeds, 1737-45:410) There now remained 150 acres of the originial purchase.

    John Thornton, age 26, witnessed a will 23 Jan 1748/49 in AC. (Nottingham Wills:152 (nunc. will of James Townsend)) He and William Davis (age 21) and John White (age 18), proved the verbal will of James Townsend.

    On 3 Dec 1774 John Thornton & wife Mary sold 50 acres of *Willises Marsh* to Shadrack Taylor for $2.00. (AC Deeds 1770-73:392) Evidently John Thornton, with his family, was living on the remaining 100 acres at the time of this deed.

    On 28 Feb 1792 John was named administrator of the estate of Samuel Owen. Arthur Whittington & Elisha Whealton were the securities. (Nottingham Wills:374 (adm. of Samuel Owen))

    John was listed as a head of household in the census of 1800 in Acc Parish, AC. He was shown as John Thornton Sen., over age 45. Listed with him were 1 male, age 0-10; 1 male, age 26-45; 2 females, age 0-10; 1 female, age 10-16; and 1 female, age 26-45. (Powell, *A C 1800, 1810, 1820 Census*)

John Thornton and Mary (N) had the following child:

       44   i. James (R.L.)[4] Thornton (Horntown), b. in AC c1754, d. 25 Jan 1834, a pensioner of the U.S. He m. Sally Cottingham 9 Feb 1786. (Nottingham, *Soldiers of the Eastern Shore*:15; AC OB1832-1836:241; ACM)

James Thornton served in the Rev War in 1776-1778; enlisted Feb 1776 in VA in the company of Capt. Thomas Snead in the regiment under Col. Matthews; discharged cFeb 1778 at Valley Forge. James Thornton Sr. was age 75 in 1829 when he applied for his pension. He was living near "Horton," on 100 acres of "very poor and mostly uncultivated land." He was single. (Nottingham, *Soldiers of the Eastern Shore*:15; AC OB1829-1832:51, 19 Dec 1829)

He left a will dated 14 Aug 1828, probated 24 Feb 1834. To wife Sally Thornton all of my estate. Wife extx. Witnessed by James S. Dunton, Samuel S. Welburne, Robert Townsend, Richard W. Guest, David Broadwater & F. Conner. AC. Sally Thornton refused to qualify & David Broadwater became admr. with Oliver Logan & Joseph Feddeman securities. (MilesW&A, p 538)

James was listed as a head of household in the census of 1830 in Acc Parish, AC. He was shown as Thornton, Jas. R.L., a head of household, age 70-80. Listed with him was 1 female, age 80-90. (Note: Perhaps "R.L." stood for "Retired from Labor.") (1830 AC census)

24. **James**[3] **Thornton Sr.** (James[2], Edward[1]), b. in AC c1725, d. after 1813. He left no will and there was no administration found of his estate. The names of his heirs can therefore only be determined accurately by finding what happened to the 42 acres of land he bought on Chincoteague in 1783 from Peggy Gillet, which he did not sell by a court deed. It is possible that James Thornton Senr. had, besides the son William Thornton, a son John Thornton, b. c1750. He would have m. about 1770 and would have been the John Thornton (of James?) in the 1800 census, age c45, with another male in the household over age 45 (his father James?). This John could have been the father of Jonathan Thornton, b. c1771, who m. 1st in 1791 Mary Owen and m. 2nd in 1806 Sally Ross, and the father of Kendall Thornton, b. c1775 who m. in 1796 Betsy Read and d. c1824. and was living on Wallops Island, under age 26 in the 1800 census and again on Wallops Island in the 1810 census.

Since his older brother John inherited their father's land near Chincoteague Inlet, James would have had to set up a household elsewhere and probably became a waterman and Chincoteague Island became his home.

On 26 Mar 1783 James Thornton first appears in AC records, when he bought, from Peggy Gillet of St. George's Parish, 42 acres for £21, of land and marsh on Chincoteague Island. (AC Deeds 1783-1788:56)

James appears on the list of tithables in AC for 1783-1792. The Personal Property Tax shows 9 Thornton men as heads of households and subject to tax.

James Thornton and Wm. Thornton Senr (father and son) were listed together with a Jacob Taylor immediately under their names. A Jacob Taylor was known to have been living on Chincoteague Island by this time. A John Thornton was listed near by.

On 24 Jun 1799 and on 28 Jun 1802 (living on Gingoteague Island), James Thornton Senr. was ordered by the AC Court to be tax free. (AC OB1798-1800:145; AC OB1800-04:274)

James was listed as a head of household in the census of 1800 in Acc Parish, AC, over age 45 with 1 male under age 10, 1 female age 10-16, and 2 females over age 45. (Powell, *AC 1800, 1810, 1820 Census*)

An indenture was made between the Overseers of the Poor and James Thornton to carry out an order made in County Court dated 25 Oct 1802 to bind Thos Russell orphan of Joshua Russell until the age of 21, unto James Thornton who will provide sufficient meat, drink, washing, lodging, and wearing apparel, teach him reading, writing and arithmetic, the trade of a farmer and also pay him $12 at the expiration of the said time. (Walczyk, *AC\ Indentures, 1798-1835*:12)

The name of James Thornton appears among the names of Chincoteague Island men on 26 Apr 1813 when votes were counted for Thomas M. Bayly for the US Congress. (AC Deeds 1812-15:113)

James Thornton Sr. had the following children:

+   45   i. William[4] Thornton Sr. (Island), b. c1746, d. Mar 1812.
+   46   ii. John Thornton , b. c1750.

28. Charles (William?)[3] Thornton (James[2], Edward[1])(Unproven), b. in AC c1732, d. after 1775.

Charles witnessed the will of Elizabeth Townsend on 29 Jan 1754. (Nottingham Wills:182) On 3 Sep 1768 he witnessed the will of William Wheelton. (Nottingham Wills:249) On 6 Nov 1773 he witnessed the will of John Smith. (Nottingham Wills:275) He left his son John Smith land in Chincoteague Neck and land near Horn Town. William (Charles?) and Charles (William?) Thornton may have been the same person. He was called William in his father James' will, but could have been the same as the Charles who witnessed 3 wills in this part of Accomack County.

Charles (William?) Thornton had the following child:

+   47   i. William (of Charles)[4] Thornton , b. c1765, d. after 1834.

Fourth Generation

33. Edward[4] Thornton (IV) (John[3], Edward[2], Edward[1]), b. in AC c1755, d. Jan 1795. (Nottingham Wills:421 (will of Edward Thornton))

He m. 1st c1775, m. **Rachel (N)** (wid. of Washburn Tunnell. In describing the ownership of tract A173 (between Wattsville and Atlantic), Whitelaw states that in 1757 Scarburgh Tunnell (wife Elizabeth) left land to his son Washpan (Washburn), and in 1772 he (wife Rachel) left to his brother

Charles. Rachel then m. Edward Thornton and 6 years later they released her dower interest to Charles, who in 1816 left his land to a son Samuel S. Tunnell. (According to Mary Frances Carey, Rachel's maiden name was Warrington.) (Nottingham Wills:421 (will of Edward Thornton); Whitelaw:1329 (tract A173))

    Rachel, b. c1750 in AC, m. c1770, **Washbourne 'Washpan' Tunnell** c1770. (Nottingham Wills:261 (will of Washburn Tunnel)) He m. **Mary Feddeman** c1784. (Nottingham Wills:421 (will of Edward Thornton) & 429 (will of Mary Thornton)) In the order of probate of the will of Edward Thornton (wife Rachel), Mary Thornton qualified. His will was written in 1782 and probabted in 1795. Evidently his wife Rachel had died and he had remarried.

    Mary , b. c1762 in AC, dau. of Meshack Feddeman and Elizabeth Matthews, d. Sep 1795. (Nottingham Wills:429)

    On 27 Nov 1759 William Beavans was named guardian to Edward Thornton, infant heir at law to his grandfather, Edward Thornton Sr. This implies that his father John (wife Rachel) had died since his grandfather wrote his will, and being the oldest son of the oldest son, Edward became the heir at law, and being underage, a guardian was appointed. He could not have been the son Edward named in the will, as that Edward was named an extr. and would have been of age to have been given that responsibility. (Nottingham Wills:195 (will of Edward Thornton Sr.))

    Edward left a will dated 2 Jan 1782, probated 26 Jan 1795.Wife Rachel Thornton extx. To wife whole estate during her widowhood. To son Henry Thornton the place where I now live, & should he offer to sell the land my son John to have it; my desire is that it shall continue in the same name, and for my son John to bequeath it to his proper heirs. Two sons Henry & John residuary legatees. Should my wife be with child that child to have things equal in value to what I have left my son John, & the rest of my estate to be divided between all three. Witnessed by John Warrington, William Burton, Rachel Thornton. (Nottingham Wills:421)

    Edward was named in a land cause 4 Nov 1795 in AC. Writ of Partition, Edward Thornton, Infant., by William Warrington his guardian appointed to defend this suit vs Henry Thornton. Whereas one Henry Thornton, father of the said Edward & Henry, was lately seized of 100 acres of land in the Parish of Accomack, and being so thereof seized on the 2 Jan. 1782, made his last will & testament and devised the said premises by the description of the place where he lived, to the said Henry, and being so seized died, by virtue whereof the said Henry entered into the said premises - That the said Edward Thornton, father of the said Edward & Henry, at the time of his death had children to-wit; the said Henry & John & also his wife enscient, who after his death brought a posthumous child, the said Edward, who was unprovided for by settlement, & neither provided for nor disinherited &c. (Nottingham, *Acc Land Causes, 1728-1825*:39)

    Edward's land was surveyed in 1796. A survey was made the year after his will was probated showed 146 acres, of which the south part of 49 acres went to Edward Thornton and the balance of 97 acres to Henry Thornton. (Whitelaw:1235)

Edward Thornton and Rachel had the following children:

48   i.   Henry^5 Thornton , b. in AC c1775, d. Sep 1816.
(MilesW&A:538 (will of Henry Thornton)) He m. 16 Mar 1798 (lic.) in WO Co. Euphama Townsend (b. c1775).
(Powell, *WO Co.Marriages 1795-1865*)

Henry was listed as a head of household in the census of 1800 in Acc Parish, AC. He was shown as Henry Thornton, of Edw'd, age 16-26. Listed with him were 1 female, age 0-10; 1 female, age 16-26; 1 female, over age 45; and 3 slaves. (Powell, *AC 1800, 1810, 1820 Census*)

Henry left a will dated 12 Jun 1815, probated 30 Sep 1816 in AC. To wife Euphamy Thornton the whole of my land & at her death to dau. Sally Thornton. To dau. Sally my Negro woman Leah & boy George &,.. To wife Euphamy Thornton remainder & a canoe during her life & then the canoe to brother's son William Thornton. To wife a gun during her life & then to brother's son Henry Thornton. Wife Euphamy Thornton & Thomas Jones extrs. Witnessed by Thomas Jones, Edward Ewell, Martha Jones & George Window. George Window & James White of Southey securities. (MilesW&A:538)

49   ii.   John Thornton, b. in AC c1780, d. Feb 1831.
(MilesW&A)

He m. 1st 6 Oct 1807 (bond) in AC, Grace Trader. Walter Wessells was the security on the M.L.B. (ACM) Grace, b. c1764 in AC, was the dau. of George Trader and Nancy (N).

He m. 2nd 30 Oct 1809 (bond), Elizabeth Hutson (b. c1790). William Hinman was the security on the M.L.B. (ACM; Carey, *The Messongo Traders;* CD309)

John 's estate was administered 1 Mar 1831 in AC by George W. Arbuckle. Joseph M. Gibb & James S. Corbin were the securities. (MilesW&A:538)

Edward Thornton and Mary Feddeman had the following child:

50   iii.   Edward Fiddeman, b. in AC, Mar 1795, d. Aug 1826.
Edward was named in his mother's will dated 24 Apr 1795 in AC. Joseph & William Fiddeman were named extrs and guardians to son Edward Thornton. (Nottingham Wills:429 (will of Mary Thornton; MilesW&A:538 (adm. of Edward F. Thornton))

Edward 's estate was administered 29 Aug 1826 in AC by James Feddeman. John Massey & Oliver Logan were the securities. (MilesW&A:538 (adm. of Edward F. Thornton))

34. John (of Edw'd)^4 Thornton (Edward^3, Edward^2, Edward^1), b. in AC c1765. He m. 1st 27 Nov 1792 in AC, **Margaret Broadwater** (b. c1770). (ACM) He m. 2nd 26 Mar 1810 (bond) in AC, **Rebecca Vernelson** (b. c1778). Thomas Collins and William Watts were the securities on the M.L.B. (ACM) Rebecca was the dau. of Elisha 'Lisha' Vernelson. (MilesW&A:555 (will of Elisha Vernelson))

John was listed as a head of household in the census of 1800 in Acc Parish, AC. He was shown as John Thornton of Edw'd, age 26-45. Listed with were 2 males, age 0-10; 1 other male, age 26-45; 1 female, age 0-10; 1 female, age 10-16; & 1 female, age 26-45. (Powell, *AC 1800, 1810, 1820 Census*)

John Thornton and Margaret Broadwater had the following children:

51   i.   John^5 Thornton, b. in AC c1795, d. Nov 1841. (MilesW&A:538 (adm. of John Thornton)) He m. 13 Dec 1822 (bond), Elizabeth Shay (b. c1790), dau. of Elias Shay and Agnes Trader. Thomas M. Bayly was the security on the M.L.B. of John Thornton of John and Elizabeth Shay of Elias. (1860 AC Census; ACM)

John was named in his grandfather's will 22 Apr 1799 in AC. (Nottingham Wills:460 (will of Edward Thornton))

John Thornton of Jno. was listed as a head of household in the census of 1840 in Acc Parish, AC, age 30-40. Listed with him were 1 male, age 10-15, 1 female, age 5-10, and 1 female, age 50-60. (Powell, *AC 1840 Census*)

John 's estate was administered 29 Nov 1841 by William Nock, in AC, William P. Moore & John C. Wise were the securities. (MilesW&A:538)

52   ii.   William Thornton, b. in AC c1800, d. 1849. The estate of William Thornton of John was administered 26 Nov 1849 in AC by David Mears. James W. Custis & Littleton A. Hinman were the securities. (MilesW&A:539)

35. William (of Edw'd)^4 Thornton (Edward^3, Edward^2, Edward^1), b. in AC c1767, d. Feb 1805. (MilesW&A:539 (adm. of William Thornton of Edward)) He m. (N)(N).

William Thornton of Edw'd was listed as a head of household in the census of 1800 in Acc Parish, AC, age 26-45. Listed with him were 1 male, age 0-10; 1 female, age 10-16; 1 female, age 26-45; and 1 free Negro. (Powell, *AC 1800, 1810, 1820 Census*)

The estate of William Thornton of Edward was administered 25 Feb 1805 in AC by Samuel Downing. David Watts & William Watts were the securities. William's estate was settled 24 Feb 1806 in AC, 27 Feb 1805 (Sale), 25 Oct

1805 (Order to Audit), 24 Feb 1806 (Rec'd) - Samuel Downing, admr. Buyers: Joshua Thornton & Molly Thornton of William. (MilesW&A:539)

    William Thornton had the following child:

      53   i. Mary 'Molly'[5] Thornton, b. in AC c1790. On 27 Feb 1805 Molly Thornton of William and Joshua Thornton were among the buyers at the estate sale of William Thornton (of Edw'd). (MilesW&A:539 (settlement of William Thornton of Edward))

40. Joshua[4] Thornton (I) (William[3], William[2], Edward[1]), b. c1755, d. Apr 1806. (Whitelaw: 1235 (tract A140); Carey, *Thornton Files*) Joshua Thornton was under age 14 in 1761 when a guardian was named and over age 14 in 1769 when he chose a guardian. (Nottingham Wills:539 (will of Joshua Thornton))

    He m. c1785, **Mary 'Molly' Wessells** (b. c1767 in AC, d. Jan 1821), dau. of William Wessells Sr. and Egnatia 'Nasha' (N). (MilesW&A:539 (will of Mary W. Thornton; MilesW&A:585 (will of William Wessells))

    On 24 Apr 1705 Joshua witnessed the will of Mary Thornton.

    Joshua inherited land c1800 in AC. In describing the owership of tract A140 (between Mappsville and Temperanceville), Whitelaw indicates that although William's will (wife Sarah) of 1758 did not mention land, he was succedded by a son William; however, the son died intestate the next year (1759), his estate being administered to his wife Anne. Both before and after the turn of the century (1800), a Joshua Thornton was shown by surveys and bounds of adjacent lands to have been the owner, so he may have been the son of the last William. In describing the owership of tract A146 (between Temperanceville, Oak Hall and Atlantic), Whitelaw indicates that in 1748 James & Hannah Wishart sold 73 acres to William Thornton Jr. A disposition by Thornton was not noted, but about 1800, a Joshua Thornton was the owner. (Whitelaw::1235 (tract A140) & 1251(tract A146))

    Joshua Thornton of Wm. was listed as a head of household in the census of 1800 in Acc Parish, AC, over age 45 with 2 males age 0-10; 1 male age 10-16; 2 females age 10-16; 1 female, age 16-26; and 3 slaves. (Powell, *AC 1800, 1810, 1820 Census*)

    He left a will dated 8 Jan 1805, probated 29 Apr 1806 in AC. To son James Thornton 75 acres adjoining James Taylor, Selby Delastatius & John Wharton & if he dies without issue, then to son David Thornton. To son Joshua Thornton the remainder of land where I now live & if he dies without issue, then to son David. To Joshua Negro girl Pagea until age 25 & then she to be free. To James Negro girl Soprah. To son David Negro boy Charles &,.. To dau. Elizabeth Matthews Negro woman Esther & if she attempts to sell her, then she to be free &,.. now in the hands of George Matthews. To Joshua & James Thornton,.. Remainder to Elizabeth Matthews, Joshua, James & David Thornton. Henry Thornton & son Joshua Thornton, extrs. Witnessed by Henry Thornton, John Thornton & Sally Thornton. (Nottingham Wills:539) William Thornton, Elias Taylor & Henry Thornton were securities.

Joshua's estate was settled 27 Jun 1808 in AC 15 May 1806 (Inventory), 16 May 1806 (Sale), 10 Jun 1808 (Audit), 27 Jun 1808 (Rec'd) - Appraisers: Solomon Ewell, Caleb Massey & Samuel Downing. Buyers: Molly Thornton, Joshua Thornton, Henry Thornton & William Thornton. Widow to have dower. Auditors: Caleb Massey & Arthur Whittington. (Nottingham Wills:539 (settlement of Joshua Thornton))

Joshua Thornton had the following children:

54   i.   William[5] Thornton, b. in AC c1770, d. c1807. He m. 19 Jul 1791 (bond) in AC, Margaret Taylor (b. c1770). Tunnell Thornton, orphan of Wm. Thronton, was bound to Joshua Thornton in 1808. (ACM; Carey, *Thornton Files*)

55   ii.   Joshua William Thornton, b. in AC c1775, d. Nov 1812. He m. 27 Jul 1807 (bond) in AC, Polly Delastatius (b. c1785). Walter Wessells was the security on the M.L.B. (Nottingham Wills:539 (will of Joshua Thornton); MilesW&A:538 (will of Joshua Thornton; ACM)

Joshua was named in the will of his sister, Esther Thornton dated 8 Sep 1804 in AC as extr. He was also given Negro girl Peggy & when she is of lawful age then to be free. She left all the money in the hands of Joshua Thornton, James Thornton & David Thornton, who were evidently her brothers. (MilesW&A:538 (will of Esther Thornton))

Joshua was listed as a head of household in the census of 1810 in Acc Parish, AC. (Powell, *AC 1800, 1810, 1820 Census*) He was shown as Joshua Thornton Jun., age 16-26. Listed with him were 1 male, age 10-16; 2 females, age 0-10; 1 female, age 16-26; and 2 slaves.

He left a will dated 14 Oct 1812, probated 30 Nov 1812 in AC. To son Joshua Thornton the plantation where I now live. To Euphamy R. Thornton £10. To Tunnell Thornton, a boy bound to me,,... Residue to my daus. Eliza Ann Thornton & Delilah Thornton. James White extr. Witnessed by James Duncan, James Thornton & Henry Thornton. David Watts & James Melvin securities. (MilesW&A:538) Joshua's estate was settled 29 Jun 1818 in AC. 30 Nov 1812 (Order to Inventory), 8 Dec 1812 (Sale), 30 Nov 1812 (Order to Audit), 29 Jun 1818 (Rec'd) - James White extr. Appraisers: Bagwell Wharton & James Duncan Jr. Buyers: Henry Thornton, Polly Thornton & James Thornton Jr. Cash paid William Thornton, guardian of

David Thornton. Auditors: B. Wharton & James
Duncan. (MilesW&A:538 (settlement of Joshua Thornton))
56   iii. David Thornton, b. in AC c1795. David was named in
the will of his sister Esther Thornton, dated 8 Sep 1804
in AC. She left all the money in the hands of the extr. to
Joshua Thornton, James Thornton & David Thornton,
who were evidently her brothers. (MilesW&A:538)
On 29 Jun 1818 when the settlement of Joshua
Thornton's estate was recorded, it showed that cash was
paid to William Thornton, guardian of David Thornton.
(MilesW&A:539 (settlement of Joshua Thornton))

Joshua Thornton (I) and Mary 'Molly' Wessells had the following children:
57   iv. Elizabeth 'Betty' Thornton, b. in AC c1785, d. before 9
Dec 1820. It was on this date that her mother Mary W.
Thornton named her 3 grandchildren Meshack, Mary
W. & Margaret Matthews in her will, implying their
mother was deceased. She m. 22 Feb 1803, Levin
(George?) Matthews (b. c1770). George Matthews was
the security on the M.L.B. (MilesW&A:539(will of Mary W.
Thornton))
Elizabeth was named in her grandfather's will dated
2 Nov 1802 in AC. (MilesW&A:585 (will of William Wessells))
Elizabeth was named in her sister's will 8 Sep 1804
in AC as sister Betty Matthews. (MilesW&A:538 (will of
Esther Thornton)
58   v. Esther 'Hesse' Thornton b. in AC c1790, d. Feb 1808 in
AC. Esther was named in her grandfather's will 2 Nov
1802 in AC. (MilesW&A:538 (will of Esther Thornton;
MilesW&A:585 (will of William Wessells))
She left a will dated 8 Sep 1804, probated 29 Feb
1808 in AC. To Joshua Thornton my Negro girl Peggy
& when she is of lawful age then to be free. Mentioned
Egnasha Bird, Mamy,.., Rebecca Russell, sister Betty
Mathuos [Matthews?]. To Joshua Thornton, James
Thornton & David Thornton all the money in the hands
of the extr. Joshua William Thornton Jr. Witnessed by
William Thornton & William Thornton. William
Thornton was security. (MilesW&A:538 (will of Esther
Thornton))
Esther (Hesse), dau. of Joshua, chose a guardian on
1806 in AC. (Carey, *Thornton Files*)
59   vi. James Thornton Jr., b. in AC c1793, m. 22 Oct 1831
(bond), Sally Mariner (b. c1810), dau. of George
Mariner. Robert Russell of Joshua was the security on

the M.L.B. of James Thornton Jr. and Sally Mariner of Geo. (ACM)

James was named in his sister's will 8 Sep 1804 in AC. (MilesW&A:538 (will of Esther Thornton)) He was shown as James Thornton in the will of Esther Thronton. She left all the money in the hands of the extr. to Joshua Thornton, James Thornton & David Thornton, who were evidently her brothers.

In 1807 James chose as his guardian William Thornton. (Carey, *Thornton Files*)

60   vii. Rachael Thornton, b. in AC c1794, m. 15 July 1815 (bond), Kendall Ross (b. c1790). John H. Watts & John Follio were the securities on the M.L.B. (MilesW&A:585 (will of William Wessells); ACM)

Rachael was named in her grandfather's will dated 2 Nov 1802 in AC. (MilesW&A:585 (will of William Wessells))

43. William⁴ Thornton Sr. (Guilford) (Thomas³, William², Edward¹), b. in AC c1760. (Carey, *Thornton Files*)

He m. c1783, **Mary Kelly** (b. c1760), dau. of Thomas Kelly and Tabitha Taham. After Thomas Kelly's death in 1784, a survey showed 180 ½ acres which were divided, the northwestern half going to Tabitha, the wife of George Clayton Hinman, and the southeastern half to Mary, the wife of William Thornton. After the deaths of William and Mary Thornton, in 1845 a William Thornton sold his 1/4 interest in 94 acres to Littleton A. Hinman, and the next year Hinman bought the 3/4 interest of Nancy Thornton at public auction. This was part of Whitelaw's tract A111 on Guilford Creek. (Whitelaw:1113 (tract A111); (Nottingham Wills:347 (will of Thomas Kelly)).

William was listed as a head of household in the census of 1800 in Acc, AC. He was shown as William Thornton, age 26-45. Listed with him were 2 males, age 10-16; 1 male, age 16-26; 1 female, age 10-16; 1 female, age 16-26; and 2 slaves. (Powell, *AC 1800, 1810, 1820 Census*)

William witnessed a will the will of Mary Bell on 16 Mar 1817 in AC. (MilesW&A:51 (will of Mary Bell))

William was named in his son's will dated 24 Dec 1821 in AC. (MilesW&A:539 (will of Thomas Thornton, Guilford))

William was named in his dau's will dated 12 Nov 1824 in AC. (MilesW&A:538 (will of Easter Thornton)) Easter Thornton left the land now occupied by her father to her brother William Thornton, provided he never sell the land and at his death to his son William.

William Thornton Sr. (Guilford) and Mary Kelly had the following children:

61   i. Easter⁵ Thornton, b. in AC c1785, d. Jan 1828 in AC. She left a will dated 12 Nov 1824, probated 25 Feb 1828 in AC. To brother William Thornton the land now

occupied by my father provided he never sells the land
& at his death to his son William. To sister Nancy
Thornton,.. & at her death to nephew William
Thornton. Witnessed by George H. Ewell, George
Clayton & George Clayton Jr. Her will was partly
proved on 28 Jan 1828 and fully proved on 25 Feb
1828. (MilesW&A:538 (will of Easter Thornton), 539 (will of
Thomas Thornton, Guilford), 539 (adm. of Nancy Thornton))

62 ii. Nancy Thornton, b. in AC c1788, d. 1838. Nancy was
named in her brother's will dated 24 Dec 1821. In his
will Thornton of Guilford gave here his entire estate
including the land & marsh which was my mother's &
which my father William Thornton now holds for &
during his life. (MilesW&A:538 (will of Easter Thornton), 539
(will of Thomas Thornton, Guilford), 539 (adm. of Nancy Thornton))

On 29 Oct 1838 Littleton A. Hinman was named to
settle the estate of Nancy Thornton. Levin Dix Sr. &
John D. Parks were the securities. (MilesW&A:539)

63 iii. James Thornton, b. in AC c1790, d. c1835, m. 10 Jan
1818 (lic.) in WO Co., Laura (Lorey) Bagwell. His
wife Laura, age 40-50, was the head of a household in
1840 census. (Carey, *Thornton Files*; Powell, *AC 1830 Census;*
Powell, *WO Co. Marriages 1795-1865*)

Laura, b. c1800 in AC, was the dau. of Charles
Bagwell and Ann 'Nancy' Grinnalds. (FA CD309;
MilesW&A:20 (will of Charles Bagwell))

James was listed as a head of household in the
census of 1830 in Acc Parish, AC. (Powell, *AC 1830
Census*) He was shown as James Thornton, age 40-50.
Listed with him were 2 males age 0-5; 2 females age 5-
10; and 1 female age 30-40.

64 iv. William Thornton Jr. (Guilford), b. in AC c1790, d.
c1839. He must have died before 10 Oct 1840, when a
Chancery suit was brought into Accomack County
Court: William Thornton's admr (Plaintiff) vs. William
Thornton' heirs (Defendants). The plaintiff was
Littleton A. Hinman, administrator of Nancy Thornton
deceased, and the defendants were William Thornton
Jr. (now age 21 years) and Spencer Drummond,
guardian to Nancy Thornton. (MilesW&A:538 (will of Easter
Thornton); Walczyk, *AC Chancery Orders, 1832-45*:100)

He m. Elizabeth Mason 19 Jan 1814 (bond) in AC.
Jesse Clayton was the security on the M.L.B. (ACM)

Elizabeth Thornton, b. c1797 in Oak Grove, AC, dau. of James Mason and Elizabeth 'Betty' Northam, d. 20 Oct 1857 in Oak Grove, AC. Her son Wm. Thorton gave the information. (WADR; Carey, *Mason Family of Kegotank*) On 16 Mar 1817 William Thornton, Richard Bundick & John Y. Sterling witnessed the will of Mary Bell. William Thornton Sr. & James Justice were securities at probate. (MilesW&A:51 (will of Mary Bell)) On 30 Sep 1819 William Riley, William Thornton Jr., & Nancy Mason witenessed the will of John Y. Sterling. (MilesW&A:505 (will of John Y. Sterling)) William was named in his sister's will 12 Nov 1824 in AC. He was shown as a brother William Thornton in the will of Easter Thornton and given the land now occupied by my father provided he never sell the land & at his death to his son William. (MilesW&A:538 (will of Easter Thornton))

65   v. Thomas Thornton (Guilford), b. in AC c1795, d. Mar 1822 in AC. He left a will dated 24 Dec 1821, probated 25 Mar 1822 in AC. To sister Nancy Thornton all my estate including the land & marsh which was my mother's & which my father William Thornton now holds for & during his life. Sister Nancy Thornton extx. Witnessed by Dennis Clayton, George Clayton & Thomas R. Clayton. (MilesW&A:538 (will of Easter Thornton) & 539 (will of Thomas Thornton, Guilford) & 539 (adm. of Nancy Thornton))

45. William⁴ Thornton Sr. (Island) (James³, James², Edward¹, b. in AC c1746. This William Thornton Senr. was evidently the eldest son of James Thornton Senr. since he apparently inherited his father land. He would have been b. c1746 and could have m. as early as 1766 or as late as 1785 as his children were born in the late 1780s. William d. Mar 1812 in Chincoteague, AC. (Carey, *Thornton Files*; MilesW&A:539 (adm. & audit of William Thornton - Island))

He brought a law suit against William Burch on 28 Sep 1784 for trespass, assault and battery.(AC OB1783-84:460)

There is no record of this William Thronton buying or selling land, but in 1832, when his son John Thornton sold land on Chincoteague, it was bordered on the East & southeast by William Thornton's heirs..

On 30 Mar 1812 James White was named to settle the estate of William Thornton. Bagwell Wharton & David Watts were the securities. On 1 Oct 1812 there was an order to audit the estate of William Thornton (Island) and James White was the administrator. John Jones, William Rowley, Charles Ewell and Thomas T. Taylor were named to appraise his estate. The auditors were Bagwell Wharton & Thomas T. Taylor. The audit was recorded on 27 Jun 1814. The list of men to whom various fees had been paid by the estate included: William Daizy, James Conner, Ocra Brainney, Thomas Hancock, Charles Carpenter, John Jones & William Sharpley. (MilesW&A:539 (adm. & audit of William Thornton - Island))

William Thornton Sr. (Island) had the following children:

66   i. John[5] Thornton Sr. (Chinco Is). d. before the census of 1870. He had a son, Rev. Wm. P. Thornton, and since the 1830 census shows him age 40-50 with 3 males in household under age 15, it is possible that Revel Thornton, b. c1815, was also a son and there were probably two others. (Carey, *Thornton Files*), b. in AC c1787 (FA CD309; 1860 AC Census)

He m. 1st 9 Feb 1813 (bond) in AC, Hester 'Hessy' Bloxom (b. c1790 in AC). Henry Thornton was the security on the M.L.B. (ACM)

He m. 2nd c1830, Susan (N) (b. c1800 in AC). When he was selling land in the 1840s his wife's name was Susan; her maiden name has not been determined. (FA CD309; 1860 AC Census)

John Thornton was listed as a head of household in the census of 1830 in Acc Parish, AC. He was age 40-50 with 3 males in his household under age 15. (Powell, *AC 1830 Census*)

On 21 Jul 1832 John Thornton bought 50 acres of land on Chincoteague Island for $50 from James S. Duntson & Eliza his wife and Thomas W. Marshall. The deed states that this land was bordered on the north & northeast by land belonging to Timothy Hill, on the East & Sourtheast by William Thornton heirs, Peter Roberts' heirs & D. Welborun's heirs and on the northwest by "the Tab lands." On 27 Mar 1833, John Thornton borrowed $100 from Daniel Jones of Chinco. Island, and put up the above land as collateral. (AC Deeds, 1830-32:535; AC Deeds 1832-34:289; Carey, *Thornton Files*))

On 9 Nov 1842 John Thornton of William, & Susan his wife, sold 20 acres of land on Chincoteague to Crippen Bowdoin Jr. & Deliala Bowdoin for $35. This land was bounded on the north by David Daizy, on the East by William Thornton, on the South by Peter Roberts' heirs and on the West by other land of John Thornton of William. Carey, *Thornton Files*; AC Deeds 1842-43:385)

On 20 Apr 1844 John Thornton & Susan of Chincoteague Island sold 10 acres of land to Wm. P.

Thornton of the same place for $12. The land was bound on the north by above Crippen Bowdin land, on the northeast by David Daizy, on the Southwest by Peter Robert's land and on the southeast by Shepherd Creek. (Carey, *Thornton Files*; AC Deeds, 1843-44:674)

On 16 Dec 1845 John Thornton Senr. & Susan his wife sold to Wm. Sharpley Senr. for $30, 20 acres of land on Chincoteague, bounded on the northeast by said Thornton, on the southeast by lands of said Wm. Sharpley Senr., on the northwest by Tabb land and on the west by Black Benny Hill, it being a part of the tract of land where John Thronton Senr. at present resides. (Carey, *Thornton Files*; AC Deeds, 1846-48:6)

On 17 Oct 1846 John Thornton of Wm. & Susan his wife sold 10 acres on Chincoteague Island to James Clayvill for $40. John Thornton of Wm. had now sold 60 acres of land on Chincoteague Island, while the records show him buying only 50 acres. (Carey, *Thornton Files*; AC Deeds, 1846-48:30)

John Thornton was listed as a head of household (HH#63) in the census of 1850 in Acc Parish, AC, a 63 year old farmer with real estate valued at $50. Listed with him were Susan Thornton, age 50; Elizabeth Thornton, age 19; and Margaret Thornton, age 8. There cold have been older daus. who had m. by 1850. He was 3 households from John D. Thornton, sailor, and 21 households from son Wm. Thornton, farmer. (FA CD309)

Jno. Thornton was listed as a head of household in the census of 1860 in Acc Parish, HH#1043, a 73 year old oysterman with real estate valued at $50 and personal property valued at $25. Listed with him was Susan Thornton, age 60. This was probably Chincoteague Island. (1860 AC Census)

67   ii. William Thornton of Chinco Is, b. in AC c1789.

He m. 1st 12 Jan 1809 (bond) in AC, Nancy Carpenter (b. c1790). Henry Hopkins was the security on the M.L.B. (Carey, *Thornton Files*; ACM)

He m. 2nd 27 Aug 1810, Sarah Hancock (b. c1790). David Watts was the security on the M.L.B. of William Thornton of Chincoteague Island and Sarah Hancock. (ACM)

46. John^4 Thornton (James^3, James^2, Edward^1), b. in AC c1750. (Carey, *Thornton Files*)

John was listed as a head of household in the census of 1800 in Acc Parish, AC. He was shown as John Thornton (W.BD.?), age 26-45. Listed with him were 2 males, age 0-10; 1 other male age 26-45; 1 female, age 0-10; 1 female, age 10-16; and 1 female, age 26-45. (Powell, *AC 1800, 1810, 1820 Census*)
John Thornton had the following children:

68   i.   Jonathan[5] Thornton , b. in AC c1771. He married three times. He m. 1st 5 May 1791 in AC, Mary Owens (b. c1772). (ACM; Carey, *Thornton Files*)

He m. 2nd 26 May 1806 (bond) in AC, Sally Ross (b. c1785). James Thornton was the security on the M.L.B. {ACM}

He m. 2nd 26 Sep 1808 in AC, Mary Jones (b. c1780). James Thornton was security on the M.L.B. (ACM)

Jonathan Thornton was listed as a head of household in the census of 1810 in Acc Parish, AC, age 26-45. Listed with him were 1 male, age 0-10; 1 male, age 10-16; 3 females, age 0-10; and 1 female, age 26-45. (Powell, *AC 1800, 1810, 1820 Census)*

On 14 Feb 1821 Jonathan Thornton gave consent for his dau. Sally to marry James Whealton of Jno. (ACM)

Jonathan Thornton was listed as a head of household in the census of 1830 in Acc Parish, AC, age 60-70. Listed with him were 1 male, age 20-30; and 1 female, age 60-70. (Powell, *AC 1830 Census*)

69   ii. Kendall Thornton, b. in AC, c1775, d. before 27 Dec 1824 when Elizabeth Thornton, widow of Kendall, m. Daniel Sturgis of Chino Island. He m. 20 Apr 1796, Elizabeth 'Betsey' Read (b. c1775). (Carey, *Thornton Files*; ACM)

Elizabeth m. 27 Dec 1824 (bond), Daniel Sturgis (Chinco Is). David Watts Sr. & William D. Cropper were the securities on the M.L.B. of Daniel Sturgis of Chinco Island and Elizabeth Thornton, widow of Kendall. (ACM)

Kendall Thornton was listed as a head of household in the census of 1800 in Wal Island, AC, age 16-26 with 2 females age 0-10; and 1 female age 16-26. (Powell, *AC 1800, 1810, 1820 Census)*

Kendall Thornton was listed as a head of household in the census of 1810 in Wallops Island, AC, age 26-45. Listed with him were 1 male, age 0-10; 1 male, age 16-26; 1 female, age 16-26. (NOTE: This could have

been either Wallops Island or Chincoteague Island.)
(Powell, *AC 1800, 1810, 1820 Census*)

47. **William (of Charles)**[4] **Thornton** (Charles (William?)[3], James[2], Edward[1]), b. in AC c1765, d. after 1834.

He m. 1 May 1821 (bond), **Polly Rowley widow** (b. c1780). William Watts was the security on the M.L.B. of William Thornton of Charles and Polly Rowley, widow of William. (ACM)

Polly m. 1st c1800, **John Young**, m. 2nd 29 Feb 1808 (bond), **William Rowley**. Obed Adams was the security on the M.L.B. of William Roley and Polly Young, widow of John. (ACM)

WilliamThornton of Charles was listed as a head of household in the census of 1800 in Acc Parish, AC, age 26-45, with 1 female age 0-10 and 1 female age 26-45. (Powell, *AC 1800, 1810, 1820 Census*)

In 1821 William Thornton of Charles conveyed land as a gift to Hessy, Polly & William Thornton. (Carey, *Thornton Files*)

William was ordered to be tax free on 1834 in AC. (Carey, *Thornton Files*)

William (of Charles) Thornton had the following children:

70   i. Hessey[5] Thornton b. in AC c1798, m. 12 Jun 1823 (bond) in AC, Nathaniel Taylor. William Watts and Zadock Selby were the securities on the M.L.B. of Nathaniel Taylor of Alexander and Hessey Thornton. (ACM; Carey, *Thornton Files*)

Nathaniel, b. c1795, m. 1st 6 Apr 1816 (bond), Euphemia Mariner. Wm. Matthews Taylor was the security on the M.L.B. of Nathaniel Taylor of Alexander and Euphemia Mariner of George. (ACM)

Nathaniel, b c1795 in AC, son of Alexander Taylor and Ann Matthews, m. 3rd 27 Jun 1838 (bond), Maria Massey. William Walston was the security on the M.L.B. of Nathaniel Taylor, widower, and Maria Henderson, widow of Joseph. (Nottingham Wills:433 (will of Alexander Taylor))(ACM)

71   ii. Polly Thornton, b. in AC c1800. Polly received land as a gift 1821 in AC when William Thornton of Charles deeded land to Hessy, Polly & William Thornton. (Carey, *Thornton Files*),

72   iii. William Thornton b. in AC c1802, m. c1833, Abagil (N) (b. c1810). (MACM:327 (marriage of son Charles Thornton); Carey, *Thornton Files*),

In 1821 William Thornton of Charles deeded land in AC to Hessy, Polly & William Thornton. (Carey, *Thornton Files*)

Descendants of Henry Trader
(Limited to the Trader surname)

Introduction
From the mid 1600s until the time of the Revolutionary War, the spelling of this family name was either Armitrader or variations thereof, such as Armitrading, Armeytrader, Armitrador, etc. Between the time of Revolution and the early 1800's a transition from Armitrader to simply Trador/Trader occurred. For the purpose of this work, the spelling of Trader was chosen as this family is now referred to. But the spelling found in the various records sited will also be shown. This work is based primarily on the research of Mary Frances Carey and letters and reports sent to her by other members of the Trader family.

First Generation
1. **Henry¹ Trader (I)**, b. c1610, d. 1663. (NC DW&c., *1657-66*:91)
 He m. 1ˢᵗ 1647, **Christian Granger** (b. c1610, d. 1650 in NC). (NC DW&c., *1645-51*:219) He m. 2ⁿᵈ c1650, **Alice (N)** (b. c1610). (Carey, *The Messongo Traders;* Purse&Person)
 Henry immigrated to Virginia in 1635. Henry 's will was probated 28 Aug 1663 in NC. (NC DW&c., *1657-66*:91) He was shown in records as Armitradinge.
 Henry Trader (I) and Christian Granger had the following child:
 + 2 i. Arthur² Trader, b. c1648.

Second Generation
2. **Arthur² Trader** (Henry¹), b. in NC c1648.
 He m. c1660, **Rose Kellam** (b. c1640). (Carey, *The Messongo Traders*)
 Arthur was living 17 Jun 1663 in NC. He was shown in records as Armitradinge.
 Arthur Trader and Rose Kellam had the following children:
 + 3 i. Richard³ Trader, b. c1674, d. Mar 1755.
 + 4 ii. Henry Trader (II) , b. c1675, d. Feb 1735.

Third Generation
3. **Richard³ Trader** (Arthur², Henry¹, b. in AC c1674, d. Mar 1755. (Nottingham Wills:182 (will of Richard Armitrader; Carey, *The Messongo Traders*)
 He m. c1700, **Elizabeth Chance** (b. c1680), dau. of Jacob Chance and Rose (N). (Carey, *The Messongo Traders;* Nottingham Wills:115 (adm. of Jacob Chance)
 On 27 Mar 1744 the widow Rose Chance was named to settle the estate of Jacob Chance. Richard Armitrader was the security. (Nottingham Wills:115 (adm. of Jacob Chance))
 Richard left a will dated 24 Feb 1755, probated 25 Mar in AC. To wife Elizabeth whole estate during her widow, then to dau. Sabrah Meersm plantation where I live. Grandsons William & Benjamin Knock. Grandau Patience Knock. Grandson Levin Knock. dau. Sabra Meers residuary legatee. Son in law John

Meers extr. Witnessed by Francis Savage, Rowland Savage, William Red. John Meers, husband of Sabra, one of the daus. & co heirs of the testator, & William Knock, son & heir at law of Rose Knock, deceased, the other dau. & co heir of the said testator, being present & having nothing to object, the said will was admitted to probate. (Nottingham Wills:182 (will of Richard Armitrader))

He was shown in records as Armitrader.

Richard Trader and Elizabeth Chance had the following children:

5   i.   Sabrah[4] Trader, b. in AC c1702, m. c1720, John Mears (b. c1690). (Carey, *The Messongo Traders*)

6   ii.   Rose Trader , b. in AC c1704, d. before 24 Feb 1755 in AC. Her children William, Benjamin, Patience & Levin Knock were also named as grandchildren. She m. c1720, (N) Nock. (Nottingham Wills:182 (will of Richard Armitrader))

4. **Henry**[3] **Trader (II)** (Arthur[2], Henry[1]), b. in AC c1675, d. Feb 1735 in AC. (Nottingham Wills:104 (will of Henry Armitrader)) (Carey, *The Messongo Traders*)

He m. c1700, **(N) Hutchens** (b. c1680). (Carey, *The Messongo Traders*) (N)

He left a will dated 13 Jan 1734/35, probated 6 Mar 1734/35 in AC. To 2 sons Liddleton & William Armitrader 300 acres purchased of John Morris. To son Henry Armitrader land & plantation purchased of Robert Taylor, also my right & title to the mill dam adjcent the land of Jacob Chance. To son Richard Armitrader land & plantation where I now live, also a piece of land adjcent Jonathan Garrison containing 60 acres. To son Richard all my land in Northampton. Son John Armitrader. dau. Roxe Willis. Son Arthur Armitrader. Son Richard residuary legatee & Exr. Witnessed by Robert Coleburn, William Spiers, Jacob Chance. (Nottingham Wills:104 (will of Henry Armitrader))

Henry Trader (II) and (N) Hutchens had the following children:

7   i.   Arthur[4] Trader (Armitrader), b. in AC c1704, d. 1742. (Nottingham Wills:114 (adm. of Arthur Armitrader)) He m. c1720, Mary (N) (b. c1700). (Carey, *The Messongo Traders*) On 16 Jan 1742/43 the sheriff was order to take charge of the estate of Arthur Armitrader and sell same at public action. (Nottingham Wills:114 (adm. of Arthur Armitrader))

+   8   ii.   Richard Trader Jr. , b. c1706, d. Nov 1762.

+   9   iii.   Henry Trader (III) , b. c1708, d. Jan 1749.

+   10   iv.   Littleton Trader (of upper AC) , b. c1712, d. Oct 1771.

   11   v.   John Trader , b. in AC c1714.

+   12   vi.   William Trader Sr. , b. c1715, d. Dec 1794.

   13   vii.   Roxe Trader, b. in AC c1716, m. c1734, (N) Willis c1734. (Carey, *The Messongo Traders*)

Fourth Generation

8. Richard⁴ Trader Jr. (Henry³, Arthur², Henry¹), b. in AC c1706, d. Nov 1762, m. c1730, **Patience Burton** (b. c1710), dau. of Thomas Burton and Amey (N). (Nottingham Wills:105 (will of Thomas Burton)) Richard Armitrader left a will dated 13 Mar 1762, probated 30 Nov 1762 in AC. Wife Patience to have use of whole estate for life, reversion to 8 children Elizabeth Harrison, Robert Armitrader, Anne Armitrader, James Armitrader, Stephen Armitrader, Susanna Burton, Richard Armitrader & Mathew Armitrader. Wife Patience & son Stephen, extrs. Witnessed by Stratton Burton, Stephen Armitrader. (Nottingham Wills:213 (will of Richard Armitrader)) Richard Trader Jr. and Patience Burton had the following children:

- 14   i. Elizabeth⁵ Trader, b. in AC c1730, m. c1750, (N) Harrison.
- 15   ii. Robert Trader, b. in AC c1732.
- 16   iii. Anne Trader, b. in AC c1734.
- 17   iv. James Trader, b. in AC c1736.
- 18   v. Stephen Trader, b. in AC c1738.
- 19   vi. Susannah Trader. b. in AC c1740, m. c1760, (N) Burton.
- 20   vii. Richard Trader, b. in AC c1742, d. 1763.
- 21   viii. Matthew Trader, b. in AC c1744.

9. Henry⁴ Trader (III) (Henry³, Arthur², Henry¹), b. in AC c1708, d. Jan 1749. He m. before 1728, **Abigail Bradford** (b. c1710, d. Jan 1752), dau. of William Bradford and Bridget Fisher. (Nottingham Wills:139 (adm. of Abigail Armitrader))

In 1728, William Bradford had given 200 acres in the Wachapreague area to his son John. The deed states that if son John should die without heirs, the land would transfer to his sister Ann Bradford and then to another sister, Abigail Armitrader. (Whitelaw:779) William Bradford left a will dated 4 July 1735, probated 1 June 1736. He left a slave named Appy or £10 to the dau. of Henry Armitrader called Comfort Armitrader when she reached age 16 years. (ADW, 1729-1737, part 1:494) These two records show that Henry Armitrader had m. Abigail Bradford before 1728.

The estate of Henry Armitrader was administered 30 Jan 1749 in AC by Abigail Armitrader. John Bradford & Samuel Beech were securities. (Nottingham Wills:135 (adm. of Henry Armitrader)) On 27 Nov 1750, Abigail Armitrader filed her husband's inventory. (AC Wills, 1749-1752:125) It consisted of £40.8.1 pence in cash, household furniture, cooking and eating utensils, livestock, farm tools and crops, "a Parcel of Leather, a Parcel of Shoe Maker's Tools, one Deerskin, one Parcel of Carpenter's Tools, and one old Testment and Printer." He was shown in the records as Henry Armitrader, Junr. In 1735 he inherited land his father had bought from Robert Taylor, 60 acres between Jonathan Garrison and Edward Kellam, and his father's right to a mill dam. This land was located in AC, between the present-day Onley and Melfa, off the highway toward Locustville.

AC records do not show Henry Armitrader, Junr. selling his land. The next owner of record was a Littleton Armitrader, presumably Henry's eldest son. (Whitelaw:850) With the exception of Littleton, nothing more has been found in AC records of the children of Henry Armitrader, Junr and his wife Abigail (Bradford) after 1752. Son Henry evidently moved to SO Co.

Henry Trader (III) and Abigail Bradford had the following children:

+ 22   i.   Littleton[5] Trader, b. c1730, d. Oct 1764.

   23   ii.   Comfort Trader, b. in AC c1732. Comfort, dau. of Henry Armitrader, was named in her grandfather's will 4 Jul 1735 in AC. (Nottingham Wills:105 (will of William Bradford))

   24   iii.   Leah Trader, b. c1735. (Carey, *The Messongo Traders*)

   25   iv.   Rachel Trader, b. c1737. (Carey, *The Messongo Traders*)

   26   v.   William Trader, b. c1739. (Carey, *The Messongo Traders*)

+ 27   vi.   Henry Trader (IV), b. 1 Jan 1741, d. c1791. (Carey, *The Messongo Traders*)

   28   vii.   John Trader, b. 1745 in AC, d. 1781, m. 1st (N)(N), and m. 2nd c1775, Elizabeth (N) (b. c1745, d. 1796). (Carey, *The Messongo Traders*) John was living in SO Co.

   29   viii.   Richard Trader, b. in AC c1747, d. 1794, m. c1765, Lavina (N) (b. c1745). (Carey, *The Messongo Traders*)

10. Littleton[4] Trader (of upper AC) (Henry[3], Arthur[2], Henry[1]), b. in AC c1712, d. Oct 1771, m. c1730, **Ann (N)** (b. c1715). (Carey, *The Messongo Traders*)

On 31 Dec 1760 Littleton Armitrader was named to settle the estate of Henry Armitrader. William Andrews was security. (Nottingham Wills:172 (adm. of Henry Armitrader))

He left a will dated 9 Oct 1771, probated 29 Oct 1771. To grandson Littleton Armitrader land where I now live, & for want of issue to my dau. Ann Bird. To son Archibold all the rest of my land I have in possession & for want of heirs to my dau. Euphamy Armitrader. dau. Comfort Morgan. dau. in law Comfort Armitrader. 4 daus. Comfort Morgan, Ann Bird, Sinah Hopman & Euphamy Armitrader residuary legatees. Son in law William Morgan, extr. Witnessed by Joseph Blake, Nehemiah Stockly. In order of probate: James Henry guardian to Littleton Armitrader, heir at law to the testator. (Nottingham Wills:258, 624 (will of Littleton Armitrader))

Littleton Trader (of upper AC) and Ann (N) had the following children:

+ 30   i.   Israel[5] Trader , b. c1732, d. May 1768.

   31   ii.   Henry Trader Jr. (of Littleton) , b. in AC c1735, d. Dec 1760. Henry 's estate was administered 31 Dec 1760 in AC by Littleton Armitrader. William Andrews was security. (Nottingham Wills:172 (adm. of Henry Armitrader); Carey, *The Messongo Traders*)

+ 32   iii.   Archibald Trader Sr. , b. c1737, d. May 1821.

   33   iv.   Ann Trader, b. in AC c1740, m. c1760, (N) Byrd. (Carey, *The Messongo Traders*) (N)

34   v. Comfort Trader, b. in AC c1742, m. c1760, William
Morgan (b. c1740 in AC, d. Nov 1781). (Nottingham
Wills:331 (will of William Morgan))

35   vi. Sarah 'Sinah' Trader, b. in AC c1744, m. c1760, (N)
Hopman.

36   vii. Euphamy Trader, b. in AC c1746.

12. **William**[4] **Trader Sr.** (Henry[3], Arthur[2], Henry[1]), b. in AC c1715, d. Dec
1794 in AC. (Nottingham Wills:421 (will of William Armey Trador))

He m. c1740, **(N) Staton** (b. c1720) in AC, dau. of Joseph Staton Jr. and
Susannah Warrington .

He left a will dated 6 Jan 1794, probated 30 Dec 1794 in AC. To son
Sacker Trador plantation where I now live and 10 acres of marsh purchased of
Abner Burton. To son William Armey Trador 1 shilling. Mentioned son George
Trador, dau. Comfort Trador, dau. Agnes Shay, granddau Peggy Trador. To dau.
Ommey (?) Young 1 shilling. Balance of estate to be divided between children
Elizabeth Lucust, Susannah Fisher, Near Taylor, Comfort Trador, Agnes Shay.
William Morgan extr. Witnesses Richard Kelly, Archibald Trador and Major
Hinman. (Nottingham Wills:421 (will of William Armey Trador))

William Trader Sr. had the following children:

37   i. Susanna[5] Trader, b. in AC c1730, m. c1750, Thomas
Fisher (b. c1720, d. Jan 1786), son of John Fisher and
Elizabeth Roberts. Thomas Fisher and his wife Susanna
sold off parts of Whitelaw's tract A134 from 1751 up
through 1767. (Whitelaw:1215; ACW&c. 1743-49:340
(settlement of the estate of Thomas Fisher' father); Nottingham
Wills:345)

After her husband, Thomas Fisher, d. ntestate in
1786, the widow Susanna joined with William and
Jenny Johnson in a sale of 65 acres to Henry Fletcher,
and the next year George and Lucretia Armitrader sold
Henry Fletcher 50 acres more. Possibly Jenny and
Lucretia were daus. and heirs of Thomas Fisher.
(Whitelaw:1215)

On 14 Aug 1786 Wm. Johnson and wife Jenny and
Susanna Fisher sold land to Henry Fletcher. (AC Deeds
1783-1788, pp. 349 & 387)

Susanna appears on the list of tithables in AC for 7
May 1787, living next door to Henry Fletcher Sr. She
was not tithable, with 1 black under 16 and 2 cattle.
She may have been listed as Sr. because her deceased
husband had a dau. Susanna by his first wife Naomi,
who would have been about age 15-17 by this time,
with a son of her own. (AC Tax Lists 1787:81, 108)

+   38   ii. Sacker Trader , b. c1736, d. Oct 1826.

+ 39 iii. George Trader , b. c1738, d. Feb 1800.
+ 40 iv. William Trader Jr. , b. c1740, d. 1826.

William Trader Sr. and (N) Staton had the following children:

41 v. Comfort Trader, b. in AC c1742
42 vi. Agnes Trader, b. in AC c1744, m. 12 Nov 1788 (bond), Elias Shay (b. c1760). (AC Mar Lic Bonds (tr), 1774-1806; ACM)
43 vii. Ommey Trader, b. in AC c1746, m. c1775, (N) Young.
44 viii. Elizabeth Trader, b. in AC c1748, m. c1775, (N) Lucas (b. c1750). (Carey, *The Messongo Traders*)
45 ix. Near Trader, b. in AC c1752, m. c1775, (N) Taylor (b. c1750). (Carey, *The Messongo Traders*)
+ 46 x. (N) Trader , b. c1754.
+ 47 xi. Staton Trader Sr. , b. c1755, d. 22 Jan 1817.

Fifth Generation

22. **Littleton⁵ Trader** (Henry⁴, Henry³, Arthur², Henry¹), b. in AC c1730, d, Oct 1764. (Nottingham Wills:139 (adm. of Abigal Armitrader))

He m. 1ˢᵗ c1750, **Ann (N)** (b. c1730). He m. 2ⁿᵈ c1764, **Elizabeth (N)** (b. c1730, d. Jun 1799). She m. 1ˢᵗ c1750, **Joseph Burton** and m. 3ʳᵈ **(N) Nock,** after 1764. (Nottingham Wills:461 (will of Elizabeth Knock))

Littleton was named as administrator of the estate of Abigal Armitrader on 28 Jan 1752. (Nottingham Wills:139 (adm. of Abigal Armitrader))

He left a will dated 11 Oct 1764, probated 30 Oct 1764. Mentioned sons Arter, Henry, and Samuel. To son Arthur Armitrader all my lands & my water mill. Mentioned daus. Abgil & Rose and an unborn child. John Tayler & Abraham Tayler extrs. Witnessed by John Coleburn, John Spiers. Littleton Trader acquired his father's estate and all his descendants remained in the Hack's Neck area of the county. (Nottingham Wills:220)

Littleton Trader and Ann (N) had the following children:

+ 48 i. Arthur 'Arter'⁶ Trader, b. c1750, d. Apr 1791.
49 ii. Henry Trader, b. in AC c1752, d. Sep 1795, m. c. 1785, Margaret (N) (b. c1765). She m. Issac Outten c1797. (Nottingham Wills:414 (adm. of Henry Trader; Carey, *The Messongo Traders*)

Henry was bound out to learn the trade of ships carpenter in 1766. He was a ship carpenter in 1784.

Henry was named in his brother's will 20 Jan 1791 in AC. (Nottingham Wills:389 (will of Arthur Armitrader))

On 29 Sep 1795 Samuel Trader was named to settle the estate of Henry Trader. Thomas Jacob & Zerobabel Hornsby were the securities. His estate was divided between his widow, brother and sister and a niece. (Nottingham Wills:414 (adm. of Henry Trader))

50   iii. Abigail Trader, b. in AC c1757.
51   iv. Rose Trader, b. in AC c1759, m. c1790, James Hamnell
       (b. c1770). (Carey, *The Messongo Traders*) James
+   52   v. Samuel Trader, b. 1763, d. 19 Feb 1810.
Littleton Trader and Elizabeth (N) had the following child:
+   53   vi. Littleton Trader, b. 1764, d. Jun 1822.
27. **Henry⁵ Trader (IV)** (Henry⁴, Henry³, Arthur², Henry¹) b. in AC 1 Jan 1741,
d. c1791. (Carey, *The Messongo Traders*)
     He m. 1ˢᵗ before 5 Apr 1771, **Agnes (N)** (b. c1745). before 5 Apr 1771. It
was on this date that Henry Trader and wife Agnes sold land to William
McClemmy. (SOD E.:142)
     Agnes d. before 12 Dec 1772 when Henry, of WO Co., sold land to John
Nelms £65. Since a wife did not cosign this deed, it is apparent that Henry
Trader had lost his first wife Agness, between the spring of 1771 and the end of
1772. (SOD E.:219)
     He m. 2ⁿᵈ 1773, **Elizabeth Smith** (b. c1750, d. 1798). On 8 Nov 1769,
Isaiah Smith had sold to Elizabeth Smith 50 acres called *Pea Patch* in Wicomico
Forrest, WO Co. On 5 May 1773, Henry Trader, of WO Co., and wife Elizabeth
Trader sold the same land to Peter Gordy. These deeds show that Henry Trader
had m. 2ⁿᵈ Elizabeth Smith by the spring of 1773. (WOD I:255)
     On the same day as the administration of the estate of Abigail Armitrader
was granted to Littleton Armitrader (30 Jan 1752), Henry Armitrader, orphan,
was bound out by the Church Wardens to William Bradford, Junr to learn the
trade of a bricklayer. This record states Henry was aged eleven years on the first
day of this month, placing his birth on 1 Jan 1741, and he was to remain with
Bradford til lawful age. (AC OB 1744-1753:566)
     Henry was named as an heir of a Rev War Veteran 1752 in AC. When his
mother's estate was settled in 1752, Henry Armitrader inherited personal
property as his share of his father's estate. The entire list consisted of : 1 horse, 1
sheep, 1 hogg, 2 geese, 3 old plates and a parcel of old books, 1 hackle and 1
small trunk, 1 pair shears, fire tons and __ forks, 2 iron wedges and 1 looking
glass, 1 kettle, 5 tubs, 7 wooden trenchers, 1 1/2 bucket of salt, 1 barrel of corn,
1 bed, 1 bed sted matt and cord, 1 pair cotton blankets, 2 pair of spectakles, and
5 pounds 3 shillings 8 pence in cash. (Acc Wills & c., 1752-1757:158) After this he
disappeared from AC records.
     On 17 Nov 1767 Henry Trader "also called Henry Armey Trader," bought
34 acres of land called *London* from David Wilson in SO Co. The deed states
that both the buyer and seller were of SO Co. (SOD D:440) The land was located
in upper SO Co., in the portion that became Wicomico Co. in 1865.
     On 19 May 1769 Henry Armatrader and wife Agnes sold 35 acres in SO
Co. called *London* to George Smith for £500. (SOD E.:23)
     On 17 Dec 1769 Henry Trader bought parts of three tracts in SO Co. from
William Stephens, 27 ½ acres called *Confusion*, 22 ½ acres called *Last
Discovery*, and 54 acres called *Maddux Fancy*. (SOD E:73) On 5 Apr 1771 Henry

Army Trader and wife Agnes sold the same to William McClemmy for £65. (SOD E:142) This deed explains that Henry Armatrader was moving.

On 19 Nov 1771 Henry Trader of WO Co. bought ¼ acre of *Pemberton's Goodwill* in Salisbury Town, SO Co., from William Winder for £10. (SOD E:148) On 12 Dec 1772 he sold this to John Nelms on 12 Dec 1772 for £65. (SOD E:219) Since a wife did not cosign this deed, it is apparent that Henry Trader had lost his first wife Agness, whose maiden name in unknown, between the spring of 1771 and the end of 1772.

On 28 Feb 1774 Henry Trader bought 147 acres called *Maddux Luck* in SO Co. from Jonathan Shockley for £160. (SOD F:129) The deed places this land "on road from Salisbury Town to Springhill Chappel." Henry Trader, of SO Co., and wife Elizabeth sold this to Benjamin Nutter on 2 Jan 1786 for £220. (SOD H:134)

On 25 Oct 1776 Henry Trader of SO Co. bought 149 acres in WO Co. called *Hypocrites Deceived* from John Gordy. (WOD K:25)

The above deeds suggest that Henry Trader moved into WO Co. after losing his first wife, but likely moved his family back into SO Co. after buying *Maddux Luck* in 1774.

Henry appears on the tax list of SO Co. for 1783, for Rewastico District, SO Co., showing he owned 147 acres of *Maddux Luck*. His household consisted of 4 males and 6 females. Apparently after he and his second wife separated in 1784. (No record has been found of this in either Princess Ann or Snow Hill.) Elizabeth (Smith) Trader and her children moved back to WO Co., where she bought land after her husband's death.

He left a will dated 7 Jul 1784, probated 29 Dec 1791 in SO Co. He left to his 3 eldest daus. Ann Trader, Mary Trader and Elizabeth Trader all his personal estate and made them joint executrices of his will. He left son Henry all my wearing clothes. He left 1 shilling sterling and my will is that he/she have no more of my estate to son Joshua Trader and Purnell Trader and daus. Milley Trader and Sarah Trader. He did not name his wife or make mention of land. Witnessess were Benjamin Hearn, Hezekiah Maddux and Samuel Hearn. Ann Trader and Mary Trader qualified as executrices.

On 14 Mar 1796, George Collins and Ann his wife and Mary Reynold (formerly Trader), extrs. of Henry Trader deceased, made a final accounting of the estate. Among the debits to the estate, James Charles had been paid £1.10.06 for making the coffin. Son Henry Trader received his father's clothes, valued at £10. Joshua Trader, Purnell Trader, Milly Trader and Sarah Trader each were paid 1 shilling & 8 pence and the balance of £116.7.5 ½ was divided between the 3 eldest daus, who were children of Henry Trader's first marriage. (SO Co. Adm. of Accounts, 1778-1796:723, 724)

Henry Trader (IV) and Agnes (N) had the following children:

54 i. Ann[6] Trader, b. c1765. (Carey, *The Messongo Traders*), (SOW 1788-1799:188)

55 ii. Mary Trader, b. c1767. (Carey, *The Messongo Traders*), (Carey, *The Messongo Traders*), (SOW 1788-1799:188)

56   iii. Elizabeth Trader, b. c1769.

Henry Trader (IV) and Elizabeth Smith had the following children:

57   iv. Henry Trader (V), b. c1774. (Carey, *The Messongo Traders*), Som Wills 1788-1799:188)

Henry was named in his father's will [see above] and his mother's will 17 Aug 1796 in WO Co. He was shown as a son Henry Trader and given land in the will of Elizabeth Trader. (WOW 1790-1799:378)

+   58   v. Joshua Trader, b. c1776, d. 1841.

+   59   vi. Purnell Trader, b. c1778, d. 1836.

60   vii. Sarah Trader, b. c1780. Sarah was named in her father's will [see above] and her mother's will dated 17 Aug 1796 in WO Co. (WOW 1790-1799:378; Carey, *The Messongo Traders*)

61   viii. Amilla 'Milley' Trader, b. c1782. Amilla was named in her father's will [see above] and her mother's will dated 17 Aug 1796 in WO Co. She was shown as a dau. Amella Johnson. (WOW 1790-1799:378; Carey, *The Messongo Traders*)

30. **Israel⁵ Trader** (Littleton⁴, Henry³, Arthur², Henry¹), b. in AC c1732, d. May 1768. (Nottingham Wills:231 (adm. of Israel Armitrader); Carey, *The Messongo Traders*)

He m. c1756, **Comfort (N)** (b. c1735). (Nottingham Wills:231 (adm. of Israel Armitrader)) She m. c1772, **William Hutson**.

On 31 May 1768 Comfort Armitrader was named to settle the estate of Israel Armitrader. Littleton Armitrader and William Morgan were securities. (Nottingham Wills:231 (adm. of Israel Armitrader))

Israel Trader and Comfort (N) had the following children:

62   i. Israel⁶ Trader, b. in AC c1758.

63   ii. William Trader, b. in AC c1760. (Carey, *The Messongo Traders*)

+   64   iii. Littleton Trader, b. c1764, d. 1826.

65   iv. Tabitha Trader, b. in AC c1766. (Carey, *The Messongo Traders*)

32. **Archibald⁵ Trader Sr.** (Littleton⁴, Henry³, Arthur², Henry¹), b. in AC c1737, d. May 1821 in AC. (MilesW&A:542 (will of Archibald Trader))

He m. 1st c1768, **Elizabeth (N)** (b. c1745). He m. 2nd c1800, **Polly (N)** (b. c1760). She c1783, m. **Eli Duncan**.

He left a will dated 18 Feb 1821, probated 29 May 1821 in AC. To Littleton A. Trader Sr. 110 acres adjoining lands of Parker Lucas & John Savage. To son Teackle Trader 70 acres adjoining the branch & mill & lands of Solomon Lucas & Parker Lucas. To wife Polly Trader all my meat & corn to support her & the family this year & also lend her Negro boy Isaac until he arrives to age 20, now 12, then Isaac to Teackle Trader until he is 31 & then to be free. My old woman Sarah to stay here on my land & if she is not able to maintain herself then my 2 sons Littleton A. Trader & Teackle Trader to maintain her. To wife Polly,.. To grandson Samuel Trader $1 &,.. To granddaus Tabitha & Sally Trader $1 each. Remainder to sons Littleton & Teackle Trader. To heirs of John Jacobs each 1 shilling. William Nock of Zadock, son Littleton Trader & Joseph Conquest extrs. Witnessed by Solomon Lucas & Eliza F. Lucas. Archibald's estate was settled 27 Jan 1823 in AC. 19 Jun 1821 (Inventory), 29 Jun 1821(Sale), 25 Jun 1823 (Audit), 27 Jan 1823 (Rec'd) - Littleton A. Trader extr. Negro boy Isaac & old woman Sarah. Appraisers: William Northam Sr., Edmund Godwin Sr. & William Nock of Z. Buyers: Littleton Trader, Polly Trader, William Trader Jr., Valentine Trader, Teackle Trader & Staton Trader. Auditors: William Northam & William Nock of Z. (MilesW&A:542)

Archibald Trader Sr. and Elizabeth (N) had the following children:

66   i.   Nancy^6 Trader, b. AC c1780, m. 8 Jul 1798, John Jacob in AC (b. c1775). Nancy was named in her father's will 18 Feb 1821 in AC. (MilesW&A:542 (will of Archibald Trader)) She was evidently deceased by this date, as Archibald Trader left the heirs of John Jacobs 1 shilling each.

+   67   ii.   Archibald Trader Jr., b. c1783, d. Jan 1815.

+   68   iii. Littleton Archibald Trader, b. c1790, d. 1826.

69   iv. Teackle A. Trader, b. in AC c1795, d. 1830 in MD. He m. 28 Feb 1818 (lic.) in WO Co., Elizabeth R. Houston (b. c1790, d. 1830 in WO Co.). (Powell, *WO Co.Marriages 1795-1865*) It was in 1830 that she died intestate and no children were named, but it was noted that her "husband's estate did not pay out."

In Teackle Trader sold 45 acres in AC, of the 70 acres that he inherited from his father, to his brother Littleton Trader.

38. Sacker^5 Trader (William^4, Henry^3, Arthur^2, Henry^1), b. in AC c1736, d. 1826. (MilesW&A:544 (adm. of Sacker Trader))

On 30 Oct 1826 Samuel S. Nock was named to settle the estate of Sacker Trader in AC. William Nock & Lewis Nock were securities. (MilesW&A:544 (adm. of Sacker Trader))

Sacker Trader had the following children:

70   i.   Jernima 'Nancy'^{6}, b. in AC c1790., m. 7 Jasn 1807 (bond) in AC, Daniel Shay (b. c1780). Staton Trader was the security on the M.L.B. of Daniel Shay and Jernina Trader of Sacker. (Lewis, *Acc MLB 1806-1835*; ACM)

71   ii. Comfort Trader, b. in AC c1806, m. 19 Mar 1827 (bond) in AC, Elijah Northam. Dan. Shay and Whittington Trader were the securities on the M.L.B. of Elizah Northam, son of Wm. of E. (who gave

consent), and Comfort Trader of Sacker. (Lewis, *Acc MLB 1806-1835*; FA CD309)

Elijah, b. c1807, d. Jul 1857 in AC, was the son of William Northam of E. and Elizabeth 'Betsy' Northam . He m. 1 Jun 1853, Margaret Wessells. He was shown as widowed and she was Margaret Young, the widow of David. (FA CD309; Lewis, *Acc MLB 1806-1835*; ACM; AC Wills 1846-1882:251)

Comfort was listed with her husband in the census of 1850 in Acc Parish, AC. She was shown as Comfort Northam, age 44 in HH#550 headed by Elijah Northam, a 43 year old farmer. (FA CD309)

39. **George⁵ Trader** (William⁴, Henry³, Arthur², Henry¹), b. in AC c1738, d. Feb 1800. (Nottingham Wills:464 (will of George Trader))

He m. c1760, **Nancy (N)** (b. c1740). (Carey, *The Messongo Traders*)

He left a will dated 15 Jan 1800, probated 24 Feb 1800 in AC. To son Parker Trader 14 acres adjcent James Abbott, but if Parker Trader never returns then to my son George Trader. To wife 1/3 of my estate To dau. Grace Trader plantation where I now live to be sold. Children residuary legatees. Robert Russell & Savage Crippin extrs. Witnessed by William Wise, John Hickman, James Rocks, William Warner. (Nottingham Wills:464 (will of George Trader))

George's estate was settled 29 Jun 1801 in AC. 14 Feb 1800/30 Oct 1800 (Sale), Oct 1800 (Order to Audit), 25 May 1801 (Audit), 29 Jun 1801 (Rec'd) - Savage Crippen & Robert Russell extrs. Various amounts to Parker Trader, George Trader, the widow, William Trader & Nancy Trader. Legacy of Gracy Trader. Auditors: Parker Barnes & John A. Bundick. (MilesW&A:542 (settlement of George Trader))

George Trader and Nancy (N) had the following children:

72   i. Parker⁶ Trader, b. in AC c1760, m. c1780, Eailsey (N) (b. c1760). (Carey, *The Messongo Traders*)
+   73   ii. George Trader, b. c1762, d. 1818.
74   iii. Grace Trader, b. in AC c1764, m. 6 Oct 1807 (bond), John Thornton. Walter Wessells was the security on the M.L.B. (ACM)

John, b. c1780 in AC, d. Feb 1831, was the son of Edward Thornton (IV) and Rachel (N) (wid. of Washburn Tunnell). He m. 30 Oct 1809 (bond) in AC, Eliza Hutson. William Hinman was the security on the M.L.B. (Nottingham Wills:421 (will of Edward Thornton); ACM; MilesW&A)

40. **William⁵ Trader Jr.** (William⁴, Henry³, Arthur², Henry¹), b. in AC c1740, d. 1826.

He m. 31 Jul 1815 (bond) in AC, **Lucy (N)** (b. c1740). She m. 1760, **(N) Baker** (wife's 2ⁿᵈ marriage). She is listed as Lucy Baker, widow, on her AC

MLB of 1815 to William Trader Senr. Purnel Cheshire was the security. (Purnel
was m. to William's dau. Lane.) (Lewis, *Acc MLB 1806-1835*)

William Trader Jr. had the following children:
+   75   i. Henry[6] Trader, b. c1768, d. 1815.
+   76   ii. Staten (of Wm.) Trader, b. c1770, d. Aug 1842.
     77   iii. Sacor Trader, b. in AC c1772. (Carey, *The Messongo Traders*)
+   78   iv. William Trader Jr., b. c1774, d. 1801.
+   79   v. Levi Trader, b. c1776, d. Jul 1815.
+   80   vi. Littleton Trader, b. c1778.
     81   vii. Colmore Trader, b. c1780. (Carey, *The Messongo Traders*),
     82   viii. Lane Trader, b. c1782, m. 21 Sep 1804 (bond) in AC, Purnell Chesser (b. c1780). (AC M.L.B. (tr), 1774-1806) He was shown as Purnell Cheshire.

46. **(N)[5] Trader** (William[4], Henry[3], Arthur[2], Henry[1]), b. in AC c1754.
(N) Trader had the following child:
     83   i. Peggy[6] Trader, b. in AC c1775, named in her grandfather's will 6 Jan 1794 in AC. (Nottingham Wills:421 (will of William Armey Trador)

47. **Staton[5] Trader Sr.** (William[4], Henry[3], Arthur[2], Henry[1]) b. in AC c1755, d. 22 Jan 1817 in WO Co. (Carey to Trader, Letter, 09/21/1999; Trader to Carey, *Letter*, 07/01/1999; WOW, 1817:22)

He m. c1774, **Susanna Taylor** (b. c1750), dau. of James Taylor (III).
(Trader to Carey, Letter, 07/01/1999) The names of Staten and Susanna appear on a deed to sell property in 1784 & on a deed to sell property on Pitts Creek, north of the MD-VA line in 1802. (WO Co. Grantor's Index, 1784:50 & 1802:504; *Taylor Family, 1663-1974*).

Staton Trader served in the Rev War c1776 under the command of Capt. Walton, WO Co. (MD Rev War Mil Lists, MF185:259)

On 24 Nov 1804, Staton Trader was bound to the state of MD for the maintenance of an illegitimate male child begotten in the body of Sarah Vezey. (WO Co.MD, X:155; Trader to Carey, Letter, 07/01/1999)

He left a will dated 15 Jan 1817 in WO Co. Elizabeth Baker was named as an heir during her widowhood and a son Staton was also named. (WOW 1817:22; Trader to Carey, Letter, 07/01/1999)

Staton Trader Sr. and Susanna Taylor had the following children:
     84   i. Teackle Taylor[6] Trader, b. in AC c1775, d. 1790-1800. (Carey to Trader, Letter, 09/21/1999)
+   85   ii. Staton Trader Jr., b. 29 Aug 1783, d. 27 Jan 1844.

Sixth Generation
48. **Arthur 'Arter'[6] Trader** (Littleton[5], Henry[4], Henry[3], Arthur[2], Henry[1]), b. in AC c1750, d. Apr 1791. (Nottingham Wills:389 (will of Arthur Armitrader))

He m. 1 Dec 1786 (bond) in AC, **Katherine Burton** (b. c1760). (AC Mar Lic Bonds (tr), 1774-1806). She m. 6 May 1794 (bond) in AC, **Stephen Drummond** (AC Mar Lic Bonds (tr), 1774-1806)

He left a will dated 20 Jan 1791 in AC, probated 27 Apr 1791 To wife Catherine whole estate during her widow to bring up my child, then to my dau. Ann Burton Armitrader. Brother Henry Armitrader, Samuel Armitrader & wife Catherine, extrs. Witnessed by John Spiers, Littleton Trader, Elizabeth Nock. Henry Trader & Catherine Trader qualified. (Nottingham Wills:389 (will of Arthur Armitrader))

Arthur 'Arter' Trader and Katherine Burton had the following child:

    86   i. Ann Burton[7] Trader, b. in AC c1790, m. 1st 30 Mar 1811 (bond) in AC, Thomas Elliott (b. c1790). Joshua Burton was the security on the M.L.B. (Lewis, *Acc MLB 1806-1835*; ACM)

She m. 2nd 12 May 1825 (bond) in AC, Thomas S. Bull (b. c1788, d. Apr 1860). William Parramore Jr. was the security on the M.L.B. of Thomas Bull and Anne Elliott, widow of Thomas. (ACM; MilesW&A:101 (will of Thomas S. Bull))

Thomas m. 1st 15 Feb 1815 (bond) in AC, Rachel Floyd. Samuel Kellam was the security on the M.L. B. (ACM)

Thomas m. 3rd 9 Jan 1829 (bond) in AC, Mary 'Polly' Mapp. George Mapp was the security on the M.L.B. of Thomas Bull and Polly Mapp of George. (ACM; FA CD309)

52. Samuel[6] Trader (Littleton[5], Henry[4], Henry[3], Arthur[2], Henry[1]), b. in AC 1763, d. 19 Feb 1810. His body was interred in Trader Plot, Pungoteague, AC. (MLAC)

He m. 19 May 1787 (bond) in AC, **Patience (N)** (b. 1 Dec 1755, d. 23 Sep 1835). (AC M.L.B. (tr), 1774-1806; MLAC) She m. 1st c1775, **Bartholomew Taylor**.

Her body was interred in Trader Plot, Pungoteague, AC. According to her tombstone in the Trader Plot near Pungoteague, Patience was the wife of Samuel Trader and the widow of Bartholomew Taylor. (MLAC)

Samuel was named in his brother's will 20 Jan 1791 in AC. (Nottingham Wills:389 (will of Arthur Armitrader))

Samuel left a will dated 14 Feb 1810, probated 25 Jun 1810 in AC. The 20 acres purchased of Eli Hornsby adjoining the land of the heirs of Zorobabel Ames to be sold. My man Shadrack may be liberated after he earns, at $25 a year, what he cost me, which was £66. My Negro man Harry may be liberated after he earns, at $25 a year, £77 which is what he cost me. All my estate to wife Patience until my son Samuel arrives at age 21. To son Samuel the plantation where I now live & also 34½ acres called *Kentucky* which I purchased of Zorobabel Taylor dec'd adjoining the land of John Milby's heirs & Salathiel West's heirs. To dau. Rosey a tract of land I purchased of John Taylor, John

Milby & Obadiah Thornman, containing 170 acres. Custis Willis & wife Patience & son Samuel extrs. Witnessed by Thomas S. Satchell & Henry S. Fisher. Prob: John Taylor, Upshur Folio & Levi Rodgers securities. (MilesW&A:544 (will of Samuel Trader))

Samuel's estate was settled 30 Dec 1811 in AC. 30 Jul 1811 (Order to Audit), 30 Dec 1811 (Rec'd) - Patience Trader extr. Named in settlement: Robert Parker (black man) & Littleton Trader. (MilesW&A:544 (settlement of Samuel Trader))

Samuel Trader and Patience (N) had the following children:

87 i. Rosanna 'Rosey'[7] Trader, b. in AC 25 Apr 1788, d. 25 Jun 1820. Her body was interred in the Trader Plot, Pungoteague, AC. Her tombstone shows her as Rosey Savage, wife of William Savage, who d. 25 Jun 1820 at the age of 32 years, 2 mos. She m. 18 Sep 1813 (bond) in AC, William Savage. Robert Pitts was the security on the M.L.B. (ACM; MLAC)

William, b. 1784 in AC, d. 15 Nov 1815. His body was interred in Trader Plot, Pungoteague, AC. His tombstone shows him as William Savage, who d. 15 Nov 1815, at the age of 31 years. (MLAC)

In addition to being named in the will of her father, Rosanna was also named in her brother's will dated 7 Apr 1818 in AC. (MilesW&A:544 (will of Samuel B. Trader))

She left a will dated 1 May 1820 in St. George Parish, probated 25 Sep 1820 in AC. To my mother Patience Trader all the land willed to me by my brother Samuel B. Trader. To son Samuel G. Savage all my estate to include the land lent to my mother & if he dies under age 21 or without issue, then to nephew George K. Taylor, son [of] John, the plantation whereon my mother at present lives & all the lands that my brother purchased of Lucinda S. Andrews & to nephew Samuel T. Taylor, son of John, all the land which I hold at present known as the Taylor land adjoining John W. Hancock, Stephen Pusey & Francis Savage Sr. & 37 ½ acres called *Kentucky* & the residue to the children of my brothers John Taylor & Major Taylor & my sister Margaret Ashby. Extr. to procure grave stones for my dec'd father, husband & brother. Mother Patience Trader extr. Witnessed by William P. Moore, Joseph Ames, James J. Teackle & Samuel W. Colonna. George Ashby, John Taylor & John G. Joynes securities. (MilesW&A:471 (will of Rosanna Savage, St. George Parish))

88   ii. Samuel B. Trader, b. in AC 1 Dec 1793, d. 15 Apr 1818. According to a stone in the Trader Plot near Pungoteague, Samuel was the son of Samuel and Patience Trader. He sailed in the schooner *William and Henry* and was lost at sea on 15 Apr 1818 at age 25. (MLAC)

He left a will dated 7 Apr 1818 in AC, probated 25 Jan 1819 in AC. To mother Patience Trader the whole of my property during her life binding her not to charge my sister Rosey Savage or her son Samuel G. Savage anything for board. At my mother's death to sister Rosey Savage the whole of my land & plantation at Pungoteague given me by my father & also the land I purchased of Miss Lucy Andrews, together with the 37 acres of land given me by my father known by the name *Kentucky* & also that piece of land which I purchased of the heirs of Eli Hornsby dec'd & after my sister takes possession she to pay my sister Margaret Taylor $300, to John Taylor $150 & to Major Taylor $150. Friend Abel R. Rodgers extr. There being no witnesses, the will was proved by oaths of John G. Joynes & Thomas R. Joynes who testified to the handwriting of Samuel B. Trader. John G. Joynes, Hutchinson Kellam & Robert Rodgers securities on the $15,000 bond. (MilesW&A:544 (will of Samuel B. Trader))

Samuel's estate was settled 27 Aug 1821 in AC. 2 Feb 1819 (Inventory & Sale), 18 & 27 Aug 1821 (Audit & Rec'd) - Abel R. Rodgers extr. Appraisers: Shadrack M. Ames, Richard Ames, John Rodgers & Dr. George Scherer. Buyer: Patience Trader. Auditors: Thomas R. Joynes, Thomas H. Kellam & Shadrack M. Ames. On 18 Aug 1821 Patience Trader acknowledged receipt of $88.93 which was applied to the credit of Samuel B. Trader. (MilesW&A:544 (settlement of Samuel B. Trader))

53. **Littleton[6] Trader** (Littleton[5], Henry[4], Henry[3], Arthur[2], Henry[1]), b. in AC 1764, d. Jun 1822. (Carey, *The Messongo Traders*)

He m. c1790), **Rachel (N)** (b. c1770). (MilesW&A:543 (will of Littleton Trader))

He was named as son and extr. in his mother's will dated 3 Feb 1798. (Nottingham Wills:461 (will of Elizabeth Knock))

Littleton Trader was listed as a head of household in the census of 1800 in AC, age 26-45 years, with no males and several daus. In the 1810 census he was listed as a head of household, age over 45 with 2 males age 10-16 and 1 male age 16-26. In the 1820 census of AC he was head of household, over age 45, with 2 males under 10 and 1 male age 10-16.

He left a will dated 2 Mar 1821, probated 24 Jun 1822. To wife Rachel Trader the use of my whole estate & at her death or marriage to my children Catharine, Elizabeth, Rosey, Littleton, Samuel & James Trader. My Negro man Charles shall not be transported out of this county by any of my children. Friend Galen Conner extr. Witnessed by William P. Moore & P. P. Watson. (MilesW&A:543 (will of Littleton Trader))

Littleton Trader and Rachel (N) had the following children:

89   i. Samuel[7] Trader, b. in AC c1790.
90   ii. Nancy Trader, b. in AC c1792. Nancy was named in her grandmother's will 3 Feb 1798 in AC. (Nottingham Wills:461 (will of Elizabeth Knock))
91   iii. Rosey Trader, b. in AC c1792.
92   iv. Catherine Trader, b. in AC c1800.
93   v. Elizabeth J. 'Betsy' Trader b. in AC c1802, m. 23 Apr 1825 (bond) in AC, John A. Coleburn (b. c1800). John W. Hancock was the security on the M.L.B. of John A. Coleburn and Elizabeth J. Trader of Littleton. (ACM; FA CD309)

Elizabeth (Betsey) Coleburn was listed as a head of household in the census of 1850 in St. George Parish, AC, HH#1081, age 48. Listed with her were the following Coleburns: Sam'l, a 30 year old sailor; Sally, age 16; Tabitha, age 14; and Margaret, age 12. (FA CD309)

94   vi. Sidney Trader, b. in AC c1810, d. young.
95   vii. Samuel Trader , b. in AC c1812. Samuel was listed with his brother in the census of 1860 in St. George Parish, AC.
96   viii. Littleton Trader, b. in AC c1814.
97   ix. James Henry Trader, b. in Pungoteague, AC c1815, d. 10 Jul 1889 in St. George Parish, AC, of unknown causes at the age of 70 years (according to death register). A friend John D. Kilmon gave the information. James m. 17 Jan 1852 (lic.) in WO Co., Elizabeth 'Betsy' Bennett (b. in Hacks Neck c1834), dau. of Covington 'Covy' Bennett Sr. and Maragaret 'Peggy' Caruthers. (WADR; Mears, *Hacks Neck & Its People*; Crowson & Hite, *AC 1860 Census*; FA CD309; Powell, *WO Co. Marriages 1795-1865*)

In 1826 Littleton Trader boarded out his son James H. Trader.

James J Trader appeared in the census of 1850 in St. George Parish, AC, a 35 year old overseer in

HH#1272 headed by Tully W. Parker, a 27 year old farmer with real estate valued at $5,000. (FA CD309) Henry Trader was listed as a head of household, HH#1243, in the census of 1860 in St. George Parish, AC, a 45 year old farm manager. Listed with him were the following Traders: Eliz't., age 29; Sidney P., age 7; Wm. H., age 4; Sam'l J., age 1; and Sam'l, a 48 year old farm laborer. (Crowson & Hite, *AC 1860 Census*)

58. **Joshua**[6] **Trader** (Henry[5], Henry[4], Henry[3], Arthur[2], Henry[1], b. c1776, d. 1841 in MD. In his will, Joshua Trader left his son John Asbury Eikel Trader the balance of his estate with instructions that he must maintain his mother. He left 25 cents each to Joshua Henry Smith Trader, William Byrd Trader and Eliza Dennis. He left $300 each to Charlotte Winder Parker and Sarah Jane Trader and two slaves each to Rufus King Trader, Levin White Trader and Thomas Bailey Trader. (Carey, *The Messongo Traders*)

He m. c1805 **Elizabeth Byrd** (b. c1785), dau. of Jesse Byrd (d. 1808). Joshua left a will dated 4 Dec 1841, probated 31 Jan 1843. (Carey, *The Messongo Traders*; MHS: CBH Turner Collection)

Joshua was named in his father's will [above] and his mother's will dated 17 Aug 1796 in WO Co. His mother, Elizabeth Trader, left him land. (WOW 1790-1799:378)

Joshua Trader and Elizabeth Byrd had the following children:

98   i.   Eliza[7] A. W. Trader, b. c1814, m. 22 Aug 1833, John Dennis (b. c1805). (Carey, *The Messongo Trader*: MHS:CBH Turner Collection)

99   ii.   Joshua Smith Henry Trader, b. 3 Aug 1808, d. 1865 in SO Co. He m. 1 Feb 1827 (lic.) in WO Co., Miranda Jenet C. Smith (b. 1806, d. 1874 in SO Co.), dau. of Isaiah Smith. (Carey, *The Messongo Traders*; Powell, *WO Co. Marriages 1795-1865*; Dryden, *SO Co. 1850 Census*; MHS:CBH Turner Collection)

      He was listed as a resident in the census report 1850 in Salisbury Dist., SO Co. (Dryden, *SO Co. 1850 Census*)

100   iii.   Charlotte Trader, b. c1811, d. 8 May 1895. She m. 1st c1830, (N) Winder and m. 2nd 7 Apr 1841, Elisha Parker. (Carey, *The Messongo Traders*; MHS:CBH Turner Collection)

101   iv.   William Byrd Trader, b. in WO Co. c1813, d. 1852, m. 5 Jan 1835 (lic.) in WO Co., Mary Ann Twilly (b. c1821). (Powell, *WO Co.Marriages 1795-1865*; Carey, *The Messongo Traders*; Dryden, *WO Co.1850 Census*)

      He was listed as a resident in the census report 1850 in WO Co. (Dryden, *WO Co.1850 Census*)

172

102   v. Sarah Jane Trader, b. 26 Sep 1825, d. 10 Feb 1899, m.
31 Jan 1843, Benjamin Burton Gordy. (b. c1815).
(Carey, *The Messongo Traders*; MHS:CBH Turner Collection)
103   vi. Rufus King Trader, b. in WO Co. c1817, d. 1884, m. 29
Jan 1845 (lic.) in WO Co., m. Nancy F. Dennis (b.
c1825). (Carey, *The Messongo Traders*; Powell, *WO Co.Marriages
1795-1865;* Dryden, *WO Co. 1850 Census*)
He was listed as a resident in the census report
1850 in WO Co. (Dryden, *WO Co.1850 Census*)
104   vii. Rev. Thomas Richard Bailey Trader, b. 13 Oct 1819 at
Wicomico, d. 10 Feb 1901. (Carey, *The Messongo Traders*;
MHS:CHB Turner Collection)
105   viii. John Asbury Eikel Trader, b. c1830, d. 1852. (Carey, *The
Messongo Traders*)
106   ix. Levin White Trader, b. Mar 1824 on the Old Trader
Farm near Salisbury, d. 26 Nov 1892, m. 6 Sep 1845
(lic.) in SO Co., Matilda Eleanor Jane Horsey (b.
c1820). (Carey, *The Messongo Traders;* Pollitt, *SO Co Marriages
1796-1871;* Dryden, SO Co. 1850 Census; MHS:CBH Turner
Collection)
He was listed as a resident in the census report
1850 in Hungrey Neck Dist., SO Co. (Dryden, *SO Co 1850
Census*)
59. **Purnell**[6] **Trader** (Henry[5], Henry[4], Henry[3], Arthur[2], Henry[1]), b. c1778, d.
1836 in SO Co. (Carey, *The Messongo Traders;* Dryden, *SO Co 1850 Census*)
He m. 8 Jan 1813 (lic.) in SO Co., **Leah Garrettson** (b. c1792, d. 1854 in
SO Co.) (Dryden, *SO Co 1850 Census;* Pollitt, *SO Co Marriages 1796-1871*)
Purnell Trader was named in his father's will [see above] and his mother's
will dated 17 Aug 1796 in WO Co. His mothe left him land. (WOW 1790-1799:378)
Purnell Trader and Leah Garrettson had the following children:
107   i. Thomas G.[7] Trader, b. c1814, d. 1871. He was listed as
a resident in the census report 1850 in Salisbury Dist.,
SO Co. (Dryden, SO Co. 1850 Census)
108   ii. Christopher C. Trader, b. c1817. (Carey, *The Messongo
Traders*)
109   iii. Freeborn G. Trader, b. c1819. (Carey, *The Messongo
Traders*)
110   iv. Adaline Trader, b. c1821. (Carey, *The Messongo Traders*)
64. **Littleton**[6] **Trader** (Israel[5], Littleton[4], Henry[3], Arthur[2], Henry[1]), b. in AC
c1764, d. by 1826. It was on this date that Littleton Trader's estate was
administered to the Sheriff. He has a son James H. Trader who was boarded out
in 1826. (Nottingham Wills:258 (will of Littleton Armitrader))
He m. c1785, **Elizabeth Byrd** (b. c1767 in Muddy Creek, AC), dau. of
Nathaniel Byrd Jr. and Naomi Watson. (Byrd, *Hist & Gene Byrd Family*)

Littleton was named in his grandfather's will 9 Oct 1771 in AC. He was given land where his grandfather lived & for want of issue to his grandfather's dau. Ann Bird. At probate, James Henry was guardian to Littleton Armitrader, heir at law to the testator. (Nottingham Wills:258 (will of Littleton Armitrader)) (Note: This implied that he was the oldest son of the oldest son.)

In 1778 Littleton Trader chose William Young as his guardian.

This Littleton Trader exchanged land left him by his grandfather for land near Accomac, in St. George Parish, in 1785 and sold this in 1788 & 1807.

Littleton A. Trader was listed as a head of household in the census of 1800 in St. George Parish, AC. He was age 26-45, with a wife of the same age. There were 4 males under age 10, 2 males age 10-16, 2 young females and 1 slave.

Littleton Trader and Elizabeth Byrd had the following children:

111   i. Israel[7] Trader, b. in AC c1786, d. Oct 1824, m. 29 Nov 1813 (bond) in AC, Tabitha Byrd (b. c1790), dau. of Major Byrd Sr. and Anne 'Nancy' Watson. Edmund Duncan was the security on the 1813 AC M.L.B. of Israel Trader and Tabitha Bird of Major. (Carey, *The Messongo Traders;* MilesW&A:543 (adm. of Israel Trader); Lewis, *AC MLB 1806-1835;* Wise, *Boston Family, 2nd Ed*)

Israel 's estate was administered 25 Oct 1824 in AC by Israel Trader. John Laws Sr. & David Baker were the securities. (Wise, *Boston Family, 2nd Ed*; MilesW&A:543 (adm. of Israel Trader))

Israel's estate was settled 27 Mar 1826 in AC 25 Oct 1824 (Order to Inventory), 2 Nov 1824 (Inventory & Sale), 6 Aug 1825 (Audit), 28 Nov 1825 (Rec'd) - William Laws admr. Auditors: William Powell & John Cole Jr. (MilesW&A:543 (adm. of Israel Trader))

112   ii. Nathaniel Trader, b. in AC c1788, d. Nov 1849 in WO Co., m. 31 May 1813 (bond) in AC, Rose A. 'Rosey' Hickman. Israel Trader was the security on the M.L.B. (Bob Jones to Miles, *Emails, 2002-03-04;* Lewis, *Acc MLB 1806-1835*)

Rose, b. c1795 in AC, was the dau. of Edward Hickman and Peggy Parker. (Dryden, *WO Co. 1850 Census*)

Nathaniel Trader was listed as a head of household in the census of 1820 in Acc Parish, AC, head of household, age 26-45, with 3 males under age 10. He was not in the 1830 AC census, so he may have relocated to WO Co. by that time.

Nathaniel 's will was probated 1 Dec 1849 in WO Co. (Bob Jones to Miles, *E-mails, 2002-03-04*)

113   iii. Edward Trader, b. in AC c1791, d. young.

114   iv. Parker Trader, b. in AC c1795, m. 26 Dec 1818 (lic.) in WO Co., Betsey Badge (b. c1800). (Powell, *WO Co. Marriages 1795-1865*)

115   v. Littleton Trader, b. in AC c1798, d. 1832 in WO Co., m. 29 Jan 1822 (lic.) in WO Co., Margaret Tull (b. c1800). (Powell, *WO Co.Marriages 1795-1865*)

116   vi. Teackle A. Trader b. in AC c1800, m. 16 Dec 1822 (bond) in AC, Ruth Delastatius. (Lewis, *AC MLB 1806-1835*) Teackle lived after 1822 in Philadelphia, PA. (Carey, *The Messongo Traders*),

117   vii. Tabitha Trader, b. in AC c1802. (Byrd, *Hist & Gene Byrd Family*)

118   viii. Ann Trader, b. in AC c1808 in AC, m. 3 Apr 1833 (bond) in AC, George Hargis. Levin Core was the security on the M.L.B. (Byrd, *Hist & Gene Byrd Family*; FA CD309; ACM)

      Ann Hargis, age 42 was listed with her husband in the census of 1850 in St. George Parish, AC, in HH#1295 headed by Geo. Hargis, a 42 year old farmer. (FA CD309)

119   ix. Samuel Trader, b. in AC c1810, d. 1842. He m. 18 Jan 1831 (lic.) in WO Co., Milly Davis. (Powell, *WO Co.Marriages 1795-1865*; Carey, *The Messongo Traders*) Samuel Trader was bound out in 1828.

120   x. James H. Trader, b. in AC c1812. In 1826 his father Littleton Trader had a son James H. Trader that was boarded out.

67. Archibald[6] Trader Jr. (Archibald[5], Littleton[4], Henry[3], Arthur[2], Henry[1]), b. in AC c1783, d. Jan 1815. (Carey, *The Messongo Traders;* MilesW&A:542 (Admin. of Archibald Trader))

He m. 3 Jul 1806 (bond) in AC, **Elizabeth 'Betsy' Northam**. Teackle Trader was the security on the M.L.B. of Archibald Trader Jr. and Elizabeth Northam, dau. of William Northam. (AC Mar Lic Bonds (tr), 1774-1806)

Betsy, b. c1785 in AC, dau. of William Northam Senr. and Nancy (N) . She m. **Henry F. Fisher** 21 Mar 1816 (bond) in AC. Teackle Trader was the security on the M.L.B. of Henry F. Fisher of Sus'a (on original) and Elizabeth Trader, widow of Archibald. Teackle Trader was security.(AC Wills 1828-46:80 (father's will); Lewis, *AC MLB 1806-1835*)

Archibald 's estate was administered 30 Jan 1815 in AC by William Northam. Thomas Kelly & Samuel Watson were securities. (MilesW&A:542 (Admin of Archibald Trader))

He was not named in his father's will of 18 Feb 1821, but his 3 children: Samuel, Tabitha & Sally Trader were given $1 each..(MilesW&A:542 (will of Archibald Trader))

Archibald's estate was settled 29 Jul 1822 in AC. 26 Jan 1815 (Inventory & Sale), No date (Audit), 29 Jul 1822 (Rec'd) - William Northam Sr. admr. Buyers: Ishmael Trader & Teackle Trader. Auditors: Southey Northam & Custis Northam. (MilesW&A:542 (Settlement of Archibald Trader))

Archibald Trader Jr. and Elizabeth 'Betsy' Northam had the following children:

121   i. Sally[7] Trader, b. in AC c1810, m. c1830, (N) McMath. (Carey, *The Messongo Traders*)

Sally was named in her grandfather's will 18 Feb 1821 in AC. (MilesW&A:542 (will of Archibald Trader))

122   ii. Tabitha Trader, b. in AC c1812. She m. 1st c1840, Samuel Mears (b. c1780 in AC, d. 12 Apr 1852), son of Bartholomew Mears and Jaquet 'Jaca' Hinman. She m. 2nd 12 Apr 1852 in AC, John D. White (b. c1810); she was shown as Tabitha Mears, widow of Samuel. (FA CD309; ACM; MilesW&A:372 (will of Samuel Mears; MilesW&A:365 (will of Bartholomew Mears))

John D. White was the son of John White Sr. and Tabitha Whealton. He m. 2nd 15 Nov 1875, Elizabeth Ann Justice in Messongo, AC. He was shown as John D. White, a 62 year old single farmer, the son of John & Tabitha White and she was shown as Elizabeth Northam, age 63 and single, the dau. of James & Millie Justice. They were m. near Messongo by T.M. Poulson. (FA CD309; Miles & Miles, *AC Marriages, 1854-1895*)

Tabitha was named in her grandfather's will dated 18 Feb 1821 in AC. (MilesW&A:542 (will of Archibald Trader)) She was named in her husband's will 3 May 1849 in AC. (MilesW&A:372 (will of Samuel Mears))

Tabitha Mears, age 38, was listed with her "brother," Thomas H. Fisher, in the census of 1850 in Acc Parish, AC, HH#986. She possessed real estate valued at $100. Thomas H. Fisher was a 22 year old farmer and evidently her half-brother. (FA CD309)

Tabitha E. White, age 48, was listed in the household of John O. White (HH#323) in the census of 1860 in Acc Parish, AC. He was a 52 year old teacher. Also listed was Sarah E. Fisher, age 12, who may have been related to her. (Crowson & Hite, *AC 1860 Census*)

123   iii. Samuel Trader, b. in AC c1814. Samuel was named in his grandfather's will 18 Feb 1821 in AC. (MilesW&A:542

176

(will of Archibald Trader))
Samuel was living in Matthews Co, VA.

68. Littleton Archibald^6 Trader (Archibald^5, Littleton^4, Henry^3, Arthur^2, Henry^1), b. in AC c1790, d. 1826 in MD.

He m. c1815, **Mary Houston Feddeman** (b. c1795 in AC, d. 22 Jan 1864), dau. of William Feddeman and Henrietta Houston (?). Her tombstone puts her birth at 1798. Her body was interred in Marshall Plot, New Church, AC. Her tombstone shows her as Mary East, who d 22 Jan 1864 at the age of 66 years. (Mark C. Lewis Files; MilesW&A:201 (will of William Feddeman); FA CD309; TUAC; Nottingham Wills:429 (will of Mary Thornton))

She m. 2nd 28 Feb 1831 (bond) in AC, **Nathaniel East**. Levin White was the security on the M.L.B. of Nathaniel East and Mary Trader, widow of Teackle. (ACM)

Littleton A. Trader was named as an heir of Rev War Veteran, William Feddeman, 27 Feb 1826 in AC. He received a legacy of $425 in the estate settlement of William Feddeman. Evidently he received this on behalf of his wife Mary. The 1889 death record of his dau. Henrietta M. Marshall, showed her as the dau. of Archibald and Mary Trader; so evidently his middle name was Archibald, as he was otherwise referred to as Littleton A. Trader. (MilesW&A:201 (settlement of William Feddeman))

Littleton Archibald Trader had the following child:

124 i. Archibald^7 Trader, b. c1810, m. 27 Dec 1827 (bond) in AC, Mary Duncan (b. c1805). Robert Twiford was the security on the M.L.B. (ACM; Carey, *The Messongo Traders*)

Littleton Archibald Trader and Mary Houston Feddeman had the following children:

125 ii. Elizabeth Trader, b. in AC c1816, m. 8 Aug 1836 (lic.) in WO Co., Walter Jones (b. c1810, d. Nov 1844), son of George Jones and Sarah 'Sally' Waters. (Carey, *The Messongo Traders*; and MilesW&A:201 (will of William Feddeman); MilesW&A:291 (adm. of Walter Jones)); Powell, *WO Co.Marriages 1795-1865*); MilesW&A:561 & 562 (will of Thomas Walter Sr.))

    Elizabeth was named in her grandfather's will 4 Oct 1823 in AC. (MilesW&A:201 (will of William Feddeman))

126 iii. Amelia Trader, b. in AC c1822. Amelia was named in her grandfather's will dated 4 Oct 1823 in AC. (Mark C. Lewis Files; MilesW&A:201 (will of William Feddeman))

127 iv. Henrietta M. Trader, b. in AC. She was named in her grandfather William Feddeman's will dated 4 Oct 1823. However, the 1850 census puts her birth at 1828; the 1860 census puts it at 1830 and her 1889 death record puts it at 1827. Henrietta M. Marshall d. 12 Jan 1889 in Acc Parish, AC. She d. of dropsy. She m. 25 Sep 1849 (bond) in AC, William H. Marshall (b. c1818, d. 10 Jun 1894). Thomas Walters was the security on the M.L.B.

of William H. Marshall, widower, and Henrietta Trader.
(MilesW&A:201 (will of William Feddeman); WADR; FA CD309;
Crowson & Hite, *AC 1860 Census*; AC M.L.B. (tr), 1847-1850)
William m. 1st c1840, (N)(N). His body was
interred in Marshall Plot, Horntown, AC. His
tombstone shows him as William H. Marshall who died
10 Jun 1894 at the age of 77 years. (TUAC; 1860 AC
Census)
Henrietta was named in her grandfather's will dated
4 Oct 1823 in AC. (MilesW&A:201 (will of William
Feddeman))
Henrietta Marshall, age 22, was listed in the 1850
census of Acc Parish, AC, with her husband, William
H. Marshall, age 32, merchant (HH#321). (FA CD309)
Henrietta, age 30, was listed with her husband,
William H. Marshall, age 40, merchant, in the census
of 1860 in Acc Parish, AC (HH#79). (Crowson & Hite, *AC
1860 Census*)
128   v. Mary Ann Trader, b. in AC c1829. age 21, was listed as
Mary East with her mother in the census of 1850 in
Acc Parish, AC (HH#861) headed by Mary East, age
55 with real estate valued at $1,000. Since she was not
named in the 1831 will of Nathaniel East, she is
assumed to have been Mary East's dau. by her former
husband, Teackle Trader. (FA CD309)
Mary was listed with her mother in the census of
1860 in Acc Parish, AC. She was shown as Mary A.
Trader, age 22 headed by William H. Marshall, a 40
year old merchant (HH#79). Also listed was Mary East,
age 60, who was evidently her mother. (1860 AC VA,
Census)

73. **George[6] Trader** (George[5], William[4], Henry[3], Arthur[2], Henry[1]), b. in AC
c1762, d. died 1818.
    He m. 1st c1780, **Lucritia Fisher** (b. c1760), dau. of Thomas Fisher and
Susanna Trader. He m. 2nd c1790, **Nancy (N)** (b. c1760). (Carey, *The Messongo
Traders; Whitelaw:1215*)
    George Trader and Nancy (N) had the following child:
        129   i. Rosey[7] Trader, b. c1800, m. 27 Mar 1819 (bond) in
AC, Walter Bloxom (b. c1795 in AC), son of Richard
Bloxom. (Lewis, *Acc MLB 1806-1835*)

75. **Henry[6] Trader** (William[5], William[4], Henry[3], Arthur[2], Henry[1]), b. in AC
c1768, d. 1815. (Carey, *The Messongo Traders*)
    He m. c1790, **Ann Smith** (b. c1770 in AC), dau. of Bayly Smith. (Carey, *The
Messongo Traders*; Nottingham Wills:446 (will of Bayly Smith))

Henry Trader first appeared on the Acc tax lists in 1792. He sold Smith land in 1797 and bought 80 acres in 1799, which he left to his three sons..

Henry was listed as a head of household in the census of 1800 in AC, age 26-45. Henry was listed as a head of household in the census of 1810 in AC, age 26-45. He had 4 sons at that time..

He left a will dated 10 Oct 1801, probated 1 Aug 1815 in AC. To my 3 sons Abbott Trader, William Trader & Parker Trader all my land I now live on. Abbott the part adjoining Bennett Mason, William the part adjoining Robert Bayly & Parker the part adjoining Solomon Boston. To dau. Sally Trader part of the land I bought on the sea side. To youngest dau. Anne Trader, my 3 sons shall pay her $50 each. Remainder to wife & at her death or marriage to my 5 children. Wife Ann Trader extx. Witnessed by Bennett Mason, Robert Chase & Molly Bloxom. Note: He said in his will he bought this land, but no deed of purchase has been found. He did not sell it between 1801 and 1815, nor has a deed been found of his dau. Sally selling the land. (MilesW&A:543 (will of Henry Trader)) Wife Ann Trader relinquished to Southey Northam who became the admr. with Jacob Kelly, Robert Chase & William Nock of Zadock securities.

Henry's estate was settled 29 Aug 1817 in 1 Aug 1815 (Order to Inventory), 9 Nov 1815 (Sale), 1 Aug 1815 (Order to Audit), 23 & 29 Aug 1817 (Audit & Rec'd) - Southey Northam, admr. Appraisers: John Riley, Thomas Kelly & William Northam Sr. Buyers: Abbott Trader, William Trader Jr., Whittington Trader, Sally Trader & Anne Trader. Named in settlement: Ishmael Trader & Levi Trader. Auditors: John Riley & Jesse Duncan Sr. AC. (MilesW&A:543 (settlement of Henry Trader))

Henry Trader and Ann Smith had the following children:

130   i.   Abbott[7] Trader, b. in AC c1790, d. 1827. He m. 1st 3 Mar 1812 (bond) in AC, Molly Bayly. Richard Hart was the security on the M.L.B. of Abba Trader and Molly Bayly. (MilesW&A:542 (adm. of Abbott Trader); ACM)

Molly, b. c1790 in AC, d. before 1846, was the dau. of Robert Bayly and Nancy (N) . He m. 2nd c1820, Ann (N). (Rev Soldiers & Sailors:32 (heirs of Robert Bayly); Carey, *The Messongo Traders*)

Abbott was the security on the M.L.B. (dated 28 Jun 1815) of Wm. Christopher and Betsey Miles. (ACM) He was also security on a M.L.B. dated 1815, of John Bayly, son of Robert and Betsy Watson dau of William. (ACM)

Abbott 's estate was administered 29 Oct 1827 in AC by James Northam. (MilesW&A:542 (adm. of Abbott Trader))

131   ii.   Sarah Ann 'Sally' Trader, b. in AC c1792, d. Jan 1850. (Mary Frances Carey; MilesW&A:544 (will of Sarah Ann Trader))

She left a will dated 27 Dec 1849, probated 28 Jan 1850 in AC. To William Marshall $45 during his life & at his death to his child now living. To Nancy Trader of William $25 &,.. To Capt. Boston $25. To Nancy Marshall,.. To Catharine Lucas,.. Dr. Francis West extr. Witnessed by Thomas A. Northam, Smith Cutler & Francis West. AC. James W. Custis & James T. Gibbons were securities. (MilesW&A:544 (will of Sarah Ann Trader))

132   iii. William Trader, b. in AC c1794, d. Dec 1845. (MilesW&A:545 (will of William Trader)) He m. 1st 10 Dec 1815 in AC, Comphrate Walker (b. c1790). (AC Marriage Register, *1805-1850*) He may have m. 2nd 7 Jan 1829 (bond) in AC, Comfort Hutson (b. c1814). Eli Chesser was the security on the M.L.B. (ACM) Although this marriage license bond was issued, it is unclear if they actually married, for in his will of 1838 William Trader referred to her and her children as Hutsons.

The 1850 census puts Comfort's birth at 1814, but her 1854 marriage puts it at 1798. (ACM; FA CD309; Miles & Miles, *AC Marriages, 1854-1895*)

She m. 28 Dec 1854 in AC, Henry C. Trader, a 57 year old widowed farmer and she was shown as Comfort Hudson, a 56 year old widow. They were m. at Comfort Hudson's by George H. Ewell. Henry was a brother to William, her first husband. (AC Marriage Register 3, *1853-1896*)

William left a will dated 30 Mar 1838, probated 29 Dec 1845 in AC. My land to Nancy Trader, George Hutson, Samuel Hutson, Alfred Hutson, Amret Hutson until Amret Hutson arrives at age 15 & then to be sold & the money to Henry Trader, Edmond Trader, Elizabeth Trader, Nancy Trader, George Hutson, Samuel Hutson, Alfred Hutson & Amret Hutson. I leave a home where I now live to Comfort Hutson 15 years. James Northam extr. Witnessed by George Parker, Parker Trader & Henry Davis. (MilesW&A:545 (will of William Trader)) The will was proved by Henry Davis. Parker Trader & George Parker the other witnesses being dead, Henry Davis made oath that the said Parker Trader witnessed the will at the same time he did. James Northam the extr. named gave bond with Littleton A. Hinman & John R. Drummond securities.

133   iv. Anne Trader, b. in AC c1796.

134   v. Parker James Trader, b. in AC, d. Nov 1843, m. 12
May 1823 (bond) in AC, Nancy Hutson (b. c1810 in
AC), dau. of William Hutson. (FA CD309; Lewis, *AC MLB
1806-1835;* Carey, *The Messongo Traders;* MilesW&A:543 (adm. of
Parker Trader))

Parker 's estate was administered 27 Nov 1843 in
AC by Nancy Trader. William Trader & William Nock
were the securities. (MilesW&A:543 (adm. of Parker Trader))

135   vi. Henry C. Trader, b. in AC c1805, d. 1861. He m. 1st 26
Dec 1829 (bond) in AC, Critty Hutson. William Trader
of Henry was the security on the M.L.B. of Henry
Trader and Critty Hutson of Wm. (ACM; (FA CD309; 1860
AC Census; AC OB1860-1862:282)

Critty, b. c1810 in AC, dau. of William Hutson,
evidently d. c1854, for her husband Henry Trader was
listed as a widower on his marriage record to Comfort
Hutson, who was probably her sister. (FA CD309; Lewis,
Acc MLB 1806-1835; AC Marriage Register 3, *1853-1896*)

He m. 2nd 28 Dec 1854, Comfort Hutson. He was
shown as a 57 year old widowed farmer and she was
shown as Comfort Hudson, a 56 year old widow. They
were m. at Comfort Hudson's by George H. Ewell.
Henry was a brother to William, her first husband. (AC
Marriage Register 3, *1853-1896;,* FA CD309; Miles & Miles, *AC
Marriages, 1854-1895.* See also entry for his brother William,
above.)

Henry Trader of H. was listed as a head of
household (HH#256) in the census of 1850 in Acc
Parish, AC, a 45 year old farmer. Listed with him were
the following Traders: Critty, age 40; Delilah, age 29;
Rebecca, age 17; Lucilla, age 15; Mary, age 12; James
H., age 4; Henny, age 4; and Elizabeth A., age 2. (FA
CD309)

Henry Trader was listed as a head of household in
the census of 1860 in Acc Parish, AC (HH#102), a 55
year old farmer with personal property valued at $400.
Listed with him were the following Traders: Comfort,
age 50; James H., age 16 and farming; Henrietta, age
16; Parker, age 15. (1860 AC Census)

76. **Staten (of Wm.)**^{6} **Trader** (William^5, William^4, Henry^3, Arthur^2, Henry^1), b.
in AC c1770, d. Aug 1842. (MilesW&A:545 (will of Staten Trader); Carey, *The Messongo
Traders*)

He m. 21 Apr 1791 (bond) in AC, **Nancy Smith** (b. c1770), dau. of Bayly
Smith and Elizabeth Taylor. (ACM; Nottingham Wills:446 (will of Bayly Smith)).

He left a will dated 29 Aug 1840, probated 29 Aug 1842 in AC. To son Teackle Trader my land by him paying $5 to my dau. Elizabeth Chesser. To my grandson Alfred Trader,.. Remainder to Ishmael Trader & Teackle Trader after paying my just debts. To son Whittington Trader $1. James Northam & Teackle Trader extrs. Witnessed by George E. Croswell & Thomas A. Northam. John Savage & David D. Abbott securities. (MilesW&A:545 (will of Staten Trader))

Staten (of Wm.) Trader and Nancy Smith had the following children:

136   i. Ishmael^7 Trader, b. in AC c1790, d. 1857, m. 22 Dec 1821 (bond) in AC, Polly Miles (b. c1800, dau. of George Miles and Comfort Taylor. William Trader was the security on the M.L.B. of Ishmael Trader and Polly Miles of Comfort. (FA CD309' Carey, *The Messongo Traders;* Lewis, *AC MLB 1806-1835;* ACM)

He left a will dated 20 May 1844, probated 26 Oct 1857 in AC To my dau. Adeline Northam one shilling. To my dau. Hetty Trader,.. To my son John T. Trader,.. To my son James W. Trader,.. Balance to my dau. Hetty Trader & my sons James W. Trader & John T. Trader. Thomas A. Northam extr. Witnessed by James W. Martin, William T. Bird & Thomas A. Northam. Edmund R. Allen & Benjamin T. Gunter were securities. (MilesW&A:543 (will of Ishmal Trader))

Ishmael Trader was listed as a head of household (HH#10-9) in the census of 1850 in Acc Parish, AC, a 60 year old farmer with real estate valued at $50. Listed with him were the following Traders: Hetty, age 30; Adeline, age 21 and John, a 16 year old laborer. (FA CD309)

137   ii. Whittington Washington Trader, b. in AC c1796, d. Jun 1847. (MilesW&A:545 (adm. of Whittington Trader)) He m. 1st 27 Jun 1816 (bond) in AC, Polly Howard (b. c1800 in AC). (Lewis, *AC MLB 1806-1835*)

He m. 2nd c1845, Rachel Northam (b. c1829 in AC), dau. of William Northam of E. and Elizabeth 'Betsy' Northam. Rachel Trader, widow of Whittington Trader, m. 17 Nov 1851 (lic.) in AC, William D. German. (Carey, *The Messongo Traders*); FA CD309; AC Wills 1828-46:474; ACM)

Rachel German d. Feb 1889 in Acc Parish, AC, from heart failure at the age of 73 years. She was the dau. of Wm. Northam, born in AC, a housekeeper, the wife of Wm. D. German. Her son Whittington Trader gave the information. (WADR)

Whittington 's estate was administered 28 Jun 1847 in AC by John W. Feddeman. David Broadwater & Nehemiah W. Nock were the securities. His wife Rachel was listed as the head of HH#1056 in 1850. (MilesW&A:545 (adm. of Whittington Trader))

138   iii. Elizabeth 'Betsey' b. in AC c1796, d. 14 Sep 1870 in Messongo, AC of old age, wife of Jas. Chesser, who gave the information for the death record. She m. James Chesser 16 Aug 1822 (bond) in AC. John & Samuel Lewis were the securities on the M.L.B. of James Chessire of William and Elizabeth Trader of Staton. (Lewis, *AC MLB 1806-1835;* 1860 AC Census; WADR; ACM)

James, b. c1795 in AC, was the son of William Chesser and Leah Marshall. (1860 AC Census; Lewis, *Acc MLB 1806-1835*)

Betsey (Elizabeth) Chesser, age 64, was listed with her husband in the census of 1860 in Acc Parish, AC, in the household (HH#278) headed by James Chesser, a 65 year old farmer. (1860 AC Census)

139   iv. Teackle Trader, b. in AC 16 May 1798, d. 8 Jan 1868. His body was interred in Trader Cem, Hallwood, AC. He m. Nancy Townsend 15 Jul 1813 (bond) in AC. Thomas Allen was the security on the M.L.B. of Teackle Trader and Nancy Powell, widow of Joseph. (MilesW&A:545 (will of Staten Trader); TUAC; ACM)

Nancy, b. 18 Aug 1796, d. 9 Mar 1875 in AC, dau. of Teackle Townsend, m. 9 Jul 1810 (bond) in AC, Joseph Powell. Edmund Bell was the security on the M.L.B. of Joseph Powell and Nancy Townsend of Teackle. (TUAC; Lewis, *Acc MLB 1806-1835; ACM*) Her tombstone shows her as Nancy Trader, 18 Aug 1796 - 9 Mar 1875. Her AC Death Record shows her as Nancy Trader, who d. 9 Mar 1874, in Atlantic Dist., of old age at the age of 79 years. She was the dau. of John & Mary Taylor, born in AC. Her dau. Emaline Rew gave the information. Her body was interred in Trader Cem, Hallwood, AC. (TUAC)

Teackle Trader, age 56, farmer, was listed as head of household in the census of 1850 in Acc Parish. He possessed real estate valued at $1,800. Listed with him were Nancy Trader, age 50 and Alfred Trader, a 24 year old laborer. Also listed were Peggy Broadwater, age 26 and black; Serena Scarborough, age 8 and black;

George T. Crippen, age 11 and black; and Abraham Thornton, age 12 and black. (FA CD309)

140   v. Valentine Trader, b. in AC c1803, d. 1880 in AC, m. 7 Aug 1823 (bond), Jane 'Jenny' Chase. He was shown as Voluntine Trader of Staton and she was shown as Jane Chace of Robt. (Carey, *The Messongo Traders*; ACM; FA CD309; Mary Frances Carey, *Research Files*)

Jane, b. c1799 in AC, was the dau. of Robert Chase Sr. and Sarah 'Sally' (N). (FA CD309; ACM)

Valentine Trader, age 47, farmer, was listed as a head of household (HH#1066) in the census of 1850 in Acc Parish, AC. He possessed real estate valued at $800. Listed with him were the following Traders: Jane, age 51 and Henry of W., a 34 year old laborer. (FA CD309) He was listed as a resident in the census report 1860 in Acc Parish, AC. (Crowson & Hite, *AC 1860 Census*)

141   vi. Patsy Trader, b. in AC c1807, m. 17 Jul 1828 (bond), William Northam (b. c1808), son of William. Whittington Trader was the security on the M.L.B. of Wm. Northam of Wm. and Patsy Trader of Staton. (Lewis, *Acc MLB 1806-1835*)

This might be Betsy instead of Patsy Trader, dau. of Staton Trader. If so, it is the same person as Elizabeth Trader who m. James Cheshire in 1822. However, she is not shown as widowed or divorced.

78. William⁶ Trader Jr. (William⁵, William⁴, Henry³, Arthur², Henry¹, b. in AC c1774, d. 1801.(MilesW&A:545 (settlement of William Trader Jr.); Carey, *The Messongo Traders*)

He m. c1795, **Diadama (N)** (b. c1775). (MilesW&A:545 (settlement of William Trader Jr.))

William's estate was settled 25 Jul 1802 in AC Jun 1802. (Order to Audit), 19 Jul 1802 (Audit), 25 Jul 1802 (Rec'd) - Deadama Trader, admx. Named in settlement: Anne Trader. Auditors: John A. Bundick & Parker Barnes. (MilesW&A:545 (settlement of William Trader Jr.))

William Trader Jr. and Diadama (N) had the following children:

142   i. Hessy⁷ Trader, b. in AC c1799. Hessy was named as an heir of a Rev War Veteran 3 Feb 1814 in AC. She was shown as Hessy Trader, an illegitimate child of Diadamey Trader, and given $20 for schooling, in the will of Sarah Bayly of Robert. (MilesW&A:36 (will of Sarah Bayly of Robert))

143   ii. William (of W.) Trader, b. in AC c1801. He m. 1ˢᵗ 29 Jan 1827 (bond) in AC, Ann Lewis (b. c1800 in AC), dau. of Isaac Lewis. William Taylor was the security

on the M.L.B. of William Trader of Wm. and Ann
Lewis, orphan of Isaac, and ward of Wm. Taylor. (Carey,
The Messongo Traders; ACM; FA CD309)

He m. 2nd c1829, Nancy West (b. c1807). (Carey, *The
Messongo Traders;* FA CD309)

William Trader of W., age 49, laborer, was listed as
a head of household (HH#1162) in the census of 1850
in Acc Parish, AC. Listed with him were the following
Traders: Nancy, age 43; Wm., a 20 year old laborer;
Samuel, an 18 year old laborer; Julias, a 16 year old
laborer; Polly, age 14; Nancy, age 12; Elizabeth, age
12; Caroline, age 9; George, age 5; and Danny, age 3.
(FA CD309) He was listed as a resident in the census
report 1860 in Acc Parish, AC. (Crowson & Hite, *AC 1860
Census*)

79. **Levi^6 Trader** (William^5, William^4, Henry^3, Arthur^2, Henry^1), b. in AC
c1776, d. Jul 1815. (MilesW&A:543 (adm. of Levi Trader); Carey, *The Messongo Traders*)

He m. c1795, **Rachel (N)** (b. c1775). She m. 2nd 29 May 1815 (bond) in
AD, **John Jester** Rachel appears as Rachel Trader, widow of "L_en," (assumed
to be Levi) on her Acc MLB of 1815 to John Jester. Jesse Miles was security.
(Carey, *The Messongo Traders*; Lewis, *AC MLB 1806-1835*)

On 31 Jul 1815 John Jester was named to settle the estate of Levi Trader.
(MilesW&A:543 (adm. of Levi Trader))

Levi's estate was settled 26 Mar 1816 in AC. (MilesW&A:543 (settlement of Levi
Trader)) 31 Jul 1815 (Order to Inventory), 23 Mar 1816 (Audit), 26 Mar 1816
(Rec'd) - Appraisers: Jacob Kelly, Isaiah Johnson Sr., William Ball & Isaiah
Johnson Jr. In inventory: Henry Trader, Whittington Trader. Auditors: Jacob
Kelly & Isaiah Johnson Sr. (MilesW&A:543 (adm. of Levi Trader)

Levi Trader and Rachel (N) had the following children:

144   i. L. Parker^7 Trader, b. in AC c1802. L. was living in
Baltimore, MD. (Carey, *The Messongo Traders*)

145   ii. Walter Trader, b. c1804. Walter was living in
Baltimore, MD. (Carey, *The Messongo Traders*)

146   iii. Colley Trader, b. in AC c1806. Colley was living in
Baltimore, MD. (Carey, *The Messongo Traders*)

80. **Littleton^6 Trader** (William^5, William^4, Henry^3, Arthur^2, Henry^1), b. c1778.
(Carey, *The Messongo Traders*)

Littleton Trader had the following child:

147   i. William^7 Trader, b. c1800. (Carey, *The Messongo Traders*)

85. **Staton^6 Trader Jr.** (Staton^5, William^4, Henry^3, Arthur^2, Henry^1), b. in WO
Co 19 Aug 1783, d. 27 Jan 1844. His body was interred in Tent Presbyterian Ch
Cem, Fairchance, Fayette Co, PA. His tombstones reads "In memory of Staton
Trader who departed this life Jan'y 27, 1844, aged 61 years, 4 months & 29
days. (Trader to Carey, *Letter, 07/01/1999*).

He m. 28 Apr 1802 in WO Co., **Sarah 'Sally' Long**. (Powell, *WO Co. Marriages 1795-1865*)

Sarah, b. 23 Feb 1775, d. 1 Oct 1838. Her body was interred in Tent Presbyterian Ch Cem, Fairchance, Fayette Co, PA. Her tombstone shows her as Sarah Trader, who departed this life Oct 1, 1838, aged 63 years, 7 months & 9 days. (Trader to Carey, *Letter, 07/01/1999*)

Staton Trader was listed in the 1800 & 1810 census in WO Co. and by 1830 was listed in Fayette Co, PA. ((MilesW&A:544 (will of Sarah Ann Trader); Trader to Carey, *Letter, 07/01/1999*)

Staton Trader Jr. and Sarah 'Sally' Long had the following children:

148   i. Ann Elizabeth[7] Trader , b. in WO Co. 24 Mar 1804., d. 9 Dec 1858 in Fayette Co, PA. (Trader to Carey, *Letter, 07/01/1999*)

149   ii. Mary Trader, b. in WO Co. 8 Aug 1805. (Trader to Carey, *Letter, 07/01/1999*)

150   iii. Susan Trader, b. in WO Co. c1806. (Trader to Carey, *Letter, 07/01/1999*)

151   iv. Teagle Taylor Trader, b. in WO Co. 10 Nov 1809, d. 30 May 1890 in Fayette Co., PA. (Trader to Carey, *Letter, 07/01/1999*)

152   v. Staton Trader, b. in WO Co. 30 Sep 1810, d. 2 Feb 1883 in Fayette Co, PA. (Trader to Carey, *Letter, 07/01/1999*)

153   vi. George Trader, b. in WO Co. c1812. (Trader to Carey, *Letter, 07/01/1999*)

154   vii. Nancy Trader, b. in WO c1814. (Trader to Carey, *Letter, 07/01/1999*)

155   viii. William Henry Trader, b. in WO Co. 15 Jan 1816, d. 1 Jun 1889 in Fayette Co, PA. (Trader to Carey, *Letter, 07/01/1999*)

Descendants of Herny Wright
(Limited to the Wright surname)

Introduction

Some of the earliest Wrights in Virginia included a Robert Wright of James City who was named "an old planter" on 1 Sep 1627, when he was granted 12 acres to the eastward of James City, part of 100 acres due him for his personal adventure. (Nugent, I:8) Robert Wright was apparently the first Wright to immigrate to the Colony of Virginia. His name is included in the Muster of Inhabitants in Virginia, taken in 1624, (Hooten:261) He came to the new country in 1608, on the *Swan*, at 45 years of age. His wife was Joane Wright and they had two children born in Virginia by 1624. A number of Wright names appeared as headrights in other parts of Virginia before 1666. Some of these men married and had families on the Western Shore of the Chesapeake Bay.

The earliest Wrights on the Eastern Shore appear to have been a Nathan Wright, who witnessed the will of Thomas Savage in 1637 (Marshall:288), and a Symon Wright, who was a headright for Phillipp Taylor in 1637. (Nugent I:74) Both Richard Wright and George Wright, with wife Anna, were named as headrights here in 1640. (Bio. Diet.) Richard Wright had died by 11 Nov 1645. (Wills and Adm. of NH Co.:17) A William Wright was a servant in Northampton County in 1652 and a Thomas Wright was named as a headright in the same year. (Bio. Diet.) Francis Wright was a headright in 1653 and Robert Wright in 1654. (Bio. Diet.)

Apparently Francis Wright moved northward into SO Co., Maryland, by 1662, where he was a trader in skins and furs. (Torrence, *Old Somerset on the Eastern Shore*:17). Other early SO Co. Wrights were: William, who m. in 1669 (p. 400); Christopher, who m. in 1673 (p. 400); John, who m. in 1677 (p. 402) and Edward, who m. in 1681 (p. 439). It seems that the only Wrights who settled on the Eastern Shore of Virginia were those whose names appeared on the early tax lists. These were: Henry Wright, William Wright, and Edward Wright, all of Accomack County.

Several factors have made tracing the Wrights in Accomack County, Virginia, difficult, especially in the early records. The spelling of the name itself has caused problems. The spelling of the family name was at times given as Right, Rite, and Ryte, necessitating a double search of the indices. Several errors have been found in secondary sources, due to these spellings, when Ryte was transcribed as Rylo (Wills and Adm.:5) and Rite as Rice (p. 84).

Whitelaw's *Virginia Eastern Shore*, page 1126, states that the land of Mary Wright, which descended to her son Henry, was left by this Henry Wright in 1785 to five children. Mr. Whitelaw has not only skipped an entire generation here, but he has named the wrong Henry Wright. The Henry who died testate in 1785 was a son of Mackwilliams Wright and not connected to this line. Mary Wright's land went to her grandson, Henry Wright, who died intestate in 1793, leaving seven children, as proved by the survey of his land. Mr. Whitelaw continues by saying the land was bought up by a son Henry, who died testate in 1848, naming his wife as Rebekah . The deeds show conclusively that Henry Wright's land was bought up by son Thomas, who died testate in 1848, naming his wife as Rebekah. In many instances family lines were determined through the use of land records. Researching deeds to prove a line is more complicated than the use of probate records and much more time-consuming.

Another error was found in WO Co., Maryland, marriage records, when this Thomas Wright m. Rebecca Hickman in 1802. Her name was given as Zebina (?) "Hickman." This is in a typed copy of the original marriage records, which are no longer available at the courthouse in Snow Hill, and the question mark after her name indicates the typist has having trouble transcribing the original recording.

Most of the research on the Wright Family of Accomack County, VA, was done by Mary Frances Carey, 31415 Horntown Road, New Church, Virginia, which she printed in a booklet on Jan 15, 1994. This was later supplemented by M.K. & Barry Miles.

First Generation

1. **Henry^1 Wright I**, b. c1645, d. c1671 in AC. (AC OB1666-70 iii:161; AC OB1671-73 iv:17)

He m. c1668, **Ann Fowkes** (b. c1639), dau. of James Fowkes . She m. 2nd c1675, **Roger Miles (I)** (d. before 1712 in AC). (AC OB1666-70iii:166; Turman & Parks, *Miles Family of Acc Co, VA;* Houston & Mihalyka, *Colonial Residents of VA's E.S.;* Whitelaw)

Henry was living 24 Nov 1669 in AC. (AC OB1666-70iii:161)

Henry Wright I and Ann Fowkes had the following child:

+ 2 i. Mary^2 Wright , b. c1670, d. c1710.

Second Generation

2. **Mary^2 Wright** (Henry^1), b. in AC c1670, probably d. c1710, leaving 200 acres of land and three under-aged sons.

She may have married twice. She could have m. **Edward Wright** c1695, who was named as a servant by Amy Fowkes in her will of 1678, although no record of a marriage has been found. Edward, b. c1645, probably d. c1703. Edward Wright likely died soon after the records show he was ill in June 1703. The AC land records prove that she had at least two sons, both Wrights.

She may have also m. c1706, **William Wright** (b. c1650), who was named as a headright for Richard Bundick" when the latter patented 1,400 acres in Parkers Neck in 1664. (Nugent I:524)

Mary Wright had the following children:

+ 3 i. Henry^3 Wright, b. c1700.
   4 ii. William Wright, b. in AC c1703, d. c1733. (AC OB1731-36:70 (Adm. of William Rite's estate to his wife Mary Rite)) He m. c1730, Mary (N) (b. c1700 in AC). William 's estate

188

was administered 6 Mar 1733 when Mary Rite was named to settle the estate of her dec'd husband William Rite. (AC OB1731-36:70 (Adm. of William Rite's estate to his wife Mary Rite); Nottingham Wills:110 (will of William Rice))

+   5   iii. Mack Williams Wright, b. c1706, d. Feb 1786.

Third Generation

3. **Henry³ Wright II** (Mary², Henry¹), b. in AC c1700.
He m. c1735, **Ann 'Nanny' Scarburgh** (b. c1704 in AC), dau. of Col. Henry Scarburgh I and Winifred Powell. (Nottingham Wills:105 (will of Henry Scarburgh); Nottingham Wills:187 (will of Winefried Scarburgh))

On 26 Jun 1751 Henry Wright and William Miles were the securities on the administration of Robert Taylor's estate to John Taylor. (Nottingham Wills:138 (will of Robert Taylor))

Henry Wright II and Ann 'Nanny' Scarburgh had the following children:

+   6   i. Henry⁴ Wright III, b. c1735, d. Jan 1794.
     7   ii. William Wright Sr., b. in AC c1740, d. 1812-1820. He m. 1ˢᵗ c1775, Comfort (N) (b. c1750). He m. 2ⁿᵈ c1800, Asha (N) (b. c1750). (Acc Dist. Ct W&D 1800-06:138)

William Wright Sen. (H.T.), age 45+ was listed as a head of household in the census of 1800 in Acc Parish, AC. Listed with him were 1 male age 10-16, 2 females age 16-26, 1 female age 45+ and no free negroes or slaves. (NOTE: H.T. would have meant Horntown.), (Powell, *AC 1800, 1810, 1820 Census*)

5. **Mack Williams³ Wright** (Mary², Henry¹), b. in AC c1706, d. Feb 1786. (Nottingham Wills:362 (Will of Mack Williams Wright))

He m. 1ˢᵗ c1730, **Mary Dix** (b. c1705 in AC). Mackwilliams Wright had m. Mary Dix, sister to William Dix, by 4 Feb 1733, when William Dix wrote his will naming their son, William Wright, as a heir. (AC DW 1729 - 1737:272)

He m. c1755, **Elizabeth (N)** (b. c1730). (Nottingham Wills:362 (Will of Mack Williams Wright))

He left a will dated 15 Oct 1766, probated 28 Feb 1786 in AC. To wife Elizabeth the use of my plantation where I live and all my personal estate during her widowhood and then the plantation where I live to my son Elijah Wright & for want of heirs to my son Abel Wright. To son Jacob Wright plantation where he lives & 60 acres of land during his natural life, reversion to my son George Wright & for want of heirs of my son Abel Wright. To son George the remaining part of my land, being 40 acres. dau. Elizabeth Wright, son Abel Wright, son Henry Wright, dau. Rachel Wright, dau. Sinah Wright & dau. Leah Wright residuary legatees. Wife Elizabeth & son Elijah, extrs. Witnessed by William Young Sr., Margaret Young & George Young. (Nottingham Wills:362 (Will of Mack Williams Wright))

Mack Williams Wright and Mary Dix had the following children:

8   i. William[4] Wright, b. in AC c1732, d. before 30 Jul 1759 in AC when the inventory of William Wright was returned by his father Mack William Wright. (AC Wills&c 1757-61:151 (Inventory of William Wright returned by his father Mack William Wright))

+   9   ii. Henry Wright , b. c1742, d. Oct 1785.

10 iii. Elizabeth Wright, b. in AC c1744.

11 iv. Rachel Wright, b. in AC c1746.

+   12   v. Jacob Wright, b. c1747, d. c1798.

13 vi. Sinah Wright, b. in AC c1748.

+   14 vii. Abel Wright, b. c1749, d. Apr 1802.

+   15 viii. Elijah Wright, b. c1750, d. Jul 1827.

16 ix. Leah Wright, b. in AC c1750.

+   17   x. George Wright , b. c1752, d. c1820.

Fourth Generation

6. Henry[4] Wright III (Henry[3], Mary[2], Henry[1], b. in AC c1735, d. Jan 1794. (Nottingham Wills:410 (Adm. of Henry Wright); Nottingham Wills:187 (will of Winefried Scarburgh))

He m. c1768, **Rachel Pettitt** (b. c1768) (b. c1745 in AC), dau. of John Pettitt and Mary (N). (Nottingham Wills:355 (will of John Pettit))

Henry was named in the will of his grandmother, Winifred Scarburgh, dated 8 Sep 1756 in AC. (Nottingham Wills:187. (will of Winefried Scarburgh))

On 27 Feb 1794 in AC Henry Wright was named to settle the estate of Henry Wright. Thomas Hickman, Constable & William Evans were the securities. (Nottingham Wills:410 (Adm. of Henry Wright))

Henry Wright III and Rachel Pettitt had the following children:

+   18   i. Henry[5] Wright IV, b. c1770, d. before 1820.

+   19   ii. Thomas S. Wright, b. c1772, d. Aug 1848.

+   20 iii. William Wright, b. c1775, d. before 1830.

21 iv. Tabitha Right, b. in AC c1776, m. 23 Jan 1796 in AC, Kendall Colony (Colonna) (b. c1775). (AC Surveyor's Record 1:251 (8 Dec 1793, division among Henry Wright's 7 children); Nottingham, *AC MLB 1774-1806*; ACM)

+   22   v. John Wright , b. c1778, d. before 1820.

23 vi. Esther 'Hessey' Wright, b. in AC c1779. (AC Surveyor's Record 1:251 (8 Dec 1793, division among Henry Wright's 7 children)

+   24 vii. Edward Wright, b. c1780, d. Feb 1844.

9. Henry[4] Wright (Mack Williams[3], Mary[2], Henry[1]), b. in AC c1742, d. Oct 1785 in AC. (Nottingham Wills:359 (will of Henry Wright))

He m. c1765, **Susannah (N)** (b. c1745). (Nottingham Wills:359 (will of Henry Wright))

He left a will dated 18 Apr 1785, probated 25 Oct 1785 in AC. Mentioned sons George Wright and Isaac Wright - Balance of estate to wife Susannah during her widowhood & then to 5 children: George, Isaac, Peggy, Scarburgh & Rachel Wright. Solomon Johnson & Elijah Wright Excutors. Witnessed by Solomon Johnson, James Wise & Elijah Wright. (Nottingham Wills:359 (will of Henry Wright))

Henry Wright and Susannah (N) had the following children:

   25 i. George⁵ Wright, b. in AC c1768, m. 1797, Bridget Simpson (b. c1770 in AC). (Carey, Wrights of AC files)

+ 26 ii. Isaac Wright Sr., b. c1770, d. Feb 1835.

   27 iii. Margaret 'Peggy' Wright, b. in AC c1770.

   28 iv. Scarburgh Wright, b. in AC c1772.

   29 v. Rachel Wright, b. in AC c1778.

12. Jacob⁴ Wright (Mack Williams³, Mary², Henry¹), b. in AC c1747, d. c1798. His widow was listed in the 1800 census as Rachel Wright. (Jacb).

He m. 19 Jun 1788 in AC, **Rachel Pettitt**. (b. c1750 in AC). (ACM)

Jacob Wright and Rachel Pettitt had the following children:

   30 i. William⁵ Wright, b. in AC c1789. (Carey, Wrights of AC files)

+ 31 ii. Dennis Wright, b. c1790.

   32 iii. Rosey Wright, b. in AC c1795, m. 29 Dec 1819 (bond) in AC, Moses Blades. Levin Hyslop was the security on the M.L.B. of Moses Blades of James and Rosey Wright of Jacob. (ACM) Moses, b. c1795 in AC, was the son of James Blades and Nelly Gray.

   33 iv. Sally Wright, b. in AC c1797, m. c1820, (N) Pruitt (b. c1795 in AC). (Carey, Wrights of AC files)

   34 v. Nancy Wright, b. in AC c1798. (Carey, Wrights of AC files)

14. Abel⁴ Wright (Mack Williams³, Mary², Henry¹), b. in AC c1749, d. Apr 1802. (Nottingham Wills:362 (Will of Mack Williams Wright)). (MilesW&A:625 (will of Abel Wright))

He m. c1783, **Lucretia (N)** (b. c1750 in AC, d. 1812). She m. 1ˢᵗ c1770, **John Nock.** (MilesW&A:626 (will of Lucretia Wright))

Abel witnessed the will of John Sparrow on 24 Jan 1771 in AC. (Nottingham Wills:282 (will of John Sparrow)) He witnessed the will of John Baker on 30 Jan 1775 in AC. (Nottingham Wills:285 (will of John Baker)) On 25 Sep 1797 he witnessed the will 25 Sep 1797 of James Delight in AC. (Nottingham Wills:438 (adm. of James Delight))

Abel Write (afse. WM.), age 45+, was listed as a head of household in the census of 1800 in Acc Parish, AC. Listed with him were 1 male age 0-10, 1 female age 10-16, 2 females age 16-26, 1 female age 45+ and 11 slaves. (Powell, *AC 1800, 1810, 1820 Census*)

He left a will dated 12 Dec 1801, probated 26 Apr 1802 in AC. Brother George Wright & wife extrs. To wife all my interest in the 3 Negroes she possessed when I m. her, no claim of dower of any of my Negroes except a girl named Rose during her natural life. Remainder to my 2 daus. Molly & Katharine subject however as to the land & my other estate, exclusive of my Negroes, to their mother's dower. Extr. to sell no part of my estate unless directed by my wife & 2 children. Witnessed by John Teackle, William Nock & Sally Justice. Isaiah Hickman & Major Hinman were securities. (MilesW&A:625 (will of Abel Wright))

Abel Wright had the following child:

35   i. Molly[5] Wright, b. in AC c1780, m. 11 Oct 1802 (bond), Thomas Justice. Rodger Miles was the security on the M.L.B. (AC Mar Lic Bonds (tr), 1798-1806)

Thomas, b. c1782 in AC, son of Richard Justice and Rachel Wimbrough, d. before 1813 in AC. (Nottingham, *Acc Land Causes, 1728-1825*; MilesW&A:382 (will of Rachel Miles, widow of Roger Miles))

Abel Wright and Lucretia (N) had the following child:

36   ii. Catherine Wright, b. in AC c1785, d. Mar 1854, m. 28 Jul 1809 (bond), James Gibbons (b. c1780, d. Oct 1833). John Teackle was the security on the M.L.B. (FA D309; MilesW&A:224 (will of Catharine Gibbons); ACM; MilesW&A:224 & 225 (will of James Gibbons))

Catherine Gibbons was named in her father's will [see above] and her mother's will dated 9 Jul 1810 in AC. Her mother also named son-in-law James Gibbons extr. and a grandson Thomas Gibbons, son of my dau. Catharine Gibbons. (MilesW&A)

Catherine was named in her husband's will dated 4 Oct 1833 in AC. (MilesW&A:224 & 225 (will of James Gibbons))

Catherine Gibbons, age 65, was living with her son James T. Gibbons, age 36, farmer, in the census of 1850 in Acc Parish, AC (HH#208). (FA CD309)

She left a will dated 2 Feb 1852, probated 27 Mar 1854 in AC. At her death slave Isaac was to be freed (provided he shall desire his freedom) at my death. To granddau Elizabeth Ann Gibbons, dau. of my son James T. Gibbons … Balance to my son James T. Gibbons. The reason I do not give my other children any portion is that I have but little to distribute among them & they desire me to give it all to their brother. James T. Gibbons extr. Witnessed by John S. Turlington & James W. Custis. William T. Parks & Samuel W. Powell were securities. (MilesW&A:224 (will of Catharine Gibbons))

15. **Elijah[4] Wright** (Mack Williams[3], Mary[2], Henry[1]), b. in AC c1750, d. Jul 1827. (MilesW&A:625 (will of Elijah Wright))

He m. c1786 **Agnes (N)** (b. c1765).

Elijah witnessed the will of Henry Wright on 18 Apr 1785 in AC. It was on this date that Richard Savage and Elijah Wright were the securities on the administration of the estate of Nancy Hinman. George Hinman was named to settle the estate. (Nottingham Wills:456 (adm. of Nancy Hinman))

Elijah Write (Guild), age 45+, was listed as a head of household in the census of 1800 in Guilford, AC. Listed with him were 1 female age 26-45 and 1 female age 0-10 and 2 slaves. (Powell, *AC 1800, 1810, 1820 Census*)

On 10 Feb 1804 Elijah Wright was the security on the M.L.B. of John Onions and Linany Littleton. (ACM)

Elijah Wright, age 45+, was listed as a head of household in the census of 1810 in Acc Parish, AC. Listed with him were 1 female age 26-45 and 1 female age 16-26 and 1 slave. (Powell, *AC 1800, 1810, 1820 Census*)

He left a will dated 22 Feb 1822, probated 30 Jul 1827 in AC. To Nancy Onions a log house & 3 acres adjoining Robert Savage heirs until her death & then to my dau. Keziah Tatham. To Nancy Onions $25. To dau. Keziah Tatham 112 acres where I now live & all of my property. Thomas Tatham, extr. Witnessed by Robert Young Sr., Robert Young Jr. & Gillett Young. (MilesW&A:625 (will of Elijah Wright))

Elijah Wright had the following child:

> 37   i.   Keziah[5] Wright, b. in AC c1800, m. 21 May 1821 (bond) in AC, Thomas Tatham (b. c1795 in AC, d. 9 Dec 1875 in Acc Parish). Elijah Wright and Gilbert M. Leatherbury were the securities on the M.L.B. of Thomas Tatham and Keziah Wright of Elijah. (FA CD309; ACM; WADR)
>
> Thomas was the son of Avery Tatham and Sallie (N). He m. Keziah Mears c1845. A friend Thos. S. Taylor gave the information. (WADR; FA CD309)

17. **George[4] Wright** (Mack Williams[3], Mary[2], Henry[1]), b. in AC c1752, d. 1800 in Acc Parish, AC. He was shown as George Wright, age 26-45. Listed with him were 1 male age 0-10, 3 females age 0-10, 1 female age 16-26, 1 female age 26-45, and 1 free negro. (Powell, *AC 1800, 1810, 1820 Census*)

He m. 3 Oct 1789 (bond) **Sally Dix** (b. c1765 in AC). (Nottingham, *Acc MLB 1774-1806*)

George was named in his brother's will dated 12 Dec 1801 in AC. (MilesW&A:625 (will of Abel Wright))

George was named in a land cause 25 Sep 1820 in AC. That a certain George Wright late of this county departed this life intestate on the _ day of _ 1820, leaving five children, viz: Your orator James Wright, your oratrixes Lovea & Henrietta & Elizabeth Northam, now wife of James Northam, and a certain Sally Wright. That the said George at the time of his death was seized in fee of four tracts of land viz: one tract where he resided containing 160 acres, part of which he purchased of George Middleton, and part was devised to him by his father; another tract containing 38 acres; another tract containing 140 acres, and another tract containing 15 acres; that the said lands descended to the said children as aforesaid &c. (Nottingham, *Acc Land Causes, 1728-1825*:125 (Partition Suit Wright &c. vs. Wright))

George Wright and Sally Dix had the following children:

38   i. Lovey[5] Wright, b. in AC c1790, m. c1813, Col. Levi Dix (b. c1790). Levi, m. 1st 1810 Catherine (N) and m. 3rd c1816, Polly (N). (WADR:119 (dau Rosey's death record); WADR:46 (son George J.'s death record shows him son of Levi & Cath); Whitelaw:1089; Carey, Wrights of AC files)

+   39   ii. James Wright Sr., b. c1792, d. Jun 1831.

40   iii. Henrietta Wright, b. in AC c1794, m. 3 Jun 1820 (bond), John C. Copes (b. c1790). Levi Dix and James Watson were the securities on the M.L.B. of John C. Copes, widower, and Henrietta Wright of Geo. (ACM) John C. Copes m. 6 Jul 1813 (bond), Ann Outten. (ACM) Henry S. Copes was the security on the M.L.B.

Henrietta was named in her brother's will 16 May 1831 in AC. (MilesW&A:626 (will of James Wright))

41   iv. Elizabeth Wright, b. in AC c1795, d. 1820 in AC, m. 1 Nov 1819 (bond), Col. James Northam who later m. her sister. Revell Parker was the security on the M.L.B. of James Northam of Jacob and Elizabeth Wright of Geo. (ACM; Turman *Admin's of AC*)

James, b. c1795 in AC, son of Jacob Northam and Sally Benson, m. 1st 5 Oct 1814 (lic.) in SO Co., Catherine Dix in SO Co. He m. 3rd 20 Oct 1822 (lic.) in WO Co., Sallie D. Wright, m. 4th 7 Mar 1838 (bond) in AC, Rosey A.G. Dix. Levi Dix was the security on the M.L.B. of James Northam, widower, and Rosey A.G. Dix of Levi. (FA CD309; Pollitt, *SO Co Marriages 1796-1871*; ACM; Powell, *WO Co.Marriages 1795-1865*)

On 25 Sep 1820 James Northam was named to settle Elizabeth's estate. Thorogood Taylor and Joseph Conquest were securities. (Turman, *Admin's of AC*)

42   v. Sallie D. Wright, b. in AC c1796, m. 20 Oct 1822 (lic.) in WO Co., Col. James Northam. [See above for his marriage to Sallie's sister and other marriages.]

Fifth Generation

18. **Henry[5] Wright IV** (Henry[4], Henry[3], Mary[2], Henry[1], b. in AC c1770, d. before 1820 when his widow, Ann Wright, was head of a household in the census of that year, which included 2 males, one 16-26 years old and another 26-45 years old, and a female 16-26 years old. (AC Surveyor's Record 1:251 (8 Dec 1793, division among Henry Wright's 7 children))

He m. c1792 in AC, **Ann 'Nancy' Savage** (b. c1770 in AC) dau. of William Savage and Elizabeth (N). She m. c1788, **(N) Bunting.** (Carey, *Wrights of AC;* Nottingham Wills:393 (will of George Savage); Nottingham Wills:328 (will of William Savage))

Henry Wright, age 26-45, was listed as a head of household in the census of 1800 in Acc Parish, AC. Listed with him were 1 male age 0-10, 2 females age 0-10, 1 female age 10-16, 1 female age 16-26, and 1 female age 26-45. (AC Surveyor's Record 1)

Henry Wright IV and Ann 'Nancy' Savage had the following children:

43   i.   Henry^6 Wright, b. in AC c1800, d. Oct 1853. He m. 22 Dec 1825 (bond) in AC, Catherine 'Caty' Bell (b. c1805), dau. of George Bell. George Bell was the security on the M.L.B. of Henry Wright Jr. and Catherine Bell of George. (FA CD309; MilesW&A:626 (will of Henry Wright); Carey, *Wrights of AC;* ACM)

          Henry Wright, age 50, miller, was listed as a head of household in the census of 1850 in Acc Parish, AC (HH#3). Listed with him were Catharine Wright, age 45; Malinda Wright, age 14; William H. Wright, age 6; Samuel C. Wright, age 3; Lucinda George, age 21 and black. (FA CD309)

          He left a will 19 Oct 1853, probated 31 Oct 1853 in AC. To dau. Melindy Wright ... balance to wife Caty Wright & son William H. Wright & son Samuel Edward Wright. James T. Gibbons extr. Witnessed by Ann Bell, Casier Russell & James T. Gibbons. (MilesW&A:626 (will of Henry Wright)) The extr. refused to qualify & Catharine Wright, widow, became the admr. with John Savage Sr. & John R. Bowdoin securities.

44   ii. Thomas Wright, b. in AC c1804, d. Oct 1848. He m. 20 Feb 1826 (bond) in AC, Eliza 'Edith' Baker (b. c1805 in AC), dau. of William Baker. Henry Wright Sr. was the security on the M.L.B. of Thomas Wright of Henry and Eliza Baker of William, dec'd. (ACM; MilesW&A; FA CD309; ACM)

          Thomas left a will dated 17 Jun 1848, probated 30 Oct 1848 in AC. To my wife the whole of my land until 1 Jan 1851 after which time I give her 1/3 of the rents of my land during her life. To dau. Prudence J. Wright my land upon the northwest side of the county road provided she does not marry contrary to the will of her mother, but if she does then to her sister Hester Ann Wright. The remainder of my land to my dau. Hester Ann Wright. One third of my personal property to my wife & the balance to my daus. Prudence J. & Hester Ann Wright. Wife & John H. Custis extrs. Witnessed by William Hope, Meshack Mears & John H. Custis. (MilesW&A:626 (will of Thomas Wright of Henry)) John H. Custis refused to qualify & Edith Wright (widow) became the admx. with John Savage Sr. & James W. Custis her securities.

45   iii. Mary 'Molly' Wright, b. in AC c1810, d. 10 Dec 1881 in Acc Parish, AC. She was shown as Mary Sparrow, dau. of Henry Wright, who died of pneumonia at the age of 70 years, a housekeeper and wife of David Sparrow. Her son-in-law, Elijah Colonna gave the information. (WADR)(Crowson & Hite, *AC 1860 Census*)

She m. 1st before 1830, Tullie Bundick (b. c1805 in AC, d. before 1850), son of Abbott Bundick and Betsy Taylor.

Molly Bundick, widow, m. 2nd 2 Feb 1857 (lic.), David Sparrow, widower (b. c1818 in AC), son of Richard Sparrow Sr. and Sarah Lewis. (1840 AC Census; MACM; FA CD309; MilesW&A:501 (will of Richard Sparrow Sr.))
He m. 1st Sarah (N) c1843. (FA CD309)

Mary was listed with her husband in the census of 1860 in Acc Parish, AC.

19. **Thomas S.**[5] **Wright** (Henry[4], Henry[3], Mary[2], Henry[1]), b. in AC c1772, d. Aug 1848. Thomas Wright and his wife, Rebecca Hickman Wright, were likely buried on his land, without tombstones, in a family plot, which today contains the stones of their two sons. (AC Surveyor's Record 1:251 (8 Dec 1793, division among Henry Wright's 7 children); MilesW&A:627 (will of Thomas Wright Sr.))

He 1st m. 16 Dec 1793 (bond) in NC, **Margaret Belote** (b. c1770), dau. of George Belote. George Belote was the security on the M.L.B. of Thomas Wright & Margaret Belote of George. (Mihalyka, *NC Marriages 1660-1854*)

He m. 2nd 27 Jul 1802 (lic.) in WO Co., **Rebecca 'Rebeckah' Hickman**
She was shown as Zebrina? (probably Rebecca) Hickman. (Carey, *Wrights of Acc Co, VA*; and Powell, *WO Co.Marriages 1795-1865*)

Rebecca, b. c1784 in AC, d. May 1866, was the dau. of Isaiah Hickman and Elizabeth Hickman. Thomas Wright and his wife, Rebecca Hickman Wright, were likely buried on his land, without tombstones, in a family plot, which today contains the stones of their two sons. (AC Wills 1846-1882:207 (will of Rebecca Wright, widow of Thomas); FA CD309)

He left a will dated 22 Jul 1848 in AC, probated 28 Aug 1848. To son Samuel Wright all my land lying westerly of a line of marked trees,.. near the market road leading to Guilford (Bayside) & near a former line between the land I purchased of Walter Wright dec'd & the land on which I now reside,.. across the land which I purchased of Colmore C. Hinman to,.. the line between my lands & the lands of Matilda Taylor & also all the houses on the land I purchased of Walter Wright if not removed by me before my decease to be removed upon that part devised to him my son Samuel Wright,... To son William Thomas Wright all my land lying easterly of said line of marked trees,.. To my dau. Elizabeth Wright Negro girl Sarah, but not her increase, the increase (if any) to my daus. Elizabeth, Catharine & Sarah. Also to dau. Elizabeth Wright ½ of the land which is my wife Rebeccah's maiden land & was her share of her father's real estate,.. To the children of my dau. Mary Ann Rew (wife of James Rew) that are living at her death $800 to make her share equal to her other sisters,.. To my dau. Catharine Wright $400 & the land known as the Selby Hickman land,.. To my granddau Catharine Hope, dau. of my dau. Nancy Hope, formerly Nancy Wright $500. To my dau. Sarah Wright $300 & the other ½ of the land which was my wife Rebekah's maiden land,.. To son William Thomas Wright,.. &,.. to my son Samuel Wright & William Thomas Wright. To my daus. Elizabeth, Catharine & Sarah Wright each,.. The remainder to my daus. Elizabeth, Catharine & Sarah Wright, the children of my dau. Mary Ann Rew & my granddau Catharine Hope in kind. Sons Samuel Wright & William Thomas Wright extrs. Witnessed by George W. Bundick, Zorobabel Chandler & James Chandler. Edmund Parks & Edmund R. Allen were the securities. (MilesW&A:627 (will of Thomas Wright Sr.))

Thomas S. Wright and Rebecca 'Rebeckah' Hickman had the following children:

46 i. Samuel⁶ Wright, b. in AC 7 Sep 1803, d. 21 Aug 1877. His body was interred in Wright Cem, Rew, AC. His tombstone shows him as Samuel Wright, son of Thomas & Rebecca Wright. (TUAC)

On 26 Feb 1844 Samuel Wright was named to settle the estate of Edward Wright. John Rew & James Justice were securities. (MilesW&A:625 (Adm. of Edward Wright))

On 30 Nov 1847, he made an agreement with Iby Curtis (Free-Negro), whereby, for $15, he purchased "her child until of proper age to be free by law," a girl named Matilda. (Deeds 1846 - 1848:698) Samuel Wright purchased 25 to 30 acres from his uncle Edward Wright's heirs in 1847. On 14 Sep 1850, Samuel bought 11½ additional acres from Colmore C. Hinman and wife Lovey. (Deeds 1849 - 1850:392)

Samuel was listed as a head of household in the census of 1850 in Acc Parish, AC. He was shown as Samuel Wright the head of HH#627, a 45 year old farmer with real estate valued at $2,500. Listed with him were William Waters, a 16 year old black laborer and Tinny Custis, age 9 and black. (FA CD309)

Samuel was listed as a head of household in the census of 1860 in Acc Parish, AC. He was shown as Sam'l Wright the head of HH#609, a 56 year old farmer with real estate valued at $2,500 and personal property valued at $3,400. Listed with him were Ester Hickman, age 60 and Tabitha Finney, a 16 year old hired servant. (1860 AC Census)

Samuel was listed as a head of household in the census of 1870 in Metompkin District, AC. He was shown as Samuel Wright the head of HH#MT160, a 66 year old retired farmer with real estate valued at $3,000 and personal property valued at $1,000. He was living alone. (Walczyk, *1870 Acc Co, Acc Parish, Census*)

He made a will 23 May 1876, probated 27 Aug 1877 in AC. He left all the lands he bought of Colmore C. Hinman, land he bought of Edward Wright's heirs and $800 to his niece, Willie Ann Wright. If she should die without heirs or under 21, then the land and cash was to go to her brother, William Thomas Wright, and her sister, Margaret S. Wright, the children of William T. Wright. He named his brother, William T. Wright, as extr. Between the time Samuel Wright wrote his will and his death, his brother had died and John J. Blackstone was named to settle his estate. (AC Wills 1846-1882:679 (will of Samuel Wright)) The land Samuel Wright inherited from his father was sold on 4 Nov 1879 to Thomas Littleton, as 70 acres at $1711. The proceeds were divided, 1/5 each to: Mary Ann Rew, Catherine Wright, Catherine Hope, Sarah Hope, and the three children of William T. Wright. (Chancery Orders 1877 - 1882:361)

47   ii. Elizabeth Wright, b. in AC 1806. (FA CD309) She d. 10 Apr 1870 in Metompkin, AC of rose cancer at the age of 64 years and 3 mos. She was the dau. of Thos. & Eliz. Wright, born in AC, an unm. housekeeper. Her brother Thomas Wright gave the information. (WADR) (Note: Her mother being named as Eliz. was evidently an error, for it is clear that her mother and the mother of her brother Thomas, was Rebecca.)

Elizabeth Wright, age 44, was listed with her brother in the census of 1850 in Acc Parish, AC, HH#469 headed by Wm. T. Wright, a 24 year old farmer. (FA CD309)

Elizabeth was listed with her mother in the census of 1860 in Acc Parish, AC. She was shown as Elizabeth Wright, age 55 with personal property valued at $800, in HH#1339 headed by Rebecca Wright, age 77. (1860 AC Census)

48   iii. Mary Ann Wright, b. in AC c1810, d. 1893. Her body was interred in Rew Cem, Rew, AC. She m. James H. Rew 5 Aug 1830 (lic.) in WO Co. (FA CD309; TUAC; Powell, *WO Co. Marriages 1795-1865*)

James, b. 25 Jan 1810 in AC, d. 6 Mar 1879, son of Charles Rew Sr. and Jane 'Jinney' (N) . His body was interred in Rew Cem, Rew, AC. (TUAC; MilesW&A:442 (will of Charles Rew) & p. 443 (will of Jane Rew Sr.))

Mary A. Rew, age 40, was listed with her husband in the census of 1850 in Acc Parish, AC in the household (HH#468) headed by James K. Rew, a 39 year old farmer. (FA CD309)

She was listed as a resident in the census report 1860 in Acc Parish, AC. (Crowson & Hite, *AC 1860 Census*)

49   iv. Catharine Wright, b. in AC c1818, d. 26 Oct 1893. The newspaper showed her as Catherine Wright, who died 26 Oct 1893 at 80 years. She was the aunt of William T. Wright. (FA CD309; (Pen. Ent., November 4, 1893 issue; Barnes & Miles, *Deaths from Newspapers 1881-1912*)

Catharine Wright, age 32, was listed in the census of 1850 in Acc Parish, AC, in the household (HH#469) headed by her brother, Wm. T. Wright, a 24 year old farmer. (FA CD309)

Catharine was listed with her mother in the census of 1860 in Acc Parish, AC as Catherine Wright, age 45, with real estate valued at $600 and personal property valued at $800, in HH#1339 headed by Rebecca Wright, age 77. (1860 AC Census)

She left a will dated 23 Jun 1890 in AC, probated on 8 Nov 1893. She left her personal estate to her nephew, William T. Wright, provided he pay her medical bills, funeral expenses and other debts, with the exception of "one pair of gold spectacles and a half dozen silver tablespoons" which were to go to his dau, Helen Wright, at his death. (AC Wills 1882-1901:263 (will of Catherine Wright))

50   v. Ann 'Nancy' Wright, b. in AC c1820, d. before 1850. (FA CD309) She was not in the 1850 census with her husband, William K. Hope. She m. William K. Hope 2

Apr 1839 (bond) in AC. James H. Rew was the
security on the M.L.B. of William Hope and Ann
Wright of Thomas. (ACM)
 William K. Hope, b. 14 Feb 1816 in AC. (TUAC;
MilesW&A:274 (will of Kendall Hope) (Note: The will stated
4 children, but they were not named. It is assumed the
K. stands for Kendall.)) was the son of Kendall Hope
and Mary 'Molly' Bundick. He m. Sarah 'Sally' Wright
4 Jul 1850 (lic.) in WO Co. (Powell, *WO Co.Marriages 1795-
1865*) (NOTE: Sally was a sister to his first wife
Ann/Nancy Wright.)
 William d. 1 May 1869 at 53 years of age. The
death records show him as Wm. K. Hope, who d. in
Apr 1868 of dysentery at the age of 56 years. He was
the son of Kendal & Molly Hope, b. in AC, married
and a farmer. His body was interred in Hope Cem,
Gargatha, AC. (TUAC; WADR)

51 vi. William Thomas Wright, b. in AC c1824, d. 18 Dec
1876. (TUAC) He was shown as Wm. T. Wright, who
died on 17 Dec 1876 in District No. 1 of typhoid fever
at the age of 50 years. (WADR) He was the son of Thos.
& Rebecca Wright, born in AC, and a farmer, the
husband of Mary. A friend Edw. Wright gave the
information. His body was interred in Wright Cem,
Rew, AC. His tombstone shows him as William T.
Wright, the son of Thos. & Rebecca Wright, who died
18 Dec 1876. (Miles & Miles, *AC Marriages, 1854-1895; WADR)*
(TUAC)
 William T. Wright m. Mary S. Carey 18 Nov 1857
in Drummond Town, AC. He was shown as a 33 year
old farmer, son of Thos. S. & Rebecca Wright. She was
shown as Mary S. Carey, age 24, dau. of Sam'l S. &
Mary Carey. They were m. at the Drummond Town
Methodist Church by J.F. Chaplain. John J. Blackstone
said both were over age 21. (TUAC; Miles & Miles, *AC
Marriages, 1854-1895*)
 Mary, b. 9 Jan 1833 in AC, d. 4 Feb 1898, dau. of
Samuel S. Carey and Mary S. 'Polly' Milliner. The
newspaper showed her as Mary S. Wright, who died at
the age of 65 years, widow of William T. Wright and
mother of C.C. Dix, Mrs. John A. Bundick and William
T. Wright. (TUAC; Miles & Miles, *AC Marriages, 1854-1895*; FA
CD309; Barnes & Miles, *Deaths from Newspapers 1881-1912*)

Her body was interred in Wright Cem, Rew, AC. (TUAC) Mary S. Wright was buried beside her husband in the Wright family plot.

William T. Wright was listed as a head of household in the census of 1850 in Acc Parish, AC (HH#469), a 24 year old farmer with real estate valued at $2,500. Listed with him were the following Wrights: Rebecca, age 66; Elisabeth, age 44; Catharine, age 32; and Sally, age 25. Also listed were Catharine Hope, age 19 and Bagwell Crippen, an 18 year old black laborer. (FA CD309)

William Thomas Wright sold no land. On 23 Jan 1851, he bought 34 acres from Matilda S. Taylor for $675, land that was bordered on the northeast by his other land and on the southeast by the public road. (Deeds 1849 - 1851:561) With this purchase, William T. Wright extended his land to present U.S. 13 (old Wallops Road).

William T. Wright was listed as a head of household in the census of 1860 in AC (HH#589), a 38 year old farmer with real estate valued at $4,000 and personal property valued at $6,500. Listed with him was Mary S. Wright, age 28. There were no children in their household. His brother, Samuel Wright, was in household 609/610. (1860 AC Census) Apparently Samuel Wright lived in the older house on their father's land and a new house was built on William's land by 1850, using the building materials of his father's will. After William m. in 1857, his mother and his unm. sisters likely went to live on the Isaiah Hickman land. Their household was numbered 1339/1335 in the 1860, census, indicating they then lived farther down the county.

In the 1870 census William (enumerated as Thomas) Wright was listed as a head of household (HH#MT182) in Metompkin District, AC, a 47 year old farmer with real estate valued at $4,000 and personal property valued at $4,000. Listed with him were the following Wrights: Mary, age 37 keeping house; Thomas, age 10 at school; Margaret, age 7; and Anna, age 9 months, born in July. Also listed was Charles Gibbons, a 23 year old black farm laborer and Mary Wright, a 17 year old mulatto domestic servant. (Walczyk, *1870 Acc Co, Acc Parish, Census*)

William 's will was probated 28 Jan 1878 in AC. His estate had been settled by his administrators, John W. Gillet and John J. Blackstone, by 28 Jan 1878, when they filed their account. (Fiduciary Accts. 1877 - 1880:270) A sum of $3164.47 was then due the estate. An appraisal of William T. Wright's personal estate had been made on 8 Jan 1877 and the items listed were sold the next day. (Inv. 1874 - 1879:298) His widow bought several items and his brother Samuel, a canoe. At the end of this six-page account appears: "A list of items under the Statue for the Benefit of the widow and infant children of the deceased." There are 28 items listed here, totaling $239.10 in appraised value. They include: "The Family Bible, Family Pictures, School Books & e," three beds and bedding, one horse, one cow, chairs, a table, knives, forks, spoons, dishes, "two Baisins," one iron pot, a spinning wheel, an axe, two hoes, five bushels corn, flour, pork, one cooking stove and utensils, three hogs and fodder (p. 304) John W. Gillet was guardian of the three underage children until they were grown. (Fid. Accts. 1877 - 1880, pp. 612, 613, 615, through 1883 - 1887)

52   vii. Sarah 'Sally' Wright, b. in AC c1825. (FA CD309) She d. Mar 1890 in Acc Parish, AC. (TUAC; WADR) She was shown as Sally W. Hope, who d. in Mar 1890 of pneumonia at the age of 70 years. She was the dau. of Thomas & Rebecca Wright, born in AC, a housekeeper, the wife of Wm. K. Hope. Her step-dau,, Cath. Hope, gave the information. Her body was interred in Hope Cem, Gargatha, AC. (TUAC) Her tombstone shows her as Sallie W. Hope, 2nd wife of William K. Hope, died 1889. She m. William K. Hope 4 Jul 1850 (lic.) in WO Co. (Powell, *WO Co.Marriages 1795-1865*) (NOTE: Sally was a sister to his first wife Ann/Nancy Wright.)

William, b. 14 Feb 1816 in AC. (TUAC; MilesW&A:274 (will of Kendall Hope) (Note: The will stated 4 children, but they were not named. It is assumed the K. stands for Kendall.)) was the son of Kendall Hope and Mary 'Molly' Bundick. He m. Ann 'Nancy' Wright 2 Apr 1839 (bond) in AC. (ACM) James H. Rew was the security on the M.L.B. of William Hope and Ann Wright of Thomas.

William d.1 May 1869 at 53 years of age. He was shown as Wm. K. Hope, who died in Apr 1868 of dysentery at the age of 56 years. He was the son of Kendal & Molly Hope, b. in AC, married a farmer. His body was interred in Hope Cem, Gargatha, AC. (TUAC; WADR)

Sarah Wright, age 19, was living in the household (HH#469) of her brother, Wm. T. Wright, age 24, farmer, in the census of 1850 in Acc Parish, AC. (FA CD309) In the 1860 census in Acc Parrish, she was listed as Sally Hope, age 37, with her husband in household, HH#714, headed by William Hope of K., a 44 year old farmer. (1860 AC Census)

20. **William⁵ Wright** (Henry⁴, Henry³, Mary², Henry¹, b. in AC c1775, d. before 1830. (AC Surveyor's Record 1:251 (8 Dec 1793, division among Henry Wright's 7 children))

He m. 28 Feb 1797, **Patience Dix** (b. c1775 in AC). (ACM)

William Write, age 16-26, was listed as a head of household in the census of 1800 in Gargatha, AC. Listed with him were 1 other male also age 16-26, 2 females age 16-26 and no slaves or free blacks. (Powell, *AC 1800, 1810, 1820 Census*)

William Wright and Patience Dix had the following child:

53   i.   Walter⁶ Wright, b. in AC c1798, d. Feb 1844, m. 5 Aug 1825 (bond), Henrietta 'Henny' Sparrow. Edmund Baker and George Littleton were the securities on the M.L.B. of Walter Wright of Wm. and Henny Sparrow of Rich. (ACM; TUAC:627)

Henrietta , b. c1800 in AC, was the dau. of Richard Sparrow Sr. and Zeporah Mears. (FA CD309; MilesW&A:501 (will of Richard Sparrow Sr.))

He left a will dated 28 Dec 1843, probated 26 Feb 1844 in AC. To my wife the whole of my land until my youngest child arrives to 21 of age. The whole of my personal property to be sold to pay my just debts & 1/3 of the remaining to my wife & 2/3 to my children. Friend John H. Custis, extr. Witnessed by John H. Custis, Griffin Savage, Zadock Mason & William Shreaves. William C. White & James Justice were securities. (MilesW&A:627 (will of Walter Wright))

22. **John⁵ Wright** (Henry⁴, Henry³, Mary², Henry¹), b. in AC c1778, probably d. before 1820 as he was not listed in the 1810 census. In this census Elizabeth Wright was given as head of a household, aged 26 to 45, with two females under 10 years and two males of 16 to 26. If these males were John Wright's sons, nothing more has been found of them. (AC Surveyor's Record 1:251 (8 Dec 1793, division among Henry Wright's 7 children))

He m. 17 Feb 1802 (bond) in NC, **Elizabeth 'Betsey' Dunton** (b. c1780 in NC). John Simkins was the security on the M.L.B. of John Wright and Betsey

Dunton. They m. between 1 Jan and 30 Mar 1802 by J. Elliott. (Mihalyka, *NC Marriages 1660-1854*)

John Wright and Elizabeth 'Betsey' Dunton had the following children:

    54   i. Tabitha[6] Wright b. in AC c1807, m. 11 Jan 1832 (bond) in AC, Richard Sparrow Jr. Edmund Baker was the security on the M.L.B. of Richard Sparrow and Tabitha Wright of Jno. (ACM; FA CD309)

Richard, b. c1806 in AC, was the son of Richard Sparrow Sr. and Zeporah Mears. (FA CD309; MilesW&A:501 (will of Richard Sparrow Sr.))

Tabitha Sparrow, age 43, was listed with her husband in the census of 1850 in Acc Parish, AC in HH#704 headed by Richard Sparrow, a 44 year old farmer. (FA CD309)

    55   ii. Elizabeth Wright, b. in AC c1810, m. Richard Bayly 31 Mar 1840 (bond) in AC. Richard Sparrow was the security on the M.L.B. of Richard Bayly and Elizabeth Wright of John. (ACM)

Richard, b. c1814 in AC, was the son of Robert Bayly and Polly (N). He m. 2nd c1845, Hetty Northam. (WADR) He m. 3rd 12 May 1868 in AC, Sally Ann Northam. He was shown as Richard Bayly, a 53 year old widowed merchant, born and living in AC, son of Robert and Polly. She was shown as Sally Johnson, age 25, born and living in AC, dau. of Gillet & Elizabeth Northam. They were m. by Montcalm Oldham. (FA CD309; MACM)

24. **Edward**[5] **Wright** (Henry[4], Henry[3], Mary[2], Henry[1], b. in AC c1780, d. Feb 1844. (AC Surveyor's Record 1:251 (8 Dec 1793, division among Henry Wright's 7 children); MilesW&A:625 (Adm. of Edward Wright))

He m. 19 Nov 1808 (bond) in AC, **Susanna Littleton** (b. c1780 in AC). Savage Crippen was the security on the M.L.B. (ACM)

On 26 Feb 1844 Samuel Wright was named to settle the estate of Edward Wright. John Rew & James Justice were securities. (MilesW&A:625 (Adm. of Edward Wright))

Edward Wright and Susanna Littleton had the following children:

    56   i. Ann[6] Wright, b. in AC c1805, m. Alexander West before 1847. She was the wife of Alexander West in 1847, when her father's land was sold. (Carey, *Wrights of AC*; FA CD309)

Ann West, age 45, was listed with her husband Alexander West (35 year old laborer), in the census of 1850 in Acc Parish, AC (HH#1210). Also listed was James Wright, age 22 and Edward Wright, age 30, who were evidently her brothers. (FA CD309)

57   ii.   John E. Wright, farmer, b. in AC c1816, d. of old age on 4 Jul 1887 in Acc Parish, AC, m. Louisa (N). He was a farmer and the husband of Louisa. His son Edw. Wright gave the information for his death record.. (WADR; FA CD309)

       John Wright was head of household in the census of 1850 in AC (HH#5), a 34 year old farmer. Listed with him were Louisa Wright, age 24; Edward W. Wright, age 8 mos., William Berry, age 14. (FA CD309)

       John was head of household in the census of 1870 in Acc Parish, AC. He was shown as John Wright, a 45 year old farmer with personal property valued at $100. Listed with him were the following Wrights: Louisa, age 45; Edward, a 19 year old oysterman; Mary, age 15; George, a 14 year old farm laborer; Anna, age 12; Susan, age 10; Betsy, age 8; and James, age 4. (Walczyk, *1870 Acc Parish, AC Census*)

58   iii.   Susanna or Louisa Wright, b. in AC c1816, m. 20 Jun 1838 (bond) in AC, Levin Pettitt (b. c1818 in AC). Thomas Hope was the security on the M.L.B. of Levin Pettet and Louisa Wright of Edward. Another record from this same source shows Levin Pettit m. Susanna Wright on 26 Jun 1838. (ACM; FA CD309; FA CD309)

       Louisa Pettit, age 34, was listed on the census of 1850 in Acc Parish, AC in HH#210 headed by her husband Levin Pettit, a 32 year old farmer. (FA CD309)

59   iv.   Edward Wright, b. in AC c1820, d. 10 Oct 1902. The newspaper obiturary showed him as Edward Wright, who d. at the age 84 years. He was the Uncle of E. Wright Jr. (Carey, *Wrights of AC*; FA CD309; Barnes & Miles, *Deaths from Newspapers 1881-1912*)

       Edward Wright, a 30 year old carpenter, was listed with his sister in the census of 1850 in Acc Parish, AC (HH#1210), headed by Alexander West, a 35 year old laborer. Also listed was Ann West, age 45, who was evidently his sister. (FA CD309)

       Edward Wright, carpenter, was listed as a head of household in the census of 1880, age 60 years. (1880 AC Census)

60   v.   George Wright, b. c1825, in AC. (Carey, *Wrights of AC;* FA CD309)

61   vi.   James Wright, b. in AC c1828. James was listed with his sister in the census of 1850 in Acc Parish, AC. He was shown as a 22 year old miller in HH#1210 headed by Alexander West, a 35 year old laborer. Also listed

was Ann West, age 45, who was evidenlty his sister. (Carey, *Wrights of AC*; FA CD309)

26. **Isaac^5 Wright Sr.** (Henry^4, Mack Williams^3, Mary^2, Henry^1), b. in AC c1770, d. Feb 1835. (MilesW&A:626 (Adm. of Isaac Wright))
He m. 1st 27 Dec 1804 (bond) in AC. **Mary Anne Satchell** (b. c1785 in AC). William H. Coxon was the security on the M.L.B. (ACM)
He m. 2nd 21 Sep 1814 (bond), **Elizabeth 'Betsy' Shield**. Thomas Chandler was the security on the M.L.B. of Isaac Wright and Betsy Wharton, widow of Charles. (ACM)
Elizabeth m. 1st 14 Oct 1806 (bond) in AC, **Charles Wharton**. (ACM) Samuel Walston was the security on the M.L.B. of Charles Wharton and Elizabeth Shield.
Isaac Write, age 26-45, was listed as a head of household in the census of 1800 in Metompkin Dist., AC. Listed with him were 2 males age 0-10, 1 male age 16-26, 1 female age 16-26, 1 female age 26-45 and 4 free negroes. (Powell, *AC 1800, 1810, 1820 Census*)
Isaac Wright, age over 45, was listed as a head of household in the census of 1820 in St. George Parish, AC. Listed with him were 3 other males and 5 females and 2 slaves. (Powell, *AC 1800, 1810, 1820 Census*)
Isaac Wright, age 50-60, was listed as a head of household in the census of 1830 in St. George Parish, AC. Also in the household were 4 other males and 5 females listed with him. He also had 6 slaves. (Powell, *AC 1830 Census*)
On 23 Feb 1835 Charles S. Snead was named to settle the estate of Isaac Wright. Edward L. Snead, George F. Snead & John Arlington were the securities. (Powell, *AC 1830 Census;* MilesW&A:626 (Adm. of Isaac Wright))
Isaac Wright Sr. had the following child:
62   i. Henry^6 Wright, b. in AC c1798. He m. 1st 20 Dec 1820 (bond) in AC, Ann Joynes (b. c1800 in AC), dau. of Zorobabel Joynes. William R. Joynes was the security on the M.L.B. of Henry Wright of Isaac and Ann Joynes of Zoro. (ACM)
He m. 2nd 9 Dec 1833 in AC, Margaret Kellam (b. c1810 in AC). Christopher C. Satchell was the security on the M.L.B. (ACM) Another record from this same source shows they were m. on 18 Dec 1833.
Isaac Wright Sr. and Mary Anne Satchell had the following child:
63   ii. Elijah W. Wright, b. in AC 5 Nov 1809, d. 20 Jun 1880 in St. George Parish of cancer, farmer, the husband of Marg't. His son Isaac T. Wright gave the information. His body was interred in Onancock Cem, AC.
He m. 27 Dec 1836 (bond) in AC, Margaret A. Snead 6 (bond) in AC. John R. Fosque was the security on the M.L.B. of Elijah W. Wright and Margaret Snead of Tully. Another record from this same source shows a

marriage of 28 Dec 1837 and he was shown as Elijah J. Wright. (MLAC; WADR; ACM)

Margaret, b. 28 Jun 1807 in AC, d. 19 Mar 1891, St. George Parish, AC, dau. of Tully Snead and Rosetta 'Rosey' (N). St. George Parish, AC. She was shown as Marg. A. Wright, who died of 'la grippe,' widow. Her son Isaac Wright gave the information. The newspaper showed her as Margaret Wright, age 84, widow of Elijah Wright and mother of Isaac T. Wright. Her body was interred in Onancock Cem, AC. (MLAC; WADR; ACM; Barnes & Miles, *Deaths from Newspapers 1881-1912*))

Elijah Wright, age 50, farmer, was listed as a head of household (HH#867) in the census of 1860 in St. George Parish. He possessed personal property valued at $5,000. Listed with him were the following Wrights: Marg't A., age 52; Rosy A., age 22; John L., an 18 year old farm laborer; Isaac, age 16; Marg't S., age 13; and Mary A., age 12. Also listed was Edw'd Beach, an 18 year old black farm laborer and Rosy White, age 81. (1860 AC Census)

Isaac Wright Sr. and Elizabeth 'Betsy' Shield had the following children:

64   iii. Elizabeth Wright, b. in AC c1815, m. 24 Dec 1838 (bond) in AC, James Colonna Doughty. Thomas J. Doughty was the security on the M.L.B. of James C. Doughty and Elizabeth Wright of Isaac. (ACM)

James, b. 16 May 1816 in AC, was the son of Jephtha Doughty and Margaret 'Peggie' Colonna . He m. 2nd 12 Dec 1842 (bond) in NC, Margaret Sarah Thomas Johnson. Richard J. Ayres was the security on the M.L.B. of James C. Doughty and Margaret S. Johnson, dau. of Thomas Johnson dec'd. Frances L. Mears, now wife of Thomas C. Mears & mother of Margaret S. gave consent. They were m. on 13 Dec 1842 by G.C. Wescoat. (WADR; MLAC; Mihalyka, *NC Marriages 1660-1854*)

James C. Doughty, farmer, d. 6 May 1887 of pneumonia in St. George Parish, AC. He was the son of Peggie Doughty, born in AC and unm. His son Jas. C. Doughty gave the information of the death record. His body was interred in Forest Grove, Pennyville, AC. His tombstone shows him as James Colonna Doughty. (MLAC; WADR)

65   iv. Thomas S. Wright, b. in AC c1815, m. 13 Feb 1839 (bond dated 7 Jan 1839) in AC, Emeline S. Mears (b.

207

c1815). William S. Sturgis was the security on the
M.L.B. of Thomas S. Wright and Emaline S. Mears,
ward of Shadrock T. Ames. Another record from this
same source shows Thomas Wright m. Emiline Mears
on 15 Jul 1837.(Carey, Wrights of AC files; ACM)

66 v. Sally Wright b. in AC c1818, m. 22 Apr 1839 (bond) in
AC, Zadock Ames (b. c1790). William S. Sturgis was
the security on the M.L.B. (Carey, Wrights of AC files)

67 vi. Susan Wright, b. in AC c1820, m. 1 Dec 1841 in AC,
John Stakes (b. c1815 in AC). (Carey, Wrights of AC files; ACM)

68 vii. Ann 'Nancy' Wright, b. in AC c1822, m. 8 Aug 1841
(bond) in AC, Ephraim Tipton (b. c1820 in MD.
Edward L. Bayly was the security on the M.L.B. of
Ephraim Tipton and Ann Wright, ward of E.L. Bayly.
(Carey, Wrights of AC files; FA CD309; ACM)

Nancy (Ann) Tipton, age 28, was listed with her
husband in the census of 1850 in St. George Parish, AC
in HH#837 headed by Ephraim Tipton, a 30 year old
coach maker, age 30 and born in MD, with real estate
valued at $1,000. (FA CD309)

31. **Dennis**[5] **Wright** (Jacob[4], Mack Williams[3], Mary[2], Henry[1]), b. in AC c1790.
(Carey, Wrights of AC files)

He m. 5 Sep 1816 (lic.) in WO Co., **Nancy Gunter** (b. c1795). (Powell, *WO Co. Marriages 1795-1865*)

Dennis Wright and Nancy Gunter had the following children:

69 i. William[6] Wright, b. in AC 29 Jun 1822, d. 12 Apr 1883
in St. George Parish, AC, of consumption, unm. farmer.
His nephew John T. Budd gave the information for his
death record. His body was interred in Budd Cem,
Accomac, AC. (MLAC; WADR)

In 1850 William Wright, age 24, farmer, was living
with the family of Jno. A. Knower in the cenus of 1850
in St. George Parish, AC, in HH#306, headed by Jno.
A. Knower, a 40 year old carriage maker. (FA CD309)

Wm. Wright was listed as a head of household in
the census of 1870 in Locust Mount PO, St.George
Parish, AC (HH#LM1581), a 47 year old farmer with
real estate valued at $250 and personal property valued
at $100. (Walczyk, *1870 Acc Co, St. George Parish, Census*)

70 ii. Sally Wright, b. in AC 14 Apr 1825, d. 10 Jan 1889.
Her body was interred in Budd Cem, Accomac, AC.
Her tombstone shows her as Sally Budd, wife of
Thomas T. Budd and the dau. of Denis & Nancy.

(NOTE: Denis & Nancy's surname was not shown.) She m. Thomas T. Budd 29 Dec 1842 in AC. (WADR:176 (death of Wm. Wright); FA CD309; MLAC; ACM)

Thomas, b. 3 Mar 1820 in AC, d. 25 Feb 1860. His body was interred in Budd Cem, Accomac, AC. His tombstone shows him as Thomas T. Budd, the husband of Sally and the son of Jno. & Sally Budd. (FA CD309; MLAC)

Sally Budd, age 24, was listed with her husband in the census of 1850 in Acc Parish, AC, HH#522, headed by Thomas P. Budd, a 29 year old farmer. (FA CD309)

39. **James⁵ Wright Sr.** (George⁴, Mack Williams³, Mary², Henry¹), b. in AC c1792, d. Jun 1831. (MilesW&A:626 (will of James Wright))

He m. 1ˢᵗ 23 Dec 1816 (bond) in AC, **Ann 'Nancy' Bundick** (b. c1792). John H. Bayly was the security on the M.L.B. of James Wright and Ann Bundick of Geo. Ann was the dau. of George 'of Metompkin' Bundick and Ann 'Nancy|Nanney' Warrington. (ACM)

He m. 2ⁿᵈ 14 Apr 1827 (bond) in AC, **Mary Ann Finney** (b. c1806 in AC). William W. Dix was the security on the M.L.B. of James Wright and Mary Ann Finney of William, dec'd. Mary was the dau. of William Finney and Sarah 'Sally' Bundick. She m. 2ⁿᵈ 17 Jun 1840 (bond) in AC, **Rev. William Laws.** Thomas P. Bagwell was the security on the M.L.B. of Rev. William Laws and Mary Ann Wright, widow of James. (ACM; FA CD309)

James Wright left a will dated 16 May 1831, probated in AC. The plantation whereon I now reside to be sold (but I reserve to my heirs & the heirs of William Finney dec'd the graveyard for a burying ground which is bounded by four stones) & the money to my wife Mary Ann Wright (to have an equal share with my children), my dau. Sarah Ann, son William Abbott, dau. Betsey, son James & son George F. Wright. Also the land in the woods which was my share of my father's land & also that which I purchased of my sister Henrietta Copes, to be sold & the money to my wife & children. Negro man Edmund to be free after my decease. Negro man Nathan to my wife & I lend my wife my Negro woman Scarburgh & her increase during her life & then to son William Abbott & my son James Wright. To son George F. Wright my Negro girl Rose (dau of Scarburgh) & her increase, but if he dies before he arrives to lawful age, then the Negro girl Rose as well as all his other estate to my living children. Friend James Northam extr. Witnessed by George Warrington Bundick, John McMath & Samuel S. Lewis. Nathaniel Topping, John Savage (of R.) & Edward W. Taylor were securities. (MilesW&A:626 (will of James Wright))

James Wright Sr. and Ann 'Nancy' Bundick had the following children:

71   i. Sarah Ann 'Sally'⁶ Wright, b. in AC c1818, m. 24 Jul 1833 (bond) in AC, Edward D. Bradford. Samuel H. Scarburgh and John Arlington were the securities on the M.L.B. of Edward D. Bradford of John B. and Sally

Wright. Edward, b. c1812 in AC, was the son of John Brown Bradford and Margaret 'Peggy' Addison. (ACM; WADR:20 (death of Ezra Bradford, son of John & Peggie Bradford was reported by his brother Edw'd L. Bradford))

72 ii. William Abbott Wright, b. in AC c1820.

73 iii. Elizabeth S. 'Betsy' Wright, b. in AC c1823. She m. 1st 6 Dec 1837 (bond) in AC, Samuel C. Hope (b. c1815 in AC). Southy Lewis was the security on the M.L.B. of Samuel C. Hope and Elizabeth S. Wright, ward of Henry P. Parks. Samuel was the son of George Hope and Nancy Taylor.

She m. 2nd 14 Dec 1843 in AC, John Hope. He was shown as John Hope, widower, and she as Elizabeth S. Hope, widow. (ACM; FA CD309; MilesW&A:272 (will of George Hope)) John, b. c1815 in AC, d. Jul 1846, was the son of Kendall Hope and Mary 'Molly' Bundick. He m. 20 Feb 1837 (bond) in AC, Ann James. Samuel Hope was the security on the M.L.B. (Grandfather Bundick's Will; ACM; MilesW&A:274 (adm. of John Hope of K.)

Betsy Hope, widow, m. 3rd 16 Sep 1850 in AC, Zorobabel Core Laws (b. c1800 in AC), son of John Laws Sr. He m. 1st 7 Aug 1827 (bond) in AC, Ann J. Coleburn. Coleburn Nock and Levin Core were the securities on the M.L.B. of Zorobabel C. Laws and Ann J. Coleburn of William. (ACM; FA CD309) He m. 2nd 8 Jan 1830 (bond) in AC, Ann Riley. Levin Core and Timothy James West were the securities on the M.L.B. of Zorobabel C. Laws, widower, and Ann Riley. (ACM)

Elizabeth was listed as a head of household in the census of 1850 in Acc Parish, AC. She was shown as Elizabeth S. Hope the head of HH#653, age 27. Listed with her were Mary A. Hope, age 9; Emma J. Hope, age 6; and Elizabeth S. Hope, age 2. (FA CD309)

In 1860 Elizabeth S. Laws, age 39, was living in the household (HH#789) of John D. Wimbrough, age 25, farmer, in Acc Parish, AC. Also listed in this household was Emma J. Hope, age 15; and Elizabeth S. Hope, age 13. (Crowson & Hite, *AC 1860 Census*)

74 iv. James B. Wright, b. in AC c1825, m. 2 Apr 1842 (lic.) in WO Co., Demariah D. Hickman (b. c1825). They supposedly m. 11 Apr 1847 (maybe 1842?). In WO Co. they were shown as James B. Wright and Demirah B. Hickman who were given a license on 2 Apr 1842.

James Wright Sr. and Mary Ann Finney had the following child:

75   v. George F. Wright, b. in AC c1830, m. 9 Dec 1851 in AC, Elizabeth W. Laws. He was shown as George T. Wright and she as Elizabeth Laws of Zorobabel Elizabeth, b. c1834 in AC, was the dau. of Zorobabel Core Laws and Ann Riley. (FA CD309; ACM)

In 1850 George F. Wright, age 20, clerk, was living with the family of Wm. Laws, a 54 year old Baptist clergyman, in Acc Parish, AC (HH#202). (FA CD309)

Geo. F. Wright was listed as a head of household in the census of 1860 in Acc Parish, AC (HH#1153), a 30 year old merchant with personal property valued at $6,000. Listed with him were the following Wrights: Elizt. M., age 26; Edwin S., age 5; Chas. C., age 3; and Mary A., age 1. Also listed was Betsey Mathews, age 19. (1860 AC Census)

ABBOTT, Amy, 48: Ann, 4, 47:
David D., 107, 181: Elizabeth,
48: George, 165: James, 165:
John, 48, 49, 66: Mary, 46:
Mason, 6: Robert, 48: Thomas,
62, 63, 65: Tommy, 69
ADAMS, Obed, 154
ADDISON, Margaret, 209: Peggy,
209
AILWORTH, James J., 118
ALLEN, Edmund R., 181, 196:
Hester Ann, 39: John, 17, 18, 19:
John H., 39: Thomas, 182
ALLENS INDUSTRY, 18, 19, 33, 35
AMES, Benjamin T., 82: John E., 83,
114, 116: Joseph, 168: Richard,
169: Sally, 207: Shadrack M.,
169: Shadrock, 207: Zadock,
207: Zorobabel, 167
ANDERSON, Esther, 108
ANDREWS, Catherine, 79: Caty, 79:
Ismael, 92: James B., 79: Lucy,
169: Mary, 93: Nancy, 79:
Rachel, 59, 60: Richard, 59:
Robert, 79: Susanna, 92:
Susannah, 93: William, 59, 93,
122,158
ANNIS, Alfred, 130: Custis, 132:
Levi, 78: Nancy, 124: Tabitha,
78
ANSIL, Elizabeth, 48, 53
ARBUCKLE, George W., 143
ARDIS, Edward, 37: Harriet F., 37:
Zadok, 17
ARLINGTON, Anna Simpson, 116:
Elizabeth, 116: John, 42, 102,
205, 208: Thomas b., 116
ASHBY, George, 168: Margaret, 168

AYDELOTTE, Benjamin, 18:
Benjamin J., 37: Mary, 105:
Polly, 105
AYRES, Edward T., 121: Richard J.,
206: Robert, 124
B—, Mordicai, 127
BACON QUARTER, 35
BADGE, Betsey, 174
BADGER, Abel, 58: Leannah, 29:
Mary, 112: Nathaniel, 112:
William, 113
BAGGALE, Gervis, 3
BAGWELL, Ann, 123, 149: Bridget,
50, 94: Charles, 50, 52, 61, 97,
99, 149: Healey Parker, 5: Isaiah,
20: Katie, 5: Laura, 149: Lorey,
149: Nancy, 149: Sadie Parker,
5: Thomas P., 208
BAILEY, Thomas, 11
BAKER, Daniel, 63: David, 173:
Edith, 194: Edmund, 202, 203:
Eliza, 194: Elizabeth, 166:
Ezekiel, 56, 87: Hetty, 64, 80:
Hezekiah, 55, 56, 68, 77: Isaiah,
87: John, 190: Lucy, 165:
Margaret, 77: Molly, 72:
Patience, 51: Peggy, 77: Preeson,
51: Rachel, 51, 72: Rachel
Bundick, 72: Richard, 51, 56, 72:
Solomon, 64: Susanna, 55, 56,
68, 77: Susannah, 80: Tabitha,
56: William, 51, 70, 72, 86, 87,
194
BALL, William, 184
BANKS, Sally, 35
BARNES, Archibald, 54, 55:
Attalanta, 55: Elizabeth, 84:
George P., 66, 67: John, 54:
Lanter, 55: Leah, 54, 55, 67:
Lydia, 130: Mary Savage, 66, 67:

212

Pamelia Mary, 130: Parker, 54,
55, 67, 165, 183: Patsy, 39:
Samuel, 130: Spencer, 54:
Susanna, 54: Susannah, 55:
William, 55
BARNS, Archibald, 48: John, 45, 46
BAYLY, Edmund, 64, 66: Edward L.,
120, 207: Elijah, 98, 99:
Elizabeth, 203: Hetty, 203: John,
14, 27, 28, 103, 107, 178: John
H., 64, 208: Matilda, 107: Molly,
178: Nancy, 99, 178: Polly, 203:
Richard, 203: Richard D., 61, 62,
74: Robert, 99, 178, 183: Sally
Ann, 203: Sarah, 183: Susanna,
99: Susannah, 98: Tabitha, 67:
Thomas, 17: Thomas M., 61, 99,
141, 144: Thomas S., 28
BAYLY'S RIDGE, 123
BEACH, Edward, 206
BEAVANS, Joshua, 134: William,
73, 92, 138, 142
BEECH, Samuel, 157
BELL, Ann, 194: Bridget, 94:
Catherine, 194: Caty, 194:
Edmund, 72, 182: Edward, 15:
Elizabeth, 15: Esther, 15:
George, 61, 194: Jacob, 15: John,
15: Joseph, 182: Keziah, 51:
Major, 15: Mary, 148, 150:
Molly, 15: Nancy, 15: Rachel,
51: Stephen, 51: William, 9
BELOTE, George, 195: John, 82, 86:
Margaret, 195: Polly, 82:
Virginia, 86: William, 116
BENNETT (Bennet), Betsy, 170:
Covington, 170: Covy, 170:
Elizabeth, 170: Margaret, 170:
Middleton, 93: Peggy, 170:
Sarah, 90, 91: Thomas, 90
BENSON, Sally, 193
BENSTON, James, 103

BERKELEY, William, 45
BERRY, Harriet, 79: Henry P., 79:
James, 124: Mahala, 79: Nancy,
79: Neary, 79: Sarah, 79:
William, 204: William H., 79
BEVANS, Mary Savage, 66: Peter,
116: Samuel, 139
BIRD (See also Byrd), Ann, 158,
173: Egnasha, 147: Jacob, 96:
Johannas, 104: John A., 130:
Nathaniel, 79: Sarah A., 130:
Solomon, 97: William, 103:
William T., 181
BISHOP, (N), 21: Esther, 21, 22:
Griffin, 98, 99: Muns, 21: Sally,
98, 99: Southy, 21, 22
BISWICK, Lewis, 92
BIVINS, John, 121
BLACKSTONE, Betsy, 80:
Elizabeth, 74, 77, 80: John J.,
197, 199, 201: William, 77, 80:
William B., 77, 80
BLADES, James, 190: Moses, 190
BLAKE, Charles, 135: Dennis, 135:
John, 135: Joseph, 135, 158:
Rebecca, 135
BLOXOM (Bloxsom), Dennis, 106,
108: Esther, 72: George, 72:
Hessy, 151: Hester, 151: John,
96: Leah, 73: Levin, 21, 108:
Littleton, 21: Margaret, 72:
Molly, 178: Nancy, 130: Peggy,
72: Richard, 177: Rosey, 177:
Simson, 138: Stephen, 97:
Thomas, 52, 97: Walter, 177
BOGGS, Francis, 29
BONNEWELL (Bonawell,
Bonnawell, Bonwell, Boniwel,
Bonwell, etc.), Alice, 27: Amelia,
27: Andrew, 39: Andrew M., 39:
Ann, 5, 6, 7, 19, 20, 26, 33, 34,

43: Ann Elba, 37: Anna, 12, 25:
Annabella, 5: Arabella, 6: Arthur,
BONNEWELL (continued)
13, 14, 15, 27, 28: Arthur R., 27:
Benjamin, 10, 16, 17, 18, 19, 34,
36, 38: Benjamin E., 37:
Benjamin P., 38: Benjamin
Purnell, 35, 38: Betsey, 11, 12,
16, 23, 24, 25, 29, 30, 31, 32:
Betsy, 31, 39, 40, 119: Bettey,
15: Betty, 8, 11, 15, 16, 23, 26:
Bordwin R., 26: Bridget, 27:
Cate, 15: Catherine, 40: Charles,
13, 14, 15, 27, 28: Cleme, 24:
Clement, 12, 16, 24, 29, 30, 31,
32, 101: Dorothy, 10: Edward,
19, 26, 40: Edward Hearn, 19,
39: Elijah, 11, 12, 22, 24, 25, 29,
30, 31, 32, 33: Elijah Clement,
33: Elijah R., 16, 24, 29, 31:
Elijah Richard, 13, 24: Eliza, 28,
35, 38: Elizabeth, 3, 4, 12, 15,
16, 20, 21, 22, 23, 24, 26, 31, 33,
39, 41, 42, 43, 49: Elizabeth M.
C., 29: Elizabeth R., 31:
Elizabeth S., 40: George, 5, 6,
13, 18, 19, 20, 26, 33, 37, 38, 39,
40, 42: Gratiana, 6, 7: Hall, 43:
Hannah, 8, 9, 13, 15, 23: Harriet,
28, 32, 33, 35: Harriett, 12, 24,
31, 32, 36, 37, 39, 40: Harriette,
33: Heely, 42: Henry, 43: Hester
Ann, 39: Hetty, 22: Isaac, 25, 26:
Isaac G., 36: Isaac Jerome, 37:
Jacob, 10, 22: Jacob Lurton, 9,
10, 21: James, 1, 2, 3, 4, 5, 7, 8,
9, 10, 12, 13, 14, 15, 16, 19, 23,
24, 26, 27, 29, 30, 31, 34, 35, 36,
39, 40, 43: James E., 37: James
W., 36, 38: James Wise, 35, 38:
Jane, 10, 34, 39: Jerome, 37:
Jesse, 20, 21, 29: Jesse b., 20:

Joachim, 8, 13: Joachim Mikeal,
7, 11, 16: John, 3, 4, 6, 7, 8, 9,
10, 13, 14, 15, 17, 19, 20, 27, 28,
29, 33, 34, 35, 38, 40, 41, 119:
Jonathan, 43: Killmon, 33: Leah,
8, 9, 12, 14, 24, 31, 32: Leah
Scarburgh, 32: Lettice, 34: Letty,
34: Levin, 12, 25: Littleton, 40:
M., 9, 16: Margaret, 22, 23, 27,
28, 41, 42, 43: Maria, 43:
Martha, 36; Martha A., 37: Mary,
3, 4, 6, 8, 9, 10, 13, 14, 15, 16,
17, 18, 19, 20, 21, 22, 25, 26, 27,
28, 34, 42: Mary Ann, 28: Mary
Jane, 10: McKeel, 9, 11, 12, 22,
23, 25, 29, 30, 31, 41, 42:
McKell, 102: Michael, 8, 9, 11,
15, 23: Michael Hall, 26, 42, 43:
Micheal, 22: Mickeel, 8, 25:
Mikeel, 9, 14, 15: Molly, 15, 21,
22, 39, 40: Nancy, 15, 20, 21, 26,
27, 33, 34, 35: Nathaniel, 28:
Patsey, 28: Patsy, 39: Pattey, 39,
40: Peggy, 11, 12, 16, 20, 21, 22,
23, 25, 27, 30: Peter, 40, 41:
Peter Lowber, 43: Polly S., 39:
Rachel, 8, 19, 20, 29, 40:
Reuben, 10: Richard, 7, 8, 9, 12,
13, 23, 25, 30: Robert, 12, 16,
24, 29, 30, 31: Rosa, 12, 25:
Rosey, 20: Sally, 12, 16, 24, 29,
30, 31, 32, 33, 35, 36: Sally R.,
32: Samuel, 42: Sarah, 1, 3, 4, 7,
8, 11, 12, 13, 19, 20, 23, 25, 30,
33, 40: Scarburgh, 11, 13: Selly,
28: Severn, 19, 33, 34, 35: Smith,
13, 15, 27, 28: Southey, 12, 23,
25, 30: Southy, 11, 12, 13, 25:
Stephen, 8, 9, 10, 19, 20, 21:
Susan, 27, 28, 34, 41, 42:
Susanna, 4, 19, 20, 27: Tabitha,
4, 12, 24, 31, 32: Thomas, 3, 5,

BONNEWELL (continued)
6, 7, 11, 12, 13, 14, 15, 16, 22,
23, 24, 25, 26, 27, 29, 30, 31, 40,
42: Washington, 37: Widow, 3:
William, 20, 21: William, 36, 40:
William C., 37: William Moore,
43
BOSTON, Captain, 179: Solomon,
178
BOWDOIN (Bowdin), Crippen, 151<
152: Deliala, 151: John R., 194
BOWMAN, David, 49: George K.,
29: John, 103, 107: Levin, 107:
Matilda, 103, 107: Tinny, 103
BRADFORD, Abel, 85: Abigail, 157:
Ann, 5, 157: Betsy, 64: Bridget,
6, 157: Edward D., 208:
Elizabeth, 82: George Bundick,
64: Jane, 82: Jinney, 82, 83:
John, 84, 157: John B., 208: John
Brown, 209: Margaret, 209:
Nathaniel, 64: Peggy, 209: Sally,
208: Sarah Ann, 208: Thomas H.,
81: William, 5, 6, 157, 161:
Zephaniah, 82, 84
BRAINNEY, Ocra, 151
BRATTEN, I., 118
BRIMER, Caleb, 105: Joseph, 105
BRITTINGHAM, Elizabeth, 7: Jane,
39: Josiah, 39: Nathaniel, 7:
Sarah, 7: William, 7
BROADWATER, Caleb, 68, 134,
135: David, 140, 182: Edward,
134, 135: Elias, 134, 135: Esther,
134: Ezekiel, 134, 135: Jacob,
135: Joseph, 134, 135: Margaret,
144: Martha, 134, 135: Mary,
134, 135, 136: Peggy, 182:
Phebe, 134: Robert J., 106:
Rosanna, 106: Sarah, 106:
Scarburgh, 134, 135

BROMWELL, George, 36: Harriet,
36: Isaac, 36: James W., 36:
Martha, 36
BRUMBLEY, Jebez, 18
BRUMLEY, Ezekiel, 18
BUDD, Betsey, 15: John, 208: John
T., 207: Major, 115: Mary, 9:
McKeel, 41: Nancy, 115: Nanny,
8: Peggy, 8: Sally, 207, 208:
Thomas P., 208: Thomas T., 207,
208: William, 15: Zorobabel, 8
BULL, Ann, 20, 117, 118: Ann
Burton, 167: Benjamin, 20:
Betsey, 12, 24: Betsy, 31: Betty,
14: Elizabeth, 31: Elizabeth R.,
31: Felix, 105: Frances, 11:
Francis A., 31: George B., 20:
George T., 20: John, 12, 22, 24,
25, 31, 70, 72, 111, 119: John
Carter, 31: John F., 29: Mary,
167: Nancy, 20, 117, 118: Peggy,
16: Polly, 167: Rachel, 167:
Richard, 41: Sarah, 41: Southey,
118: Southy W., 69, 119:
Thomas S., 167: Tobias, 11
BUNDICK, (N), 49: Abbot, 94:
Abbott, 46, 47, 50, 51, 55, 56,
68, 77, 78, 79, 87, 195, Agnes,
53, 67, 68: Amanda A., 85: Ann,
45, 46, 47, 50, 51, 52, 53, 62, 63,
64, 83, 86, 97, 208: Ann Custis,
67: Anne, 49, 54: Attalanta, 55:
Beersheba, 52, 57, 58: Betsy, 59,
60, 61, 63, 64, 77, 80, 195:
Betty, 68: Bridget, 53, 54:
Catherine, 79: Caty, 79: Charles
B., 84, 85: Damaris, 61: David,
72: Dorothy, 44, 45, 46:
Edmund, 59, 86: Edward, 87:
Elias, 51, 52, 72, 87: Elijah, 82,
87: Elijah Russell, 87: Elijah
Thomas, 81: Eliza, 86: Elizabeth,

BUNDICK (continued)
44, 45, 48, 49, 52, 53, 59, 61, 63,
65, 66, 68, 72, 76, 78, 80, 81, 84,
86: Elizabeth S., 84, 85: Esther,
49, 72: Fluranna J., 85: George,
46, 47, 48, 52, 53, 54, 55, 56, 58,
59, 60, 62, 63, 64, 67, 68, 69, 70,
71, 72, 74, 77, 80, 81, 208:
George E., 85: George E. L., 85:
George Gilchrist, 68: George T.,
70: George W., 63, 66, 196:
George Warrington, 62, 63, 65,
208: Grace, 45, 46: Jabez, 78:
James E., 84, 85: Jane, 82, 83:
John E., 87: John F., 84: Jinney,
82, 83: John, 49, 50, 53, 54, 55,
56, 57, 58, 61, 70, 83, 97, 105;
John A., 54, 63, 64, 65, 66, 67,
165, 183: John Abbott, 48, 49,
52, 53, 54, 66: John B., 83, 84,
85, 114: John F., 61, 85: John H.,
85: John P., 83: John S., 58, 66,
67, 82, 83: John Satchell, 68:
John T., 61: Joseph, 72: Justice,
47, 52, 55, 56, 68, 71, 72, 74, 77,
80, 98: Justis, 47: Keziah, 47, 51,
87: Lanter, 55: Lany, 70: Leah,
51, 55, 67, 80: Levin, 51, 58, 59,
87: Lewis, 67: Long, 50, 57, 58:
Lucretia, 55, 56: Luke, 71:
Lukey, 55, 56: Mahala, 79:
Margaret, 72: Margaret E., 84,
85: Margaret R., 84, 85: Mary,
47, 51, 76, 78, 82, 83, 195, 199,
209: Mary J., 84, 85: Mary
Savage, 66, 67: Milly, 62, 63:
Molly, 70, 72, 76, 78, 195, 199,
209: Mrs. John A., 199: Nancy,
53, 58, 60, 62, 63, 64, 66, 69, 70,
71, 73, 74, 75, 76, 77, 86, 208:
Nancy Mears, 75: Nancy
Warrington, 63: Nanney, 62, 63,

208: Neary, 79: Noah, 70:
Patience, 51: Peggy, 72: Peggy
Bagwell, 51: Piper, 50, 55, 56,
63, 71, 77: Polly, 74, 86, 87:
Rachel, 48, 51, 58, 59, 60, 61,
71, 81, Richard, 44, 45, 46, 47,
48, 50, 52, 53, 55, 56, 57, 59, 60,
61, 62, 63, 68, 70, 71, 72, 77, 87,
97, 122, 150, 187: Richard A.,
61: Robert, 49: Ruth, 44, 45:
Sally, 51, 55, 57, 59, 60, 64, 70,
76, 81, 82, 86, 208: Sally A., 81,
82: Samuel, 81, 82: Samuel C.,
81: Sarah, 52, 55, 57, 58, 59, 64,
70, 81, 86, 87, 208: Sarah A., 81:
Shady, 55: Sophia, 51, 94:
Southy, 49: Suanna, 47:
Suisanna, 58: Suke, 55, 56:
Susan, 82, 83, 84, 85: Susan J.,
86: Susanna, 46, 47, 48, 50, 55,
56, 58, 97: Susannah, 52:
Tabitha, 47, 48, 51, 52, 53, 54,
60, 63, 64, 71, 78: Thomas E.,
87: Tullie, 78, 195: Virgie B., 85:
William, 53, 54, 55, 56, 59:
William, 66, 67, 68, 71, 74, 75,
76, 77, 80, 81, 82, 84, 85:
William H., 66: William S., 81,
84
BUNTING, Ann, 194: Betsy, 119:
Elizabeth, 119: John, 96: John
A., 62: Jonathan, 57: Luther,
119: Nancy, 194: Rachel, 71:
Rosey, 119: Sally, 81: Sarah, 81,
82: Solomon, 71, 81, 82
BURCH, William, 150
BURTON, Abner, 159: Amey, 157:
Elizabeth, 160: J., 27: John, 68:
Joseph, 160: Joshua, 84, 167:
Katherine, 167: Patience, 157:
Stratton, 157: Thomas, 157:
William, 135, 142

IRONMONGER, Betsy, 101:
Elizabeth, 101: James, 118:
Major, 14: Zadock, 101
JACOB (Jacobs), Isaac, 45: John,
164: John B., 77: Nancy, 77,
164: Richard, 45: Thomas, 45,
160: William B., 75
JAMES, Ann, 209: Betsy, 86, 113:
David, 5, 6, 105, 106: Elizabeth,
6, 86, 106, 113: Emma, 114:
George W., 85: Hester, 106:
Hetty, 106: Levin, 114: Margaret,
114: Mary, 5, 106: Mary A., 114:
Molly, 114: Patience, 113:
Robert, 5, 51, 106, 108: Sarah,
114: Sarah Ann, 106: Thomas,
114: William, 5, 58, 106, 113,
114
JENIFER (Jenefer), Colonel, 50:
Daniel, 5, 46: Elizabeth, 5: St.
Thomas, 5
JENKINS, Francis, 18
JESTER, John, 41, 184: Joseph, 41,
42: Margaret, 42: Matilda, 107:
Rachel, 184: Susan, 41: Tinny,
107
JOHN RUSSELL RIDGE, 123
JOHNSON, Alfred F., 117: Amella,
163: Amilla, 163: Isaac S., 35:
Isaiah, 104, 184: Isoial, 104:
Jenny, 159: Margaret Sarah
Thomas, 206: Mary, 105, 106,
117: Milley, 163: Polly, 105:
Sally, 117, 203: Sarah, 35:
Solomon, 104, 190: Thomas,
206: William, 1, 105, 106, 159
JONES, Ann, 33: Daniel, 151: David,
46: Eliza, 34, 38: Elizabeth, 176:
Evitt, 45: George, 176: Giles, 35:
Isaac, 34, 38: John, 44, 150, 151:
Martha, 143: Mary, 153: Robert,
52: Robert F., 34: Ruth, 44:

Sally, 176: Sarah, 176: Thomas,
44, 46, 143: W., 36: Walter, 176
JOYNES, Ann, 205: John, 16, 24,
111, 119: John G., 14, 27, 115,
168, 169: John J., 111: Levin, 26:
Levin L., 14: Levin S., 14, 15,
29, 115: Sally, 60: Sarah, 60:
Thomas R., 14, 15, 21, 29, 118,
169: William, 60: William R.,
205: Zorobabel, 28, 205
JUSTICE (Justis), Bernette, 124, 125:
Betsey, 127: Betsy, 123:
Elizabeth, 123: Elizabeth Ann,
175: Harriet, 125: Isaiah, 123,
124, 126, 129: James, 107, 150,
175, 196, 202, 203: Josiah, 126:
Mary, 46, 124, 129: Mary A.,
123: Millie, 175: Molly, 191:
Netty, 124: Noah, 127: Parker,
122: Priscilla, 125: R., 107:
Rachel, 191: Ralph, 46, 50, 97:
Richard, 94, 123, 191: Sally,
123, 124, 126, 129, 191: Samuel,
122, 124, 129: Samuel R., 125:
Sarah, 123, 126, 129: Susanna,
46, 47, 97: Tabitha, 126:
Thomas, 191: Thorowgood, 123:
William, 76, 81, 123
KELLAM (Kellum), A.J.T., 121:
Benjamin, 28: Betty, 40:
Catherine, 40: Dolly, 40:
Edward, 157: Elizabeth, 40, 81,
155: Francis, 120: Henry, 155:
Howson, 40: Hutchinson, 169:
James, 58: John C., 115:
Margaret, 205: Melnida, 86:
Polly, 114: Richard, 155: Robert,
114: Rose, 155: Samuel, 167:
Thomas H., 169
KELLY, Jacob, 178, 184: Mary, 148:
Richard, 159: Richardson, 117:

MEARS (continued)
Gillett, 75: Jaca, 175: Jaquet,
175: Jennie, 126: John, 126, 156:
John W. A., 121: Jonathan, 105:
Joseph G., 86: Keziah, 192:
Margaret, 77: Mary, 126: Mary
S., 77: Meshack, 75, 77, 195:
Nancy, 75, 76, 77, 126: Peggy,
77: Rachel, 8: Sabrah, 156: Sally,
121: Samuel, 175: Sukey, 75:
Susan, 86: Susannah, 75:
Tabitha, 175: Thomas C., 206:
Virginia, 86: William, 82:
William W., 77: Zeporah, 202,
203
MEERS, John, 156: Sabra, 155, 156:
Sabrah, 155
MEKEALL, John, 7
MELSON, Isaac, 48: Joseph, 78:
Robert, 22: Sarah, 12, 13:
Scarborough, 12, 13: Smith, 12,
13
MELTEN, John, 135
MELVIN, James, 146
MERRILL, Asa J., 132: Jacob, 17
METCALF, Adeline, 128: Jesse, 33:
Patty, 33: Sally, 33: Sarah, 33
MICHAEL, Anne, 4, 6: Gratiana, 6,
7: John, 4, 6: Simon, 4: Susanna,
4
MIDCASS, Patty, 33
MIDDLETON, Eleanor, 92: George,
192: Thomas, 92
MIKEAL, Roger, 3
MILBY, John, 167, 168
MILES, Ann, 187: Betsey, 178:
Comfort, 181: George, 181:
Jesse, 184: Polly, 181: Rodger,
191: Roger, 187: Tabitha, 78:
William, 188
MILLIGAN, John, 92
MILLINER, Mary S., 199: Polly, 199

MISTER, Catherine, 102: Caty, 102:
James F., 102: Rachel, 102:
Susanna, 110, 111: William, 112
MITCHELL, George, 128
MONGER, Betsy, 101: Elizabeth,
101: Zadock, 101
MOORE, Mary, 42: Mary Ann, 28:
Mathey, 28: Peter, 28: William,
42: William P., 144, 168, 170
MORGAN (Morgon), Arnold, 97:
Comfort, 158, 159: William, 158,
159, 163
MORRIS, Gilbert, 135: John, 135,
156
MOUNTNEY, William, 2
MYCHELL, Susana, 4: Susanna, 3
NANCY, Hetty, 106
NEGRO (Does not include Free
Blacks with surnames. They are listed
alphabetically by surname.), Abram,
29: Adah, 118: Ansley, 118: Appey,
157: Bett, 104: Bill, 20: Candis, 110:
Charity, 104: Charles, 145, 170:
Charlotte, 41: Chloe, 123: Comfort,
29: Dick, 118: Edmund, 104, 208:
Esther, 107, 145: George, 118, 143:
Harry, 167: Henry, 118: Isaac, 110,
163, 164: Judah, 104: Keziah, 104:
Leah, 104, 143: Letty, 110: Levi, 28:
Love, 104: Lucy, 104, 110: Mary, 83,
118: Moses, 110, 118: Nathan, 208:
Pagea, 145: Peggy, 146, 147: Peter,
20, 110: Philip, 49: Rachel, 118:
Raner, 118: Rose, 191, 208: Sarah,
110, 163, 164, 196: Scarburgh, 208:
Shadrack, 167: Simon, 110: Sophrah,
145: Sybal, 49: Tamer, 110
NELMS, John, 161, 162
NELSON, Lany, 70
NICHOLLS, John, 2
NICHOLS, John, 7

NIXSON, Ann, 46: Edward, 46:
Richard, 46: Thomas, 46
NOCK (Knock), Ann, 50, 97:
Benjamin, 155, 156: Bridget, 53:
Elizabeth, 160, 167: George, 50:
John, 50, 52, 57, 97, 190: Levin,
155, 156: Lewis, 164: Littleton,
130: Lucretia, 190: Nehemiah
W., 182: Patience, 155, 156:
Rose, 50, 156: Samuel S., 164:
Sarah, 70: Susannah, 62:
William, 50, 53, 97, 107, 118,
144, 155, 156, 164, 178, 180,
191: Z., 107, 164: Zadock, 123,
130, 164, 178
NORTHAM, Adeline, 181: Betsy,
165, 174, 175, 181: Betty, 88,
102, 103, 107, 150: Catherine,
193: Comfort, 164, 165: Custis,
175: E., 164, 181: Elijah, 164,
165: Elizabeth, 102, 103, 107,
150, 165, 174, 175, 181, 192,
193, 203: Gillet, 203: Henrietta,
192: Hetty, 203: Jacob, 104:
James, 178, 179, 181, 192, 193,
208: Margaret, 165: Patsy, 183:
Rachel, 181: Sallie D., 193:
Sally, 193: Sally Ann, 203:
Southey, 104, 175, 178: Southy,
88: Sukey, 75: Susannah, 75:
Thomas A., 179, 181: William,
164, 165, 174, 175, 178, 181,
183
NORTON, Frances, 6
NOTTINGHAM, Mary, 44: Richard,
44
NUTTER, Benjamin, 162
OHIO (tract of land), 17
OLDHAM, Montcalm, 121, 203
ONIONS, John, 47, 192: Nancy, 192:
Richard, 52: Sally, 56, 68, 77:
Susanna, 47: Susannah, 47:

William, 55, 68, 77: William
Selby, 57
ONLEY (Only), Francis, 102: John
F., 63: Margaret R., 102: Peggy,
111
OUTTEN (Outton), Ann, 193:
Ephraim, 111: Isaac, 160:
Margaret, 160: Susanna, 58:
William, 58
OWEN (Owens), Mary, 140, 153:
Samuel, 139
PARADISE, John, 34: Milby, 34:
Nancy, 34, 38: Parker, 34, 36,
38: William, 35, 38
PARKER, Agnes, 132: Charlotte
Winder, 171: Elisha, 172:
Elizabeth, 125: George, 11, 179:
John, 15, 17, 18, 132: Littleton,
118: Mary, 16, 17: Mary H., 114:
Peggy, 173: Philip, 8: Revell,
193: Robert, 15, 168: Sacker, 16,
17, 18, 132: Sarah, 11: Susan J.,
113: Susannah, 55: Tully W.,
171: William, 18
PARKERS NECK, 97
PARKS, Benjamin, 61, 96, 125:
Bernette, 125: Daisy, 61:
Edmund, 78, 196: Eleanor, 96:
Henry P., 209: John, 62, 123,
125: John D., 149: Nelly, 96:
Parker W., 123: Rachel, 121,
123: William T., 191
PARRAMORE, Margaret, 80:
William, 54, 80, 167
PATTERSON, William, 139
PAYNE, Betsy, 39: Elizabeth, 39:
Polly S., 39: Samuel A., 39
PEA PATCH, 161
PEARSON, (N), 47: William
Bundick, 47, 50
PEMBERTON'S GOODWILL, 162
PEPPERS VEXATION, 35

PERRY, Thomas, 133
PETTITT (Petitt, Pettit), Elizabeth
   D., 76: John, 189: Levin, 204:
   Louisa, 204: Mary, 75, 76, 189:
   Mary Jane, 76: Molly, 75, 76:
   Rachel, 189, 190: Susanna, 204:
   William M., 76
PHILLIPS, Ann, 116: Elizabeth, 30:
   Elizabeth M. C., 29: Laban, 30:
   Laben, 58: Mary, 116: Molly,
   116: Nancy, 58, 116: Rachel, 30:
   Sarah, 112: Smith, 30: Susannah,
   41: Tabby, 116: Tabitha, 116:
   William, 30, 116, 117
PILCHARD, Ann, 92, 93: Francis, 93
PITTS (Pitt), Jabez, 104: Pamelia,
   132: Robert, 168: Sarah, 110,
   111
POCOMOKE SWAMP, 89
POULSON, Edward, 117: Elizabeth,
   5, 11: Erastus, 5, 131: James, 14,
   20, 27: John, 131: John Edward,
   130: Katie, 5: Mary E., 130:
   Robert J., 42: T. M., 175
POWELL, James, 133: John T., 85:
   Joseph, 182: Nancy, 182: Samuel
   W., 191: William, 103, 173:
   Winifred, 188
PREESON, Thomas, 92
PRESCOTT, Polly, 74: Thomas, 74
PRUITT, Sally, 190
PURNELL, Benjamin Purnell, 37
PUSEY, Stephen, 168
RACKCLIFFE, Nathaniel, 133
RAYFIELD, Ann, 116: Custis, 120:
   Levi, 116: Levi R., 116
READ, Betsey, 153: Betsy, 140:
   Elizabeth, 153: Richard P., 121
RED, William, 156
REDDEN, Elizabeth, 34: John, 17,
   36: Nathaniel, 36: Stephen, 35,
   38

REED, William Bundick, 58
REVELL, John, 90: John K., 20
REW, Charles, 64, 198: Emaline,
   182: Hetty, 64: James, 196:
   James H., 198, 199: Jane, 198:
   Jinney, 198: John, 196, 203:
   Mary Ann, 196, 197, 198:
   Reuben, 103, 107: Richard P.,
   42: Sally, 64: Sarah, 64
REYNOLD, Mary, 162
RICHARDSON, Ezekiel, 33: Harriet,
   33: Isaiah, 33: John, 33: Peggy
   Mears, 9: Rachel, 9: William
   Martial, 9
RIGGEN, Joshua, 17
RIGGS, John, 52, 55: Nancy, 130
RILEY, Ann, 209, 210: Charlotte, 36:
   Jacob, 36: John, 17, 18, 178:
   Mary, 98, 99: Molly, 98, 99:
   Raymond, 62: Thomas, 49:
   William, 98, 150
ROBERTS (Robert), Ahah, 121:
   Edwin, 83: Elizabeth, 159: Peter,
   151
ROBINS, Alice, 27: Arthur, 26:
   Mary, 26: Michael, 41: Tillar, 26
ROBINS HOLE, 61, 63, 123
ROBINSON, Tully, 7
ROCKS, James, 165
RODGERS (Rogers), Abel R., 169:
   Betsy, 110, 111: Elizabeth, 111:
   Emma, 61: Eunice P., 61: George
   S., 121: John, 110, 111, 169:
   Levi, 168: Major, 111: Peter,
   111: Reuben, 21: Richard, 92:
   Robert, 52, 169: Sarah, 16, 19:
   Susannah, 49: Tabitha, 52:
   Zorobabel, 15
RONE, Daniel, 111
ROSS, Kendall, 148: Rachael, 148:
   Sally, 140, 153
ROTTEN QUARTER, 18, 19

ROWLEY, Polly, 135, 154: William,
135, 150
RUSSELL, Abe, 22: Abel, 22: Casier,
194: Elijah, 87: George, 12, 13:
James, 119: Joshua, 141, 147:
Leah, 22: Margaret, 22, 23:
Peggy, 11, 12, 13: Rachel, 29:
Rebecca, 147: Robert, 12, 13,
147, 165: Sarah, 11, 12, 13:
Thomas, 141
RYLEY. See Riley
SACKER, Bridget, 18
SALISBURY, Catherine, 102: Caty,
102: Margaret, 41, 42
SAMUEL TAYLOR'S ISLAND, 137
SAMUEL TAYLOR'S MARSH, 137
SANDERS, Mary, 51: Rachel, 51:
Richard, 51
SANDFORD, Thomas, 104
SANDREWS, Rachel, 52
SATCHELL, Anne, 49: Christopher
C., 205: Elizabeth, 48, 53, 54:
Esther, 49: Henry, 48, 52, 53:
Mary Anne, 205: Molly, 49:
Rachel, 48, 49: Southey, 19:
Southy, 49: Thomas S., 168
SAULSBURY, Robert, 102
SAVAGE, Ann, 78, 194: Elizabeth,
66, 194: Francis, 156, 168:
Griffin, 202: Griffith, 13: John,
103, 163, 181,194, 195, 208:
Mary, 116: Mary Anne, 106:
Molly, 116: Nancy, 78, 106, 194:
R., 208: Richard, 192: Richard
R., 106: Robert, 109, 192:
Robinson, 17: Rosey, 168, 169:
Rowland, 156: Sally, 106: Sally
C., 106: Samuel C., 107: Samuel
G., 168, 169: Sarah, 13: Thomas,
186: William, 168, 194
SAVAGE'S, 75

SCARBURGH (Scarborough),
Americus, 67: Ann, 188: Charles,
90: Edmund, 45, 90: Elizabeth,
90: George, 16, 111: George P.,
118: Henry, 188: Nanny, 188:
Samuel H., 208: Serena, 182:
Winifred, 188, 189
SCHERER, George, 169
SCOTT, Elizabeth, 42: George, 83:
George W., 42, 83: John T., 27:
Nancy, 27: Sacker, 70
SELBY, Zadock, 154
SEYMOUR, William, 14, 16, 20, 27,
28, 58
SHARPLEY, Tabitha, 134: William,
134, 151, 152
SHARROD, Elizabeth, 21: Thomas,
21
SHARWOOD, Nancy, 26
SHAY, Agnes, 144, 159, 160: Daniel,
164: Elias, 144, 160: Elizabeth,
144: Jernima, 164: Mary, 41:
Molly, 41
SHEPHERD, Nancy, 115
SHIELD, Betsy, 205, 206: Elizabeth,
206
SHOCKLEY, Jonathan, 162
SHREAVES, Mary J. W., 100:
William, 202
SILVERTHORN (Silverthorne),
Sebastian, 4: Susanna, 4: Mary,
4: Tabitha, 4
SIMKINS (Simpkins), C., 27: John,
202
SIMPSON, Bridget, 190: Elizabeth,
116
SMITH, Ann, 177, 178: Bayly, 177,
180: Carmine, 29: Charles, 120,
121: Edward, 79: Edward C., 79:
Eliza, 120: Elizabeth, 10, 161,
162, 163, 180: Elizabeth J., 120:
Francis S., 85: George, 119, 161:

Isaiah, 161, 172: James, 18:
John, 7, 14, 19, 141: John W.,
42: Mahala, 79: Miranda Jenet
C., 172: Nancy, 180: Neary, 79:
Sally, 121: Samuel, 79: Susan, 79
SNEAD, Ann, 114: Anna, 12, 25:
Borden, 25: Bowdoin, 114:
Charles, 20: Charles S., 205:
Edward, 29: Edward S., 14:
George, 64: George F., 205:
Isaac, 12, 25, 26: John, 66: John
L., 71: Margaret, 206: Margaret
A., 205: Mary, 25: Nancy, 114:
Polly, 114: Rosetta, 206: Rosey,
206: Tabitha, 71: Thomas, 14,
27, 40, 102, 140: Tully, 205, 206
SOMERS, Elizabeth, 62
SPARROW, David, 78, 195: Henny,
202: Henrietta, 202: John, 190:
Mary, 78, 195: Molly, 78:
Richard, 195, 202, 203: Sarah,
195: Tabitha, 203: Zeporah, 202,
203
SPIERS, John, 160, 167: William,
156
STAKES, John, 207: Susan, 207
STALL, Dorman, 2
STANLEY, Christopher, 133:
Elizabeth, 133
STANTON, John, 3
STATON, (N), 159, 160: Joseph,
133, 159: Susannah, 159:
Warrington, 138
STEAVENS, William, 49
STEPHENS, Elizabeth, 48: Kesire,
105: William, 161
STERLING, John, 98, 99: John Y.,
150: John Young, 100: Lovey,
98, 99, 100: Mary, 134, 135:
Polly, 110, 111

STEVENS, Christopher, 49:
Elizabeth, 49: George, 49: John,
49: William, 18, 49
STOCKLEY (Stockly), Ann, 5:
Charles, 67; George, 6: John,
133: Nehemiah, 158; William,
133: Woodman, 136
STRAN, Mary P., 121, 122, 123
STRATTON, Elizabeth, 133: John,
133
STRINGER, John, 2
STURGIS, Ann, 46: Betsey, 153:
Daniel, 45, 153: Dorothy, 46:
Elizabeth, 45, 153: Jacob, 54:
John, 45: Jonathan, 45, 46:
Martha, 49: Richard, 45:
Susanna, 48: William S., 207
TANKARD, John, 6
TARR, Betsy, 108: Charley, 36:
Elizabeth, 108: John, 108
TATHAM, Avery, 192: Ayres, 62,
63: Keziah, 192: Sallie, 192:
Tabitha, 148: Thomas, 192
TAYLOR, Abraham, 160: Alexander,
154: Ann, 154: Ann Custis, 67:
Ann Mary, 134: Bartholomew,
136, 167: Beersheba, 52: Betsy,
77, 195: Caty, 78: Charles, 78,
82: Charles W., 83: Comfort,
181: Crippen, 53, 123: Edward
W., 208: Elias, 145: Elizabeth,
129: Euphemia, 154: George, 58,
81, 82, 83: George K., 168:
George Trewet, 56: Hessey, 154:
Isaac, 77, 78: Jacob, 141: James,
59, 78, 124, 145, 166: Jane, 82:
Jeminia, 137: Jinney, 82:
Johanna, 11: John, 52, 160, 167,
168, 169, 182, 188: John T., 38:
Kesziah, 104: Major, 168, 169:
Malinda, 86: Margaret, 169:
Maria, 154: Mary, 182:

WHITE (continued)
175: Lacey, 80: Levin, 176:
Lucy, 80: Mary A., 129: Rosy,
206: Sally, 76, 81: Samuel C.,
23: Southey, 143: Tabitha, 175:
Tabitha E., 175: William, 29:
William C., 76, 77, 81, 202
WHITTINGTON, Arthur, 139, 146
WHITTY, John, 89
WHITTY'S LOT, 89
WILKINS, Ann, 112: Henry, 112:
John, 2, 6: Sukey, 112: Susanna,
112
WILLIAMS, Elizabeth, 7: Mary C.,
121: Robert W., 121: Thomas, 3
WILLIAM'S ISLAND, 137
WILLIAMSON, David, 91
WILLIS, Custis, 168: Patience, 168:
Rose, 156
WILLISES MARSH, 139
WILLITS DISCOVERY, 35
WILSON, David, 161: Rachel, 135:
William, 47
WIMBROUGH, Beersheba, 57, 58:
John, 50: John D., 209: Joseph,
57: Rachel, 191: Solomon, 94:
Susanna, 50
WINDER, Charlotte, 172: William,
162
WINDOW, George, 143
WISE, Ann, 4: Betsey, 16, 24:
Dorothy Edmunds, 5: Elizabeth,
5, 16, 24: Elizabeth Bagwell, 5:
Healey Parker, 5: Henrietta
Sarah, 5: Henry A., 102: Isaiah,
4: Isaiah Evans, 4: James, 20,
190: Jennings Cropper, 4:
Johannes, 112: John, 3, 4, 10,
112: John C., 102, 144: John
Evans, 4, 5: John Hastings, 5:
Leah, 31: Lucy Parker, 5:
Margaret, 4: Mary, 3, 4, 13, 15:

McKeel, 12, 24: McKeely, 16,
24: Molly, 28: Nancy, 20: Sarah,
3, 4, 13: Susan, 4: Susanna, 8,
19, 20: Susey, 20: Thomas, 17:
William, 4, 7, 10, 13, 165:
William E., 4: William Thomas,
5
WISES ADDITION, 7
WISHART, Hannah, 145: James, 145
WOODSON, Deniy A., 129: Drury
A., 130
WRIGHT, Abel, 188, 189, 190, 191:
Agnes, 192: Ann, 64, 78, 187,
188, 193, 194, 198, 199, 201,
203, 205, 207, 208: Anna, 186,
200, 204: Asha, 188: Betsey,
203, 208: Betsy, 202, 204, 205,
206, 209: Bridget, 190:
Catharine, 196, 198, 200:
Catherine, 191, 194, 197: Caty,
194: Charles C., 210:
Christopher, 186: Comfort, 188:
Demariah D., 209: Dennis, 190,
207: Edith, 194, 195: Edward,
186, 187, 189, 196, 197, 199,
203, 204: Edward W., 204:
Edwin S., 210: Elijah, 70, 188,
189, 190, 191, 192, 206: Elijah
J., 206: Elijah W., 205: Eliza,
194: Elizabeth, 188, 189, 192,
193, 196, 197, 198, 200, 202,
203, 205, 206: Elizabeth M.,
210: Elizabeth S., 209: Elizabeth
W., 210: Emaline S., 207: Esther,
189: Francis, 186: George, 64,
67, 186, 188, 189, 190, 192, 193,
204: George F., 208, 210:
George T., 210: Helen, 198:
Henny, 202: Henrietta, 77, 81,
192, 193, 202: Henry, 78, 186,
187, 188, 189, 192, 193, 194,
195, 205: Hessey, 189:

WRIGHT (continued)
Hester Ann, 194, 195: Isaac, 189,
190, 205, 206: Isaac T., 205,
206: Jacob, 189, 190: James, 64,
192, 193, 203, 204, 208, 210:
James B., 209: Joane, 186: John,
186, 189, 202, 203: John E., 204:
John L., 206: Katharine, 191:
Keziah, 192: Leah, 188, 189:
Louisa, 204: Lovea, 192: Lovey,
193: Lucretia, 190, 191: Mack
Williams, 188, 189: Malinda,
194: Margaret, 190, 195, 200,
205, 206: Margaret A., 206:
Margaret S., 197, 206: Mary, 78,
186, 187, 188, 195, 200, 204:
Mary A., 206, 210: Mary Ann,
64, 196, 198, 208, 210: Mary
Anne, 205: Mary S., 199, 200:
Melindy, 194: Molly, 78, 191,
195: Nancy, 64, 78, 190, 194,
196, 198, 201, 207, 208: Nanny,
188: Nathan, 186: Patience, 202:
Peggy, 190: Prudence J., 194,
195: Rachel, 188, 189, 190:
Rebecca, 195, 196, 198, 199,
200, 201: Rebecca Hickman,
195: Rebeccah, 196: Rebeckah,
195, 196: Rebekah, 187: Richard,
186: Robert, 186: Rosey, 190:

Rosy A., 206: Sallie D., 193:
Sally, 64, 190, 192, 193, 199,
200, 201, 207, 208: Samuel, 195,
196, 197, 200, 201, 203: Samuel
C., 194: Samuel Edward, 194:
Sarah, 188, 196, 199, 201, 202:
Sarah Ann, 208: Scarburgh, 190:
Sinah, 189: Susan, 204, 207:
Susanna, 203, 204: Susannah,
189: Symon, 186: Tabitha, 189,
203: Thomas, 186, 187, 194,
197, 199, 200, 201: Thomas S.,
189, 195, 196, 206, 207: Walter,
195, 196, 202: William, 45, 186,
187, 188, 189, 190, 201, 202,
207: William Abbott, 208, 209:
William H., 194: William T.,
197, 198, 200, 202: William
Thomas, 196, 197, 199, 200:
Willie Ann, 197
WYATT, Andrew, 120: Andrew B.,
120: Betsey, 120: Elizabeth, 120:
Jane, 120: John, 120
WYLIE, John, 90
YOUNG, David, 165: George, 188:
Gillett, 192: Isaac, 103: John, 47,
135, 154: Keziah, 47: Margaret,
165, 188: Ommey, 159, 160:
Polly, 135, 154: Robert, 192:
William, 49, 61, 173, 188

www.ingramcontent.com/pod-product-compliance
Lightning Source LLC
Chambersburg PA
CBHW071349280326
41927CB00040B/2432